INSIGHT GUIDE

France

APA PUBLICATIONS
Part of the Langenscheidt Publishing Group

L

INSIGHT GUIDE France

ABOUT THIS BOOK

Editorial

Project Editor
Fiona Duncan
Managing Editor
Cameron Duffy
Editorial Director
Brian Bell

Distribution

UK & Ireland
GeoCenter International Ltd
The Viables Centre
Harrow Way
Basingstoke
Hants RG22 4BJ
Fax: (44) 1256-817988

United States
Langenscheidt Publishers, Inc.
46–35 54th Road
Maspeth, NY 11378
Fax: (718) 784-0640

Worldwide
APA Publications GmbH & Co.
Verlag KG (Singapore branch)
38 Joo Koon Road
Singapore 628990
Tel: (65) 865-1600
Fax: (65) 861-6438

Printing

Insight Print Services (Pte) Ltd
38 Joo Koon Road
Singapore 628990
Tel: (65) 865-1600
Fax: (65) 861-6438

© 1999 APA Publications GmbH & Co.
Verlag KG (Singapore branch)
All Rights Reserved
First Edition 1986
4th Edition 1999

CONTACTING THE EDITORS
Although every effort is made to
provide accurate information in
this publication, we live in a
fast-changing world and would
appreciate it if readers would
call our attention to any errors or
outdated information that may
occur by writing to us at:
**Insight Guides, P.O. Box 7910,
London SE1 8ZB, England.
Fax: (44 171) 620-1074.**
e-mail:
insight@apaguide.demon.co.uk

With an excess of ambition,
perhaps, this book attempts
to encapsulate the nation about
which everyone has a different opinion. "France is the most civilised
country in the world and doesn't
care who knows it," proclaimed
writer John Gunter. But Shakespeare
described it as a "dog-hole", Joseph
Addison accused it of having
"infected all the nations of Europe
with its levity" and Tobias Smollett
declared "they have not even the
implements of cleanliness." Mark
Twain added: "France has neither
winter, summer, nor morals – apart
from these drawbacks it's a fine
country."

The dirt that the world's critics
like to fling at France doesn't seem
to stick, however. It remains
Europe's biggest tourist attraction –
both in terms of its size as Europe's
largest country and of the number
of annual visitors.

The reasons for such popularity
are plain to see from a quick
perusal of this book: France's diversity of landscape is overwhelming;
its monuments are among the most
famous in the world; its arts are of
the top quality, and its cuisine is
unsurpassable.

A face of rural France

How to use this book

The book is carefully structured both to convey an understanding of France and its culture and to guide readers through its sights and activities:

◆ To understand France today, you need to know something of its past. The first sections, **History** and **Features,** cover the country's culture in lively, authoritative essays written by specialists.

◆ The main **Places** section guides you around the country region by region, describing all the main sights and places of interest, and many of the lesser known ones. The principal places of interest are co-ordinated by number with full-colour maps.

◆ The **Travel Tips** listings section at the back of the book provides a convenient point of reference for information on travel, hotels, restaurants, nightlife, shopping and festivals. Information may be located quickly by using the index printed on the back cover flap – and the flaps themselves are designed to serve as useful bookmarks.

◆ Photographs are chosen not only to illustrate the geography, the architecture and history of France but also to convey the many moods of the country and the everyday activities of its people.

The contributors

This new edition was edited by **Fiona Duncan**, who has lived in both Paris and Provence. She has devised, written and edited several guides to France.

Writer, broadcaster and *Insight Guides* regular with a special interest in France **Lisa Gerard-Sharp** contributed all the new history and feature essays, as well as the chapter on Le Nord.

Many of the photographs are by *Insight Guides* regulars **Catherine Karnow**, **Bill Wassman** and **Lyle Lawson**.

Anne Roston was the editor of the original edition, and contributors included **Ted Widmer, Mary Deschamps, Marguerite Morley, John Wain, John Smith, Francois Dunoyer de Segonzac, Rodger Goodson, Rosemary Bailey, Diana Geddes, Susan Bell, Philip Hyman, Mary Hyman, Jim Keeble, Peter Graham, Grace Coston** and **Jill Adam.**

Map Legend

—— - -	International Boundary
——	Regional Boundary
- - - -	Département Boundary
⊖	Border Crossing
— • —	National Park/Reserve
- - - -	Ferry Route
Ⓜ	Metro
✈ ✈	Airport: International/Regional
🚐	Bus Station
🅿	Parking
❶	Tourist Information
✉	Post Office
✝ ✝	Church / Ruins
✝	Monastery
☾	Mosque
✡	Synagogue
🏰	Castle / Ruins
∴	Archaeological Site
∩	Cave
𝕀	Statue/Monument
★	Place of Interest

The main places of interest in the Places section are coordinated by number with a full-colour map (e.g. ❶), and a symbol at the top of every right-hand page tells you where to find the map.

CONTENTS

Castelnau
in the
Dordogne

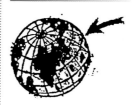

Travel Tips

EUROPE'S OLDEST NATION

Exuberant and charming? Or enigmatic and arrogant?

France's character is as tantalising as ever

Neatly symmetrical – almost hexagonal – in shape, France, the world's fourth richest country, is Western Europe's largest nation, although it would fit quite easily into the state of Texas. It is a rural country, with the population of 57 million thinly spread through the land, at an average of 104 people per sq. km (the UK averages 240 per sq. km). Some 56 percent of the land is farmed and 25 percent under forest. The nation's largest industry is the business of food production.

There's one huge and famous urban area: almost 9 million people live in and around Paris, one of the world's finest and favourite - destinations, but the second and third French cities – Lyon and Marseille – are very much smaller, with populations of 1.2 and 1.1 million respectively.

France is also Europe's oldest nation, existing in its present form since the 15th century. The nation's boundaries are largely natural ones, with the English Channel to the north, the Atlantic to the west, the Pyrenees and the Mediterranean to the south, and the Alps, the Jura mountains and the Rhine to the east. These all contrive to make the nation almost insular, and the overwhelmingly Catholic people are perhaps not as cosmopolitan as other European countries with more openly shared borders. And yet France has immense cultural influence on the rest of the world, and the existence of several minority languages within the country – Breton, Basque, Catalan, Elsass-dutch and Provençal – plus the fact that it is the only nation which is at once in northern and southern Europe suggest something of the extraordinary variety that is to be found within its borders.

France has 56 million visitors a year, making it Europe's most popular tourist destination. These visitors are attracted by its superb landscape and historic cities, its unsurpassable food and wine, its unique culture and elegant shopping. In an increasingly conformist world, the nation with a genius for living well – and the one that gave us the word "elite" – retains its unique allure. ❑

PRECEDING PAGES: grape picking at Santenay, Burgundy; equestrian outing at Arnac-Pompadour; sunset at Mont-St-Michel; fun by the Eiffel Tower, Paris.
LEFT: exterior sculpture in the chapel at Kermaria, Brittany.

LA BELLE FRANCE

From the windswept coastline of Brittany to the scented, sun-baked hills of Provence, France is a rich and beautiful amalgam of European landscapes

Considering the English Channel, Atlantic, Pyrenees, Mediterranean, Alps and Rhine as preordained natural boundaries, the French often compare their plot of earth to a divinely shaped hexagon that absorbs and unites all the different parts of Europe. Indeed, France is at once a northern and southern European country, connecting the cold Atlantic Ocean with the warm Mediterranean Sea, and the empyreal Pyrenees with the Flemish flatlands. A detailed map of France, using different colours to describe regional characteristics, would bear a striking resemblance to an Impressionist painting.

The French are proud of their country's proportional symmetry. Recognising disparate attributes and uniting them in a way that makes such good sense, they see in France's shape a national character that may at times be quirky and erratic, but is supremely ordered.

At 550,980 sq. km (212,741 sq. miles), France is the world's 37th largest country. It escaped the gouging glaciers of the Ice Age, so its landscape is generally mellow and pastoral with gentle hills and plateaus, carved by deep river valleys. Imposing mountains lie only along the eastern and southern frontiers. It is a remarkably rural nation, with the population spread thinly over huge areas, which is perhaps why French farmers have such political power.

The rock and its rolling

Later geophysical development in the large southeastern Garonne region left profound impressions between younger and older hills, providing perfect conditions for the formation of valuable minerals as well as oil and natural gas. To add to France's fortune, the existence of an extensive network of rivers, like the Garonne, promises an eternal fertility unmatched by other countries; France has the highest percentage of arable land in Western Europe.

PRECEDING PAGES: spring in Gascony.
LEFT: the Atlantic coast at the Pointe du Raz.
RIGHT: Aquitaine agriculture.

To the northwest lie Brittany and Normandy, each with independent peoples and traditions dating back millennia. The thatched huts, bent apple trees and locally produced cheeses and ciders of Normandy contribute to its popularity as a place to visit. Many painters, understandably, have been drawn to the gentle green

countryside, dotted by black and white cows under a dramatic and often stormy sky, as well as to the colourful fishing ports along the coast.

Further west, the craggy coastline and harsh landscape of Brittany still conjure up the druidical presence of its original Celtic population, although today's descendants are relatively unwarlike fishermen. Particularly intriguing are the mysterious fields of megaliths and the pink granite rocks of the Corniche Bretonne.

Border country

To the northeast are the old provinces of Alsace and Lorraine. The Rhineland is the least well-defined of the six borders of the hexagon, and the result has been an unending series of nasty disputes between France and Germany ever since these two countries first came into existence. Alsace is especially valuable because its mines have turned France into the world's third largest producer of iron ore. The city of Strasbourg, which houses the European Parliament, has a German feel in its architecture and its culinary specialities, but is nonetheless defiantly French. Indeed, the paragon of French patriotism, Joan of Arc, hailed from neighbouring Lorraine, although she was martyred by the English in Rouen.

Not far south rise the gentle Jura mountains

and below them the French Alps, which stretch all the way down to the Alpes Maritimes and Côte d'Azur. The icy white peak of Mont Blanc, at 4,810 m (15,780 ft), is the highest mountain in Europe, its broad-shouldered shape, once seen, never forgotten.

The longest river

The subdued Loire valley, dug out by France's longest river (980 km/609 miles), is one of the country's chief tourist attractions. The splendid châteaux and gardens of Touraine still boast the glory of the *Ancien Régime* and its aristocratic pleasures.

Directly south is the enormous Massif Central, which lies in the heart of the country and supplies France with much of its grain. The strange *puys* of Auvergne (steep conical hills, caused by volcanic eruption during the earth's formation) contrast pleasantly with the rolling hills, plateaux and deep river valleys of neighbouring Périgord and Limousin, just over to its west.

That the particularly lush Dordogne river valley, in Périgord, has been alluring mankind for thousands upon thousands of years is evidenced by the prehistoric cave paintings found in its grottoes, particularly the enigmatic depictions of horses, elk and bison surrounded by arrows and strange symbols in the Lascaux cave complex, discovered in 1940 by two boys out walking their dog.

Further south still, basking under blue skies, is the sunny Midi. The landscape here, with its reds, yellows and browns, is very different again, with sun-baked clay buildings and a slower pace of life. Not that even the south is visually uniform: the wide, yellow fields that seem to stretch forever, the even rows of plane trees and charming red towns of Languedoc meld into the impossibly verdant Pyrenean mountain range towards the Spanish border, or the Cévennes and Ardèche national parks away to the east.

Many of the old southern cities, like Toulouse, Montpellier and Nîmes have been quick to embrace the modern age, although there is still an indefinable languor about all of them. Montpellier is perhaps the most dynamic, with its many new buildings and a thriving university and medical school, while Toulouse is famous for its aerospace industry and Nîmes has imaginative new housing and facilities for the arts. There is certainly no languor about the bustling seaport of Marseille, the jet-set towns of the Côte d'Azur and, of course, the cosmopolitan principality of Monaco, tucked between France and Italy.

The Mediterranean island of Corsica not only *seems* like a separate country to the northerner, it would even become one if the independence movement had its way. Its wild, barren landscape, steep cliffs and mountains and lovely beaches make it an interesting destination for the traveller and the sun-seeker, though a difficult one to traverse.

Many French towns and provinces are most

Eye of the hurricane

Paris has been called everything from a whore by Henry Miller to "one of the most noble ornaments of the world" by Montaigne. It is certainly the centre of everything French and the nexus of French transport (all distances are measured from the square in front of Notre-Dame Cathedral). It is the world's fashion capital; it is revolutionary in its grand arts and architectural projects but it also has one of the best preserved city centres in Europe. It has a distinctive population – stylish, intellectual and difficult – and very different from the rural French. But more of that later. ❑

famous for the splendid wines that bear their name. Yet that delightfully bubbly stuff is only one of Champagne's patriotic offerings; the entire northeast is a major industrial region producing coal, oats and sugar beet. Similarly, the long river valley running parallel to the eastern frontier and connecting the Saône with the Rhône river, not only cradles the vineyards of Burgundy and towns like Beaujolais, it also aids communication between the north of the country and the south.

LEFT: heading up into the Alps on the mountain train.
RIGHT: reflections in the Dordogne at Beynac-et-Cazenac.

A VARIED CLIMATE

The French climate is temperate, and varied, as one might expect in a country with so many different faces. In the northwest, the Atlantic ocean is the dominant influence, bringing high winds and driving rain as well as warm winters and cool summers. Eastern France, closer to the heart of Continental Europe, has marked seasonal changes, with cold winters and very warm summers, while the west enjoys a high proportion of sunshine, particularly along the Atlantic coast. The south has a Mediterranean climate, its winters mild, its summers hot, characterised by sudden fierce winds and dramatic storms.

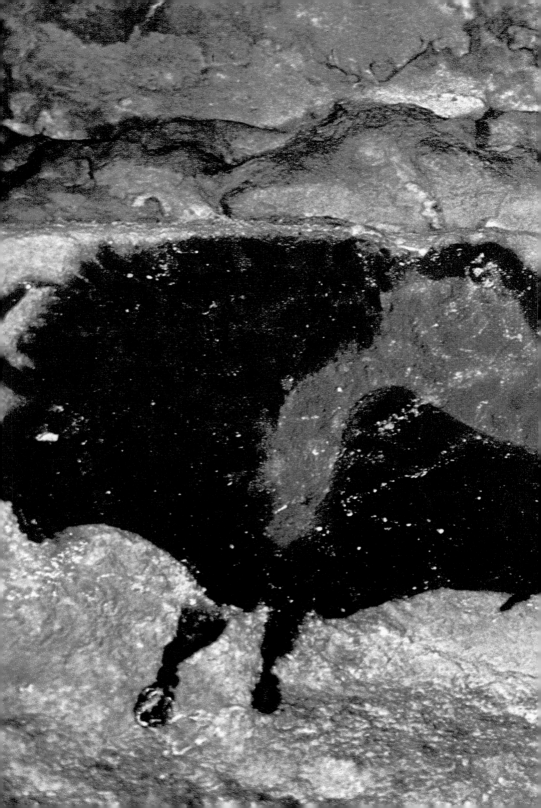

Decisive Dates

PRE-ROMAN AND GALLO-ROMAN ERA
600 BC: Greeks found the settlement of Massalia (Marseille).
Circa **300 BC:** Celts conquer southern Gaul.
121 BC: Romans cross the Alps and annex Provence.
Circa **58 BC:** Gallic tribes, under the leadership of Vercingetorix, are conquered by Julius Caesar.
AD 3rd–5th century: Barbarian invasions of Roman Gaul by, amongst others, Goths, Vandals and Franks.

4th century: Growing Gallo-Roman settlement on the Seine banks; Lutèce becomes Paris. Christianity arrives.
476: Overthrow of the last Roman emperor leading to the fall of the Roman empire.

THE DARK AGES
496: Clovis the Frank, first ruler of the Merovingian dynasty, converts to Christianity.
Circa **630:** First Benedictine monasteries were established.
751: Pepin the Short becomes first ruler of the Carolingian dynasty.
800: Pepin's son, Charlemagne, is crowned Holy Roman Emperor.

843: The Treaty of Verdun divides the Carolingian empire into three parts.

THE MIDDLE AGES
910: Foundation of the Benedictine monastery at Cluny.
987: Hugh Capet becomes the first ruler of the Capetian dynasty.
1066: Norman conquest of England.
1152: Henry Plantagenet (future Henry II of England) marries Eleanor of Aquitaine, with the result that one third of France falls into English hands.
1180: Philip Augustus begins a reign lasting 43 years.
1214: Philip Augustus wins the Battle of Bouvines, enabling him to claw back French territory from the English.
1226: Start of the reign (until 1270) of Louis IX, later canonised as St Louis.
1285: Philip IV, the Fair, is crowned.
1305: The Papacy is transferred from Rome to Avignon.
1328: Philip VI becomes the first Valois king.
1337: Start of the Hundred Years War with England.
1348: The Black Death.

THE RENAISSANCE
1415: French defeat by Henry V of England at the Battle of Agincourt.
1429: Joan of Arc leads French troops against the English at Orléans, and the Dauphin (Charles VII) is crowned at Reims.
1431: Joan of Arc burned at Rouen.
1453: End of the Hundred Years War.
1494–1559: Italian Wars – France and Austria fight over Italian territories.
1515: The Renaissance prince, François I, begins his reign; introduces the finest Italian artists to his court.
1562–1598: Wars of Religion setting Huguenot (Protestants) against Catholics.
1594: Henry of Navarre, having converted to Catholicism, is crowned Henry IV.
1624: Cardinal Richelieu becomes Minister of State, represses Protestants and involves France in the Thirty Years War with the Hapsburgs.
1643: Accession of Louis XIV, with Cardinal Mazarin as Minister of State.
1715: Accession of Louis XV.
1756–1763: The Seven Years War; France loses her North American colonies.
1769: Annexation of Corsica.

1774: Accession of Louis XVI.
1778–1783: French support for the 13 colonies in the American War of Independence.

THE FIRST EMPIRE AND RESTORATION
1789: Storming of the Bastille.
1792: Overthrow of Louis XVI. Declaration of the First Republic.
1793: Execution of Louis XVI; Robespierre's Reign of Terror, ending in his execution in 1794.
1804: Napoleon crowned as Emperor; introduction of the Code Napoleon. First Empire.
1815: Napoleon's One Hundred Days; he is defeated at the Battle of Waterloo and exiled to St Helena.
1830: Revolution deposes Charles X in favour of the July Monarchy of Louis-Philippe.
1848: Louis-Philippe, the Citizen King, deposed. Second Republic.

THE SECOND EMPIRE AND THIRD REPUBLIC
1851: Coup d'état by Louis Napoleon Bonaparte, Napoleon's nephew. Second Empire.
1870: Franco-Prussian War; overthrow of Louis Napoleon Bonaparte (Napoleon III).

THIRD REPUBLIC
1871: Uprising by Paris Commune with 25,000 people killed. Third Republic.
1889: Universal Exhibition of Paris; construction of the Eiffel Tower.
1897–1899: The Dreyfus Affair.
1914: Start of World War I.
1916: Battle of Verdun.
1918: End of World War I.
1919: Treaty of Versailles.
1939: Outbreak of World War II.
1940: Paris is bombed and occupied by the Germans. General de Gaulle, in London, calls for resistance to the occupiers.
1944: Allied landings in Normandy on D-Day. Paris is liberated and General de Gaulle heads a Provisional Government until 1946, when a Fourth Republic is declared.
1945: End of World War II.
1946: War commences in Indo-China.
1954: France withdraws from Indo-China. Start of the Algerian insurrection.

PRECEDING PAGES: Lascaux cave paintings.
LEFT: the crowning of Clovis.
RIGHT: the St Bartholomew's Day Massacre, which took place in 1572.

1958: The Algerian crisis topples the Fourth Republic.

THE FIFTH REPUBLIC
1959: General de Gaulle elected the first president of the Fifth Republic.
1962: Algerian independence.
1965: De Gaulle re-elected president.
1968: Strikes and student riots in Paris against the university system and the Government forces de Gaulle into an election. He wins but resigns in a year.
1969: Georges Pompidou elected president.
1974: Valérie Giscard-d'Estaing elected president.

1981: François Mitterrand elected president.
1986: Right-wing Jacques Chirac becomes prime minister in a unique "cohabitation" with a socialist president, reaffirmed in 1988 when socialists regain power.
1989: Bicentenary celebrations of the Revolution herald a the opening of the Louvre Pyramid, Grande Arche and Opéra Bastille – Mitterrand's *Grands Projets*.
1995: Jacques Chirac elected president.
1997: Socialist Lionel Jospin becomes prime minister, creating a second "cohabitation".
1998: Regional elections confirm a political polarisation, with the mainstream right losing out to the extremist National Front. ❑

...lio cesare imperante · A theodoto dimensa · nominatur pars terci
...ed uere est quarta · na asia ētnē partes duas ⁊ affrica teia europā
...abe europa maria XI · īsulas XL · prouincias XX · oiētes XXVI
...utē opida CXX · flumina XXI · Gentesq; diuersas numero XX
...egna ū que si colore rubeo circūscripta ad romanos frācosq; pertinent in
EVROPA dicta ē ab europpa filia agenoris regis lybie · uxoris iouis ·

Hunī osofia Grecia Macedonia etruria
Vvandali Recia dardania Achaia Sclauia
gothi norica dalmacia Atheis Apulia Rooa
Septem
trion Panonia italia capania
Scannia Dacia Sclaui albadus Tuscia Lauinia
Norweis
Suenia Bauaria
Saxonia histria willa Bur gun di na
Alemania a qui ta nia
Germania gallia gallia gallia
Germania gallia Narbona
Gallia
colonia
Gallia
neustria
Flandria hispania hesperia
tincona
Galicia lusitania

THE EARLY YEARS

As fossil finds and cave paintings attest, France has been inhabited for millennia.

The Gauls settled it, the Romans usurped it and the French made it a nation

After the glaciers receded from Europe, around 450 BC, France was populated from the east by a large influx of Celtic peoples. These were the legendary Gauls, or Galli, celebrated in every French language classroom from Paris to Martinique as *nos ancêtres les Gaulois* (our ancestors the Gauls). Renowned for long hair and fighting naked in battle – and for cartoon heroes Asterix and Obelix – the Gauls were a strong and independent people who left an indelible stamp on the French character.

The southern part of the country, meanwhile, received the attention of the classical civilisations. The coast was hellenised by Greek merchants who founded the port of Massilia (Marseille) around 600 BC. In 121 BC the Roman Senate assumed a protectorate over the region, expanding its influence into Provence. Then in 58 BC, the Gallic tribes were invaded by an ambitious Roman proconsul seeking prestige through conquest, Julius Caesar. The Gauls, under the famed Vercingetorix, put up a brave fight, but in the end Caesar triumphed.

The Romans

The Roman occupation of Gaul brought such refinements as roads, architecture and urbanisation, especially in the southern Midi, Nîmes and Arles. Lyon became a capital of sorts, and the French language began to develop from Celtic and Latin. On the Seine sprang up a small town called Lutetia, that would someday grow to be the great metropolis of Paris.

Attracted by relative peace and prosperity, many "barbarian" peoples migrated to Roman Gaul from the 3rd to 5th century. Among these were the Franks (whence France derived its name), the Burgundians, the Goths (Visi and Ostro), the badly-behaved Vandals, and the Alan. In 451, the growing town of Lutetia narrowly escaped total destruction by Attila the Hun through the intervention of its patron saint,

Genevieve. In the 5th and 6th century Britons from Cornwall and Wales emigrated, giving the peninsula of Brittany its name.

The incoming barbarian presence began to undermine flagging Roman authority and, in 486, a Frankish king, Clovis, attacked and defeated the Gallo-Romans at Soissons. He

consolidated his power by defeating the Alemanni at Tolbiac in 496 and the Visigoths near Poitiers in 507. Converting to Christianity and moving his capital to Paris (507), Clovis was an important precursor of the French state, which he called "Francia". His descendants, however, were weak leaders, and when Charles Martel led the French troops to victory over the invading Muslims at Poitiers (732), the groundwork was laid for a new dynasty. His son, Pepin the Short (whose wife was called Big-footed Bertha) crowned himself King of the Franks, beginning the Carolingian succession.

Pepin's offspring was Charlemagne, whose papal coronation at Rome in 800 created the

LEFT: a medieval map places Burgundy at the centre of Europe.

RIGHT: the Roman Pont-du-Gard in Provence.

Holy Roman Empire. Charlemagne doubled his domain to include what later became Germany, by fighting the pagans of western Europe in the name of Christianity. He is also known for unifying the Franks and Gallo-Romans under his leadership and encouraging education in his court. The *Chanson de Roland* (*see below*) later celebrated the bravery of his knights.

The problem of succession plagued Charlemagne as it had Clovis, and in 843 the Treaty of Verdun divided the empire into three. After a weak and unstable period, the Count of Paris, Hugh Capet, declared himself king in 987 although at that time his jurisdiction extended

only to the region around Paris. He was, however, the founder of a long-surviving dynasty: 806 years later, his descendant Louis XVI was addressed as "Citizen Louis Capet" before his execution.

LA CHANSON DE ROLAND

The *Chanson de Roland* is the epic tale, written around 1100, of the death of one of Charlemagne's brave knights, commander of his army when its rearguard was crushed by the Basques in the Pyrenees in 778. The work traditionally marks the conception of both French literature and the chivalrous ideal of a *douce* France worthy of self-sacrifice.

The Middle Ages

Religious fervour inspired the erection of some of France's most impressive monuments. The Romanesque church at Mont-St Michel was built from 1024 to 1144. France accommodated the rise of monasticism with two of the greatest orders: the Benedictines at Cluny and the Cistercians at Cîteaux. Although it was destroyed during the French Revolution, the abbey church at Cluny was the largest of its kind until the construction of St Peter's in Rome.

French participation in the Crusades (1096–1291) bolstered nationalism (*Gloria Dei per Francos,* or the Glory of God through the French, was the motto of French crusaders) and worldliness, and the Romanesque style was strongly influenced by Eastern architecture. The 1066 invasion of England also expanded French influence and marks the last time England was occupied, although strictly speaking this was more the result of Norman than French foreign policy.

French fortune was checked, however, by the 1152 marriage of Eleanor of Aquitaine to England's Henry II, and his consequent possession of this huge chunk of France. The accession of Philip II (Augustus) to the throne in 1180 greatly strengthened the monarchy, and his victory at Bouvines in 1214 helped win back from England some of its French possessions as well as some sense of a national identity. Philip much improved the status of his capital by advancing the construction of Notre Dame cathedral (1163–1320), the University of Paris (founded in 1120) and the Louvre fortress.

In 1253 the Sorbonne was established. The growth of cities and universities was complementary, and signalled a shift away from the dominance of monasteries and feudalism. New rational thinkers such as Pierre Abélard emerged, although the castration he received for tutoring his student Héloïse a bit too affectionately illustrates the precariousness of the intellectual's position versus the orthodoxy of the church. Nevertheless, his example also proves the zeal with which the French pursued scholarship and romance. Concomitant with the growth of cities was the construction of majestic Gothic cathedrals (*see page 31*). Those at Chartres, Rouen, Reims and Amiens are among the most impressive buildings in the world.

The monarchy and kingdom grew stronger under forceful leaders such as Louis IX (St

Louis, 1226–70), who established the Parliament, built Sainte Chapelle and fought the infidel; and Philip IV (the Fair, 1285–1314). Yet France remained a confusing hotchpotch of independent duchies for some time. The southern region of Languedoc suffered vigorous repression at the hands of northerners angered by the Albigensian and Waldensian heresies.

The Hundred Years' War

This war, which began in 1337, was a long and protracted struggle to remove the English presence in France. Supported by the truculent Burgundians, the English tried to get a conti-

Instead of being able to temper the growing conflict between the dukes of Burgundy and the dukes of Orléans, he managed only to increase their bitterness.

In 1415, the English army under Henry V, composed largely of archers and light infantry, routed the more numerous but less mobile French at Agincourt. Seven years later, when Charles VI died, the French crown was awarded to his grandson, the English King Henry VI, rather than the French Dauphin. The end of the Hundred Years' War (which actually lasted 116 years) in 1453 essentially marks the end of the medieval period. ❑

nental foothold, and it was not until 1558 that they were finally kicked out of Calais. Indeed, it was not until 1802 that the British sovereigns relinquished the title "King of France and England". Internal matters were complicated by the decimating Black Death (1337–50) and by the so-called Babylonian Captivity (1309–78) when the papal seat was transferred to Avignon to escape the petty intrigues of Rome. Then, to worsen matters, Charles VI (son of Charles the Wise) began to lose his mind in 1392.

LEFT: Abélard and Héloïse.
ABOVE: Joan of Arc, the Iron Maiden martyred in 1431 by the English.

JOAN OF ARC

The tide of French affairs during the Hundred Years War with the English seemed at its lowest ebb when a peasant girl from Lorraine appeared on the scene, Joan of Arc. Inspired by heavenly voices and an angelic vision, she led the French troops to raise the seige of Orléans and crown the Dauphin king at Reims in 1429. She was captured by the English and burned at the stake in Rouen in 1431 (at the remarkable age of 19) but Joan's defiant patriotism illustrated the people's growing sense of national identity. The words which were spoken at her trial, "God will send victory to the French", inspired the nation.

ARCHITECTURE: A GOLDEN AGE

Fuelled by the explosion of church building, the Romanesque and Gothic styles represent the richest period of French architecture, lasting from 950 to 1500

To the medieval mind, the Romanesque church represented a spiritual journey, with a symbolic lifting of the veils suggested by the architecture. In this Bible written in stone, the narthex (vestibule) was Galilee and the choir Jerusalem: a passage from witness to transcendence. Yet curiously, the mas-

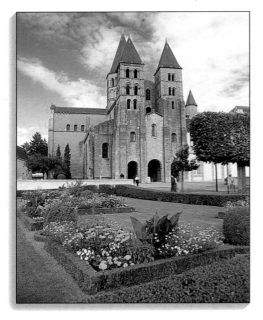

terpieces of Romanesque art also sprang from the religious materialism of the Middle Ages. The building boom from 1050 to 1350 saw the creation of 80 cathedrals, 500 major churches and countless smaller ones.

The medieval builders were inspired by the remains of Roman buildings languishing in French cities. During the Romanesque period, from 950 to 1150, recycled Roman stone found its way into round arches and thick walls, conical spires and solid belfries. The buildings were simple or majestic, with austere crypts or exuberantly frescoed walls.

Unsurprisingly, the Romanesque tradition had its greatest flowering in regions with a rich

Roman past or in places which had close contact with Italian civilisation. The Romanesque style spread to France from northern Italy, led by the Lombards, skilled master-craftsmen. The Roman basilica was the prototype, a simple structure with radiating aisles. However, in fertile French soil, the Romanesque soon had its vernacular forms that surpassed many Italian models. The triumph of the Romanesque also reflects a spiritual resurgence and the spread of monasticism.

Local stone was used, whether golden-hued limestone or grey granite, pink sandstone or rosy southern bricks. In France, stone vaults were commonplace, both as a prevention against fire and as a means of creating spatial unity: the seamless effect achieved was one no timber ceiling surmounting stone walls could match. Barrel-vaulting was the favoured system, a continuous vault of semi-circular or pointed sections, unbroken by cross-vaults. Stone carving flourished, with crude capitals giving way to more sophisticated forms, including the lavish carving of the tympanum.

Although Christ in Majesty and the Last Judgment predominate in major pictorial scenes, equally symbolic designs feature foliage or mythical beasts.

Regional styles

Burgundy remains a treasure trove of the Romanesque. Paray-le-Monial is a scaled-down version of the lost abbey at Cluny, once the largest church in Europe. Tournus is a masterpiece of early Romanesque, the surpassingly lovely basilica at Vézélay being its sole rival. Fontenay represents the perfect Burgundian abbey.

While the greatest concentration of inspiring Romanesque architecture is found in Burgundy, many regions boast individual treasures, from the Auvergne to Alsace, Languedoc to Provence. While the Burgundian style was creative, the Provençal style was conservative, one of tall, narrow churches. Alsace was influenced by the more cumbersome Rhineland Romanesque whereas Languedoc favoured domes. In general, northern Romanesque was more progressive, choosing naves with aisles and twin towers to mask the ends of the aisles. By contrast, southern Romanesque was more resolutely Roman, preferring domes and aisleless naves.

In Anjou, Fontevraud is the most impressive medieval abbey in France, essentially a Romanesque complex with Gothic additions.

Further south, French Romanesque is often infused with a Moorish flavour; such as the cathedral at Le Puy. The majority of such sites lie on the pilgrimage route to Santiago de Compostela in Spain.

Provence produced a golden age of Romanesque, visible in a cluster of Cistercian abbeys. As for St-Trophime in Arles, its Romanesque structure and cloisters were clearly inspired by the surrounding Roman remains. However, the greatest Romanesque complex in the South of France is the abbey church of Sainte-Foy in Conques.

Gothic glory

Arguably Europe's most influential style, Gothic originated in the Ile-de-France, close to the centres of royal power. The finest testament to the glorious Gothic period lies in the airy northern cathedrals of Paris and Chartres, Amiens and Reims, Beauvais and Bourges, Laon, Le Mans and Strasbourg.

However, the transition between Romanesque and Gothic is already evident in the Burgundian abbey of Pontigny, a well-preserved Cistercian foundation built between 1150 and 1212. As the English writer Barry Miles has pointed out, the Burgundian discovery of rib-vaulting, the pointed arch and the flying buttress "paved the way to Gothic, with its unbroken columns soaring towards heaven, and huge windows beyond the wildest dreams of Romanesque builders".

Gothic was a form forged from the restrictions of the Romanesque tradition and a natural quest for wider, higher, lighter churches. In striving for a soaring, vertical effect, the Gothic ideal echoed the quest for God. The style is characterised by ribbed vaulting, pointed arches and flying buttresses. By stabilising the thrust and orchestrating space, buildings could be more ambitious. The new techniques enabled space to be freed for larger windows, leading to the sublime stained glass of Chartres Cathedral, the most complete collection of medieval glass in Europe.

Early Gothic, from 1180 to 1250, is symbolised by Chartres, which adopted flying buttresses, pointed arches and new window space. Chartres is called "the mind of the Middle Ages made manifest", the most coherent of Gothic cathedrals.

Reims Cathedral boasts a taller nave than Chartres, as well as a *claire voie* (open-work) gallery crowned by statues of mythical beasts.

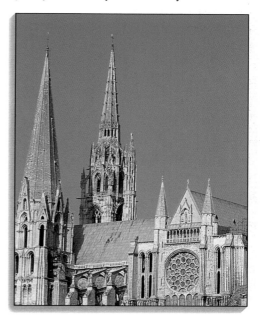

The clerestory windows, with their slender bars of stone, pioneered Gothic tracery.

High Gothic, the golden age of cathedral building, lasted from 1250 to 1375, and represented a vertiginous spectacle of tall clerestory windows and luminous naves, as in Beauvais Cathedral. In its final, exuberant phase, Gothic became Flamboyant, thanks to its flame-shaped columns and ornate window tracery.

Ornamental excess embraced a forest of statuary and gables, encrusted by pinnacles and purely decorative archways. Strasbourg Cathedral encompasses the entire period, from a Romanesque crypt to a frothy spire and west facade, a masterpiece of Gothic tracery. ❏

LEFT: the Romanesque Basilique du Sacré-Coeur at Paray-le-Monial, Burgundy.
RIGHT: the Gothic Chartres Cathedral.

LVDOVICO MAGNO

IVC. ET NAVAR. REX CHRISTIANIS

Ludovico Magno

THE AGE OF ABSOLUTISM

The 17th and 18th centuries saw the rise and apogee of the monarchy, and a golden age of learning before the storm clouds of revolution set in

The reign of shrewd Louis XI (1461–83) prepared the way for the French Renaissance. It saw the elimination of much opposition to royal authority, adding Maine, Provence and Burgundy to the realm, thereby uniting most of present-day France (the duchy of Brittany was annexed in 1491 on the marriage of Anne of Brittany to Charles VIII).

The 16th century brought important changes to France in almost every area. The discovery and absorption of the Italian Renaissance inspired great artistic activity at the courts of Francis I (1515–47) and Henry II (1547–59). Leonardo da Vinci himself spent his final years at the royal château of Amboise in the Loire valley, and writers such as the poet Ronsard, the essayist Montaigne and the bawdy comedian Rabelais all contributed to the growth of French literature. Explorer Jacques Cartier (and later Samuel de Champlain) carried the fleur-de-lis (symbol of France) into the North American wilderness. The reformed teachings of Martin Luther and John Calvin took hold, especially in the south of France. Even more important was the general rise in knowledge, particularly outside the aristocracy and church.

The latter part of the 16th century was marred by fierce religious wars between the Protestants, called Huguenots, and the Catholics, culminating in the St Bartholomew's Day Massacre (1572), when thousands of Protestants were slaughtered by royal troops as they prayed. The blame for this has been laid on Catherine de Medici, the scheming Florentine who exerted power through her husband Henry II and her sons, Francis II, Charles IX and Henry III.

A strange sequence of deaths and assassinations among Catholic rivals to the throne brought the crown to the Protestant Henry of Navarre (Henry IV), destined to be one of France's greatest kings. To appease the worried citizenry, he converted to Catholicism with the memorable declaration that "Paris is worth a mass." The womanising Henry, whose tongue had been sprinkled with wine and garlic at his baptism to give him proper spirit, endeared himself to France with his leadership and boisterous behaviour. He declared there should be a

chicken in every pot, and improved the religious climate with the Edict of Nantes (1598), granting some tolerance to the Protestants. All France mourned when he was stabbed to death in 1610 by the fanatic Ravaillac.

The rigorous Richelieu

The tender age at succession of Louis XIII (1610–43) made his reign vulnerable to the wily machinations of interlopers such as Cardinal Richelieu, a humourlessly strong-minded man who got his daily exercise jumping over the furniture of his apartments. Richelieu, nonetheless, did much to strengthen the central authority of the monarchy. Indeed, the combi-

PRECEDING PAGES: Burgundian Romanesque church.
LEFT: Louis XIV, the Sun King.
RIGHT: Cardinal Richelieu.

nation of royal power and longevity that char-acterised the 17th and 18th centuries led this period to be known as the Age of Absolutism.

As Grand Master of Naviga-tion and Commerce, Richelieu also bolstered France's mercan-tile status, expanded its Ameri-can holdings and founded the Académie Française (1653). At the same time, the wars and in-trigues pursued by Richelieu caused great misery among the people. The Thirty Years War (1618–48) was expensive and inconclusive, and Richelieu

> ### WORSHIP THE KING
>
> The nobility became mere courtesans at Louis XIV's court. The role of one was to pass the king's shirt at the Levée, of another to cry "The king's meat!" as it passed to the table.

monarchy, and stories of the luxury surround-ing Louis are legion.

Determined to escape the complications of Paris, which was becoming so important a city as to be inde-pendent of all authority, Louis decided to build a royal court so magnificent that it would require the presence and conse-quent submission of the aris-tocracy. The construction of the palace at Versailles accom-plished this very well.

Louis judiciously chose his ministers from

ended the tolerance of Henry IV with the seige of the Huguenot city of La Rochelle.

The Sun King

The death of Louis XIII left his five-year-old son Louis XIV on the throne. Destined to rule longer than any king of France, his reign began somewhat inauspiciously with a regency presided over by his mother, Anne of Austria, and Richelieu's successor, Cardinal Mazarin. The nobility sought to regain its former power during the rebellion of the Fronde (1648–53), but was ultimately subdued. Yet, in spite of these difficulties, the reign of *Le Roi-Soleil* (Sun King) marks the apogee of the French

the bourgeoisie and petty nobility to keep the nobles in their place. He gave France the largest army in Europe. He was indeed the state, as he boasted. Yet under him the "state" also grew somewhat distant from the people. The bour-geoisie became envious of the opulence of Ver-sailles, while workers and peasants grew jealous of the bourgeoisie. The revocation of the Edict of Nantes (1685) renewed hostility toward the Protestants, many of whom left the country for good (including 200,000 artisans France could scarcely afford to lose). There was a renewal of hostilities between the sects in the Cévennes to the south (1702–05), and a brief peasant uprising in Brittany was crushed. The famines of 1662 and 1693 underscored societal differences.

In spite of these ethnic problems, the age of Louis XIV witnessed a great revival of popular interest in classical learning and art. The theatre of Corneille and Racine, the fables of La Fontaine, the comedies of Molière, the oratory of Bossuet, and the brilliant thought of Pascal and Descartes all brought to French literature a refinement that it had not known before.

Louis's death in 1715 left his five-year-old great-grandson Louis XV on the throne, who in turn reigned until 1774. Despite Louis XV's personal mediocrity, France's reputation as the

associated American idealism with their own Enlightenment.

Discontent brewing

The success of the relationship between France and America was offset by the war's enormous cost, and the taxation proposed by Louis XVI's ministers Turgot and Necker during his reign from 1774 to 1793 grated on a populace that had become less tolerant of inequality. Discontent was fuelled by the bad harvests of the 1780s, and for reasons that remain murky even today, France plunged into a revolution that changed the course of history.   ❑

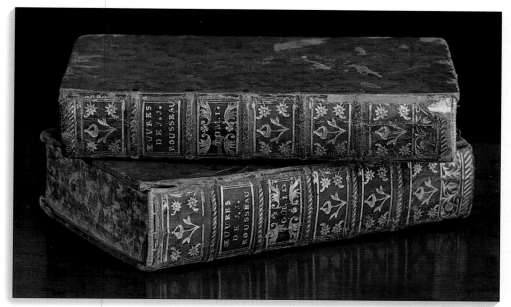

most sophisticated nation on earth grew steadily in an age known as the Enlightenment.

The acquisition of knowledge apparently did not quite extend to military matters, however, for France lost its North American possessions to England after the Seven Years War (1756–63). The French did, however, later gain a sort of revenge by aiding the American rebels in their subsequent War of Independence.

The philosophical import of this American revolution was not lost on the French, who

LEFT: the opulent Hall of Mirrors at Versailles.
RIGHT: significant and weighty tomes from the philosopher Jean-Jacques Rousseau.

THE ENLIGHTENMENT

The Enlightenment spawned unprecedented cultural activity, and Paris saw itself as a beacon illuminating the rest of civilization. The fight for intellectual progress took place on several fronts. Montesquieu argued for representative law and political reform. Diderot and d'Alembert directed the mammoth *Encyclopédie* from 1750 to 1780. Buffon studied natural history, and the Montgolfier brothers recorded the first balloon flight in 1783. Rousseau suggested sweeping changes in society and education and Voltaire, perhaps the brightest light of all, virulently satirised oppression and intolerance wherever he saw it.

REVOLUTION AND THE REPUBLIC

As the rich grew richer and the poor had nothing, discontent exploded into revolt.
Heads rolled in the First Republic. Then along came Napoleon...

What we refer to as the French Revolution began in 1789, but it actually consisted of several different power struggles that overlapped and fed off one another. To settle the fiscal crisis, Louis XVI convened an assembly of deputies elected by the nobility, clergy and Third Estate (everybody else). The bourgeoisie seized the occasion to create an assembly charged with electing a new constitutional government.

On 14 July 1789 a Parisian mob stormed the Bastille prison, long a symbol of royal power. Inspired by this audacity, peasants organised themselves across the country and the bourgeois National Assembly abolished the privileges of the nobility and clergy. The Declaration of the Rights of Man and the Citizen, signed on 26 August, was the culmination of a century of enlightened thought.

In this spirit of reform, France was reorganised into a constitutional monarchy and its ancient provinces were converted into 83 smaller departments. The republican *tricolore* replaced the royal fleur-de-lis as the national flag. Meanwhile, however, Queen Marie-Antoinette had secretly requested intervention from her brother, the Emperor of Austria, and so war was declared. Counter-revolutionary activity in Brittany, the Vendée and Lyon confused matters further.

A new assembly, called the Convention, angrily abolished all royal authority, instituted the metric system, adopted the "Marseillaise" as the national anthem, and declared 1793 to be Year One of the Republic.

With a new system of months and dates to replace the Julian calendar, not even time was held sacred by the zealous insurgents. Louis and his family were arrested while they were trying to flee, and on 21 January 1793 the King of France was guillotined in the name of his people in the Place de la Concorde.

PRECEDING PAGES: Delacroix's Revolution.
LEFT: Napoleon Bonaparte.
RIGHT: Robespierre beheading the executioner.

To maintain control, the Convention, under the direction of Robespierre, assumed draconian powers and executed any who challenged its authority (the final death toll was around 40,000). This period, known as the Terror, ended only after the execution of Robespierre himself (1794).

Napoleon Bonaparte

A young Corsican general who had distinguished himself in battle – one Napoleon Bonaparte – took advantage of the climate of confusion by seizing power in 1799. He quickly consolidated his power by enacting a sweeping body of civil legislation known as the Code Napoleon. This code remains the backbone of the French legal system even today. In addition, Napoleon reformed the French educational and monetary systems, founded the Bank of France, appeased French Catholics frightened by the revolution and reunited the divided country. His popularity enabled him to crown himself emperor in 1804. He also sold a large chunk of middle America to Thomas Jefferson in 1803.

Unfortunately, these early successes led Napoleon to believe he could create an empire of the order of Charlemagne's, and, although he almost succeeded, France became embroiled in an unending succession of wars that culminated in the disastrous expedition into Russia in 1812. Defeated and exiled to Elba, Bonaparte escaped and made a dramatic return during the short-lived "Hundred Days", but the alarmed European powers defeated him once and for all at Waterloo (1815). Napoleon's wars had reduced France to poverty.

Restoration and rebellion

The Bourbon kings were placed back on the throne by the victors and initiated a period of great interest in palatial repair, which is why their reign is known as the Restoration. The bourgeoisie, however, were unhappy to serve a fat king again after the great expansion of their importance under the Revolution and Napoleon.

When Charles X (1824–30) unwisely curtailed the freedom of the press in July 1830, students and workers erected barricades in Paris and began three days of rioting in protest. The King was forced to flee, and his cousin Louis-Philippe, who claimed to support republican principles, was appointed to replace him and was publicly embraced by the ageing Marquis de Lafayette before the Hôtel de Ville. France became a constitutional monarchy again.

The emotions that precipitated the "July Days" of 1830 were in many ways the legacy of the unfinished Revolution. The desire for individual expression and modernity was also translated into an exciting new body of literature that defied classical rules (*see below*).

Technological innovation and urban growth consolidated the dominance of the bourgeoisie and fostered the development of a large, urban working class. Photography was invented by Joseph Niepce in 1816 and advanced by Louis Daguerre in the 1830s. The railways (1832) revolutionised transportation in France as they enhanced the capital city.

Aware of the changes taking place, complicated class doctrines were advocated by philosophers such as Saint-Simon, Auguste Comte, E.P. Fournier and Pierre Proudhon that were later to serve as an inspiration to Karl

ROMANTICISM

Feeling restless with the complacency of the Restoration, a new generation of writers sparked rejuvenated interest in literature and sought to stage an intellectual revolution to parallel the political ones that had taken place. Led by the young Victor Hugo, these writers emphasised the power of the imagination in distinct contrast to the rationality of the 18th century *philosophes* such as Jean-Jacques Rousseau.

The most important literary form of the romantic period was that best equipped to describe and appeal to the now-powerful bourgeosie: the *roman* (the French word for novel, which of course corresponds closely to the French word

romantisme). Allowing free expression, the novel was well-suited both to paint exotic pictures of foreign lands and less flattering ones of a progressively industrial and aggressive French society.

Authors such as Stendhal and Honoré de Balzac disparagingly exposed the rapacity and snobbery of their fellow citizens and subjected them to minute analyses of character and appearance.

During the July Monarchy these social changes accelerated, the dominance of the bourgeoisie was consolidated and Paris became the capital not only of Europe but of the 19th century.

Marx. History writing, as exemplified by Jules Michelet, Alexis de Tocqueville and François Guizot became a newly respected mode of expression. The caricatures of cartoonist Auguste Daumier also reflected the changing nature of the times.

In spite of 17 assassination attempts in 18 years and several serious urban riots (Paris, 1831 and 1834; Lyon, 1831), opposition from extremists of the left and right, and growing class tension, the July Monarchy was at least able to avoid foreign conflict. Moreover, the government, led by Louis-Philippe's minister Guizot, presided over a steady economic combined to remind workers of their inferior status. In February 1848, Guizot forbade an anti-government banquet to be held in Paris and provoked public rioting and barricades similar to those of 1830. The National Guard supported the demonstrators, and suddenly Louis-Philippe had to flee the country just as unceremoniously as his predecessor.

The poet Lamartine proclaimed the founding of the Second Republic, and a provisional government was formed that shortened the working day, declared universal male suffrage and abolished slavery. After initial elections were won by moderate republicans, workers of

growth. Responding once to a complaint that his government favoured the rich, Guizot earned a measure of notoriety by responding to the plaintiff, "Then make yourself rich!"

The Second Republic

The downfall of Louis-Philippe remains as difficult to explain as the previous revolutions. Again, one of the issues at stake was the unhappiness of those who felt strangled by society. The 1847 fiscal crisis and unfair voting laws

LEFT: caricature of Victor Hugo by Faustin.
RIGHT: Daumier believed that incarceration did not always produce the best results.

the far left rioted during the so-called "June Days" of 1848. Barricades again went up in Paris, but this time the insurrectionists were crushed and 4,000 of them killed. A presidential election conferred power upon the surprisingly popular nephew of Napoleon, Louis Napoleon Bonaparte. A man without the dynamism that his name suggested, Bonaparte declared himself emperor and arrested his opponents in a coup on 2 December 1851. The idealistic republic ended where it had started, with yet another monarchy.

The Second Empire continued much of the expansion, both industrial and intellectual, that had taken place under Louis-Philippe. France acquired Savoy and Nice from Italy in 1860, the importance of which should be fully realised by the many topless sunbathers on the Côte d'Azur today. The Crimean War against Russia (1854–55) was inconclusive, but nevertheless France began to extend its influence into other regions, including China, Mexico and northern Africa.

Having learned the importance of street barricades in overturning governments, Louis Napoleon entrusted the Baron Haussmann with the beautification of Paris. Haussmann changed the face of the city by widening its avenues, eliminating its congested areas and creating large public parks like the Bois de Boulogne. The result was a truly grand, international metropolis that also happened to be a much harder place to stage a good riot.

The status of the Second Empire ended abruptly in 1870. Tricked into a precipitous declaration of war against Prussia by the insulting Ems Telegram, which allegedly made sport of his moustache, an overconfident Bonaparte established his lack of military ability once and for all by leading his troops to a cataclysmic defeat at Sedan.

Following this debacle, the entire superstructure of the Second Empire promptly collapsed, whereupon a provisional republican government was formed that tried in vain to perpetuate the war against the better-equipped Prussians. Although this attempt failed, wounded French pride was assuaged somewhat by leader Léon Gambetta's escape from besieged Paris in a balloon. Victory for Bismarck's army was inevitable, however, and the French were forced to cede the eastern provinces of Alsace and Lorraine.

The Commune

In Paris, a feeling of patriotic indignation, combined with resentment towards the extreme hardship that had been inflicted upon the capital during the Prussian war, created a climate of bitter discontent. When the provincial government, temporarily seated at Bordeaux, surrendered to the Prussian demands, exasperated Parisians declared the formation of an independent workers' commune. With the support of its National Guard, the Commune refused to comply with orders to surrender to the French Army based at Versailles. The result was a bloody two-month civil war in which Paris was

again besieged and which only ended after 20,000 *communards* gave their lives to protect their city from their fellow countrymen. The northeast wall of the Père Lachaise cemetery, Mur des Fédérés, where the last insurgents were gunned down, has since become a pilgrimage site for members of the left.

In spite of the disastrous conditions which spawned it, the Third Republic continued for 70 years and escorted France confidently into the 20th century. In the aftermath of the violent Commune, the republicans chose to concentrate on stability both at home and abroad. Basing its power among the enormous petty

NOVEL CRITICISM

The retrenchment of the monied bourgeoisie under Louis Napoleon gave added fodder to the novelists and government critics who had thrived under the July Monarchy (see page 42). Indeed, the republican Victor Hugo was forced to live in exile in the English Channel Islands. The description of social mores received further refinement at the hands of Gustave Flaubert, whose *Madame Bovary* and *Sentimental Education* shocked readers by their graphic accounts of adultery and avarice. The poet Charles Baudelaire, too, excited indignation by his celebration of sensuality and the morbid attraction of death.

bourgeoisie, the Republic nevertheless made important concessions to workers such as allowing unions in 1884. The Ferry Laws (1880–81), moreover, granted free public education across France. The Republic also managed to atone somewhat for the loss of Alsace and Lorraine by developing an enormous colonial empire in Africa and Asia. At its greatest extent, the French network of overseas possessions was second only to that of Britain.

Measured against the industrial and military

> ## BELLE EPOQUE
> The late 19th century witnessed an artistic flowering that foreshadowed the cultural preeminence Paris would enjoy for the next half-century.

ceased to enjoy or worked especially hard to dispel. Attributable in part to the excitement generated by its artistic and literary communities, in part to the prodigious amounts of *absinthe* and opium consumed by them, in part to the many nightclubs open to connoisseurs of the *demi-monde*, stories of "Gay Paree" titillated listeners around the world.

Although the stability of the Third Republic was conducive to this sort of activity, it would be misleading to ascribe the cultural ascen-

standards of Germany, Britain and the United States, France's worldwide importance diminished somewhat during this period. There are many other indices of a nation's greatness, however, and during the *belle époque* the French inspired the envy of the world with their ebulliance and *joie de vivre*.

Absinthe and opium

It was about this time that Paris began to cultivate the racy, *risqué* image that it has never

dancy of Paris to any particular government. The true genius of French culture seems to lie in its ability to weather political hurricanes without losing equilibrium. At any rate, Paris reminded the world of its importance with Universal Expositions in 1855, 1867 and 1889. The chief attraction in 1889 was the new Eiffel Tower, with its 1,792 steps painfully reminding visitors of the weight of their history. Some thought the Tower ugly; others hailed it as a sign of the country's energy.

The Dreyfus affair

The atmosphere of modernity did not, however, disrupt the cherished French tradition of polit-

LEFT: *The line for rat meat,* Cham's cartoon on the Commune.
RIGHT: *Le Moulin de la Galette* (1876) by Renoir.

ical divisions. A minor tremor occurred in the late 1880s when General Boulanger excited great patriotic fervour and seemed capable of upsetting the political balance. This only served as a prelude, however, to the Dreyfus affair.

Suspected of assisting German spies, and convicted in part because of his Jewish background, Captain Alfred Dreyfus became the focal point of an outbreak of national paranoia that severely rocked the French Army, Republic and standing order. Defended by the ever-volatile intelligentsia, summoned to the cause by Emile Zola's incendiary letter entitled "*J'Accuse!*", the Dreyfus affair was somewhat

similar to the American experience with McCarthyism and the Rosenberg Trial in that it aroused vehement emotions that greatly transcended the importance of the specific case.

The struggles between right and left, the military and the intellectuals, ceased altogether with the inevitable, yet unexpected outbreak of World War I (1914) and the chance for revenge upon the Germans. Opening the floodgates of patriotism, the war proved to be as shattering to the French as it was to all the other parties involved.

Quick German penetration of France was stopped by the Allies at the Marne. Protracted trench warfare followed, with tremendous losses sustained by both sides. Abortive campaigns in Champagne and Artois were followed by the costly victory of Verdun, in which there were 700,000 casualties. Ironically, Verdun was also the site of the partition of the Carolingian empire that had originally created France and Germany.

While most of the war was a bloody stalemate, the harsh terms imposed on Germany by President Georges Clemenceau in the Treaty of Versailles (1919) allowed the French to perceive it as a glorious victory in the grand tradition of Vercingetorix, Roland, Joan of Arc and Napoleon. Besides claiming enough reparations to gild the Eiffel Tower, the French were able to reunite Alsace and Lorraine under the *tricolore*. The heavy price of the victory, however, may still be seen in the lengthy list of names inscribed on the solemn memorials you find in every French village.

The années folles

Paris emerged from the catastrophe with characteristic élan and the decade which followed, the 1920s, proved to be one of the most lively in the city's history.

Unfortunately, the ebullience of the 1920s, known in France as the *années folles* (crazy years) did not serve as an accurate barometer of the rough weather ahead. The depression of the 1930s hit France hard. The collapse of the European money order, accelerated by the unstable cycle of reparation payments following the war, wreaked havoc on the French economy and political structure. ❑

AMERICANS IN PARIS

The emergence of Paris in the 1920s as a hothouse of literary talent was in great part due to the large expatriate colony whose attention had been called to France by the Great War. Ernest Hemingway, F. Scott Fitzgerald, Gertrude Stein, James Joyce and Henry Miller all spent considerable time imbibing French culture and enjoying a bohemian lifestyle away from the glare of publicity at home.

French writers, too, were well-represented during the interbellum. The novel profited from the craftsmanship of old masters like Marcel Proust and André Gide, while André Malraux injected adventure.

LEFT: Shakespeare and Company today.
RIGHT: the winter season, Nice.

NICE

FRENCH ART

French painters have been at the vanguard of most important artistic movements since the 17th century, from Rococo to Impressionism and beyond

The writer Emile Zola defined a work of art as "a corner of nature seen through a temperament". As befits their revolutionary sensibilities, French temperaments have been at the forefront of most major artistic movements since the 1600s. French art has dabbled in the Rococo, Neo-Classicism, Romanticism,

Realism, Impressionism and Cubism. However, as Gustave Courbet (1819–77) declared, "There can be no schools; there are only painters…"

Golden age

The 17th century was a golden age for European art: Italian painters were finally overshadowed by Rubens, Rembrandt, Velasquez and Poussin. Like his contemporaries, Nicolas Poussin (1594–1665), France's first great artist, succumbed to the lure of Rome, still the artistic capital, where the Classical and Christian worlds collide. Since his mind was at home in antiquity, the "philosophical painter" chose the grand manner, a nostalgic vision of calm, dig-

nified landscapes, dreamland pastorals inspired by the bygone age of classical art. As Poussin intended: "The subject-matter shall be grand, as are battles, heroic actions and divine things". Yet the breadth of the painter's vision is more easily compared with musicians and poets, notably Bach and Milton, than with contemporary artists. His search for structure and form concealed great power and deep reserves of emotion. As a result, Poussin influenced French artists from David and Ingres to Cézanne.

Claude Lorrain (1600–82) was equally enamoured of Rome but more dedicated to the pursuit of the picturesque. Whereas Poussin was passionately rational, Lorrain's landscapes were poetic and poignant. By contrast to these voluntary exiles, artists fêted in France were enslaved by the courtly tradition. Charles Lebrun (1619–90) acted as master of ceremonies to Louis XIV and produced portraits of great pomp. His successor, Pierre Mignard (1612–95) painted the court of Versailles with considerably more charm.

The flighty spirit of Rococo flourished in 18th-century France. Antoine Watteau (1684–1721) reflected the decorative tastes of the French aristocracy, painting a fantasy world of court revelries and bucolic bliss. In this shimmering, artificial society, even Watteau's shepherdesses wore silk. Yet Watteau's gift is great enough to infuse the genre with delicacy, refinement and a soft melancholy, perfectly expressed in his *Pierrot* (1719). As the art historian Ernst Gombrich says, "His awareness of the transience of beauty gave his art that intensity which none of his many admirers and imitators could equal".

Still, Jean-Honoré Fragonard (1732–1806) conveys a silken charm with his dancing, cavorting, amorous figures. He outlived his era, however, and, reduced to poverty after the Revolution, he died forgotten. François Boucher (1703–70), the celebrated court painter, was influenced by the Flemish artist Rubens and patronised by Madame de Pompadour, but is best known for his creamy, voluptuous nudes.

Revolutionary art

The erotic games of the *ancien régime* were swept away by the political correctness of 1789 *(see page 41)*. Jacques-Louis David (1748–1825) was the official artist of the Revolutionary government.

An ardent supporter of Robespierre, David acted as a glorious propagandist, revelling in the patriotic themes that befitted such heroic times. He claimed his elevated Neo-Classical style celebrated "a people guided by reason and philosophy; a reign of liberty, equality and law". In truth, his austere and academic art was as much a reaction against the excesses of the Rococo.

The Neo-Classical tradition was also embraced by Jean-Auguste Ingres (1780–1867), a follower of David. Noted for his cool clarity, technical assurance and academic precision, Ingres was a conservative who decried the conflicting current of the age: Romanticism. In response to entreaties to "follow our century", Ingres retorted: "But suppose my century is wrong?".

Eugène Delacroix (1798–1863), the high priest of Romanticism, was convinced that he and his century were as one. "I see in painters prose writers and poets", he declared. "Cold exactitude is not art; ingenious artifice, when it pleases or when it expresses, is art itself".

His passionate canvases rebelled against bloodless perfection. Instead of classical nobility, fine draughtsmanship and restraint, his creed was colour, exoticism and free reign to the imagination. *Liberty on the Barricades* is considered the last successful allegory ever painted.

Delacroix's visionary, melodramatic style is echoed by the energy and exoticism of Théodore Géricault (1791–1824). His fondness for spectacular effects and natural restlessness predisposed him to a revulsion against the rational. His Romantic masterpiece, *The Raft of Medusa* (1819), created a scandal with its gruesome depiction of grieving, hysteria and doom. Indeed, with the triumph of the Romantic movement, the artistic baton definitively passed to France, a preeminence the country still claims.

LEFT: *Landscape with Orpheus* by Poussin (1659).
RIGHT: *Les Baigneuses* (Bathers) by Jean-Honoré Fragonard (*circa* 1765–70).

Realism

The Revolution was slow to radicalise the hierarchical nature of public art. Hitherto, pride of place was given to dignitaries and heroic figures while peasants were relegated to genre scenes. Only after the 1848 Revolution was there a concomitant revolution in subject matter: painting began to portray the people. Although considered the architect of Realism, Gustave Courbet (1819–77) demurred: "the title of realist has been imposed upon me". Instead, he saw his instinctive naturalism as a quest for truth, at one with his desire to challenge staid conventions and (shake the people).

François Millet (1814–75), best-known for his peasant paintings, worked in the same genre. *The Gleaners* (1857) is his quintessential work: a dignified composition of heavy-limbed women toiling in the cornfields. Millet was a member of the Barbizon School, a group of landscape painters who, reacting against pretension, were drawn to the glades of Fontainebleau.

Edouard Manet (1832–83) heralds 20th-century art and was a precursor of Impressionism. Manet was not afraid to discard outmoded conventions, trusting his eyes rather than traditional ways of seeing. His forceful pictures focused on social life and pleasure, exposing his subjects to harsh sunlight without the moral lessons expected by a bourgeois public. According to Ernst Gombrich, Manet showed that when studying nature in the open air, individual objects blur into "a bright medley of tints which blend in our eye or really in our mind". His most famous painting, which shocked at the time, is *Déjeuner sur l'Herbe* (1863), in which a nude model picnics on the grass with two formally dressed gentlemen, holding the onlooker in her frank stare. The picture is a bold assertion of the right of the artist to depict whatever he pleases for the sake of aesthetic effect.

THE BEST MUSEUMS OF ART

France has many fine museums of art. Two exceptional ones which include decorative arts and objects as well as paintings are the Musée de Cluny, Paris (medieval art) and Château d'Ecouen, Ile de France (Renaissance art).

Others which concentrate on painting are:
- Musée du Louvre, Paris
- Musée d'Orsay, Paris
- Musée Picasso, Paris
- Fondation Maeght, St Paul-de-Vence
- Musée des Beaux-Arts, Lyon
- Musée des Beaux-Arts, Lille

Impressionism

"Since the appearance of Impressionism, the official salons, which used to be brown, have become blue, green and red". Claude Monet (1840–1926), the master of colour and light, and founder of the new movement, focused on the changes in colour brought about by this return to nature. Monet's *Waterlilies* series are reveries of colour and light, a shimmering restlessness of atmospheric effects and beautifully balanced tones and colours.

La Gare de St-Lazare (1877) depicts a locomotive belching against a background of golden light streaming through the roof. The movement's preoccupation with the fleeting moment exposed painters to the charge of neglecting the solid forms of nature.

Although this lack of finish was dismissed as slapdash, Monet took comfort from the fact that Delacroix, Courbet and Millet had all been scorned in their day. In time, the public was won over by these puzzling pictures, retraining their eyes to appreciate Camille Pissarro (1831–1903). The painter tried to see his bird's eye views of Parisian boulevards with the shock that first stunned his contemporaries: "If I walk along the boulevard, do I look like this? Do I lose my legs, my eyes and my nose and turn into a shapeless blob?".

Although sympathetic to Impressionism, Edgar Degas (1834–1917) was more drawn to movement, space and spontaneity. His off-centre compositions captured the atmosphere of cafés, circuses, the races and ballet. His dispassionate studies of dancers in a range of unexpected postures cannot be dismissed as mere prettiness. Pierre-Auguste Renoir (1841–1919) began as an Impressionist but later came under the more Classical influence of Cézanne. Like Degas, his penchant for the picturesque often blinded critics to the artistry of his ravishing forms dissolving into sunlight and air.

With Paul Cézanne (1839–1906), French art almost came full circle *(see page 48)*. The "father of modern art", aimed at painting "Poussin from nature", capturing in his canvases the balance, harmony, grandeur and serenity of the previous painter without losing any of the colour or modelling of the Impressionist movement. ❏

LEFT: *Fruits* by Paul Cézanne (1879).
RIGHT: *L'Absinthe* by Edouard Manet (1859).

POST-WAR FRANCE

*Emerging from the misery of war, France has striven to overcome instability,
and to become a cohesive nation at ease with itself*

The military build-up in Germany and Italy under Hitler and Mussolini not only threatened the European balance, but resulted in the humiliating German repossession of the Rhineland in 1936. The Spanish Civil War greatly aroused the ire of French intellectuals, but they were powerless to lift a finger to dispel the rising storm. In 1938, France joined Britain in appeasing Hitler at Munich, and, after Poland was invaded on 3 September 1939, World War II was declared.

France at war

Much of the blame for this sequence of events lay in the irrational certainty with which the French believed their country to be impregnable. So confident were the French that the Maginot Line, a fortified wall stretching across Alsace and Lorraine, was inviolable that today it has become synonymous with the idiocy of relying too heavily on only one line of defence.

After eight months of the "Phoney War," during which neither France nor Germany dared to attack the other, the German *blitzkrieg* penetrated deeply into France from Belgium and rendered the vaunted Maginot Line useless by encircling and capturing it.

The armistice signed on 22 June 1940 created a German occupation zone in the north and a nominally autonomous region in the south with its capital at Vichy. The famous World War I general Marshal Henri Philippe Pétain was given full leadership powers in this region, and the constitution of the Third Republic was abrogated. At the same time, General Charles de Gaulle, the Under-secretary of State for National Defence, had fled to London to organise the Free French in their resistance effort. The British were forced to scuttle the French fleet moored in Algeria, although this action produced painful hostility between the allies. Under General de Gaulle's leadership, the

Resistance grew steadily throughout the war, and the troops of the Free French were instrumental in the North African and other campaigns. It would be inaccurate, however, to suggest that the Resistance enjoyed widespread support from its inception. The beloved Marshal Pétain was one of France's most respected men and appealed to the country's strong traditions of agriculture, family and Catholicism.

The collaboration (a word avoided in the 1990s) with the Nazis was deemed the least painful means of coexistence, even if it implied the deportation of Jews and other French citizens. This question still has ramifications of almost unbearable delicacy for the French conscience, and it has been agonisingly debated. The question of allegiance was solved, by the successful invasion of France by the Allied troops in 1944. Although the D-Day assault on Normandy on 6 June was the most dramatic moment of the invasion, there was also a slow, arduous penetration from Provence in the south.

PRECEDING PAGES: World War II cemetery, Normandy.
LEFT: Picasso and Françoise Gilot, Golfe Juan, 1948.
RIGHT: General de Gaulle in office.

LIBERATION

The liberation of Paris on 25 August 1944 was one of the craziest and happiest days in the city's chequered past, partly because the Allied commander, Dwight D. Eisenhower, diplomatically allowed the French troops, under the leadership of General Leclerc, to be the first to enter the city. Needless to say, French participation in the invasion of Germany was sweet revenge.

The aftermath

In spite of this happy conclusion to the most tragic chapter of French history since Californ-

The instability of the Fourth Republic was proven by the succession of 24 ministries from 1945 to 1958, during which French Indo-China was lost to the Viet Minh at the battle of Dien Bien Phu (1954) and the Algerian independence movement grew out of hand. It was this latter fiasco that prompted the imperial return of de Gaulle, who had earlier withdrawn from the political stage, and who summoned up all of his prestige and six feet four inches to bulldoze the National Assembly into passing a new constitution, creating the Fifth Republic and giving him the authority he desired.

General de Gaulle urged France to "marry

ian wine was invented, the nation's position in the world of 1945 was more precarious than it had been in centuries. First, its cities and most precious architectural treasures had been mercilessly razed by the German and Allied invaders. Second, and more important, the fragile national ego had been shattered by defeat and collaboration, and now surveyed a world dominated by the US and the Soviet Union.

After a brief period of intense self-analysis, during which thousands of suspected collaborators were executed, France looked to the future. Massive urban rehabilitation projects were undertaken – mostly, despite financial constraints, with typical good taste.

the century" and adapt to the modern world. Yet in typically French fashion, his period in office offered several salient contradictions. In spite of his militaristic appeal, he presided over a gradual withdrawal from Algeria (completed in 1962). Notwithstanding his staunch nationalism, he supervised the dismantling of the French colonial empire. Despite his wartime allegiances, he vehemently rejected the leadership of the United States and Great Britain, ejecting NATO from Paris (1967), vetoing Britain's membership of the European Economic Community (1963) and organising a rapprochement with Germany in order to reassert European independence.

During the post-war period French culture underwent a resurgence. The existentialist philosophy of Jean-Paul Sartre, Simone de Beauvoir and Albert Camus electrified the world with its chic pessimism. The *nouveau roman, nouvelle cuisine* and *nouvelle vague* all brought important innovations. Inspired by French cinema, the world's youth again looked to Paris as the hippest city on the planet.

May 1968

The year 1968 should not have been as chaotic as it was, but the study of French history hastily teaches one to abandon the confines of ratio-

events and by his failing foreign and economic policy, de Gaulle relinquished power to his former prime minister Georges Pompidou in 1969. Later known chiefly for the cultural centre at Beaubourg bearing his name, Pompidou died after a long illness in 1974.

The Presidents

The ensuing presidential election saw the Gaullist Valéry Giscard d'Estaing win against Socialist François Mitterrand. Despite his rightist nature, Giscard's seven-year presidency incorporated reforms desired by the left: less restrictive divorce laws, legalised abortion and

nality. In the month of May, a general feeling of malaise and spring fever erupted into aggressive demonstrations against the Vietnam War, government control of the media and the stagnant values of the adult generation. The tension increased when the students removed paving stones in the Latin Quarter, built barricades in the finest French revolutionary tradition, and occupied the Sorbonne. Joined by the workers of the left, the student demonstrations escalated into a national crisis. Shaken badly by these

LEFT: General Charles de Gaulle and Winston Churchill meet during the war.
RIGHT: the Liberation of Paris, 1944.

widely available contraception, and an 18-year-old voting age. Although an élitist patrician, Giscard was also a modernist and technocrat with an international outlook.

In 1981, the tables were turned when Mitterrand defeated Giscard, bringing the left to power for the first time under the Fifth Republic. Like Giscard, Mitterrand surprised those unfamiliar with the vagaries of French politics by maintaining close ties with the United States and advocating only limited nationalisation of French industry. As the longest-serving president in French history, Mitterrand (*see page 59*) played a significant role on the world stage, from the Falklands to the Gulf War and Bosnia.

In foreign policy, he cemented the Franco-German axis at the heart of the European Union. The relationship with Chancellor Helmut Kohl was forged on common defence interests, a dread of war and a shared enthusiasm for full European integration. At home, however, his second administration was plagued by recession and scandals.

No real change

Despite the very real differences between General de Gaulle, Pompidou, Giscard and Mitterrand, France continued to function in much the same way along several fronts. The government

period of cohabitation (*see below*), with a right-wing president facing a radical left-wing administration led by Lionel Jospin.

Future challenges

If it is difficult to see a clear progression in such turbulent history, it is largely because the country has always been such a patchwork of polarised groups and political swings. Yet France has both dazzled and bewildered the world with its brilliance and absurdity. As it faces the challenges of the 21st century, it is still striving to quell its revolutionary spirit and become a cohesive nation at ease with itself. ❏

continued to develop its independent *force de frappe* rather than cower beneath the Nato nuclear umbrella, most controversially with the resumption of nuclear testing in the Pacific. France also asserted its right to forge its own distinctive foreign policy.

In 1989 France celebrated the bicentennial of the Revolution, which led to an orgy of self-congratulation and analysis. It was a heady era that ended with the election of the former Mayor of Paris, the right-wing Jacques Chirac as president in 1995. Mitterrand died soon after, honoured to the end despite increasing disquiet about his personal integrity. The victory of the left in the 1997 elections provoked another

COHABITATION

Since 1986, when right-wing Jacques Chirac became prime minister during the presidency of socialist president François Mitterrand, France has had to come to terms with an unusual and potentially uneasy political situation: cohabitation, the concept of overlapping terms of office of a president and a premier who come from opposing political camps.

As the president has a seven-year mandate, and the National Assembly has a five-year one, cohabitation was inevitable at some point. Yet given the checks and balances of the process, the public is generally favourable to this moderating mechanism.

Mitterrand's Legacy

As an untainted politician with a distinguished war record, François Mitterrand spoke to a new generation when he became Socialist president (1981–1995). Yet at heart he was an urbane intellectual of the old school, with a literary bent and philosophical outlook.

As a wily statesman, his ideals were tempered by principled pragmatism: he wanted to make his mark. After de Gaulle, Mitterrand was the politician who most shaped 20th-century French society, transforming the Paris skyline along the way.

All French presidents have had pet projects but in modern times none were more bombastic than Mitterrand's *grands projets*. The visionary leader declared, "Visitors will come to see the Paris of architecture, sculpture, museums and gardens; a city open to imagination, ideas and youth".

If Mitterrand was suffering from a Louis XIV complex, Giscard d'Estaing had a witty, and somewhat scathing, rebuke: "He is trying to leave monumental traces so that his other deeds can be forgotten".

The president's legacy encompasses such landmarks as the controversial glass pyramid of the Louvre, a shimmering cut glass and steel diamond of fantastic transparency and light. As the most harmonious *grand projet*, the pyramid provides an elemental solution to infusing an ancient institution with a more modern spirit.

"The city must rediscover its unity," Mitterrand declared, "with the centre put in touch with the periphery and marginal neighbourhoods." Social engineering French-style took a symbolic rather than practical form: his Grande Arche de la Défense was designed to lift the desolation of a neglected district, linking marginal with mainstream Paris, and literally leading to the explosive triumphalism of the Arc de Triomphe.

The National Library in east Paris was a project close to the President's heart, intended to revive a depressed working-class area. Finished after Mitterrand's death, the

LEFT: modern art from Jean Cocteau.
RIGHT: François Mitterrand.

building boasts L-shaped towers designed to resemble four open books. Architecturally more successful is the Arab Institute (1981), where architect Jean Nouvel first made his mark. The centre, a celebration of light filtered through glass, is intended to foster cultural exchanges between Islam and the West. As Mitterrand stated, "For me, architecture is the premier art; more than anything, it is useful art".

This was particularly true of the ultra-modern Science Museum in La Villette, an exciting urban renewal project. By contrast, the new opera house is a testament to the

president's audacious policies in the arts. Opéra Bastille (1989) was intended as a "people's opera" but became a Parisian *bête noir*, blighted by shoddy finishing and beset by orchestra strikes. Whatever its failings, it has helped turn a traditional working-class area into the liveliest and most *branché* (coolest) quarter of Paris.

Mitterrand, a self-proclaimed agnostic, faced his death with stoicism: "I'm not frightened of death, but I love life. This comes too early". As for posterity, the jury is still out on Mitterrand's political legacy but the dazzling new Parisian cityscape remains a fitting personal memorial. ❑

THE CONTEMPORARY SCENE

The Chanel suit is still ineffably chic, the Burgundy vintages are better than ever,
yet France today is introspective and slightly unsure of its identity

Loyd Grossman, the food critic, comments "the French used to treat cooking almost as an extension of foreign policy, and used it to establish a French cultural hegemony over the rest of the world". Certainly, France prides itself on capturing the cultural high ground, whether upholding intellectual standards or making a simple salad dressing *comme il faut*.

At its best, the French way of life is deeply civilised, embracing beguiling patterns of thought, a penchant for the arts and philosophy and a gift for food and fashion. Rationalism and humanism, Republicanism and conservatism, provincialism and intellect are the pillars of the French tradition. At heart, citizens are traditionalists who enjoy debate, demonstrations and destruction but disapprove of shifts in behaviour. In Republican mode, they would agree with the dictum that the urge to destroy is a creative urge. In bourgeois mode, they believe in *douceur de vivre*, the seductive notion of the Gallic good life.

One of the world's most prosperous countries is currently undergoing an identity crisis and a mood of introspection. Not that the casual observer need notice: the Chanel suit is still ineffably chic; the Burgundy vintages are better than ever; and French films are a byword for lucid humanity..

Yet the tension between faddishness and familiarity is clear in the French approach to cuisine: an admiration for exotic new gastrodomes is undercut by a desire for old regional comfort food. France at the *fin de siècle* may be wallowing in nostalgia yet can still produce some of the boldest modern architecture. This dichotomy runs deep in the national identity, typified by the French traits of intellectual rigour and romantic inconsistency. It remains to be seen if France's unexpected victory in the World Cup in July 1998 really does lift the country out of its gloom, dispel

PRECEDING PAGES: the *boules* team; Riviera bikers.
LEFT: Left Bank *intéllo*.
RIGHT: *l'art de vivre* in the city.

racial tension and propel the country towards economic prosperity.

The world stage

As staunch Europeans, the French were among the architects of the Maastricht treaty, the blueprint for European integration. Yet, in a Mitter-

rand referendum, the French only narrowly voted to remain in the European Union. In the late 1990s, the relationship with Europe remained troubled as the country struggled to control the bloated public sector and prepare for monetary union.

On the wider stage, the French have a love-hate relationship with the United States and Canada, having owned much of the former and populated much of the latter. As the gospel of growth has faltered, France feels overshadowed by the American economic model. Le *modèle anglo-saxon* is disparaged as a hire-and-fire culture with little compassion for the weak.

French identity feels threatened by Americanisation and a globalisation perceived as Anglo-Saxon cultural imperialism. However, national pride and the counter-cultural streak in French culture ensure that the country is fighting back. La Francophonie, the organisation of French-speaking countries, is a useful vehicle of cultural conquest. The French are aware that the association represents 450 million people compared with the Commonwealth's 1.6 billion. In supporting so many unsavoury regimes, the French adhere to the John Foster Dulles school of realpolitik: "They may be bastards but at least they're our bastards". Yet whereas the British imperial legacy

was democracy and the rule of law, the French have always stressed culture in the fullest sense.

La gloire and la patrie

On the domestic scene, presidential power is a hallmark of the French system. Such is presidential prerogative that citizens shudder at the thought of a philistine leader. No president personifies an archetypal Frenchness more than de Gaulle. He set the tone for future generations by propounding paternalism, chauvinism and national destiny. His belief in *la gloire* and *la patrie* form an assumption of superiority and of the supremacy of French civilisation.

THE REVOLUTIONARY SPIRIT

Storming the barricades is an honourable French tradition. In Paris, there is a different demonstration every week by the Matignon, the Prime Minister's residence. To an outsider, France often seems to be on the brink of insurrection spurred by latter-day sans-culottes. During protest marches, boulevards are often filled with demonstrating workers flaunting banners.

While some campaigns are genuinely revolutionary, many are token protests. Foreign correspondent Kate Muir reported on the tame nature of a recent journalists' gathering: "Riot police hooted in derision and swapped their truncheons for salami baguettes".

The 30th anniversary of the May 1968 student riots revived nostalgia for left-wing militancy. Social unrest often acts as a safety valve for discontent against an aloof government. At heart, an old Manichean spirit pervades French public life, a mistrust of authority and intolerance of differing views. Winter 1997 witnessed renewed social tension. In Paris, Fouquet's gourmet restaurant was invaded by unemployed protesters demanding foie gras for all. Fouquet's later delivered free dinners to an occupied benefits office.

The support for strikers is proof of a French belief in solidarity and social cohesion, a variant on fraternity.

GOD AND THE GENERAL

When de Gaulle died, Noel Coward was asked what he thought God and the general would find to talk about in heaven. Coward replied: "That depends on how good God's French is." Although outdated, the witticism captures French nationalism at its most confident.

De Gaulle aside, World War II continues to tarnish national pride and cast a shadow over contemporary France. As a compromised and collaborationist society, France was slow to confront its Vichy past. As a result, the nation's war wounds have been slow to heal. The trials of Klaus Barbie in the 1980s and Maurice Papon in the 1990s have forced the French to re-examine their wartime records. As actor Daniel Auteuil said of his role in a Vichy epic, *Lucie Aubrac* (1997): "France is ashamed of this period and we can't escape the shame so there is always controversy."

"L'Etat c'est moi"

The might of the state has been a familiar feature of French history. Louis XIV's proclamation found favour with Napoleonic France and has resonance today. If France remains a fairly centralised state, it is partly as a response to the Jacobin tendencies in society. The French civil service has been a stabilising force, providing a tradition of continuity irrespective of changes of government. However, it suffers from over-manning, employing 5 million people, one in four of the French working population.

The civil service has tripled its workforce since 1960 and the country boasts both the largest police force in Europe, and the one working the fewest hours. A short working week and generous holiday entitlements are a feature of the French civil service. Since the 1980s, however, devolution has been presented as a welcome departure from the long tradition of centralisation.

Capital versus country

The rift between Paris and the provinces has been a perennial French concern. Taine put it in a nutshell in 1863: "There are two peoples in

LEFT: young bloods out for the night at St Germain-des-Prés in Paris.
RIGHT: Parisian self-confidence.

France, the provinces and Paris: the former dines, sleeps, yawns, listens; the latter thinks, dares, wakes and talks; the one dragged by the other like a snail by a butterfly, now amused, now worried by the capriciousness and audacity of its leader". Certainly, France experienced post-war urbanisation relatively late and Paris traditionally acted as a brain-drain from the provinces. Recently, there has been a reversal of the trend, with the relative rise of the regions. As a result, the provinces have lost their old inferiority complex: for example, virtually every bookshop now boasts a regional section.

Alsace, Burgundy, Normandy and Langue-

doc are just a few of the regions to maintain a strong identity. However, Corsica, Brittany and the Basque country are the regions with the deepest sense of difference, underlined by an ancestral mistrust of Paris. Brittany feels its Celtic roots strongly, in its separate language, music, culture and traditions. Corsica's difference is recognised in the considerable degree of autonomy it enjoys. Nonetheless, recent, if sporadic, bomb attacks by Corsican, Breton and Basque separatists attest to the disaffection felt by these complex and misunderstood regions.

Although historically France has only paid lip service to devolution, considerable decentralisation took place in the 1980s: banks and state departments were moved to the provinces. Regional autonomy is making progress, with regional assemblies, as well as cultural and social services administered on a local level. Ninety-five *départements* are grouped into 22 viable economic regions, with most dominated by the regional capital. These *grandes villes* have a history of asserting themselves, particularly the biggest conurbations, known as *métropoles*. Traditionally, big city mayors run regional fiefdoms and often play a national role. Lille, Lyon, Strasbourg and Bordeaux have often been power-bases for government ministers who repay their electorate by bringing

economic specialisation and investment to the city.

The cultural revival of the regions is not matched by the sleepy countryside. *La France profonde,* "deepest France", has long been a victim of the rural exodus. France can therefore no longer be described as a nation of small farmers: family farmers or wine-growers often rely upon their wife's income or on tourism in the form of *gîtes* or *chambres d'hôtes*, bed and breakfast. The countryside is increasingly a city playground, with farmsteads converted into second homes or simply abandoned. *"La vie paysanne"* is cultivated by those who have long since stopped being peasants. Commentator

John Lichfield sees paralysed rural France as a barometer of the national mood, with its "desire for change matched by a terror of change". Tourism has already brought a new lease of life to beautiful but deserted mountainous areas and this remains the main hope for the future - until the French discover down-shifting.

In the past, the typical village was like a 19th-century novel, ruled by the chatelain, the curé, schoolteacher, doctor, and lawyer. But these notables have drifted away and been replaced by the romanticism of ancient regionalist sentiments. It is a nostalgia tinged with complacency, a comforting sense of belonging without the need to live there and endure the constrained life of a Flaubert novel.

Made in France

After the post-war economic miracle, France overtook Britain in 1967 and remains the world's fourth largest economy, with a healthy balance of trade. However, liberalism struggles to compete with the ancient traditions of *dirigisme* and *étatisme* (statism). As *The European* newspaper says: "Whenever any public figure is brave enough to say that what France needs is a strong dose of economic deregulation, privatisation and labour flexibility, they are howled down by the mob as if they were proposing a return to 19th-century *laissez-faire* capitalism". Thierry Flandin, a politician in the Loire, captures the national mood: "We know in our hearts that France needs to become less taxed, less bureaucratic, less state-controlled. But there is also a fear that we may lose the things that make us French."

France's future lies in an increasingly service-based economy and the selling of French *savoir-faire* abroad. For all the vineyards in Beaujolais and Burgundy and the appparent power wielded by French farmers, only five percent of the workforce remains in agriculture. Unemployment and urban insecurity are the current French social concerns, followed by race and the polarisation of right and left.

In the late 1990s, unemployment passed the three million mark, affecting 12.5 percent of the working population, with the jobless figure double amongst the under-25s. In fathoming the special status of the French unemployed, commentator Susannah Herbert says: "Rather like being an intellectual or an aristocrat, being jobless is not a predicament but a position." The introduction of the 35-hour working week was the platform upon which the Socialist government was elected, a measure it claimed would provide for fairer redistribution of work. Nonetheless, the policy is bitterly opposed by French conservatives and most foreign observers, who claim it will only exacerbate unemployment.

A bourgeois paradise?

Being bourgeois is a way of life rather than a social status. "What the French like about it is the security, the lack of vulgarity, the reliability, the continuity of life. What they detest is the predictability, the lack of curiosity, the respectability", claims writer Michel Syrett of the inner conflict that taxes citizens. France prides itself on being a classless society, despite the rituals and rigid hierarchies of certain social groups, and the formal relations between subordinates and superiors.

The privileged *grande bourgeoisie* still possesses considerable power and forms the executive class, dominating the upper echelons of business and the civil service. These bureaucracies presume clearly defined rights and privileges, just as the best *lycées* are still the preserve of the same class. Below, comes the *bonne bourgeoisie*, the backbone of the middle class, who make up the majority of *cadres* or professionals. The *petite bourgeoisie* are a more nebulous group of minor civil servants, skilled workers and traders, a class traditionally derided by intellectuals. Nonetheless, the narrowness but richness of bourgeois life is a cause for literary celebration, from Balzac to Colette.

"Let them eat cake"

Despite the Revolution, a segment of snobbish society is still in awe of the declining ranks of the *noblesse d'epée*, from the Comte de Paris to the d'Orléans dynasty. Contrary to popular opinion, the French are as snobbish as most other races. As song-writer Boris Vian declares: "I suffer from snobbery, I'm riddled with the microbe, and when I die, I want a Dior shroud." While the aristocracy might be an irrelevance, a *grande-bourgeoise* background stands a citizen in good stead, from attendance at the

---

LEFT: *l'art de vivre* in the provinces.
RIGHT: vineyard worker with his mechanical grape-picker in Chalonais.

> ### LA GAUCHE CAVIAR
>
> The new aristocracy is *la gauche caviar*, French "champagne socialists". This mix of media people, left-wing intellectuals and politically correct celebrities are in the ascendancy. In this cosy world, television interviewers may be married to ministers, with the resulting political debate somewhat stiffled.

right state *lycée* to entrance to the right *grande école* (elite university). Although social status reflects merit and education rather than class privilege, France is a meritocracy in which being born into the right background helps.

The taste of new aristocracy is often indistinguishable from *grande bourgeoise*: homes adorned with Aubusson tapestries and oriental rugs, exquisite panelling and sculpted fireplaces. In Paris, St Germain is the traditional enclave of the intelligentsia, the haunt of those who "want to be in the heart of the city but hear only birds singing". Luminaries such as Sartre and Simone de Beauvoir have given way to Christian Lacroix and Catherine Deneuve, Jane Birkin and Jean-Paul Belmondo. Led by *chanteuse* Juliette Greco, the champagne set are fighting against the encroaching commercialism of their precious *quartier.*

The *cadres*, essentially the new middle class, represent twenty-five percent of the population, corresponding to the growth in the service sector. As salaried managers not employers, they enjoy a high standard of living and job security. The prestigious *cadres supérieurs* may control a department while *cadres moyens* control a smaller unit. Teachers are also considered cadres, with a higher social status than in many other countries. There is greatest social mobility amongst *cadres moyens*, who come from a variety of backgrounds. Unlike the traditional *grande bourgeoisie*, this new middle class tends to be consumerist and less conservative. Yet

according to Michel Syrett, these bourgeois "are snobbish about where they shop, eat, play tennis, take dancing lessons, holiday, and go to church". But what makes French snobbery easier to accept is that "it is based on good taste rather than on an hereditary principle of certain things being right".

French homes reflect the traditional lifestyles of their owners: thus, the homes of the *grande bourgeoisie* are studies in coffee table conservatism, radiating tranquillity and gracious living. The French have fallen for the patterns of modern suburbia, with three-quarters of all Parisians becoming *banlieusards*, suburbanites. In terms of residential districts, there is a great polarisation between mainstream society and the alienated underclass. Immigrants, the unemployed and a lost generation of urban youth tend to live in the *quartiers difficiles*, the sink suburbs, the doughnut of deprivation that surrounds a host of provincial cities.

Race relations

Several million Muslims live in France, mainly Beurs, the offspring of North African immigrants who settled there in the 1950s. Although classed as French citizens, les Beurs face pervasive discrimination and suffer from disaffection and social exclusion. Youth unemployment is as high as 80 percent in the concrete jungles around major cities. For young Muslim militants, the estates are a breeding ground for drug addiction and crime, fundamentalism and terrorism. The neo-fascist National Front discriminates against immigrants from its stronghold in the western Mediterranean area and recently polled well in other regions. Not that the picture is wholly bleak: since the 1980s, there has been a groundswell of solidarity for young French Algerians and youthful protests against racism.

Vive la différence

In romantic matters, the French place passion over morality, and mock the puritanical Anglo-Saxon code. In The Tyranny of Pleasure, philosopher Jean-Claude Guillebaud is a lone voice, charging his fellow-countrymen with cultivating the illusion of decorous infidelity while berating the rest of the world for being puritanical. During the days of customary illicit liaisons and leisurely time-keeping, the traditional post-work affair was described as the *cinq-à-sept*, a moment of passion before the

FAMILY VALUES

In its "France for the French" policy, the National Front discriminates in favour of "French" families. Even without such dubious help, the population is predicted to overtake Britain's by the year 2000. Divorce, birth control and abortion were all legalised in 1975.

Today, the birthrate of 1.72 children per family exceeds the European average but remains a source of concern for the state: every "*famille nombreuse*" (that is, blessed with three children or more) is rewarded with a range of extra benefits. These include nursery provision, subsidised public transport, car tax and school meals, as well as free admission to museums.

bourgeois banker returned to the bosom of his family. In keeping with the times, the urban affair has now become the business-like B&B (*baiser et breakfast*), a functional interlude embracing sex and a shared croissant. The rise of the mobile phone and the decline of the mistress culture have put paid to plush boudoirs and the sophisticated etiquette of infidelity.

Yet the French still pride themselves on separating sex and love, pleasure and appearances, honouring the social status of the wife, while respecting the secret power of the mistress. To critics, this is a value-free zone in which neither moral scruples nor suffering are recognised. In My Husband's Mistress, Madeleine Chapsal laments the passing of the classic *ménage à trois*, the complicity between wife and mistress. After willingly sharing her media magnate husband with the Minister for Culture, she regrets the way that a passionate affair has been downgraded to "*une aventure*", a convenient interlude for undemanding career women and colleagues: "Desire hasn't changed but the way of accommodating it has".

Political correctness has little place in a charmingly chauvinistic society. In general, the French fear that feminism is a threat to femininity and the flirtatious game between the sexes. The downside is that sexism remains rife in public life, hardly surprising in a country where women finally only won the vote in 1944. Indeed, before 1965, no married woman could accept a job or open a bank account without her husband's permission. Sexual harassment has only been an offence in France since 1992: office flirting remains a pleasurable duty without set limits.

As for public life, until the Socialist government came to power in 1997, France had few female politicians, and was 72nd in the world league of female representation, behind Uganda and Togo. However, 11 percent of MPs are currently women, including a clutch of senior ministers. Their impact is already clear, from the businesslike approach of Cathérine Trautmann, mayor of the showcase city of Strasbourg, to the radicalism of Martine Aubry, the tough, plain speaking Minister for Employment. "When a woman says what she thinks, she is

annoying", she said recently. "When it's a man, he has character ".

Cocooning

The family unit may be functioning adequately but the average individual is troubled and inward-looking. Cocooning, the retreat into privacy known as *le repli sur soi*, is not uniquely French. However, it represents an intense reaction against consumerist culture, with its tempting terrace cafés and glittering designer shops. Troubled by *fin de siècle* angst, economic insecurity and a society in transition, many French people are languishing in a mood of introverted

provincialism. Yet this loss of *joie de vivre* can also be seen as a search for a deeper personal identity and a better quality of life.

Je pense donc je suis

French intellectuals glory in their flawless Cartesian logic and love of conceptualising. The education system focuses on transmitting knowledge and training intellects, not on fully developing the individual. The stereotype of floppy-haired philosophers sipping pastis in smoke-filled cafés still prevails. However, citybred *intéllos* are chic counter-culturalists and self-indulgent purveyors of post-structuralism. Jean Baudrillard makes statements such as "I

LEFT: North African restaurateur in Dijon.
RIGHT: in a pensive mood while waiting for a train at Bastille Métro station.

feel like a witness to my own absence", but to his fans, this famous philosopher is ever-present. French philosophers are notoriously *médiathiques*, in love with the limelight. Bernard-Henri Levy, the left-wing media personality, is as popular for his dashing looks as for his opaque opinions on Jacques Derrida.

Culture vultures

In the land of Proust and arcane philosophy, popular culture has never been a French forte. Singer Johnny Hallyday, ageing Gallic rocker and patron saint of provincial bars, is ridiculed abroad, as are French rappers. Ironically, the

chanson, the traditional popular song or ballad, accommodates wit and irreverence but does not travel well. France currently feels outshone by the resurgence of British culture, compounded by the success of the Anglo-Saxon economic model. "Britain is on ecstasy while France is on prozac", declares one French commentator. The British literary novel is fêted in France for being baggy and inviting rather than arid and academic, like recent prize-winning French works. Writer John Ardagh bemoans the lack of cultural creativity: "Where are the new novelists, playwrights and painters?" before indirectly answering his own question: "Arts and ideas flourish best in times of settled prosper-

ity". In the meantime, the French are struggling to reconcile tradition with modernity, rampant consumerism with rural culture and heritage.

In the fashion world, the British may have blown away the cobwebs of *haute couture* in the houses of Dior and Givenchy, but traditional couture survives in Chanel and Yves Saint Laurent. French television suffers from underfunding and over-regulation, with under-resourced cable channels and a history of political interference.

In a recent poll, two-thirds of the sample said television insulted their intelligence. Despite its glorious past, the French film industry is currently criticised for being moribund, only redeemed by the talent of individual actors. Still, while Parisian cinemas continue to offer a choice of 350 films a day, the country looks set to remain a cinephile's paradise.

Café society

Compared with the trendiness of eclectic cuisines in London, Sydney or New York, French cuisine is traditional, relying on classic dishes enlivened by robust regional cooking. The greatest French chefs are content to spend a lifetime perfecting a small repertoire of dishes. However, a new generation has grown up with "*le fast food*", and without the gastronomic *savoir-faire* that was once their birthright. The cost and uneconomical nature of gourmet cuisine are also threatening the future of certain "*temples de la gastronomie*".

When Paul Bocuse became the first chef to delegate in the kitchen, it was seen as an affront to French culinary heritage. In the end, tradition usually prevails: just as many minimalist cafés often revert to classic bistros, so most masterchefs remain wedded to tradition. By the same token, despite anti-smoking legislation, nicotine-stained bars boast "*espace non-fumeurs*" signs swathed in clouds of smoke. *Plus ça change*.

Culturally, France is searching for a new momentum. Even if the country is wallowing in misplaced nostalgia, however, all is not lost: as historian Theodore Zeldin says, even "French cooking has repeatedly transformed itself by searching for old regional recipes". ❏

LEFT: Fontaine de Stravinski, on the Right Bank in Paris.
RIGHT: the face of an elegant nation.

French Cinema

I f Cannes represents the showcase of international cinema, then Paris is the film capital of the world. In France, there has always been an intellectual passion for film. The country pioneered cinematography in the 1890s and film has been considered an art form ever since. As writer John Ardagh says, "The cinema combines lyricism with documentary to a higher degree than any other art, and this duality appeals to the French". Given the dire state of the novel, drama and painting in contemporary France, the cinema is arguably the most

vibrant art form, and certainly the one with the most credibility.

The Lumière Brothers made their first film in Lyon in 1885, featuring local factory workers. Yet the first flowering of French cinema was in the 1930s, marked by the films of Jean Renoir. This era was only surpassed by innovative New Wave cinema of the late 1950s and early 1960s. Since then, French cinema has come to be equated with the unique artistic vision of the *auteur*. Resnais, Godard, Chabrol and Truffaut had no qualms about considering themselves creative artists.

Internationally, Brigitte Bardot inflamed post-war passions in a sultry star vehicle, *And God Created Woman* (1956), an ode to pleasure-seeking

directed by Bardot's mentor, Roger Vadim. Alain Resnais' *Hiroshima Mon Amour* (1959) was a more questing and inspired work, a masterpiece of modern cinema. In the same year, the term *nouvelle vague* was coined to cover the distinctive and lyrical voice of New Wave films. Jean-Luc Godard's *A Bout de Souffle* (1959), with Jean Seberg and Jean-Paul Belmondo, was a classic twist on a tale of love across the tracks. (The film was later reborn as *Breathless*, in a Hollywood remake starring Richard Gere). François Truffaut's *Jules et Jim* (1961) was a *nouvelle vague* classic, a *ménage à trois* starring Jeanne Moreau.

The best film-makers have not been beguiled by foreign promise. As Lyonnais Bertrand Tavernier says, "I am against phoney internationalism in films; one should stick to one's cultural roots". Lyon has been used as a backdrop in countless films, including *The Unbearable Lightness of Being* (1990) and Tavernier's *Around Midnight* (1986), the jazz film for which he is best-known abroad. As sacred *terre de cinéma*, the Lyonnais has attracted such contemporary directors as Claude Lelouch and Patrice Leconte, drawn to the lakes and the mountains.

Paris is equally well-served by cinema, from Louis Malle's *Zazie dans le Métro* (1960), a New Wave extravaganza, to Luc Besson's *Subway* (1985), a modish depiction of the dark underbelly of the City of Light.

Since the New Wave heyday, the best French films have tended to be intimate, small-scale works on conventional themes, distinguished by a certain artistry. Tavernier is a champion of this style, believing in "the minor heroism of daily life". This approach is also reflected in the work of Eric Rohmer, whose beguiling moral fables recount the psychosexual dilemmas of articulate young couples. *Claire's Knee* (1970), shot in the Lyonnais, is typical of his subtle vision.

The veteran *monstres sacrés* of New Wave cinema also appear comfortable with this humanistic approach: François Truffaut's *Woman Next-Door* (1981) explores a rekindled love affair between Gérard Depardieu and Fanny Ardant. As Truffaut said of his creed: "The best of the permanent subjects is love". An intimate canvas is also favoured by Claude Chabrol's *The Ceremony* (1995), featuring Isabelle Huppert and Sandrine Bonnaire.

Louis Malle had a more distinctive vision, beholden neither to French nor American traditions. His *Souffle au Coeur* (1971), depicting an incestuous mother-son relationship, shook the *grande bourgeoisie*, the class he came from, while *My Dinner with André* was just that, an urbane discussion about life. At the other end of the cinematic scale, Maurice Pialat, a Cannes prize-winner, makes resolutely bleak films about the human condition. Vastly superior, though in a different genre, is Claude Lanzmann's *Shoah*, a chilling documentary based on living testimony, and arguably the greatest film about the Holocaust ever made.

Cathérine Deneuve, currently the face of Marianne, the French figurehead, personifies cool perfection. In her heyday, she was a perfect foil to Yves Montand's warm Gallic charm. Her spiritual successor is Carole Bouquet, the face of Chanel, and mistress of the ineffable chic. In Claude Berri's *Lucie Aubrac* (1997), she and Daniel Auteuil play resistance fighters in Lyon, the final film in a wartime trilogy inspired both by major events and by Berri's wartime childhood.

The versatile Auteuil is also superb in *La Reine Margot,* a seamless historical epic, as is Isabelle Adjani, an actress who convincingly portrays passion. Auteuil, Depardieu and Emmanuelle Béart also star in Berri's *Jean de Florette* (1985) and *Manon des Sources*. These glowing Pagnol canvases depict Provençal life in all its rustic glory, achieving accolades and box office success in other countries.

Foremost amongst older French character actors is Philippe Noiret, whose lugubrious features haunt many a feature film.

Erstwhile heart-throbs such as Yves Montand and Alain Delon have given way to Vincent Lindon, who featured in the erotic *37.2 Le Matin* (*Betty Blue*, 1986) by Jean-Jacques Beneix, director of the whimsical *Diva* (1981). Despite their age and unconventional looks, both Gérard Depardieu and Daniel Auteuil regularly play romantic leads. Depardieu is the most versatile French actor of his generation and the only one to achieve international fame. Even so, he shines in such tales as *Cyrano de Bergerac* rather than in English-speaking roles. His son Guillaume is following in his famous father's footsteps.

Amongst French actresses, Isabelle Huppert (*Madame Bovary* and *The Lacemaker*), Fanny Ardant, Miou-Miou, Sophie Marceau, Sandrine Bonnaire and Isabelle Adjani are names to conjure with. Emmanuelle Béart is convincing, both in

Provençal pastorals and in Claude Sautet's *Nelly and Monsieur Arnaud* (1995), which explores a curious relationship between a young woman and a retired businessman.

Juliette Binoche, who is known for her integrity and enigmatic vulnerability, has starred in numerous fine films, as well as becoming the first French actress to win an Oscar: for her performance in *The English Patient* (1997). In Hollywood, she has confounded the stereotypical perception of French actresses as glamorous but heartless *femmes fatales*. Cool contemporary directors such as Léos Carax (*Les Amants du Pont Neuf*) and André Téchiné (*Alice and Martin*, 1998) frequently use

Binoche as a muse. Indeed, Téchiné recently praised her as having "her feet in the mud and her head in the stars".

Veteran film-makers have been criticised for seeing the world through privileged white bourgeois eyes. As if in response, recent French cinema has confronted social issues such as Aids, crime, poverty and race. "And realism is probably here to stay" remarks the French film magazine *Première*. However, some critics argue that the pendulum has swung too far away from the arty, humane, personal vision of respected *auteurs*. No matter how irredemably bourgeois, Tavernier, Rohmer and Bertrand Blier (*Merci La Vie*) still deserve a treasured place in French cinema. ❑

LEFT: Brigitte Bardot in *Et Dieu Créa la Femme*.
RIGHT: photo opportunity outside the Carlton Hotel, at the Cannes Film Festival.

LA CUISINE

For the French, eating is more a way of life than of keeping alive. The purchase and
preparation of the country's abundant produce is all part of the art de vivre

Food and wine, from the humblest cheese or *vin de pays* to *foie gras* or vintage claret, are the subject of constant interest, assessment and discussion. The French are also gastronomic chauvinists – but then they have good reason to be. True, there have been alarming developments in recent years: the advent of the perfidious microwave and of pre-prepared chilled products has been a boon to lazy restaurateurs; and those who forecast that fast food would never catch on in France have had to eat their words, particularly in Paris. Even so, French standards of cooking, both in restaurants and in the home, are still comfortably ahead of those in most countries.

The French nation's love of good food is only natural, for France offers an enormous variety of produce. It is able to do so because it is a land of great climatic and agricultural diversity and its coastline is washed by both the Atlantic Ocean and the Mediterranean, which together offer a temptingly wide variety of seafood.

Regional strengths

Each region has its specialities, both animal and vegetable. With its high concentration of restaurants and demand for fine produce, Paris is surrounded by a belt of top-quality market gardens. They provide the capital with many early vegetables, from tender green peas and carrots to crisp spinach and new potatoes.

The Loire valley, site of many of France's most famous châteaux, offers fresh salmon from its river, cultivated mushrooms from the caves around Saumur, and a rich variety of game and wild mushrooms from the lake-studded woods of Sologne, in addition to a host of fruit and vegetables – plump asparagus, cherries, plums – as befits a region called "the garden of France". The full-flavoured specialities of the Southwest include *foie gras* (goose liver pâté) from Gascony, truffles from Périgord, raw

ham from Bayonne and cured anchovies from Collioure, while Provence is the home of fragrant Cavaillon melons, sun-gorged tomatoes and pungent basil, which gives *pistou* soup its distinctive flavour.

One of the delights of visiting small restaurants and bistros all over France is tracking

down unusual regional specialities found only rarely in Paris, let alone the rest of the world. In the Pyrenean town of Castelnou, you may find a dish called *cargolada*, a grill of local snails, sausages and lamb chops cooked successively over a fire of vine cuttings and eaten in the open air. Some restaurants in Nice still feature *estocaficada*, a pungent dish of stockfish (dried cod), tomatoes, peppers, potatoes and black olives. In the Auvergne, salt pork is poached in wine and served with tiny Puy lentils. *Baeckeoffe*, an unusual stew of mixed meats (beef, lamb and pork) and potatoes, can still be found in the local country inns of Alsace, washed down, of course, with fine Alsace wine.

PRECEDING PAGES: olives and their oil.
LEFT: chef Paul Bocuse.
RIGHT: dishes from the Nivernais.

Fresh is best

The French calculate freshness in hours, not days, which is why French markets are such good sources for local specialities. This also shows in dishes such as *plateau de fruits de mer*, a sumptuous platter of raw shellfish and cooked crustaceans that brings with it the tang of the sea. If you eat at restaurants in seaside resorts like Deauville in Normandy and Bouzigues or Cassis on the Mediterranean, you are quite likely to see fishermen wandering in with buckets of fresh seafood for the chef.

It is always a good idea, when sizing up a strange restaurant from the menu posted out-side, to see if any attempt has been made by the chef to give his dishes a regional touch: pride in one's origins can often stimulate that extra bit of care and effort.

Nowadays even France's grandest restaurants – Georges Blanc in the Burgundy village of Vonnas, Troisgros in Roanne, Paul Bocuse out-side Lyon and L'Oustau de Baumanière in Les Baux-de-Provence, to mention but four – will provide their own versions of regional fare alongside the more sophisticated *haute cuisine* their customers expect.

Blanc's menu regularly features snails from the Burgundy vineyards and frog's legs from

TEMPLES OF GASTRONOMY

Famed French restaurants, whose much venerated chefs have won them the ultimate accolade of three Michelin stars include: *L'Espérance, St Père, Vézelay

- ☛ Troisgros, Roanne
- ☛ Georges Blanc, Vonnas
- ☛ Boyer "Les Crayères", Reims
- ☛ Côte St Jacques, Joigny
- ☛ Paul Bocuse, Collonges au Mont d'Or, Lyon
- ☛ Lameloise, Chagny
- ☛ Côte d'Or, Saulieu
- ☛ Les Prés d'Eugénie, Eugénie-les-Bains
- ☛ Auberge de l'Ill, Illhaeusern

the nearby Dombes lakes, while Bocuse offers France's finest (and most expensive) poultry, chicken from Bresse, in various guises. The famed local Alpilles lamb at L'Oustau de Bau-manière is accompanied by vegetables and herbs full of Provençal scents and flavours.

More perhaps than in any other country, French specialities of food and drink are named after the towns and villages that produce them. Many a cheese carries the name of the place where it originated – Camembert, Roquefort and Munster, for example. The highly-prized *belon* oyster is called after the Belon river in Brittany. Cognac is a town as well as a world-famous brandy, Calvados an administrative department as well as a prized applejack. And of course many a fine wine reveals its place of origin in its name.

Anyone driving through France cannot fail to be struck by the overwhelming importance of food in daily life. Whenever they can, the French prefer not to stock up at a supermarket for the week, but to shop carefully for the next meal or two. Outdoor markets selling anything from fruit and vegetables to meat, fish and cheese are regular weekly events in towns both large and small. They are also social occasions which give people a chance to catch up on the latest gossip, discuss the latest developments

whether the peaches are ripe he will often let you taste one, free of charge, so you can decide for yourself.

Seasonal fare

A common sight along major roads are the roadside stands that sell just-picked peaches, apples and plums, homemade preserves, home-cured olives, or honey from local hives. There are also large signs pointing enticingly to nearby farms, where eggs, poultry, goat's cheese or homemade *foie gras* and *confits* are available. Some filling stations even offer customers a selection of surplus vegetables (let-

on the political scene and talk about the weather (which the French do just as much as the British). Such exchanges usually take place in the packed neighbourhood or village café, over a glass of pastis or wine.

Food merchants take a loving interest in their wares. The fishmonger does not merely sell fish – he may offer a recipe for, say, grilling bright fresh sardines in tender vine leaves. The fruit and vegetable merchant knows which potato variety is best for a gratin, and if you ask

LEFT: seasonal offerings on a market stall in the heart of Paris.
ABOVE: *saucisson sec* for sale.

tuces, tomatoes, young white onions, shallots) from the owner's garden. And of course wine estates and cider producers also put up signs to make their presence known.

Each food has its season. When asparagus from the Loire valley appears in the shops you can be certain that spring is in the air. The charming Pyrenean village of Céret produces the first-of-the-season cherries in mid-April. Come May, juicy new garlic comes on the market (garlic lovers like to roast the cloves, then spread them like butter on freshly toasted bread).

If driving through France in the month of June, you may find the road blocked by a herd of cows or a flock of sheep with clanging bells round their necks. They are being led up to their summer pastures in the mountains, where they will feast on sweet grasses and wild flowers. In Savoie, the milk of Tarine cows is best for the finest cheese of the region, mountain Beaufort, which is made into huge wheels like Gruyère. At local markets, merchants discuss the age of a Beaufort as seriously as wine buffs compare vintages. As a Beaufort matures (over a period of anything up to eight months), its flavour gets better, nuttier and more profound.

By July, towns and villages come alive with the first of the harvest festivals. The peach is

celebrated in the Roussillon village of Ille-sur-Têt. In August the entire spa town of Digne, in the Alpes-de-Haute-Provence, turns out for a lavender festival, while in November the inhabitants of the Normandy village of Beuvron-en-Auge gather to sample the new crop of apple cider.

Even wine has its season. On the third Thursday of November, in wine bars, cafés and restaurants and at private tables all over France, the first wine of the season, Beaujolais Nouveau, is eagerly tasted. At its best it is a light, fruity, uncomplicated tipple, ideal for washing down an improvised meal of dry pork sausage and buttered country bread with friends.

BIG APPETITES

The French get through 109 kilos (240 lbs) of meat per person per year (only slightly less than the Americans) 22 kilos (48 lbs) of cheese, 62 kilos (137 lbs) of bread and a world record 80 litres (21 gallons) of wine.

The daily diet

The French spend about 20 percent of their income on food and wine. In such a culturally varied nation as France there is no absolutely typical meal, though there are typical local eating patterns. The biggest dividing line is between city and country.

Although generalisations are always suspect, it's fair to say that most French begin the day with a large bowl or mug of white coffee and a *tartine* (a slice of bread or a rusk spread with butter and jam). Farmers and other country-dwellers who get up early and do manual work will usually follow this up with a *casse-croûte* (snack) of bread (often half-rye) and sausage or pâté at about 9.30am. A substantial three- or four-course lunch comes next, often beginning with soup based on a homemade vegetable or chicken broth, and almost always comprising a meat course. Supper is often a light meal, with more soup, followed by cheese.

Many office workers lunch in company canteens, which are usually a cut above such establishments in other countries. The food on offer is generally designed to cater for the weight-conscious as well as those who do not need or want to care about their figures. Some office workers make do with just a sandwich (usually ham or cheese, or both, in a buttered *baguette*) and a glass of wine.

With more and more working mothers, the evening meal will often consist of something simple like *bifteck frites*, which has almost become a national dish in recent years, or frozen fish (sold complete with its sauce), followed by cheese or a fruit yoghurt.

As in many countries, Sunday lunch provides an opportunity to let rip with a big meal. But even then the fare is likely to be straightforward and traditional – roast beef or leg of lamb, often with a tart or cake bought from the local *pâtisserie* for dessert. ❑

LEFT: *charcuterie* delights in Bayeux, Normandy.
RIGHT: buying a chicken on market day.

FRENCH CHEESES – A CROWNING GLORY

"Nobody can bring together a nation that has 265 types of cheese," complained General de Gaulle. *It's even worse: France has more than 365 cheeses.*

Cheeses are one of the crowning glories of France. They come in all shapes and sizes: square, pyramid, heart-shaped or in a crottin. Certain cheeses are often displayed on straw mats (*paillons*), while others are wrapped in walnut or chestnut leaves. Classic cheeses are given *appellation d'origine* labels, which are as prestigious as those accorded to wine. Regionalism is everything since the concept of terroir prevails in French cheese, as it does in wine. The regional repertoire is formidable, from creamy camembert to cheeses rind-washed in beer, or the blue-veined champions, roquefort and bleu d'auvergne. Given such splendours, it is easy to overlook the piquant disks of goat's cheese, the Swiss-style cheeses from the Alps (such as emmenthal francais and raclette) or the monastic cheeses from Citeaux in Burgundy or the Trappist abbaye de belval.

Blue cheeses, made from cow's or ewe's milk, are blue-veined, with a sharp, spicy aroma. Bleu d'auvergne is similar to roquefort, but made from cow's milk, while bleu de bresse is a factory-made blue cheese. Certain cheeses with a rind develop an edible crust and become runny as they age. Apart from camembert, characterisic examples are brie de meaux and chaource, both from Champagne. By contrast, rind-washed cheeses are more pungent: these unpressed cheeses have rinds soaked in beer or eau de vie. Maroilles, munster, époisses and livarot all have distinctive flavours. Hard, pressed cheeses, like cantal and other alpine cheeses, are made from cow's and ewe's milk. Such cheeses are mild but acquire a crust and a pungent flavour.

▷ **BRITTANY BOARD**
A Brittany cheeseboard includes St Paulin, a smooth cheese with an orange rind, and Campénéac.

△ **TASTE OF PROVENCE**
Bannon goat's cheese market. Bannon, named after the place, is made from ewe's or goat's milk and wrapped in chestnut leaves tied with raffia.

△ **BURGUNDIAN FEAST**
The king of Burgundian cheeses is the brandy-soaked *époisses*; it partners a full-bodied red Burgundy beautifully. Chambertin is similar, but milder, creamier and rind-washed in *marc de bourgogne*.

▽ CAMEMBERT COUNTRY
The most famous French cheese was supposedly created after a rebel priest, fleeing the French Revolution, passed on the secret of the cheese to a Norman farmer's wife.

FARMHOUSE FROMAGE

▽ CHEWING THE CUD
Normandy is quintessential dairy country. These brown and white dairy herds give the creamiest milk, ideal for camembert. Both Normandy butter and cream also have *appellation d'origine* status.

"Fromage fermier" is a mark of quality, a farmhouse cheese made from unpasteurised milk. Compared with cheeses from large-scale dairies, the taste of these "lait cru" cheeses is infinitely deeper and subtler. Each cheese has its own time-honoured traditions and process. The cheese-makers use milk from their own or neighbouring herds. *Brie de meaux* from Champagne takes 20 litres of milk to produce one cheese 35 centimetres in diameter. To produce *cantal* in the Auvergne, curds are traditionally turned and pressed through cheese-cloth by hand. After being curdled, drained and hard-pressed, cantal is aged for over a year. Unlike mass-produced *camembert*, *camembert fermier* is moulded by ladle. Unpasteurised milk is heated and coagulated with rennet before the rich curds are ladled into camembert moulds. Then the cheeses are removed from their moulds, dry-salted, and sprayed with a bacterium to encourage the ripening process. After a month, they develop their ripe bloom.

◁ GOAT'S CHANCE
Chèvre fermier (farmhouse goat's cheese) can be flavoured in many ways. Popular additives include herbs, peppercorns, ash or wrapped in walnut or chestnut leaves. In Provence it can come *aux herbes de provence*, coated with local herbs.

◁ NORMAN FEAST
A feast of creamy camembert and pungent *livarot*, a rind-washed cheese with a reddish crust and deep flavour. These are matched by pont l'eveque.

▽ FEELING BLUE
Roquefort is considered the world's finest blue cheese. In France, the intense aroma is usually paired with a sweet wine, such as a Beaumes-de-Venise.

THE WINES OF FRANCE

Wine is more than a drink in France; like bread, it is inseparable from life and fine wines are a civilising pleasure which speak to the palate and to the mind

One cannot visit France without gaining a profound respect for wine. It is omnipresent. It fills shop windows, is served at every meal and is offered as a gift. Vineyards line the roads, not only in Burgundy and Bordeaux but along the Mediterranean coast, the length of the Loire, near the German border, and can be found even in Paris itself. Visitors are struck not only by the vast amounts of land devoted to grape growing but to the quality and diversity of the wines produced.

The wine stain on the map

A map of France showing the grape-growing regions looks as if someone had spilled a glass of wine on it. A large ring-shaped stain covers roughly two-thirds of the country. The ring starts just below Paris, extends westward to the Atlantic, curves inland along the Mediterranean then swings up north again to where it began. Being a stain, it is far from regular. Indeed, portions are very thick, particularly towards the top and western half of the ring, and numerous dribbles seep out along the lower rim covering most of the Mediterranean coast. A large drop just east of Paris (Champagne) and a streak in the far east near the German border (Alsace) are clearly visible.

This spill does not touch the Brittany peninsula, nor any of the area along the English Channel. Indeed, most of the Belgian border is stain-free, as is the very centre of the ring roughly equidistant from La Rochelle in the west and Grenoble in the east. At the time, the spill was clearly a dramatic one since even Corsica was dampened, especially in the north, but large patches are prominent both on the southeast coast and inland from Ajaccio as well as on the extreme southern tip near Bonifacio. In all, very few regions were spared and regardless of where you are in France, you will never be more than 160 km (100 miles) from an area in which wine is being made.

The range and density of vineyards account for the extraordinary variety of French wines. There is no one wine-making region – virtually the entire country makes wine – and, given the diversity of climates and soils, it is not surprising that France produces wines with "personalities" as different as those of the people who tend the vines. The fruit of an Alsatian Riesling is as different from that of a white Graves as the red-faced Alsatian peasant is from an austere château-owner in Bordeaux.

This said, similarities exist on occasion and though one can quickly learn to recognise wines with very strong personalities, only those who have taken the subject seriously enough to participate in many wine tastings can accurately distinguish one Bordeaux from another or pin a name on a glass of fine Burgundy.

Wine is so much a part of French life that people in France could no more imagine studying wine than studying how bread is made – both products are so readily available and so

---

LEFT: *Habit de Vigneron*, the spirit of the grape.
RIGHT: a wealthy *domaine*.

frequently consumed, they believe that through the sheer extent of their exposure they know how to evaluate both. The general consensus is that those who drink poor wine, or repeatedly purchase a rubbery *baguette*, essentially deserve their fate.

Insofar as quality goes, one can confidently purchase wine in France and generally expect it to be fairly decent, without much knowledge of how it is made or even precisely from where it comes. Fortunately, you can't go far wrong because wine is quite good throughout the country. This said, one should

> **WINE BUYING TIP**
>
> As a general rule, most wines are best savoured in or near the vineyards of their origin.

regions: Bordeaux, Champagne, Burgundy, Beaujolais, Alsace, Rhône Valley, Loire Valley, Provence, Languedoc-Roussillon, the South-west and Franche-Comté. Although the fame of the first four has long spread throughout the world, the rest enjoy varying degrees of celebrity and the products of some have an extremely limited market even within France itself. Inevitably, the non-specialist asks: what makes each of these regions special? And what is one to do when faced with the hundreds of bottles bearing similar names?

not conclude that all French wines are fine wines – not by any means. Within such famous regions as Burgundy and Bordeaux the truly fine wines form only a small percentage of the total production.

Indeed, most French wine comes from neither of these regions (production is most heavily concentrated along the western half of the Mediterranean), and part of the pleasure of exploring France is discovering the many "obscure" wines that are rarely exported and often have remarkably specific tastes. Anyone, for instance, who has not sampled the sherry-like whites of the Jura is in for a surprise.

France possesses 11 major wine-producing

Understanding grapes and wines

Though grape varieties are thought by many to be the key to understanding and identifying wines, many fine French wines are made by blending varieties to temper their individual tastes (this is systematically the case in Bordeaux). Even in regions where only one grape variety is employed, results can vary enormously from vineyard to vineyard. France is a country of micro-climates and this, combined with strong Gallic personalities, means that neighbours often produce wines bearing similar labels but with strikingly different flavours.

This is particularly evident in Burgundy. The Clos de Vougeot vineyard, for example, is archetypical in that it counts over 100 owners. Like almost every other vineyard in Burgundy, it has been divided and subdivided so many times that, every year, there are potentially a hundred different Clos de Vougeot wines to choose from. In reality, some of the plots are so small that their owners simply sell the grapes to a shipper (*négociant*) who combines them with others from the same property to make a Clos de Vougeot under his own label. Hence, unlike Bordeaux where each famous growth belongs to an individual owner, and one bottle of 1982 Château Latour is like another, in Burgundy the quality of a bottle of Clos de Vougeot

and Alsace. Though the former can produce sublime bottles, the latter two regions make simply pleasant red wines which are as much curiosities as anything else. Nonetheless one can never discount grape varieties where quality wines are involved and wines made, for instance, with the Gamay grape (such as the wines of Beaujolais) rarely attain the finesse of those made with Pinot Noir.

Constant change

Despite the emphasis on tradition, French wines have evolved and continue to change (generally for the better) in the 1990s. Champagne,

depends on which of the many individual owners or shippers made it. Within a given *appellation*, some plots of land are better than others and some wine-makers are more talented than others. In short, in Burgundy, the name of the wine-maker is as important as the wine itself.

The contrast is even greater when the same grape variety is used in different regions of France. The same Pinot Noir grape, for example, used in all the finest red Burgundies, is also used to make the still red wines of Champagne

LEFT: wines such as these Burgundies can be the product of several local vineyard owners.
ABOVE: checking out the crop.

CHARACTER VERSUS QUALITY

Though "noble" grape varieties flourish in France (Cabernet Sauvignon, Pinot Noir, and Chardonnay to name but the top three) they cannot be grown successfully everywhere and, indeed, very strict wine legislation governs the better French wines and even forbids the use of these noble grape varieties in certain *appellation contrôlée* wines in regions where other grape varieties have traditionally been grown. One might go so far as to say that the French emphasis is not necessarily on producing the highest quality wine in every region, but a distinctive wine in every region. This, for the most part, is the case in the 1990s.

for instance, was actually one of the great red wines of France until the 18th century when the method for making sparkling wines was perfected and then eclipsed the reds. And in the 17th century, the *clairet* (claret) wines of Bordeaux were not ruby red but pale, almost rosé.

In recent years, the greatest changes have occurred in the far South where the wines of Languedoc-Roussillon (a vast area extending from the Spanish border all the way to Montpellier) have attained "name wine" status. This has occurred thanks to the proliferation of new *appellations contrôlées* (wine legislation controlling the way in which wines with specific place names are made). Until the 1960s, most of these wines were cheap table wines sold under brand names rather than their own. The 1990s Côtes de Roussillon, Minervois, Fitou or Corbières may not bring tears of joy to your eyes but many are excellent value and particularly good when served with local food.

Wine and food

It is a truism in France to say that local wines are at their best with local food. The idea of drinking an Alsatian Riesling with a *bouillabaisse* in Marseille would not even occur to a normally constituted French brain. A Burgun-

TASTING WINE

Throughout the country, French vineyards are planted not only with grapes but with signs inviting travellers to stop and sample their wine. Accepting such invitations is the best way to learn what French wines are all about but both tact and caution are required.

A French proverb warns: *à bon vin, pas d'enseigne* (good wine, no sign). In other words, wines of high quality don't need to advertise. Indeed, many of the best growers (particularly in Burgundy) live in unpretentious homes with little or no indication that their wine is for sale. Despite such discretion, most will receive visitors (though it is highly advisable to telephone before dropping in), but don't

consider such a visit a simple occasion for a free drink. Serious tasters don't even swallow the wine they are offered – they politely spit it out onto the gravel floor of the cellar or into the spittoon which is frequently provided for this exact purpose. Wine cellars are for tasting not drinking and, if the language is not a barrier, listening as well.

Owners and growers will invariably taste their wines with you and you will quickly discover the respect that wine receives in the depths of these French *caves*, though it is only at the table that wine blossoms into the taste experiences that make bottles memorable.

dian shivers at the thought that the most potently aromatic cheese of his region (Epoisses) could be served up with a glass of Bordeaux. When travelling in France, the golden rule – "local wines with local food" – must be rigorously observed – or else expect your waiter not only to frown but shown signs of despair.

What if there are no local specialities on the menu? This is frequently the case in the finest restaurants that pride themselves on serving creative dishes and little, or no, local fare. In this case, two other golden rules should help you make your choice: white wines are served

Choosing the wine

The elegant choice, regardless of the region you are in, is Champagne (the drier the better) as an apéritif; the more realistic choice will be a local white wine, probably of a recent vintage. Afterwards, best drink the local wines anyway even if the food takes a creative turn. Nevertheless, if your budget permits, remember that the finest white wines come from Burgundy (Meursault, Puligny Montrachet), the best red Rhône wines (Hermitage, Côte Rôtie) can be excellent value; sweet wines such as Sauternes, Jurançon, or Monbazillac are not fashionable but outshine the reds with *foie gras*; the great

before red and the best wine is always served last. Reflect on the implications: both rules suggest that in a well orchestrated meal at least two different wines will be served.

The allusion to both white and red hints that both a fish and a meat course will be presented and, lastly, if the best wine is served last it is to accompany not dessert, but cheese – in short, a three- to four-course meal is in the making. Now, the difficulty is always which wine to choose?

LEFT: a glass of wine is an essential ingredient at social gatherings.
ABOVE: château tasting.

red Bordeaux *are* the great red Bordeaux, and late-vintage wines are a must in Alsace or anywhere else they might be proposed.

Lastly, grower-bottled (*propriétaire*) wines should always be preferred to shipper-bottled (*négociant*) wines and, in better restaurants, don't hesitate to engage your *sommelier* (wine steward) in intense discussion ("Was that a good year in the Loire?"). Remember, wine is not just a drink – otherwise it would suffice to order "red" or "white". Each sip includes a drop of French culture and each glass potentially contains sensory memories that will live on long after it has been emptied and the bottle has entirely disappeared. ❏

FUTURISTIC FRANCE

The French are a fiercely patriotic people, with an eye for beauty and design. They love to set the pace and take pride in the nation's innovative achievements

In a petition against the construction of the 300-m (984-ft) Eiffel Tower just over a century ago, 300 of France's most illustrious literary and artistic figures cried: "We protest against this column of iron sheets bolted together, this ridiculous vertiginous chimney glorifying the vandalism of industrial enterprise." But their outcry was to no avail, for Gustave Eiffel had official backing for his startlingly ambitious project, chosen from among 700 others, to commemorate the 100th anniversary of the French Revolution. Had not the prime minister himself asked for "something sensational, the like of which has never been done before?"

Well, he got it, and on 31 March 1889, Gustave Eiffel, followed by a panting band of government and city officials, climbed the 1,792 steps to the top of what was then the world's tallest tower and hoisted the French flag to the patriotic strains of the *Marseillaise*. Instead of later being pulled down, as its detractors hoped, France's "Iron Lady" has lived on to become the nation's most popular public monument.

Controversial change

If the Eiffel Tower was the symbol of French industrialisation, the Pompidou Centre (1974) represented the emergence of high-tech France. President Pompidou created this futuristic complex but fortunately died before his plans for unaesthetic skyscrapers and freeways could ruin the Parisian cityscape. The Centre had few fans at its inception: its bizarre inside-out jumble of multi-coloured pipes and steel scaffolding reminded many of an oil refinery, not an art museum. Yet by the time of its restoration for the millennium, the complex had become an accepted part of the Paris cityscape. In the same vein, I.M. Pei's glass pyramid in front of the Louvre, with its brilliant use of light and space, has long since won over most people.

PRECEDING PAGES: La Défense, Paris.
LEFT: Futuroscope, the science park near Poitiers.
RIGHT: the Louvre pyramid.

In giving Paris a futuristic face, recent administrations have been deeply respectful of the past. The "route royale", leading from the Louvre to La Défense, will be restored for the millennium. La Défense itself, an area of bleak office blocks, is completed by the Grande Arche de la Défense, an arch echoing the glo-

rious Arc de Triomphe. As for private architecture, Jean Nouvel's modernist Fondation Cartier (1994) is an office block built around a protected 17th-century cedar tree.

Paris of the 1980s and 1990s was characterised by presidential *grands projets*. However, in the millennial capital, much of the public works budget is spent on restoring and maintaining such projects, including putting tiles back on the Opera Bastille. Recent projects have been practical, if equally prestigious. The captivating new Stade de France is an 80,000-seater football stadium created for the 1998 World Cup Final. The spaceship-like structure sits in St Denis, an industrial northern suburb. Aided by air cushions and hydraulic lifts, the stadium's lower stand can be retracted to reveal an athletics stadium.

Avant-garde race

The French take a personal pride in the nation's innovative achievements, whether in the fields of architecture, *haute couture*, or high tech, particularly if such projects are on a grand scale. The Suez Canal, the Concorde supersonic aircraft, the Channel Tunnel, the Ariane space rocket, the TGV *(train à grande vitesse)* are the kind of projects at which the French excel. France has the advantage of possessing both a

become the most "nuclearised" nation in the world, with three-quarters of its electricity and over a third of its total energy being supplied by nuclear power. However, pressure by the Green lobby has led to a decision to dismantle certain fast-breeder reactors, beginning with the Superphénix near the Swiss border in 2005.

Telecommunications represents a successful partnership between *dirigisme* (state control) and native French technological flair. In the early 1970s, France had one of the most backward telecommunications systems in Europe, with fewer telephone lines per capita than Greece. In the 1990s, thanks again to massive

powerful, highly-centralised state with the vision required to back such projects, and an elite corps of engineers trained at the nation's most prestigious universities (the *grandes écoles*) with the imagination and skills required to carry them out.

In the past, France has often been in the forefront of scientific discovery. The country has produced leading pioneers in many fields, including radiology, biotechnology, medicine and pasteurisation, as well as in aeronautics, photography and nuclear physics. In 1978, at the time of the first oil shock, nuclear power accounted for less than two percent of France's basic energy needs. By 1998, France has

investment, it has one of the most efficient and advanced systems in the world.

Of particular note is the success of its home viewdata system, Minitel, launched in 1984. With more than five million subscribers (the terminals are provided free of charge), it has become the biggest videotex system in the world, providing access to over 16,000 database services ranging from train timetables to advice on where to get the best fresh *foie gras* and a chance to participate in erotic, multi-

ABOVE: home of the 1998 World Cup Stade de France
RIGHT: the Géode at La Villette, the futuristic science museum in Paris.

party, screen conversations (the famous *messageries roses*). However, since the advent of the English-language dominated Internet, Minitel has suffered somewhat.

Getting there fast

In transport technology, France is a world leader. As well as holding the world rail speed record (with a top speed of 514 kph or 320 mph), its TGV train is a model of comfort and efficiency. Opened on specially-constructed track between Paris and Lyon in 1981, the TGV service has since been extended westwards to Tours and Nantes and northward to Lille and Calais to link up with the Channel Tunnel. With an average cruising speed of 300 kph (186 mph), journey times have often been slashed by half or more. A high-speed Paris bypass now links the northern TGV line directly with the south, including stops at Charles de Gaulle airport and the Disneyland Paris leisure park.

Flying high

In aeronautics, France has long set the pace. The first man to fly the Channel was Henri Blériot, in 1909. France has been the driving force behind the highly successful, wide-bodied Airbus commercial aircraft, produced by a six-

THE CHANNEL TUNNEL

The Channel Tunnel, one of the engineering achievements of the century, was pioneered by President Mitterrand and the British. The chairman of TML, the French contractors, recently declared: "For both economies it is a great success because traffic is booming and freight is cheaper". Since the flagship project opened in 1994, the road and rail link has carried at least a third of the traffic between France and Britain. The French smugly point out that while their rail link is fast and efficient, the British service is sluggish, due to their failure to build a new rail link.

In 1984 the French President and the British Prime Minister, Margaret Thatcher, agreed to create the grandest of *grands projets*: the Channel Tunnel. But for the personal chemistry between the two leaders, the project would not have gone ahead since Mrs Thatcher loathed Mitterrand's predecessor, Giscard d'Estaing. Instead, she succumbed to François's Gallic charm and wit, despite being described as having "the eyes of Stalin and the mouth of Marilyn Monroe".

However, when the British style guru and restaurateur Terence Conran suggested Britain could be inspired by the *grands projets*, Mrs Thatcher invited him to design a table. Such was the gap between French philosophising and British pragmatism.

nation European consortium. Concorde, the Franco-British supersonic aircraft, represents another triumph for French aviation technology. France has also been the prime mover behind the European space effort, providing the bulk of both the funds and technology for the Ariane space rocket.

Science matters

France prides itself on its presentation of accessible science. Futuroscope, near Poitiers, is an imaginative theme park and interactive celebration of the moving image. The huge success of Paris's "hands-on" science museum, the Cité

des Sciences in La Villette, bears witness to the French fascination with technological marvels. Nearby is La Cité de la Musique, a futuristic conservatoire and concert hall. In France, even music is regularly presented in a resolutely modernist setting.

Not that France neglects pure science. The Centre National pour la Recherche Scientifique is one of the biggest and best centrally-financed pure science research bodies in the world. Thanks to the state-financed *grandes écoles*, France also has an elite class of engineers and applied scientists. Yet these practitioners have traditionally remained woefully isolated from one another. Recently, there has been a big

effort to remedy this failing, notably by setting up *technopoles* to bring academic research scientists and industrialists together. Based on the university-centred science parks in the US and Britain, the first French *technopole* was set up in Grenoble in the late 1980s. The idea caught on like wild-fire. In 1998, there are 50 such centres, and no French city now considers itself complete without its own *technopole*.

Glittering cities

The political decentralisation of the 1980s helped to accelerate this trend. The result was a veritable orgy of spending as towns vied with one another in the splendour of their new opera houses, pedestrian zones, museums, sports stadiums, new-age public transport systems and high-tech research facilities.

The state also had social engineeering in mind, in an attempt to boost depressed districts. In 1989, to kick-start urban regeneration in the neglected east of Paris, the Ministry of Finance was transferred from the Richelieu wing of the Louvre to a new complex at Bercy, dubbed "the Gulag" by disgruntled *fonctionnaires*. Nonetheless, regional renewal over the past decade has been impressive. The legendary sleepy, backward, French provincial towns are now largely in the past.

Despite their historic quarters, Lille and Lyon are at the forefront of futuristic design. Lille has experimented with Euralille, served by its own train station. Set amid mirror-glass reflections, it is a bold and ostentatious business district. Lyon boasts the thrilling airport of Satolas, its spreading wings symbolising the meeting of the TGV train and a plane. The city acts as a magnet for the finest French architects: the 19th-century opera house has gained a glass and steel dome by Jean Nouvel. Renzo Piano, who co-designed the Pompidou Centre, recently created Lyon's La Cité, a graceful new riverside sector in the spirit of an Italian piazza. The pavilions and passageways act as a showcase for the "secret" Interpol building. The French also readily welcome foreign architects.

More than most countries, revolutionary France gives the impression of rushing headlong towards the future. ❏

LEFT: the Sophia-Antipolis technology centre on the Côte d'Azur.
RIGHT: striking design is part of everyday life.

PLACES

*A detailed guide to the entire country, with principal sites
clearly cross-referenced by number to the maps*

France is divided into 22 regions, each of which has its own distinctive landscape and which break down into a total of 96 *départements*. The country is laced with 806,000 km (500,000 miles) of roads, 7,000 km (4,500 miles) of autoroute or motorway and 50,000 km (31,000 miles) of long-distance path; it has 5,000 km (3,000 miles) of coastline, ranging from the wild and rocky Breton coast in the north to the sandy beaches that enhance the Mediterranean coast in the south. Its longest river is the Loire, at 980 km (610 miles), with some 300 glorious châteaux spread out along its lazy length. Mont Blanc in the French Alps is the highest mountain in Europe at 4,800m (15,780 ft).

And yet, despite these nationwide statistics, France is essentially a regional country. Each area has its own individual characteristics, perhaps best exemplified by French food, which is a particular source of pride and the nation's principal export: every town has its own market, reflecting the produce of the surrounding land, and its own butchers, bakers and regional cuisine. And although the fast food culture has begun to make inroads, nationwide food chains still remain an anathema, indeed, nationwide anything is relatively unimportant compared to other European countries.

Therein lies the nation's charm for the traveller, and the following pages attempt to do justice to the character of each region. The chapters are grouped into seven sections which reflect particular areas of touristic interest: Paris, the city of lovers; the West, including the Loire river valley that became the seat of kings; the North, rugged, remote and charismatic; the Northeast, lands of verdant vineyards and peaceful villages; Central France and the Alps, with high resorts and lakes, rolling hills and Massif; the Southwest, from the pastoral landscape of Périgord and Gascony to the white Basque beaches and steep, dramatic Pyrenees; and the South, the scented, sun-baked hills of Provence and Europe's sumptuous playground on the Côte d'Azur. And finally there's a brief introduction to Corsica, France's island in the Mediterranean.

It would take an enthusiast a lifetime to get to know the length and breadth of France. For those who don't have a lifetime to spare, this book provides a full-colour tour of the nation. Choose what you want, and go. ❏

PRECEDING PAGES: a calm moment on the canal at Gissy-sur-l'Ouche in Burgundy; fishing on the Mayenne, Loire Valley; the Gros-Horloge, Rouen.
LEFT: picnic in the Pyrenees.

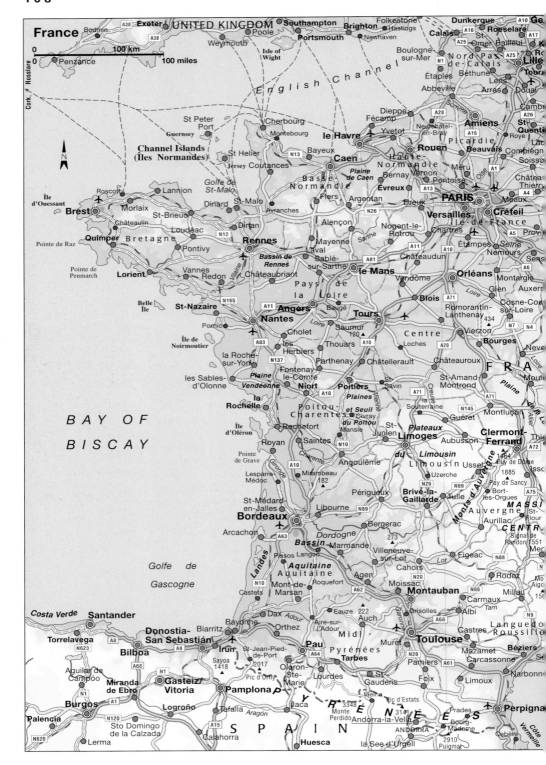

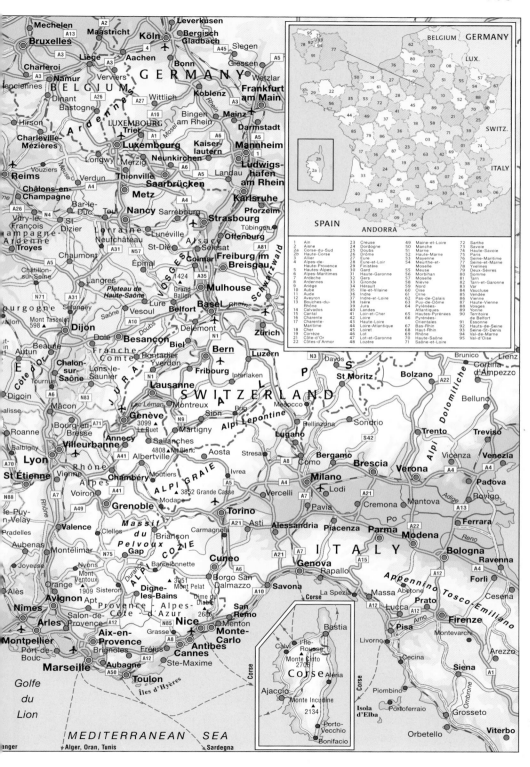

PARIS AND SURROUNDINGS

As Victor Hugo put it: "It is in Paris that the beating of Europe's heart is felt. Paris is the city of cities." Certainly, it is at the heart of France. In terms of urban sprawl, it is, in Europe, second only to London. Where matters of French administration, politics and cultural life are concerned, it plays an absolutely dominant role. It is also the world capital of chic. For all these reasons and more, Paris is so unlike much of the rest of its own country that it has been described as virtually a city-state in its own right.

Largely undamaged by two world wars, Paris has been created by centuries of inspired planning. Its street corners reek of history, its monuments and museums are well-known to people from all over the world and its inhabitants are an endless source of controversy. In this French capital, every pavement is a theatre on which daily life is played out.

Perfectly preserved though it is, Paris is a city unafraid of change. I.M. Pei's pyramid in front of the Louvre and the massive development at La Défense are evidence of that. But there are regrets in this process of evolution – in the city where Voltaire was reputed to drink 40 cups of coffee a day at Le Procope, the café culture is threatened by the fast-food invasion, and the number of cafés has drastically fallen from a total of 12,000 at the beginning of the 1980s to fewer than 5,000 in the 1990s.

Paris has a reputation for being a city of romance, a city of arts *par excellence* and a city of fun. There's endless entertainment here for the observant, who will learn as much about Paris and its inhabitants from walking the streets as from visiting the great museums.

One of the benefits of Paris is a superb public transport system, and it is thanks to the RER and SNCF that the region surrounding the city is so easily accessible. Day trips to such essential sights as Chartres, Monet's garden at Giverny and the palace at Versailles are described in the **Around Paris** chapter (*page 147*). And France's biggest tourist attraction, **Disneyland Paris**, is also profiled (*page 157*). ❑

PRECEDING PAGES: the Seine winds its way round the Ile de la Cité.
LEFT: a young Parisienne.

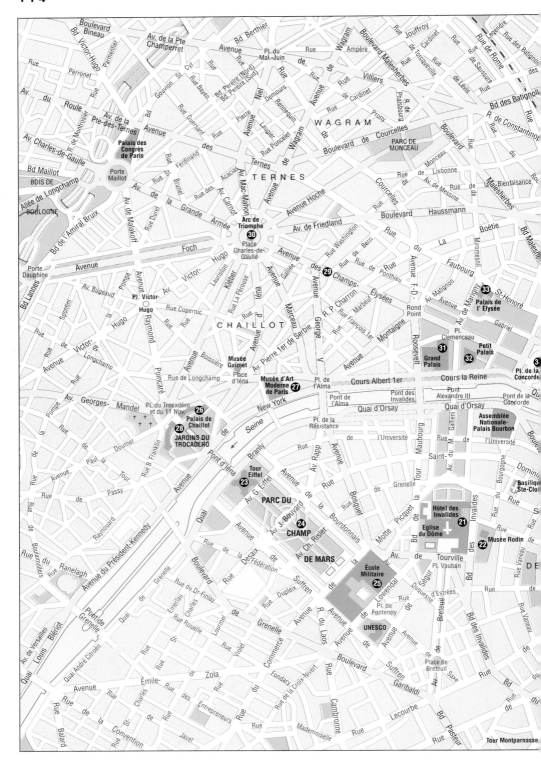

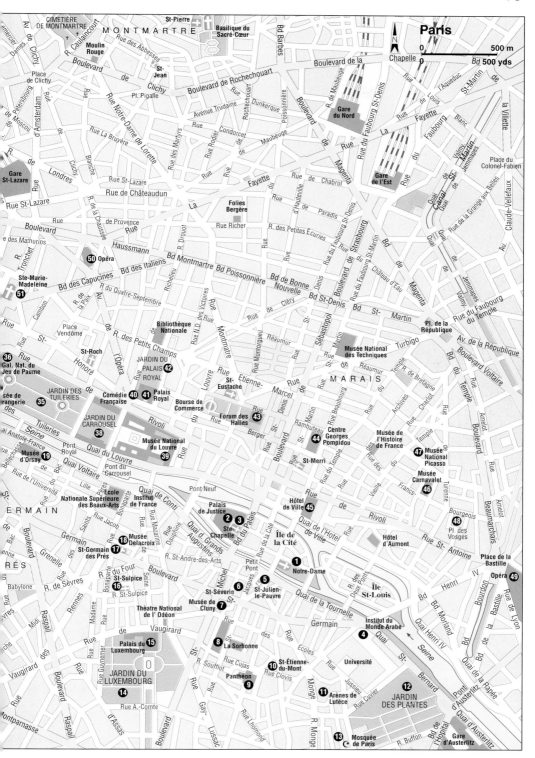

PARIS

Perhaps the grandest and best-preserved, certainly one of the most beautiful cities in the world, Paris is loved for its inimitable atmosphere and its many pleasures, from culture to cuisine

Map on pages 114–5

Paris

Paris is the hub of Europe, and its most densely populated capital. One-fifth of France's 57 million people live in and around the city, along with immigrants, students, artists, teachers, business people and political refugees from around the world. The expatriate community is active; theatre, cinema, arts and news publications abound in various languages, including English. So many of the people living in the cosmopolitan region come from foreign lands and the provinces of France that the native *parisien* is a rare beast.

The first to arrive in this enchanted spot were the Parisii, a tribe of Gaulish fishermen and boatmen. The appearance of the Roman Empire brought about the strange mixture of Latin and northern civilisation that makes France unique. Though the Romans imposed their tongue, their official name for the city, Lutetia, disappeared from use over the years. Since then the number of emperors, philosophers, ambassadors, adventurers and outcasts who have arrived in this city is as uncountable as the lights bedecking it by night.

Strollers' city

Lovers know the city best. Silent green courtyards, the river's edge, the misty air are all accomplices to seduction. Some visitors never see the inside of a museum or monument, yet they know and love Paris deeply. It is a city ideal for strolling, tucked inside a 34-km (21-mile) perimeter. It is divided into 20 *arrondissements*, or districts which are used in postal codes and which begin in the centre with the *premier* (1er) *arrondissement* and spiral out in a clockwise direction. The city is also defined by its *quartiers*, Montmartre, Montparnasse, St Germain, Quartier Latin and so on, each with its own style and character. The River Seine divides the north from the south of Paris into what is known as the *rive droite* (right bank) and *rive gauche* (left bank).

Everything is accessible by public transport, though the elderly and those in wheelchairs will encounter difficulties. Free maps are widely available, but they won't show you the lanes of Montmartre or the key outer districts such as La Défense or La Villette.

Beginnings

Paris was founded on the **Ile de la Cité**, the primitive cradle of the city. Some of the ancient soul remains in the island's celebrated monuments. The **Cathédrale Notre-Dame ❶** (open daily; entrance fee for towers) was built during the 12th and 13th centuries, and extensively restored in the 19th. The original Lady of the Cathedral was a "black virgin", a popular ancient fertility figure. This dark, hooded lady was already credited with several miracles before disappearing

LEFT: Paris rooftops.
BELOW: permanently perched on Notre-Dame.

The devilish gargoyles scowling down from the upper gallery are not medieval nightmares but playful creations of the 19th-century Gothic revivalist architect – Viollet-le-Duc.

BELOW: Notre-Dame in the spring.

during the Revolution. A 14th-century statue of unknown origin stands in the same place (to the right of the choir) and is venerated still.

The building is a masterpiece of Gothic art. The tall central spire (82 m/270 ft) is flanked by two square towers. Visitors may climb all the way up during daylight hours and see the **Bourdon**, the 16-ton brass bell that the hunchback Quasimodo rang in Victor Hugo's novel, *Notre-Dame de Paris* (The Hunchback of Notre-Dame). The view from the top, alongside the devilish stone gargoyles, is a heavenly reward after the long climb up the spiralling stone staircase.

Between the towers stretches a long gallery, and below this the central **Rose Window** has a diameter of 9 m (31 ft), forming a halo above a statue of the Virgin Mary. The window surmounts the **Galerie des Rois**, 28 modern statues of the kings of Judah and Israel. The statues were all decapitated during the Revolution. Only recently were the heads discovered in a nearby construction site; they are now on display at the Cluny Museum. On a level with the *parvis*, the paved terrace in front of the cathedral, the three doorways of Notre-Dame are, left to right, the **Virgin's Portal**, the **Judgment** and **St Anne's Portal**. Each is covered with intricate carvings relating biblical tales and the lives of the saints.

A number of events from French history took place both on the *parvis* and inside the cathedral. In 1430, the young Henry VI of England was crowned king of France in the middle of the Hundred Years War. French King Henry IV arrived at the cathedral after abjuring Calvinism to receive the coveted crown. His cynical remarks caused the population to doubt the sincerity of his belated conversion. Nevertheless Henry le Grand rode fearlessly to the altar, surrounded by troops in full battle dress.

The coronation of Napoleon I in 1804 was certainly the most grandiose cer-

emony witnessed here. The gilded imperial coach materialised out of the snow. The gathered crowd saw nothing more than the curtained windows – Josephine and Napoleon drove to the back of the building to don their coronation robes in the wings. In the rear of the cathedral nave, they mounted the specially constructed double staircase to their thrones. The privileged guests, ladies bursting out of their low-cut gowns, gentlemen in uniform and high black boots, were accommodated on tiers of seats. Pope Pius VII agreed, for diplomatic reasons, to be present at the three-hour ceremony, but balked at performing the actual crowning. In fact, after the Pope's blessing, Napoleon simply crowned himself as the crowd cried "*Vive l'Empéreur!*"

More recently, on the liberation of Paris in 1944, Charles de Gaulle came to give thanks at Notre-Dame, while the Bourdon bell tolled joyously and sniper shots rang out in celebration.

Lining the walls of the cathedral are 29 chapels. The large main altar represents the **Offering of Louis XIII.** It commemorates the birth of the king's heir. To the left and right of the Nicolas Coustou Pietà are statues of Louis XIV (who completed the memorial) and Louis XIII.

Notre-Dame exhibits

The **Trésor de Notre-Dame** (open daily; closed Sun am; entrance fee) contains richly ornamented robes and chalices. Outside, the **Musée de Notre-Dame** (open Wed, Sat, Sun; entrance fee) charts the history of the cathedral and has exhibits of ancient pottery found beneath the parvis. In the **Crypte Archéologique** (open daily; entrance fee), underneath the parvis, are excavations of buildings dating back to the 3rd century.

Map on pages 114–5

TIP

Each Sunday at 5.45pm, the organ master fills Notre-Dame with classical music, soaring to paradise out of the 112-stop instrument. Classical concerts are also given in Sainte Chapelle.

BELOW: high-vaulted elegance of the central nave.

*Stained glass
perfection at
Sainte Chapelle.*

BELOW: painter on
the Pont des Arts.

In Memoriam

Behind the cathedral on the eastern tip of the Ile de la Cité, a small park was inaugurated in 1962. It harbours a monument by Pingusson honouring the 200,000 French martyrs who died in concentration camps in World War II. The **Mémorial de la Déportation**, moving in its simplicity, marks an unknown grave.

The western end of the island is almost entirely occupied by the **Palais de Justice ❷** (open Mon–Fri), a huge Gothic structure (much restored and rebuilt) where the first 12 Capetian kings lived. At the corner of the Quai de l'Horloge, the **Tour de l'Horloge** dates from the 15th century and is echoed on the northern facade by three round towers which mark the entrance to the **Conciergerie** (open daily; closed public hols; entrance fee). Many a death sentence was pronounced in the shadows of this infamous prison of the French Revolution. In one dark room the prisoners ate (the more fortunate had dinners sent in) and slept, struggled to keep warm and clean in the general squalor, and sometimes died of fear before reaching the guillotine. One of the last to go was Fouquier-Tinville, president of the Revolutionary Tribunal, who sent 2,278 men and women to the guillotine before him.

Queen Marie-Antoinette was held here, in a cell now open to visitors and replete with royal relics of her last days. She left the Conciergerie, hair shorn and wrists bound, in a dirty cart, sitting with her back to the horse so that the crowd might insult her to her face.

On the Boulevard du Palais, an ornate 18th-century gate opens onto the **Cours de Mai**, with **Sainte Chapelle ❸**, a glittering jewel of Gothic art, rising up amid the stark walls of the high court. The church was constructed in 1246 by Saint Louis to hold the Crown of Thorns and other purported relics, which he

purchased from the Emperor of Constantinople. The lower chapel was frequented by the palace servants and the upper by the royal household. Above, 15 great stained-glass windows fill the room with the precious coloured light that has given the chapel its renown. The walls soar up 31m (102 ft) and seem to be made of sparkling glass held by the scantiest skeleton of ornately carved stone. (Open daily; closed public hols; entrance fee.)

Ile de la Cité connects with the **Ile St Louis** by the Pont St Louis. The iron bridge leads to the smaller of the two Seine islands, soaked in 17th-century calm. Along the quiet streets the visitor will discover small art galleries, some intimate restaurants and tea rooms, and **Berthillon**, home of what is reputed to be the best ice-cream in Paris, which is just at the end of the bridge.

The left bank

Several bridges link the two islands to the *rive gauche* and *rive droite*. From the **Pont de la Tournelle** on the Ile St Louis, the view onto the left bank is dominated by the glass and steel edifice of the **Institut du Monde Arabe ❹**, an avant-garde, curved construction celebrating French ties with the Orient. The top floor of this museum, library and conference centre is a terrace café, offering exceptional views of the Seine and Notre-Dame. Next door is the famous restaurant **La Tour d'Argent**, and the same view as the Arab Institute.

Closer to Notre-Dame, the **Petit Pont** links Cité to the *rive gauche*. The shortest bridge in town has the longest history, reaching back to the origins of Roman Lutetia. Originally a wooden bridge, it was burned down many times in the course of numerous battles. In 1718, the bridge and its surroundings blazed up once more, under strange circumstances. A custom of the times was to seek the

Map on pages 114–5

Vedettes du Pont Neuf (tel: 01-46 33 98 38) run cruises along the Seine lasting about one hour. Boats leave from Square du Vert-Galant every half hour in high season.

BELOW: Sainte Chapelle, jewel of Gothic art.

A section of the six-panel, 15th-century tapestry, La Dame à la Licorne in Hôtel de Cluny.

repose of a loved one's soul by casting a bowl containing bread and a candle into the river. The mother of a drowned child did so, setting a barge piled with straw afire, and the bridge, packed with wooden houses, blazed out of control. This tragedy led to a law banning all buildings on bridges, which changed the face of the city.

Facing the Petit Pont on Rue de la Bûcherie is the bookstore **Shakespeare and Company**, named after the famous shop Sylvia Beach founded as a lending library in the 1920s. Many great and near-great authors have walked through the doors since; some of their pictures adorn the walls of the shop. Poetry readings are held in the upstairs sanctum, often by candlelight, and the atmosphere probably hasn't changed much since James Joyce's day.

Around the corner is one of the most affecting churches in Paris, and the oldest. **St Julien-le-Pauvre ❺**, small and squat, tucked into a corner of its little garden, looks like a humble country church which has somehow been transported to the city. Begun in 1170, it is now a Greek Catholic church. The interior is modest but beautiful, with elegant capitals.

The **Pont Neuf** (New Bridge) at the eastern end of the Cité is, despite its name, the oldest bridge standing in Paris, completed in 1607. It was the first bridge to be built entirely in stone, the widest, and the only one to be equipped with raised pedestrian walkways. These qualities, plus its central location, made the Pont Neuf a popular meeting place for peddlers, acrobats, tooth-pullers, musicians, pick-pockets and prostitutes. From the lower *quai* or aboard a *bateau mouche* tour boat, notice the 900 faces carved along the sides of the bridge, each one unique, and some of them particularly expressive.

BELOW: George Whitman, owner of Shakespeare and Company.

The Latin Quarter

The heart of the *rive gauche*, is the **Quartier Latin**, an area which is made up of the 5th and 6th *arrondissements*. In the early Christian era, the Roman city of Lutetia could no longer be contained by the protective confines of the small islands and spread to this southern hillside.

Here in the 13th century a number of schools opened their doors, most notably the **Université de Paris**, which still draws students to the quarter, though they no longer speak scholarly Latin. The main boulevards are **St Michel** and **St Germain**, both lined with shops and cafés and packed with people. The labyrinth of smaller streets winding around them is full of activity. Students and young people wander in and out of the bookshops and cafés all day long. At night, they head for Greek, Chinese and Italian restaurants, cinemas and nightclubs. On **Rue de la Huchette** a tiny theatre has been playing Ionesco's *La Leçon* and *La Cantatrice Chauve* for more than 40 consecutive years. The smell of cous-cous and the jangle of oriental music have become a permanent part of the production. Classical music sometimes wafts out **St Séverin ❻**, another magical medieval church, harmoniously proportioned and delicately decorated.

Clustered around St Séverin are little streets lined by Greek restaurants in an area known as **Little Athens**. Staff stand in doorways, imploring you to enter, and their house specialities are displayed in pavement cabinets and in the window, along with piles of broken crockery to indicate that "traditional plate-smashing goes on here" although in truth you will find the waiters loath to let you break their plates.

At the corner of Boulevards St Michel and St Germain is **Musée de Cluny ❼**, housing the ruins of the Roman Lutetia, including the **Roman Baths**. The *hôtel* (residence) itself is one of the few medieval mansions remaining in Paris and contains artifacts from castle and church life, such as the exquisite tapestries of *La Dame à la Licorne* (The Lady and The Unicorn). (Open Tues–Sun; closed public hols; entrance fee.)

Seat of learning

The heart of the Quartier Latin is dominated by **La Sorbonne ❽**, one of the most famous and distinguished institutes of learning in the world, founded in 1253 as a college for poor theological students. A few blocks down the Boulevard St Germain to the right, the austere facade of the **chapel of La Sorbonne** welcomes the curious. Cardinal Richelieu is buried here along with his hat suspended above, which will fall, so legend has it, when he is released from hell. Further along Rue St Jacques, to the left, the **Panthéon ❾** sits at the top of the Rue Soufflot. This 18th-century monument marks the top of **Mont Ste Geneviève**, the outer limits of the Roman city. The Panthéon is where illustrious Frenchmen are put to rest, and these include Victor Hugo, Voltaire, Rousseau, Zola and Resistance leader Jean Moulin.(Open daily; entrance fee.)

Close by, the attractive church of **St Etienne du Mont ❿**,with a superb rood screen, contains the remains of Racine and Pascal, commemorated by plaques,

Map on pages 114–5

TIP

For a wonderful panoramic view of Paris, and a relatively easy ascent, climb to the dome of the Panthéon, the city's most rewarding tall buiding.

BELOW: chapel in Place de la Sorbonne.

F. Scott Fitzergerald finished his most famous novel, The Great Gatsby, *(1925), portrayed on screen by Robert Redford and Mia Farrow (above), at 58 Rue de Vaugirard, just south of the Jardin du Luxemburg.*

BELOW: arriving for mint tea at the Paris Mosque.

and an ornate shrine to Ste Geneviève, patron saint of Paris. Life is less serious on the **Place de la Contrescarpe**, ringed by cafés, and the **Rue Mouffetard**, a long, winding street with a bustling daily market.

The only other Roman vestige in Paris proper (besides the Baths at Cluny) is the **Arènes de Lutèce ⓫**, the ancient arena. Tough Roman combatants have been replaced by peaceful *boulistes*, playing France's most popular game. *Pétanque* is a good spectator sport too, and the Arènes is a lovely park to rest.

Nearby, the **Jardin des Plantes ⓬** is a good place for a stroll. Within the garden the **Musée National d'Histoire Naturelle** and its contents have been restored, and a new gallery, the Grande Galerie de l'Evolution, added (open Wed–Mon; entrance fee). To the southeast along the Seine is the Quai de Bercy, an area of new development centred on the Bibliothèque Nationale de France François Mitterrand (nicknamed TGB, **Très Grand Bibliothèque**). This was Mitterrand's last *Grand Projet*, which cost nearly 8 billion francs to build. Near the labyrinth exit, down the Rue Quatrefages, is the **Mosquée de Paris ⓭** (open Mon–Thurs, Sat, Sun; closed Muslim hols; entrance fee). The Moorish mosque includes Turkish baths, open to the public, and a tea room.

The Luxembourg Gardens

The Sixth *arrondissement* lies on the opposite side of the Boulevard St Michel from the area described above. It has a more formal atmosphere, beginning with the **Jardin du Luxembourg ⓮** (open daily: dawn to dusk).The **Palais du Luxembourg ⓯**, constructed in the 17th century for Marie de' Medici, today houses the French Senate. In the park, children are more in evidence than politicians, sailing boats on the carp-filled pond.

North of the park, the great bulk of **St Sulpice** ⓰ looms amongst the narrow streets, harmonious except for its ill-matching towers.

"Lost Generation" readers will wander wistfully down the **Rue de Fleurus** to stop at No. 27, Gertrude Stein's home of many years; and **Notre Dame des Champs**, where Hemingway lived in a flat above a sawmill in the 1920s. His favourite café, the **Closerie des Lilas**, is still operating to the south at 171 Boulevard Montparnasse and serves excellent meals inside or on the terrace.

The crossroads at the 11th to 12th-century church of **Saint Germain des Prés** ⓱, once one of the most powerful abbeys in the land, is another gathering place, the most chic in the Latin Quarter. The **Cafés Flore** and **Deux Magots**, favoured by well-dressed intellectuals, face the **Brasserie Lipp**, where (rumour has it) only the most famous authors are invited to sit by the windows. There are a number of fine shops in the streets around here. Behind the abbey, on the delightful **Rue de Furstenberg**, the **Musée Delacroix** ⓲ shows that painter's work in his *atelier* (open Wed–Mon; entrance fee).

Chic St Germain

Lively and stylish streets abound in St Germain. **Rue de Buci** is thronged with people shopping in its colourful daily market (except Mon). **Rue de Seine, Rue Bonaparte, Rue Jacob** and **Rue des Beaux-Arts** (where Oscar Wilde expired in a seedy hotel, now a luxury one), are full of contemporary art galleries. The **Ecole des Beaux-Arts**, facing the river, is the country's foremost school of art. In between the Ecole des Beaux-Arts and the Musée d'Orsay, **Quai Voltaire** is lined with antique shops and was once home to Wagner, Sibelius, Baudelaire, Wilde and Voltaire.

Map on pages 114–5

TIP

There is something for everyone in the Luxembourg Gardens. Attractions include: boating, model sail-boating, a bandstand, shady outdoor café, bee-keeping school, donkey rides, puppet theatre, and an adjacent riding centre.

BELOW: Café de Flore.

CAFÉ LIFE

The café is the Parisian's decompression chamber, easing the transition between *dodo-Métro-boulot* – sleeping, commuting and working. It provides a welcome pause in which to savour a *petit noir* (espresso) or an apéritif, to empty the mind of troublesome thoughts and to watch the people go by. The café is also the place to meet friends, have a romantic tryst or even to do business in a relaxed atmosphere.

The first café ever to open was Le Procope in 1686 (13 Rue de l'Ancienne-Comédie) and the literati soon started to congregate there, keen to discuss ideas with each other. More establishments quickly sprang up and during the 18th century, the neighbourhood "zinc", named after its metal counter, became part of the fabric of French life. In Paris, each café developed its own character, attracting different types of clientele, and with the widening of the boulevards in the 19th century, the tables spilled out on to the pavements.

Although authentic "zincs" are still to be found, and many are thriving, café life is now in serious danger of extinction: in Paris alone, 1,000 have closed in five years. Go to a genuine one soon; unless you do, you cannot claim to appreciate the traditional essence of Paris.

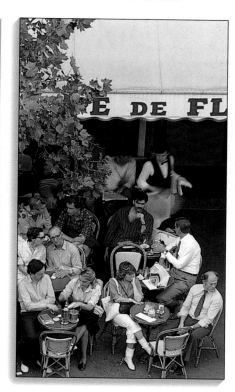

La Closerie des Lilas, at 171 Boulevard du Montparnasse, was a favourite haunt of Jean-Paul Sartre (above). The mad 19th-century poet Gérard de Nerval used to walk his pet lobster on a lead at La Rotonde (No. 105).

BELOW: dinner at La Coupole.

The long-abandoned train station, Gare d'Orsay, was given a new purpose when it became one of the city's foremost art galleries, **Musée d'Orsay** ⑲ (open Tues–Sun; entrance fee). Preserving the building's *belle époque* architecture, Gae Aulenti redesigned the inner space into several exhibition levels, while keeping the airy majesty of the original train station. Devoted to works of the last half of the 19th century, it includes famous canvases by Monet, Manet, Renoir, Van Gogh and Cézanne. Do not miss the opulent restaurant.

Sacré Parnasse

The southern end of the Latin Quarter is dominated by **Tour Montparnasse** ⑳, a shiny black skyscraper shooting up above the Montparnasse train station. The 58-floor complex, completed in 1973, certainly changed the artists' haunt of the 1920s, and Picasso, Boris Vian and F. Scott Fitzgerald might say for the worse. But what the quarter lost in old-fashioned charm it has regained in dynamism. Today, Montparnasse is a nocturnal hot spot still favoured by artists. In the tower, an elevator will whisk you to the top floor in 40 seconds. There you can view the panorama of Paris from the terrace or inside the rooftop restaurant.

A short walk down the bright and busy **Boulevard Montparnasse** brings you to **La Coupole**, a spacious, popular café-restaurant with a low-key dance hall. Singles beware (or be brave): La Coupole is one of the biggest pick-up joints in town. The scene goes on until 2am, often animated by heated debates between colourful regulars. The nearby **Select** and the **Dôme** have similar atmospheres, but the Coupole remains the king of cafés.

Elsewhere in Montparnasse the controversial Rodin **statue of Balzac** stands at the crossroads of Boulevard Montparnasse and Avenue Raspail, and the

Map
on pages
114–5

Cimetière du Montparnasse accommodates Sartre and Baudelaire. Under the lion at Place Denfert-Rochereau stretch the **Catacombs**, miles of underground tunnels containing six million skeletons, stacked against the walls (open Tues–Sun; closed public hols; entrance fee).

The Emperor's tomb

The Boulevard du Montparnasse divides the Latin Quarter from the 14th to 15th *arrondissements* and turns northeast to the Boulevard des Invalides. Though most people who visit the **Hôtel des Invalides** ㉑ approach this impressive monument from the north side, facing the river, a less sterile and imposing first view offers itself from the perspective of the **Avenue de Breteuil**. Laid out in 1680, this avenue rolls forth like a long green carpet to the **Place Vauban**. As one nears the dome, its vast proportions become evident.

Louis XIV ordered the construction of the Hôtel des Invalides in 1671, to serve as a home for disabled soldiers. In fact, it functioned as a clearing house for veterans, many of whom, despite their infirmities, were sent to guard fortified places all over France. The regimen was fairly strict: those who arrived late for meals sat at isolated tables in the middle of the refectory, drinking only water.

The graceful dome, topped by a spire reaching 102 m (336 ft), originally capped the Royal Church. Today, the building has the tombs of French military heroes, including Napoleon I, Vauban, Turenne and Foch, and contains the **Musée de l'Armée** (open Oct–Mar: daily; closed public hols; entrance fee), the world's largest military museum. In the former dining hall, now the **Salle des Armures**, magnificent suits of armour are displayed, and in the same wing is a fine collection of early arms and battle dress. The facing wing is dedicated to the world wars, and includes some of the famous Marne Valley taxis – cabs which were mobilised in World War I and contributed to the key victories in the valley.

The Invalides is probably most widely known for the **Tomb of Napoleon I**. In 1840, King Louis-Philippe gave permission to bring the emperor's remains back to Paris. A roaring crowd greeted the funeral chariot on 15 December. According to Victor Hugo, it resembled a "mountain of gold". Decorated with eagles, golden bees and 14 statues of victory carrying the symbolic coffin, the gilded creation weighed 11,818 kg (26,000 lbs). The coffin was then set in the church of the **Dôme** for 10 days as admirers filed through. The present sarcophagus in red porphyry was designed shortly afterwards by Visconti and has since stood directly under the dome.

Eve in the garden

A more peaceful spot is the nearby **Musée Rodin** ㉒ (77 Rue de Varenne; open Tues–Sun; entrance fee), in the **Hôtel Biron**, where the sculptor lived and worked. The setting is sublime, and visitors can admire a number of Rodin's most celebrated works (*The Thinker, The Gates of Hell, Eve, The Burghers of Calais*) in the charming garden of roses, trees and ponds. Inside, the various models for his statue of Balzac, which

"Everything that exists elsewhere exists in Paris."
— Victor Hugo

BELOW:
Les Invalides.

*Sculptural detail,
Palais de Chaillot.*

Balzac, which shocked the city officials, are alongside the collection of drawings, etchings and studies. Early critics accused the artist of making plaster-casts of real bodies and pouring his bronze into them. The museum is a magical place to savour the master's work, especially in the late afternoon, when the guard with his long black cloak circles the garden ringing his bell.

A short walk away is Paris's most famous monument: **La Tour Eiffel** (1st and 2nd levels open daily until 11pm – midnight July and Aug; 3rd level open until 8pm; entrance fee). Recently tons and tons of rust have been scraped off her and "Eiffie" looks better than ever. She won her fame the hard way, however. Erected for the Universal Exhibition of 1889, the 300-m (985-ft) tower designed by Gustave Eiffel was snubbed and disdained by the stylish and intellectual crowd. But ordinary people grew fond of the tower as it rose up slowly over two years, and cheered when Eiffel himself climbed up to plant a French flag on the top. The stormy aesthetic debate raged on for years. Ultimately, the telegraphic communication saved the Eiffel Tower, which became a relay station and is still used for radio in the 1990s.

There is a choice of eating places in the tower, one very expensive. You can visit the elevator machinery, and a small museum on the first floor shows films of the tower. The view is dynamite, whether you stand at the bottom and watch the iron framework whooshing up, or look down at Paris from above. The best city-gazing is about an hour before sunset.

BELOW: The Eiffel Tower from the Palais de Chaillot.

The rectangular park at the foot of the tower is the **Champ de Mars** ㉔. The large field has been used for popular celebrations (the first Bastille Day commemoration was held here on 14 July 1790) and military exercise. Indeed, the park runs from the Seine to the **École Militaire** ㉕, an 18th-century edifice designed by Jacques-Ange Gabriel.

Trocadéro

As you stand at the foot of the Eiffel Tower, your eye is carried across the river by the elegant span of the **Pont d'Iéna**. The buildings and terraces spread along the riverside on the far side of the bridge are known as the **Trocadéro**. The site was a wooded hill when Catherine de Medici built a palace there, and Napoleon planned to build an imperial city, "a Kremlin a hundred times more beautiful than that of Moscow", on the spot. In 1827, Charles X had a fantastic stage-set installed where the re-enactment of the battle of Fort Trocadéro in Cadiz was played out. The name remained when the site was prepared for the Universal Exhibition.

The present buildings of the **Palais de Chaillot** ㉖ crowning the hilltop date from the 1930s. One wing holds the **Théâtre National de Chaillot**, devoted to monumental productions of both classical and modern plays, and was home to the Musée du Cinéma until it burned down. In the other wing are the **Musée de l'Homme** (anthropology; open Wed–Mon; closed public hols; entrance fee) and the **Musée des Monuments** (open Wed–Mon; entrance fee).

Whether you cross the Seine by foot, or take the elevated Métro at Bir Hakim you will find yourself in the ultra-chic **16th *arrondissement***. The 16th is home to the *grande bourgeoisie* of Paris, as a quick look around at the sumptuous apartment buildings, expensive boutiques and exotic food markets will confirm. The area has been an enclave of wealth for over a century. When it was incorporated into the city of Paris, the area was given *arrondissement* number 13. But the influential residents made short work of obtaining a more desirable number for their address. Visitors will find the Trocadéro a bustling spot, alive with tourists and kids on roller skates. But at night-time, the residential nature of the 16th makes it quite a bore.

The **Musée d'Art Moderne de Paris** ㉗ (open Tues–Sun; closed public hols; entrance fee), which has been rather sparsely frequented since the opening of the Pompidou Centre, is inside the **Palais de Tokyo** (another vestige of the 1937 Exposition). In the **Jardins du Trocadéro** ㉘, an **aquarium** has been cut into the hillside.

Also cut into the hillside, though at a much earlier date (13th century), are the *caves à vin* located near the Passy Métro station on Square Charles Dickens. Today the ancient cellars are home to the **Musée du Vin** (Wine Museum; open daily; entrance fee), where visitors can study the tools of wine-making and the evolution of different bottles and glasses. The walls are covered with engravings, posters, sketches and water-colours, some of them quite funny. There is a shop with mouthwatering merchandise, and you can taste wines and have a light meal at the **Caveau des Echansons**.

On the top of the Passy hillside, the **Maison de Balzac** (open Tues–Sun; closed public hols; entrance fee) has been converted into a museum where visitors can see mementos and manuscripts of the famous writer. The house was ideally suited for the ever-indebted author; while creditors knocked at the main entrance on Rue Raynouard, he slipped out the back on to Rue Berton.

In the woods

One reason the wealthy prefer to live in the 16th is its proximity to the **Bois de Boulogne**, a lovely 872-hectare (2,500-acre) park on the western edge of Paris. The several lakes and the many paths through the woods as well as the **Longchamps Racetrack** are all popular with city dwellers. Especially beautiful is the **Pré Catalan** with its outdoor theatre, the **Jardin Shakespeare**. In this enchanted spot, gardeners have tried to plant every type of tree, bush and flower that the Bard spoke of in his plays. There are plays and concerts in the Pré in the summer season, in an unforgettable setting.

The **Jardins de Bagatelle** are bewitching in the rose season, when every species blooms along the fragrant paths. This corner of the park has long been the city's frivolous Lovers' Lane, and *faire la bagatelle* means what lovers do together. There are a few high-class restaurants in the park, but unless you're headed for one it's wise not to venture into the woods after dark. Prostitution and concomitant crime are rampant.

On the edge of the park, on Rue Louis Boillu, the **Musée Marmottan** (open Tues–Sun; closed public hols; entrance fee) holds more than 130 works by Impressionist painter Claude Monet. About 30 of the pic-

Map on pages 114–5

TIP

Queues for the Eiffel Tower can be up to two hours long in summer, so get there early. The best, and certainly most romantic place to see the Eiffel Tower is from Trocadéro at night, when it is gloriously lit up and in full view at the end of Champs de Mars.

BELOW: a quiet corner in the Bois de Boulogne.

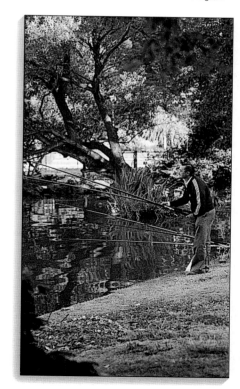

Guarding the Palais d'Elysée.

tures represent his house at Giverny and the water lilies that inspired him. Quite a few paintings from the series on Rouen Cathedral are hung here, too, a startling revelation of Monet's advanced colour technique. Of particular interest is the painting *Impression,* which gave the whole movement its name.

Further west beyond the Périphérique sprawls the space-age city of **La Défense**. Europe's largest business centre and a testimony to the French inclination to innovate, the district found its focus with the opening in 1989 of **La Grande Arche de la Défense**, one of Mitterrand's *grands projets* which mirrors the Arc de Triomphe. Glass elevators whisk you to its summit, from where there is a dramatic view back to central Paris. The **Esplanade de la Défense** is crowded with business people during the week and tourists at weekends, when the **Sculpture Park**, **Automobile Museum** and **Imax Dome** (the world's largest wrap-around cinema screen) come into their own.

Famous promenade

Avenue Foch leads from the Bois straight down to the **Champs Elysées** ❷❾, the famed promenade crowned by the **Arc de Triomphe** ❸⓿, in the centre of **Place Charles de Gaulle-Etoile**.

The Arc de Triomphe was completed in 1836, and commemorates the victories of the Napoleonic Empire. In 1920, an unknown soldier was buried beneath the arch and a flame marks his grave. If you want to climb to the top for the view and the **museum** (open daily; entrance fee) do take the underground passage to the arch – the roundabout is notorious for heavy traffic.

Stroll down the prestigious avenue or sit on a terrace in the sun. The Champs-Elysées is one of the world's best people-watching places. The window shopping

BELOW LEFT:
La Grande Arche de la Défense.
BELOW RIGHT:
the Arc de Triomphe at night.

is grand too, and a number of covered galleries and arcades make it a pleasure in any weather. About half-way down, you will find the elegant **Hôtel Georges V** (on the avenue of the same name) a dignified luxury hotel with beautiful sitting rooms and a fine courtyard restaurant. Some of the city's most exclusive eateries are found on side streets off the Champs, but the over-priced fast-food bistros on the avenue are mostly pretty awful.

The lower half of the avenue runs through majestic chestnut trees. Several fine theatres and restaurants are set among the trees. The **Grand Palais** ③① (open Wed–Mon; entrance fee for exhibitions) and the **Petit Palais** ③② (open Tues–Sun; closed public hols; entrance fee), two distinctive glass- and steel-domed museums have changing shows and 19th- and 20th-century painting. Across the other side of the avenue, at the end of Avenue de Marigny, the **Palais de l'Élysée** ③③ is the official residence of the President of the Republic.

Continue walking and you will emerge onto the **Place de la Concorde** ③④. The central **Obelisk**, which graced the tomb of Ramses II at Luxor 3,000 years ago, was erected on this spot in 1836. The great drama of the *place* was on 17 January 1793 when King Louis XVI was guillotined here. At 10am, the king arrived in a cart with his confessor and two gendarmes. He took off his coat and tie and mounted the scaffold. As the terrible roar of soldiers' drums filled the air, the king cried out "*Je suis perdu!*" (I am lost!) His severed head was then held up for the crowd's inspection.

The Louvre

The arcaded pavements of the **Rue de Rivoli** are always busy. Facing the arcades, the **Jardin des Tuileries** ③⑤ stretches down to the Louvre. At the Con-

Map on pages 114–5

TIP

The Champs-Elysées is made for parades and it looks its best during the Bastille Day (July 14) parade; also at night when the Arc de Triomphe and Place de la Concorde are impressively floodlit.

RIGHT: Place de la Concorde.

Aristide Maillol (1861–1944) started sculpting at the age of 40, concentrating his efforts on large, bronze, nude women – 20 of which adore the Tuileries.

corde end of the gardens, the small **Jeu de Paume** ❸ (open Tues–Sun; entrance fee) has temporary exhibitions, and opposite, the **Musée de l'Orangerie** ❸ contains Monet's "Waterlilies" series, as well as Cézannes and Renoirs (open Wed–Mon; entrance fee). The Tuileries were designed by landscape artist André Le Nôtre, who also conceived the park at Versailles and other royal gardens. The wide paths and small lawns in the midst of trees are dotted with stately stone statues. Between the palace wings in the **Jardin du Carrousel** ❸ the **Arc de Triomphe du Carrousel** completes one of the longest architectural vistas in the world, stretching all the way from this small arch past the obelisk and Concorde, through the Arc de Triomphe to the Grand Arche at La Défense, ghost-like in the distance.

The pyramid

There is an obelisk at Concorde, so why not a pyramid at the **Musée National du Louvre** ❸? Conceived by the American I.M. Pei, the **Louvre Pyramid** was inaugurated in 1989. Whether loved or despised, the design ingeniously disperses daylight round the ancient courtyard around it and the foyer below, as well as providing multiple entrances to the Louvre's mighty galleries. The original 13th-century palace was a royal residence until 1793, when it was turned into the world's largest museum. The collections are seemingly infinite, from Roman, Greek, and Egyptian artifacts to Renaissance painting, and without a floor-plan it is easy to get lost. One of the most dramatic features of the major ongoing renovation of the Louvre is the Richelieu wing with its two splendid light-flooded sculpture courts. The old favourites, however, are well signposted – *Mona Lisa* ("La Joconde" in French), *Winged Victory* and *Venus*

BELOW: the Louvre's distinctive pyramid.

de Milo (open Wed–Mon; entrance fee). A recent development is the opening of the **Musée de la Mode et du Textile**; another is the decision to give the Mona Lisa her own room.

The medieval city which succeeded the ancient Roman Lutetia huddled close about the walls of the Louvre. The maze of lanes and dead-end streets was so confusing that Queen Marie-Antoinette, preparing to flee Paris, wandered lost for two hours before discovering the royal coach waiting on the Rue de l'Echelle. Bonaparte made clearing the area around the Louvre an important part of his vast urban programme.

At the Ritz

The **Place Vendôme**, two blocks off the Rue de Rivoli, is a 17th-century marvel of harmony. Under the stone arches, the **Ritz Hôtel** is well suited to its surroundings. Its opulence created the word "ritzy". Hemingway once hoped that heaven would be as good as the Ritz; his ghost still haunts the bar which is named after him (prices have risen since Ernest's day). Now the hotel has earned worldwide notoriety through being where Diana, Princess of Wales, spent her last hours before her fateful car journey with the hotel owner's son, Dodi al-Fayed, in August 1997.

Further along the Rue de Rivoli, overlooking two squares named after famous French writers, Colette and Malraux, the **Comédie Française** ❹ is the revered classical theatre founded by Molière. Beside it, the **Palais Royal** ❹ was built by Cardinal Richelieu in the 17th century and willed to the king at his death. Anne of Austria moved here with her son, the future Louis XIV, because she so much preferred it to the gloomy Louvre. The **Jardin du Palais Royal** ❹ behind

Map on pages 114–5

TIP

Each evening, 45 minutes before curtain-rise at the Comédie-Française, 112 tickets are sold at low prices at the booth just off the square on Rue de Montpensier behind the theatre.

BELOW: Coco Chanel, who revolutionised Paris fashions in the 1940s.

PARIS FASHIONS

Poiret, Chanel, Dior... most of this century's best-known fashion houses have been French. At the end of World War II, discreet salons and their *vendeuses* gave way to the bright lights of the catwalk as Dior's New Look burst on to the scene with full skirts and luxurious, voluminous fabrics. During the 1950s, Chanel's commitment to freer, more carefree clothing paved the way to a more liberated style for women. But the revolution came in the 1960s with Yves Saint Laurent and fashion for the future followed by the fun fashions, plastic and chain-link dresses of Courrèges and Paco Rabanne.

With the extravagant styles and brilliant colours of Christian Lacroix in the 1980s, Paris hit the big time again. It now treads a tightrope between the traditional glamour of its image and the radical chic of many of today's designers, with avant garde foreigners Paul Galliano and Alexander McQueen heading Dior and Givenchy.

Today, haute couture designs are worn by a handful of rich women. The designs, however, provide inspiration for a designer which can then be applied to accessories, perfumes and cosmetics — the real money spinners.

the palace is a bright and sunny park. In the shaded gallery at the north end is the **Grand Véfour** restaurant, perhaps the most beautiful in Paris. The 18th-century décor is listed, and its food merits two Michelin stars.

At the far end of the park, you can cross the street and enter two unusual *galleries*, covered streets lined with shops. The **Galeries Colbert** and **Vivienne**, spacious and quiet, covered with high glass roofs, are an oasis in the crush of midtown. Tea or lunch at **A Priori Thé** in the Vivienne Gallery is guaranteed to soothe the most jangled nerves.

Just a few blocks down from the 17th century lies the 20th in the form of the **Forum des Halles** ❸. This modern, glass and steel commercial centre is on the site of the old Paris market and has become a crowded retail centre, and a seedy gathering place for drop-outs and drug addicts. Some of the old atmosphere does still exist, for example at **Pied de Cochon** (Rue Coquillière),which serves meals and hot onion soup night and day, as it did when the market kept the quarter lively around the clock, and in pedestrianised **Rue Montorgeuil**, where a colourful daily street market still operates. The **Square des Innocents** occupies the site of the city's oldest cemetery, dating from the Gallo-Roman period. A ghastly spot surrounded by charnel houses, the cemetery absorbed some two million corpses before it was emptied in 1786. Perhaps the Euro-tramps in motley attire who soak their feet in the fountain don't look so very different from the area's 15th-century wanderers.

In the Quartier de l'Horloge, a pedestrianised area just north of the Pompidou Centre, is a huge Defender of Time clock in brass and steel. On the hour, a life-size soldier does battle with either the dragon of earth, the bird of air or the crab of the sea. At 6 and 12, all attack.

Contemporary culture

There's always a colourful crowd around the **Centre Pompidou** ❹, known locally as Beaubourg. Designed by an Italian-British team of architects (Piano and Rogers), the building presents a glass facade supported totally by an external skeleton. Though some Parisians claim to detest it, the inside-out museum rapidly became the most visited attraction in town. Currently the building is closed for renovation until 1999. The escalators which run up the side of the building in clear tubes remain open, as does an exhibition space, while the library is being housed temporarily in a building nearby.

When the building reopens it will again operate as a multifunctional arts centre, with lots of off-beat exhibits centred around its **Contemporary Art Collection**. Music, cinema, theatre and poetry all have a place on the museum's varied programme.

BELOW: escape artist in front of the Pompidou Centre.

Old Paris

The **Marais** (literally, "swamp"), was *the* place for nobles to live in the 16th and 17th century. The charming streets were then neglected for 300 years, and the grand residences crumbled. Since 1962, the quarter has been renovated, and is now a mixture of rough charm and refined elegance.

The ornate Gothic **Hôtel de Ville** ❺ (City Hall) on the Rue de Rivoli, is the most monumental reminder of the neighbourhood's heyday. The original 16th-century structure was burned to the ground on 24 May 1871 by angry *Communards*. One year later, architect Viollet-le-Duc directed a scrupulous restora-

Map on pages 114–5

tion. Recently scrubbed clean and beautified by a fountained esplanade, the Hôtel de Ville has added a visitor's centre with documentation and exhibits of the city.

Behind the Hôtel de Ville and off the Rue de Rivoli, the **Rue Vieille du Temple** wanders into the oldest section of the Marais. The street takes its name from the Knights Templar, an ancient secret order of powerful princes of finance. The Knights went underground in 1312, but their temple, until it was destroyed in 1811, was a sort of safe house where police did not penetrate. The young son of Louis XVI was held there when his parents were tried – prisoner or guest? – and mysteriously disappeared. Likewise, the fabulous treasure they were supposed to have amassed over the years, including the Holy Grail, has never been found.

The **Rue des Rosiers** is the heart of the Jewish quarter. The kosher restaurants and shops sell products from Eastern Europe and North Africa.

The Mémorial du Martyr Juif Inconnu (Memorial to the Unknown Jew) stands on Rue Geoffroy l'Asnier, south of the Jewish Quarter. Its eternal flame in an underground crypt is a poignant reminder of the Holocaust.

The story of Paris

To discover even more about the Marais, visit the **Musée Carnavalet** ㊻ (23 Rue de Sévigné; open Tues–Sun; entrance fee), the historical museum of Paris, which also has information about local activities; the Marais has retained a strong cultural identity and is the site of many special festivities. The house itself once belonged to Mme de Sévigné, 17th-century authoress and vicious gossip, whose *Letters* revealed the intricacies of aristocratic life at court. She was born, baptised and married in the Marais, where she also died.

Nearby, at Place Thorigny, the **Musée National Picasso** ㊼ occupies the restored **Hôtel Salé**, built by a wealthy tax collector. Picasso's family donated a

BELOW: *circa* 17th-century Hôtel Salé, housing the Musée Picasso.

BELOW: singing for her supper in the Place des Vosges.

large collection of his works to the state, in lieu of huge inheritance tax payments due after the painter's death. The well-organised collection is displayed in this beautiful Renaissance setting (5 Rue de Thorigny; open Wed–Mon; entrance fee).

Behind the *hôtel*, down the Rue Birague, is charming **Place des Vosges** , named after the first region to pay taxes to the new Republic. The rectangular *place*, the oldest in Paris, is where Victor Hugo lived. You can visit his house, **Maison Victor Hugo** (open Tues–Sun; entrance fee) at number 6, and see not only manuscripts and notes, but also his drawings and handmade furniture. The view of the square from his windows probably hasn't changed much since Hugo gazed out seeking inspiration.

Bastille

The limits of the Marais are marked by the **Place de la Bastille**. This was the site of the dreaded prison constructed in the 14th century, whose walls were about 11 m (30–40 ft) thick in some places, protected by high battlements and heavy artillery. Despite the apparently impregnable walls, the Bastille fell before the onslaught of the furious population on 14 July 1789. "Is it a revolt?" asked Louis XVI. "No sire," he was told, "a revolution." The hated jail was completely destroyed and in its place was eventually erected, in 1840, the towering **Colonne de Juillet** commemorating the victims of the Revolution.

Dominating the Place de la Bastille is the new **Opéra de Paris Bastille** ❹, another monument to glass and concrete, opened in 1989. The "opera of the people" has been dogged by scandal and criticism, but has led to a gentrification of the Bastille quarter (to the consternation of some of its more colourful residents). This is the upwardly trendy corner of Paris.

From the **Port de l'Arsenal**, the city's marina on the south side of the Place de la Bastille, you can catch a canal boat northwards underground to **Place de la République**. The canal emerges there and continues through several locks to Port de la Villette. Here, the old slaughterhouses have been transformed into one of the capitals most enjoyable high-tech parks, **Parc de la Villette** (open Tues–Sun; entrance fee). The **Géode**, a 37-m (120-ft) diameter geodesic dome covered with polished steel mirror surfaces, houses a hemispheric cinema screen which takes you on a journey from the galaxies to the depths of the oceans, whilst next door the **Cinaxe** is a giant flight simulator, not for the easily sick.

The **Cité des Sciences** is a futuristic museum, celebrating man's ingenuity with numerous interactive exhibits. In contrast, the solidly 19th-century **Grande Halle** on the other side of the canal seems a relic from the age of iron.

Père Lachaise

Memories of the past are preserved with more reverence at the **Cimetière Père Lachaise**, beyond the Marais. This graveyard with its streets and boulevards, above-ground monuments and regular visitors feeding the wild cats, is like a miniature city. You can buy a map of some of the many famous gravesites. These include the tombs of Abélard and Héloise, Rossini, Chopin, Edith Piaf, Gertrude Stein, Molière, Oscar Wilde, Sarah Bernhardt, Marcel Proust, Simone Signoret and Yves Montand and *Doors* lead singer Jim Morrison.

The French who visit the cemetery usually make a point of seeing the **Mur des Fédérés**. In 1871, the last of the insurgents from the *Commune de Paris* took a stand among the sepulchres of the hilly cemetery. They were trapped and executed against the wall, which still bears the marks of the fatal rounds. Rumour

Map on pages 114–5

The most visited grave in Cimetière Père Lachaise is that of Jim Morrison, which has become a shrine for his fans. Graffiti ensures you will not miss it and security has had to be implemented to protect it from further vandalism.

BELOW: fast food, Paris style.

was that some of the *Communards* had escaped detection and were living in Père Lachaise secretly. Even today, there are rumours of strange and unwholesome goings-on after nightfall.

In fact, the area around the cemetery, the 20th *arrondissement*, is a popular residential zone and the Ménilmontant *quartier* is becoming a lively area of off-beat art galleries, shops and cafés. The pavements of Ménilmontant were the first stage for Edith Piaf, who hit the streets singing aged 12. Her forceful, emotional style won many admirers. Popular slang uses her name – *piaf* – to mean a singing bird. The tiny **Musée Edith Piaf** is at 5 Rue Crespin-du-Gast (tel: 01-43 55 52 72; open Mon–Thur pm by appointment). About the only other trace of her is a tiny *place*, east of the cemetery, recently rebaptised in her honour. Another famous singer, Maurice Chevalier, wandered through the quarter as a youngster. He sang, "*Oh, les rues de Ménilmontant, sont-elles toujours montantes?*" – in reference to the steep hill that starts up from the Belleville district to peak at that most Parisian hilltop, **Montmartre**.

This particular *mont* is dominated by the distinctive white domes of the **Basilique du Sacré-Coeur** Ⓐ which was built in 1876 on the site of the bloodily vanquished *Commune de Paris*. Few Parisians are very fond of the monument, perhaps by association with the repression of the popular uprising. It certainly occupies a choice spot: the highest in the city, on its northern rim.

A Picasso party

Upper Montmartre residents long considered themselves a village apart from the rest of the town. Painters Toulouse-Lautrec and Utrillo, and later Picasso, Matisse, poet Guillaume Apollinaire and pianist Eric Satie enjoyed the image of

"I want my heart to be preserved in a pitcher of Vin de Beaujolais in the restaurant in Place du Tertre on the summit of Montmartre."

– JOHN DOS PASSOS

BELOW: Père Lachaise Cemetery.

the free-thinking hilltop and made it the happiest and most condusive place for artists to live in Paris.

If the Commune was the greatest political expression of the Montmartre temperament, the *banquet Rousseau* must sum up her artistic glory. Picasso decided to give a banquet in his studio to honour naive painter Henri Rousseau. The young Spaniard was full of admiration for the older painter's work, but the dinner party grew into an event to celebrate an epoch, not just one man. Amongst the guests were Apollinaire (who escorted the guest of honour), Gertrude and Leo Stein, Alice B. Toklas, Max Jacob, Georges Braque, Maurice de Vlaminck and Marie Laurencin. The guests met beforehand and were feeling very festive by the time they left the bar. The evening progressed (despite the caterer's failure to deliver the food, and perhaps because of the quantities of wine served), through a number of songs, poems and dances performed in honour of Rousseau, who sat on a high platform playing his violin tearfully. One of the guests fell into the pastries, another ate a lady's hat, and no one was surprised when a donkey wandered in for a drink.

Lingering memories

The innocent drunkenness of the time is still lingering in the atmosphere of the **Au Lapin Agile** ❸, a Montmartre cabaret on Rue des Saules. The Lapin is one of the last places in Paris you can hear a complete repertoire of popular French music. Guests sit elbow to elbow at rough wooden tables. Everyone is served a *cerises à l'eau de vie*. One by one, the singers, actors and comics do their gigs, then hurry off to another cabaret or restaurant. The piano player and the boss keep things rolling between acts. It opens late and fills up quickly.

ABOVE AND BELOW:
Au Lapin Agile,
where artists and
intellectuals used to
congregate.

The Dutch painter Vincent Van Gogh (1853–90) lived in Rue Lepic between 1886 and 1888. Here, he painted his Self Portrait with a Gray Hat. While in Paris, he taught himself the French Impressionist techniques, breaking away from his dark painting to make better use of colour.

Rue Cortot was home to Satie (No. 6) while he was composing his delightful piano pieces, and to Utrillo, who lived there with his mother, artist Suzanne Valadon. He captured many of *La Butte's* houses and cafés in his work. At No. 12 is the **Musée de Montmartre** (open Tues–Sun; entrance fee) which is housed, along with the **Montmartre Cultural Centre**, in an 18th century-manor house. Its windows overlook the **Montmartre Vineyard**, the only remaining vineyard in Paris, and Rue St Vincent. Every October, there is a big harvest celebration here.

You will find more entertainment on the crowded main square, **Place du Tertre** . Besides a flock of painters, there are bars, cafés and restaurants aplenty, most offering music. For a truly retro evening, stop at **La Bohème** on the *place* for dinner or drinks. There you can polka and Charleston and cha-cha-cha to the strains of the accordion, and join in loud and joyful French drinking songs. Leaving Place du Tertre where it meets Rue Poulbot, you will pass **Espace Montmartre** (open daily; entrance fee), home to over 300 works by Salvador Dali, and its popular shop.

Windmill turned dance hall

On the corner of **Rue Lepic** and Rue Girandon stands the **Moulin de la Galette** . The windmill was made into a dance hall in the 19th century, and celebrated in a painting by Renoir. Van Gogh lived with his brother in a pretty little house, No. 54 Rue Lepic, before moving south. Lepic turns into a lively market street that will carry you down the hill to lower Montmartre, or you may prefer to use the funicular, which runs from near Place d'Anvers at the bottom of the hill to Sacré-Coeur at the top.

BELOW: art for sale in Montmartre.

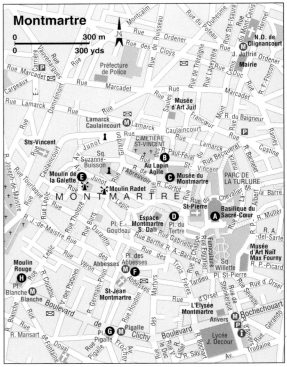

On the way down, detour to Place Emile-Goudeau to see the old piano factory, **Bateau-Lavoir**, which was where many of the great artists of the day had their extremely shabby, ill-equipped studios. It was here, for example, that Picasso painted *Les Demoiselles d'Avignon*, considered to be the precursor of Cubism. In 1970 the original building burnt down, but it was replaced with a replica, in which modern day artists may rent space.

Further down, **Place des Abbesses** , named for the nuns of the abbey which stood here in the Middle Ages, is a pretty square with a noteworthy Métro entrance, one of only two to retain its original glass roof. Designed by architect Hector Guimard, it is a picturesque evocation of early Art Nouveau with its green wrought-iron arches and amber lights.

Red lights

This is **Pigalle** (*Pig Alley* to two generations of American and British soldiers), a gaudy red-light district going as far as Place de Clichy. Beware of the numerous Live Shows along this sexy strip. Though they lure you in with low prices, they hit you for a stiff drink minimum inside.

The famous **Moulin Rouge** is on Place Blanche. The windmill is neon now and most of the audience arrive by tour bus. Though they still perform a version of French can-can, the girls are wearing feathers these days (mostly on their heads). Champagne obligatory. If you want a more modern scene, Pigalle is still the place to be: it's changing all the time as new clubs emerge from seedy pasts to become disco temples. **La Locomotive**, next door to the Moulin Rouge, is Paris's biggest dance venue, on three stories. Its Sunday afternoon Gay Tea Dance, formerly held at Le Palace, is a Parisian institution.

TIP

The ideal way to see Montmartre is on foot, but the Montmartro-bus and tourist train provide a less exhausting slice of the district and start from Place Blanche.

BELOW:
Place du Tertre.

Map on pages 114–5

A flock of fashion designers have their principal houses in Rue Faubourg St Honoré: Christian Lacroix at No. 73, Sonia Rykiel at No. 70, Yves St Laurent at No. 38 and Japanese Ashida at No. 34. For scarves and leather goods, try Hermès at No. 24.

RIGHT: shop window at Hermès.
BELOW: gypsy musican.

The Grands Boulevards

Boulevard Montmartre is at the heart of the **Grands Boulevards**, traced out by Baron von Haussmann under Napoleon III. The boulevards were designed to open up the city centre and beautify Paris. Most of the buildings along the boulevards date from 1850–70 and create the image of Paris that we still have today. Emile Zola, prolific novelist of the period, described the immense fortunes that were made on property speculation as Haussmann's plan for the city was implemented.

The **Boulevard des Italiens**, leading up to the Opéra, posed problems. Though level and straight today, it was once a small hill. The hill, wound about with narrow streets and hovels and rife with the odour of the pig market, completely blocked the view of the Opéra. There were few complaints when Haussmann knocked down the slums and levelled the ground, carting the surplus earth away to even out the Champs de Mars.

The beautiful **Opéra de Paris** ⑳, designed by Charles Garnier and completed in 1875, splendidly occupies the central point where the great boulevards converge. This is a favourite quarter for strolling, shopping, or sitting on a café terrace. The opera house is glorious and romantic. Inside, the majestic staircase and rich marble decorations evoke visions of swirling gowns, tuxedos and top hats. On rehearsal days, you can only peep through small portals at the auditorium and stage. But if it's possible, go in to look at the surprising **Marc Chagall Ceiling**. The modern painter's pearly blue image of heaven presents a striking contrast with the gilded luxury of the theatre. At the back, an entrance off Place Charles Garnier leads to the little-known **Musée de l'Opéra** (open daily except during matinées and events; entrance fee), for lovers of lyric arts.

You may be irresistibly drawn to the pavement of the **Café de la Paix**. Known to be the most expensive café in town, it is also admitted to be the most attractive. Two of the largest and best known department stores are nearby on Boulevard Haussmann, **Galeries Lafayette** and **Printemps**.

Boulevard de la Madeleine is a fashionable artery leading to the church of **La Madeleine** ㉛. This imposing and squat 19th-century "Greek temple" sets an austere tone, but a flower market and some smart shops dress up the square. One of the most appealing windows is at **Fauchon**, where you can drool over the displays of delectables from around the world, presented with inimitable French flair.

Returning to the city's heart

From Place de la Madeleine, Rue Royal leads back into the centre of town, crossing **Rue St Honoré** and **Rue Faubourg St Honoré**, the city's most exclusive shopping area where *haute couture* shops, each with elegant window displays, jostle for attention.

Back at Place de la Concorde, the visitor can look up the majestic, glittering Champs-Elysées, and down through the Jardin de Tuileries to the Louvre, getting a good general feeling for the city's soul. Over on the left bank, the cafés and open spaces will be full of students and lovers, all contributing to the *joie de vivre* that pervades the great city of Paris. ❑

OTHELLO
GIUSEPPE VERDI
THIERRY BRUET

TREASURES OF THE LOUVRE

The largest palace in Europe, the Louvre has assembled an incomparable collection of old masters, sculptures and antiquities

One of the world's greatest museums, the Louvre is immense in scale, the size of its collections (well over 200,000 pieces) and the crowds that invariably throng its galleries (5 million visitors each year), make it one of the more challenging Parisian sights. It is impossible to try to see everything in one visit, although many people manage to cram in the edited highlights in one morning. This, however, does little justice to the wealth of exhibits, which range from European sculpture and painting to antiquities, decorative arts and objects.

HISTORY OF THE COLLECTION

The Louvre's collection was built up through patronage, gift-giving, requisition and other methods of appropriation. François I (pictured above, by Jean Clouet) was a Renaissance king who amassed a superb array of mostly Italian contemporary and classical works, and patronised artists such as Leonardo da Vinci. Louis XIV similarly made patronage a royal duty and added to the collection. Nationalisation of most French works of art after the Revolution led to the Musée de la Rèpublique being opened to the public in 1793. The greatest contribution to the Museum was made by Napoleon I, who brought back the spoils of his various campaigns. Louis XVIII acquired works including the Venus de Milo, but in 1848 the Louvre once again became the property of the State.

◁ **DYING SLAVE**
One of a pair of sculptures by Michelangelo, thought to represent the Arts, held captive by Death, after the death of Pope Julius II, a great arts patron.

▷ **THE BATHERS**
It is thought that Fragonard painted this canvas in the 1760s following his first trip to Italy. Fragonard was greatly influenced by Rubens in his use of colour, the fullness of his figures, and the painting's sensual and joyous theme was enhanced by the use of scumbles and glazes. Donated in 1869, the canvas is today part of the museum's comprehensive collection of European painting.

△ **OBJETS D'ART**
This 13th-century reliquary of St Francis of Assisi is one of the fabulous items found in the eclectic department of Objets d'Art.

▷ **ANTIQUITIES**
During the 18th and 19th centuries, antiquities were seen as the greatest art form, although the Louvre's core collection contains pieces which belonged to François I.

CASTLE, PRISON AND PALACE

The Louvre building, thought to be named after an area where wolves were hunted, has been enlarged and remodelled by French rulers for more than 800 years. The first building on the site was Philippe-Auguste's 12th-century fortified castle, known popularly as the "Tour de Paris", which contained the state treasury, archives and the royal storeroom. It also served as a prison. As medieval Paris grew, and the monarchy established other residences, the Louvre's importance declined.

In 1527, François I commissioned a Renaissance palace – the first example of French Classical architecture – to replace the château. By the end of the 17th century there was hardly an original stone left standing. The buildings surrounding the Cour Carrée predate 1715, and comprise the oldest parts of the building. In the 19th century, Napoleon I added the Galerie du Nord, and the buildings which flank the north and south sides of the Cour Napoleon date from the time of Napoleon III. The most recent addition to the Louvre's landscape is I.M. Pei's dramatic glass pyramid, which has become the museum's 20th-century emblem.

▷ **FONTAINEBLEAU SCHOOL**
This 16th-century painting of the Duchess of Villars and Gabrielle d'Estrée, attributed to the School of Fontainebleau, is a fine example of the then popular portrait genre. It shows the two sisters taking a bath. The Duchess, in a symbolic gesture, is announcing the future birth of her sister's child, the illegitimate son of Henry IV.

◁ **TOMB OF PHILIPPE POT**
A star of the collection of European sculpture is this unusual late 15th-century piece by Antoine le Moiturier. Philippe Pot was the Great Seneschal of Burgundy, an official of considerable rank. His imposing tomb, which was formerly in the Abbey of Citeaux, shows him dressed in armour, being carried on a shield and supported by eight weeping figures dressed in mourning garb.

▽ **SARCOPHAGUS OF THE RECLINING COUPLE**
Standing more than a metre high, this painted terracotta sarcophagus is one of the most impressive of the museum's Etruscan treasures. It depicts in detail everything from the folds of the garments to enigmatic smiles. The base of the sarcophagus is a couch, used by guests at an Etruscan banquet.

AROUND PARIS

*Ile-de-France, the region which encircles Paris, is a rich
mix of glittering palaces, castles and cathedrals, stately forests and
quiet villages, all within striking distance of the city*

Map
on page
148

You don't have to travel far from Paris for a taste of the amazing diversity which characterises the French landscape. A daytripper can choose from the glories of the palace of Versailles or Chartres cathedral, the tranquillity of Monet's garden or the forest of Chantilly, or the sheer fun of Disneyland Paris (*see page 157*). All the destinations are easily reached by RER or train.

An overwhelming display of splendour lies in store at **Versailles ❶**. As you approach, the fabulous **Château de Versailles** (open Tues–Sun; entrance fee; tel: 01-30 84 74 00) glitters on the hilltop. Louis XIV transformed the simple village and small château into an unequalled expression of wealth, privilege and absolute monarchy. At Versailles, the French court could amuse itself well away from the stench and conspiracy of Paris. As a result, the monarchy became out of touch: historians debate whether Marie-Antoinette actually said of the starving population during the Revolution, "Let them eat cake," but angry crowds did drag Louis XVI and his wife back to Paris, and later, in 1793, they were publicly executed. The château was ransacked, but saved from ruin.

Inside, the tour takes you through the **King's Apartments**, including his bedchamber, placed in the centre of the symmetrical palace. Other rooms, including Marie-Antoinette's, are furnished in matchless Louis XIV style. The astonishing 70-m (233-ft) **Hall of Mirrors** is lined on one side by a series of arches filled with reflecting glass, and on the other by French windows overlooking the terrace.

The park was designed by André Le Nôtre, the landscape artist who created the image of the royal garden *à la française.* From the palace steps, you can look down the length of the **Grand Canal** in the form of a fleur-de-lis, which divides the park in two. On each side of the central alley leading to the garden's main focus, **Apollo's Pool**, the woods are sprinkled with delightful statues, secret groves, goldfish ponds, fountains, and flowerbeds. Here nature is tamed, and the Sun King reigns supreme, represented as the god Apollo.

The beauty of the palace is best appreciated from the bottom of the park, at the far end of the canal. The building floats on air, buoyed up by the fluffy mass of the trees on either side, capturing the sunlight in its bright windows and gilded ornaments. Don't be fooled by the tricks of perspective the gardens can play – it's nearly 5 km (3 miles) around the canal. On the northern side, Louis XIV built a smaller residence, the **Grand Trianon,** where he could escape from the stiff etiquette of the court. Nearby is the **Petit Trianon**, added on by Louis XV, and the **Hameau**, a make-believe village where Marie-Antoinette played milkmaid.

LEFT: Versailles.
BELOW: looking up
to Louis XIV.

TIP

The SNCF runs a bike rental service (Train + Vélo) at many stations – when you buy your train ticket, reserve a bike, which you pick up at your destination. This is the best way to visit Giverny. Or SNCF runs a train/car hire service (Train + Auto).

If all this puts you in a mood to pamper yourself, try the tea room at the top of the Grand Canal. From the Le Nôtre terrace there is a spectacular view of the Forêt de St Germain, which surrounds **St Germain-en-Laye** ❷. Perched above the Seine, this is the most chic and affluent of the city's suburbs, with a **château** that was another royal retreat.

Giverny

To the northwest of here, near the town of Vernon, a pink and green country house sits basking in sunlight and flowers. This is **Giverny** ❸, home of painter Claude Monet until his death in 1926 (open Apr–Oct:Tues–Sun; entrance fee; tel: 02-32 51 28 21). The little pond and Japanese bridge, the wisteria, azalea and water lilies inspired some of Impressionism's greatest works. Nearby is the **Musée Américain** (open Apr–Oct: Tues–Sun; entrance fee) which demonstrates the influence of Impressionism on American art.

From the Paris Gare du Nord, you can catch a train north to the great forests.

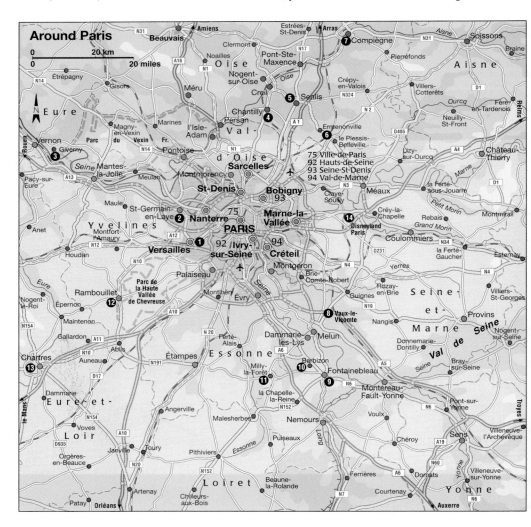

Around Paris

In the delightful **Forêt de Chantilly**, the **Château de Chantilly** ❹ nestles in a grove. Wild ducks settle in the moat around the blue and white palace. Inside, the **Musée Condé** (open Apr–Oct: Wed–Mon; Nov–Apr: pm only Mon–Fri, all day Sat, Sun; entrance fee) displays the art collection of the château's last private owner and includes works by Botticelli, Raphael, Giotto and Holbein. The magnificent stables are occupied by the the **Musée Vivant du Cheval** (open May–Aug: daily; Sept–Apr: Wed–Mon; entrance fee). On Sunday afternoons in summer, waltzing thoroughbreds offer an impressive display of horsemanship under the magnificent dome.

Map on page 148

Around Chantilly

Northeast of Chantilly is the attractive town of **Senlis** ❺, with its **Cathédrale Notre-Dame**. Across the A1 Autoroute, children will enjoy **Parc Astérix** (open Apr–Aug:daily; Sept–mid-Oct: Wed, Sat, Sun; entrance fee) where they can step into Roman Gaul to meet comic-strip hero Asterix and his friends, and experience Europe's most gut-wrenching roller-coaster ride. South of Chantilly, off the N16, mention must be made of the superb **Musée National de la Renaissance** in the **Château d'Ecouen** (open Wed–Mon; entrance fee), which displays rich collections of art, tapestries and furnishings from the 16th century.

The **Forêt d'Ermenonville** ❻ has several attractions, the most unusual of which is the **Mer de Sable** theme park, which offers acres of sand and Wild West fun. The largest of the great forests circling Paris is the **Forêt de Compiègne** covering 15,380 hectares (38,000 acres) with oak and beech, ponds and streams, and the hunting trails of kings. The ancient city of **Compiègne** ❼ on the banks of the Oise was long a royal residence, as its **château** (open

Horses abound in Chantilly: its race-course, created by the horse-crazy aristocracy of the last century, is one of the most fashionable in France.

BELOW: Hôtel de Ville, Compiègne.

André Le Nôtre (1613–1700) is France's most celebrated gardener. Creator of the French formal garden, he designed those at Versailles, Vaux-le-Vicomte and the Jardin des Tuileries in Paris, where his family had gardened for three generations.

BELOW: gone fishing at Etangs de St Pierre.

Wed–Sun; public hols; entrance fee) testifies, but it is the late Gothic **Hôtel de Ville** which steals the spotlight. At the top of its central spire, the oldest bell in France is struck by three figures in pantaloons known as Picantins.

Forest excursions

From the centre of the aristocratic little city you can make a number of excursions into the forest. Just outside town, stop at **Les Beaux Monts** for a bird's-eye view of Compiègne and the Oise valley below. From here, a pedestrian circuit has been marked out to guide you through the forest and back in one or two hours. North of the N31, **Musée Wagon de l'Armistice** (open Wed–Sun; entrance fee) is located in the clearing where, in a railway coach, both the 1918 and 1940 Armistices were signed between France and Germany. A replica railway coach stands inside the small museum which also houses a collection of photographs and newspaper records from both World Wars. Some of the earlier pictures have to be viewed on stereoscopes. This curious presentation takes nothing away from the photographs themselves, surely among the most eloquent statements on the wars in existence.

The nearby village of **Vieux Moulin** is the perfect place to stop for refreshment after a woodland promenade. Empress Eugénie preferred to relax by fishing at the **Etangs de St Pierre**. Not far from the *étangs* (ponds) lies the picturebook **Château de Pierrefonds** (open July–Aug: daily; Nov–Mar: Mon–Sat; Sept, Oct, Apr–June: Wed–Sun; closed public hols; entrance fee). It is a strange monument: a medieval castle built in the late 19th century. Architect Viollet-le-Duc undertook the vast restoration for Napoleon III, who used it for hunting and entertaining. At the fall of the Second Empire, the castle became

government property. Empress Eugénie, known as the Countess of Pierrefonds, returned to visit the château in 1912. She stood with other tourists in the emperor's bedroom, where gilded bees and hunting frescoes adorn the walls. She looked again at the spacious reception hall, blue and red and satiny gold, and wept.

Château de Vaux-le-Vicomte ❽ (open Feb–mid-Nov: daily; entrance fee) was also brutally separated from its owner, but in different circumstances. Nicolas Fouquet was appointed treasurer to Sun King Louis XIV in 1653 and used his privileged position to amass a fortune. A patron of the arts, he supported Molière and Jean de la Fontaine, and organised extravagant parties that were the talk of the town. When he decided to build a country palace, he called on the finest designers: architect Le Vau and landscapist Le Nôtre.

They chose a site near the ancient town of **Melun** (by car on N4 or 6 or by train from Gare de Lyon). The park was Le Nôtre's first major work and the elegant symmetry of the garden is echoed by the château. The blue water in the pools, the green velvet lawns and the sandy pathways set off to perfection the warm stone and slate blue roofs of the building.

When it was completed in 1661 Fouquet organised a grand *fête* to celebrate the king's birthday and inaugurate his exquisite new home. The fountains spewed, musicians played, torchlight sparkled every-

Map on page 148

where. A fantastic show, including dancing horses (some of them drowned in the moat), was given for the king's enjoyment. But Louis was not amused. He was outraged at the display of Fouquet's wealth and *panache*. His aide Colbert assured him that the treasurer's fortune had been stolen from the king's own coffers. That same night Fouquet was arrested and imprisoned at Vincennes.

Louis's pride still wasn't satisfied. He ordered Le Vau and Le Nôtre to build another, bigger palace, sparing no expense. They did, and while Fouquet grew old and died in prison, the Sun King and his court shone at Versailles. Visitors can relive the château's history on Saturday nights from May to October.

Melun sits on the northern edge of the **Forêt de Fontainebleau**, 20,230 hectares (50,000 acres) of oak, beech, birch and pine. There are weird giant rock formations in the forest, complete with local alpinists and climbers who stay in shape by scurrying up them. The station (from Gare de Lyon) is in the suburb of Avon, in the heart of the woods. This is a starting point for cyclists, picnickers, mushroom hunters and bird watchers.

Sounds of satin

The centre of **Fontainebleau** ❾ is dominated by the rambling **Château de Fontainebleau** (open Wed–Sun; entrance fee; tel: 03-60 71 50 70). The first royal residence was erected in the 12th century and every subsequent royal inhabitant left his mark on the hunting palace. The most remarkable work was commissioned by François I in the 16th century. In the long, airy gallery and ballroom, you can almost hear the swish of voluminous skirts, the satin dancing slippers, and the music drifting out to mingle with the sounds of the forest.

Perhaps the château bid adieu to regal splendour in 1814, when Napoleon I,

Fontainebleau has been called "a rendezvous of châteaux" because it incorporates buildings of so many different periods.

BELOW: Fontainebleau in winter.

Map on page 148

Jean Cocteau is buried in Chapelle Ste Blaise. The inscription on his tomb is moving in its simplicity: "Je reste avec vous" – "I am still with you".

RIGHT: Cocteau's chapel in Milly-la-Fôret.
BELOW: bringing home the bread.

who fled here from Paris when his government collapsed, parted company with the Imperial Guards in the aptly named **Cour des Adieux**. Tourists can witness the haughty magnificence of his **Throne Room** and his private apartments.

Close by, **Barbizon** ❿ is a village famed for its links with 19th-century artists, when landscape painters Rousseau and Millet settled there and formed the Ecole de Barbizon. The **museum** of the school is located in the Auberge du Père Ganne (open Oct–Mar: Wed–Mon; Apr–Sept: Sat, Sun; entrance fee), while Rousseau's studio is open for occasional exhibitions. In **Milly-la-Fôret** ⓫, there is an impressive **market-place** where people have been shopping beneath the massive wooden *halles* since 1479. Now the square is surrounded by high-priced antique shops and property agents, none offering anything as beautiful as the rough-hewn beams of the simple shelter.

Another old tradition in the area is the cultivation of medicinal herbs and flowers. These plants, known as *simples*, were first grown around a 12th-century leprosarium. When it was demolished, only the **Chapelle St Blaise** remained (open Easter–Nov: Wed–Mon; Nov–Easter: Sat, Sun) and it still stands today. Poet Jean Cocteau decorated the chapel in 1958. Flowers grow straight up the walls, around tiny stained-glass windows glowing like lamps in the cool, dim chapel; a frisky cat is poised to leap into the holy water font. Above the altar, Cocteau painted the resurrection of Christ in pure lines and delicate colours.

Northwest of Fontainebleau, in the lovely *département* of Les Yvelines, the ivy-clad **Château de Rambouillet** ⓬ (open Wed–Sun;closed public hols and during official residence; entrance fee) is the summer home of the president of France.The **Forêt de Rambouillet** is the region's richest hunting ground, reserved today for the *Chasse à Courre*, running with the hounds.

Chartres

Another favourite daytrip from Paris is to **Chartres** ⓭, 97 km (60 miles) southwest of the city. The attractive medieval town sits upon a plateau hemmed in by wheatfields, on the banks of the Eure. The first glimpse of the lofty spires of the **cathedral** (open daily) rising above the rich plain – exactly as 13th-century pilgrims must have seen them – is unforgettable.

Begun in 1194, the cathedral took only 30 years to construct, lending it an architectural unity and an air of perfection.Before you enter, be sure to take a look at the intricate carvings on the door known as the **Portail Royal**. The 13th-century **stained-glass windows** represent the world's most remarkable collection, measuring a total of 2,499 sq. m (26,900 sq. ft). The three large **Rose Windows** fill the cathedral with changing patterns of light and colour. Traces of an ancient labyrinth mark the floor; penitents and pilgrims followed it on their knees to reach the altar. Parts of the crypt below date from the 9th century. Having plumbed the depths of this intensely beautiful building, climb to the top of the tower, where sunlight and shadows will make your spirits soar.

Chartres is a protected site; the old city has been sensitively restored, and the banks of the Eure offer a pleasant promenade after lunch. There are gardens and stone bridges, and views of the cathedral. ❑

DISNEYLAND PARIS

The most popular tourist destination in France is designed to enrapture children, but its many attractions also stimulate a more sophisticated imagination

Map on page 148

Located at Marne-la-Vallée, 32 km (20 miles) east of Paris on a 1,943-hectare (5,000-acre) site one-fifth the size of the city itself, **Disneyland Paris** has finally taken off after a rocky start in 1992 when bankruptcy threatened. (Open daily; entrance fee; the best option is to purchase a two- or three- day Passport which does not have to be used on consecutive days, has no date limit and is more economical; tel: 01-60 30 60 30). To get there you can take RER line A to the end, or a regular TGV train from Roissy-Charles de Gaulle airport (15 minutes), or a shuttle bus from Orly airport.

Following the success of Tokyo Disneyland, opened in 1983, Europe was scoured for a suitable site for another non-American venture. The Disney empire eventually chose the land of Napoleon. France was somewhat of a homecoming, suggest Disney officials, since Walt's family originally came from Isigny-sur-Mer on the Normandy coast – d'Isigny (from Isigny) evolved to Disney once in America. Generous financial incentives from the French government might also have influenced the final decision.

Practicalities of Disneyland

With 40 attractions – 11 of them built since the opening – the whole site will not be fully developed, if present plans are maintained, until 2017, when there will be an MGM studio theme park, another new golf course and 13,000 more hotel rooms. But the resort is still impressive enough. Aside from the park itself, there is a complex of American theme bars, shops and restaurants known as Disney Village, six hotels situated just outside the main turnstiles, a campsite and a 27-hole golf course.

Disneyland can be a daunting place, especially for mild-mannered Europeans unaccustomed to American-style fun. On popular days, the Magic Kingdom can receive more than 40,000 visitors (the park opens at 9am in the summer holidays and closes at 11pm). The best way to approach getting the most out of your time here is to decide on what you want to do in order of priority and get there early, as by midday lines of restless pilgrims at the most popular rides can be quite long. The longest wait can be up to 45 minutes, but the queues are well regulated and there is plenty to see while you gradually shift along. Heading round the park in an anti-clockwise direction avoids the bigger crowds, since the circular train chugs clockwise.

The gardens are immaculate, as is the entire complex, with teams of roving cleaners ensuring nothing sullies the Disney brilliance. The code of cleanliness also extends to the employees across the board who are not permitted facial hair, dangly earrings, tattoos or short skirts.

PRECEDING PAGES: Disney's squeaky-clean park. **LEFT:** Sleeping Beauty's Castle. **BELOW:** Big Thunder Mountain gives a screaming good ride.

There are 150,000 trees in Disneyland, as many as in the whole of Paris. Many are North American varieties, such as Red Cedar, Honey Locust and Giant Sequoia, as well as Judas trees, Monkey Puzzle, cacti and palms. The palms survive the winter insulated in foil painted to look like bamboo.

Getting your bearings

Disneyland Paris theme park is divided into five main areas, or "lands", each with attractions, restaurants and shops following a particular theme. Designed by "Imagineers", artistic and mechanical wizards who spend their lives thinking up weird and wonderful attractions, this is Disney's most technologically advanced park yet, benefiting from state-of-the-art robotics called "Audio-Animatronics", where life-size, life-like figures speak, sing and dance.

Once through the Victorian turnstiles, already humming along to ubiquitous Disney music, you enter **Main Street USA**, an evocation of 19th-century small-town America. **City Hall**, on the left, is the central information centre, contact point for lost children and property. Here too is the **Main Street Station**, from where the train circles the park. The station is often crowded, and it is better to board it at one of the other stations en route, such as Frontierland. The bandstand in Main Street square is the best place from which to view the daily parades which traverse the park.

Many of the most popular attractions in the park are found in **Frontierland**, to the left of Main Street, so head here first. **Phantom Manor**, home to some of Disney's most spectacular audio-animatronics, provides a high-tech rollicking ride through a haunted house. If the house itself seems familiar, it may be because it is copied from Hitchcock's *Psycho*. The "dead" tree outside is not actually dead, but has been specially treated by Disney botanists so that it grows no leaves.

The **Rivers of the Far West**, an artificial lake in the midst of Frontierland, can be enjoyed by Mississippi paddle-steamer, keelboat, or Indian canoe. The Indian canoe station, a quiet dead-end, verdant and full of birdsong (taped, but it fools

BELOW: Main Street USA.

Map on page 148

the real birds) is a tranquil contrast to the roller-coaster ride. Frontierland leads almost imperceptibly into **Adventureland**. Sparse scrub gives way to lush bamboo and flowers, the twang of Wild-West guitar fading into the beat of African drums. Here is another top attraction, the unforgettable **Pirates of the Caribbean** (queues usually move quickly).

Rival to Big Thunder Mountain, Disney's first-ever 360° looping roller-coaster, is **Le Temple du Péril**, near **Explorers' Club Restaurant**. Hold onto your stomach as the ore carts plunge through rain forest, and turn upside down above a mock archaeological dig inspired by the *Indiana Jones* saga. Elsewhere, Adventureland offers the ultimate tree-house, **La Cabane de Robinson**, and an **Adventure Isle** based on Robert Louis Stevenson's *Treasure Island*. More sedate amusement is found in the **It's a Small World** kingdom, where national stereotypes live in a cheerful puppet kingdom of singing children. Children will love **Fantasyland**, containing the park's centrepiece **Sleeping Beauty's Castle**.

The final stage of the journey, unless you've decided to go anti-clockwise, is **Discoveryland**, providing an assortment of futuristic high-tech experiences. Space Mountain is a roller-coaster ride into outer space inspired by Jules Verne's novel *From the Earth to the Moon* and **Star Tours** offers a trip into space with George Lucas's *Star Wars* characters. Next door's **CinéMagique** lets you sample Michael Jackson's feet in your face, with a 3-D motion picture of Captain Eo and his merry band of dancers. For a voyage through time in 10 minutes join the robotic time-keeper at the **Visionarium**, where a wrap-around screen provides a panoramic view of Europe, from the Swiss Alps to Gérard Depardieu's nose. The view of Paris 200 years from now is the most interesting and disturbing feature of the show. ❑

Open until the early hours, Disney Village, between the park and the hotels, is a complex which buzzes with shops, restaurants, night-clubs and a massive multi-screen cinema.

BELOW: part of the parade.

THE WEST

The romantic image of the **Loire Valley** (*pages 164–175*) is quintessentially French; the gentle France of medieval tapestries, the hunt of the Sun King, splendid Renaissance châteaux, Rabelais and gargantuan feasts. What was once a valley of kings has given way to a more bourgeois paradise that can be enjoyed by all, with food and wine of a quality to delight the most discerning traveller.

Between Giens and Angers the Loire Valley is a lush and fertile region, fought over for centuries by a succession of French and foreign protagonists. All along the banks of the might river is the architectural evidence: châteaux which range from the gloomy defences of Langeais or Chinon to the exquisite Renaissance detail of Azay-le-Rideau or Chenonceau, built at a time when pleasure began to predominate over protection. Here too is Chambord, with its spectacular roof once described as the "skyline of Constantinople on a single building," and Villandry, with some of the finest formal gardens in France.

Beyond this rich panoply of floodlit battlements and luxurious interiors more rural pleasures await: the gentle landscape of Anjou; the misty woodland of the Sologne; the Orléanais with its half-timbered farmhouses and rolling vineyards; the quiet meanderings of the Loire's lesser tributaries; the Indre, Cher, Vienne and Indrois; and the lovely Loir, not to be confused with its greater namesake, which runs through the region from Ile-de-France to Anjou.

The bucolic charms of the region are easily matched by the sophistication of its cities which provide a wealth of magnificent architecture, superb restaurants and elegant shopping. Don't miss the old quarter of Blois, the fine museums of Tours, or the grand parks of Orléans. But perhaps one of the greatest joys is simply to sit on the river bank and watch the "*avenue qui marche*" flow slowly by on its inexorable journey to the sea.

Southwest of the Loire Valley lies the gentle landscape of **Poitou Charentes** (*pages 178–181*), source of that great "drink for heroes": Cognac. The region encompasses the magical waterworld of the Marais Poitevin and stretches to the Atlantic coast, with its atmospheric islands of Oléron and Ré, and the delightful port of La Rochelle. ❑

PRECEDING PAGES: formal ornamental gardens at Villandry.
LEFT: Chambord, jewel in the night.

Map on page 166

Paris

THE LOIRE VALLEY

The wealth and beauty of this lush valley were once denied to all but a privileged few. Today, the private domains of the Loire are a public showcase of French civilisation

Once the setting for the French court, the Loire valley attracted counts and courtiers who wanted easy access to the king, and built their grandiose homes within striking distance of the royal palaces. Where all was once designed to exclude the many and please a few, today the visitor is welcomed in the châteaux and their parks. Between visits to them, you can enjoy the quiet pleasures of a beautiful, and little changed, landscape, and the rivers which define it.

Beginning at the eastern end of the Loire, the small town of **Gien** ❶ owes much of its beauty to Anne de Beaujeu, daughter of Louis XI. She was responsible for building the château, the bridge, the cloisters and church in the late 15th century. The château now houses a museum of hunting, the **Musée International de la Chasse** (open daily; entrance fee).

The red and black brick of the château, laid in geometric patterns, is one of the typical styles of the valley. The streets of this bustling little Renaissance town are hung with flags and lined with flowers. *Faiencerie de Gien* (earthenware) is well-known for its bright designs and long history. The riverside factory can be visited only by request (write in advance or telephone 02-38 67 69 69), but the museum and shop are open daily.

Castles and churches

About 23 km (14 miles) downstream from Gien lies the château of **Sully-sur-Loire** ❷ (open Mar–Nov: daily; entrance fee). Seemingly afloat along with the ducks and swans around it, the castle has two distinct parts: the early 14th-century fortress and the 17th-century wing added by Sully, finance minister to Henry IV. In the older section, three vast rooms on succeeding floors tell of life in the Middle Ages. Furniture was reduced to large chests which served for storage, seating, even sleeping; dining tables were planks laid over simple trestles; the court slept as many as 12 to a bed. The big draughty rooms were lined with tapestries, which were also used as hanging partitions.

The high, keel-shaped timber roof, made of chestnut, is 600 years old. The great tree trunks were soaked and salted, heated and bent, a process which took as long as 50 years. In the 17th-century wing, the rooms are of more human proportions. The beams are hidden by painted ornamental ceilings and the floors panelled in wood.

Sully-sur-Loire is a rare example of a château with the contrasting architecture of both medieval defensive fortress and Renaissance pleasure palace.

A little further downstream, you should pause to see not a château but a church: that of **St Benoît-sur-Loire** ❸, one of the finest Romanesque buildings in

BELOW: Bastille day parade.

France. Most remarkable is the square belltower which forms the porch, embellished with three aisles of arches decorated with carved capitals. The crypt contains the relics of St Benedict, brought from Italy in the 7th century – a monastery was founded here in AD 650.

A little further along the river is **Germigny-des-Prés ❹**, a diminutive church dating from the time of Charlemagne (9th century, except for the 11th century nave). It contains a wonderful Byzantine glass mosaic, also 9th century, which was uncovered in 1840. Glowing with colour, it depicts the Ark of the Covenant.

The Maid of Orléans

At the point where the Loire leaves its northward course to flow southeast stands **Orléans ❺**, a modern city whose heart was bombed out during World War II. Its soul, however, lives on in the cult of Joan of Arc; it was here that she successfully resisted the English army before being burnt at the stake at Rouen. Deprived of its historic buildings, Orléans is now strewn with memorials to her. In the handsome but desolate **Place du Martroi** there is an equestrian statue of the heroine, and the site where she stayed in 1429 has become the **Maison Jeanne d'Arc** (3 place Général de Gaulle; open Tues–Sun; closed public hols; entrance fee), where scenes from her life are recreated with the help of audiovisuals.

Just 18 km (11 miles) outside busy Orléans is quiet **Beaugency ❻**, where an 11th-century bridge provides a view of the river and the town. The tiny streets still have a medieval feel. Market days, with local produce and handicrafts, the smell of roast meats and fresh bread, are particularly atmospheric.

The 15th-century **Château de Dunois** has certainly remained unchanged,

Every year on 29 April and 7–8 May, Orléans celebrates its liberation from the English by Joan of Arc with a pageant and a service of dedication in the cathedral.

BELOW: Orléans seen from the river.

except for slight damage sustained during the French Revolution. The museum of traditional regional crafts inside gives an idea of life outside the castle walls (open Wed–Mon; closed public hols; entrance fee). The collection includes nearly 100 *coiffes*, the finely embroidered linen bonnets local women wore religiously until the onset of World War II – when they ran out of starch.

Chambord and Cheverny

In the **Fôret de Chambord**, deer, boar and other wild animals roam the national game reserve freely, and observation towers have been set up for the public. In all, the park covers 5,463 hectares (13,500 acres), surrounded by the longest wall in France.

Chambord ❼ itself is the largest château on the Loire, built for François I, an airy pleasure palace in such a variety of styles that it has been called "the skyline of Constantinople on a single building". The most striking feature is the double-spiralled staircase in the centre of the castle, where lords and ladies played naughty games of hide-and-seek. (Open daily; closed public hols; entrance fee; tel: 02-54 50 40 00).

From Chambord to Blois, the traveller can take a delightful route past some less grandiose châteaux, of white tufa stone and slate. At the end of a long alley of stately trees, **Cheverny** ❽ rises up gracefully. Though it is still inhabited – by the same family since the early 16th century – visitors can tour the sumptuous 17th- and 18th-century rooms, richly hung with Aubusson and Flemish tapestries. The Viscount and Viscountess Arnaud de Sigalas perpetuate the hunting tradition, and a special *son et lumière* recreates the atmosphere of the royal hunt (open daily; entrance fee).

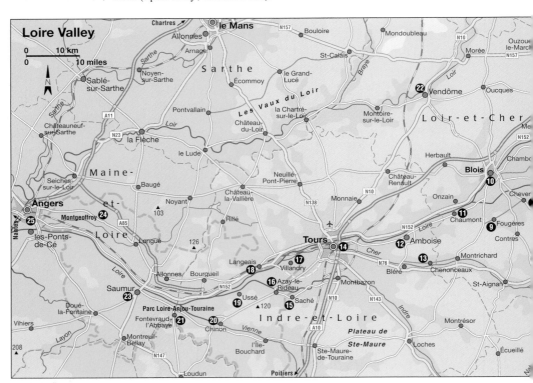

A short distance away is **Fougères** ❾, a charming village off the track of most tourists. At the feudal **château** (open Wed–Mon; closed public hols; entrance fee), the *son et lumière* includes fireworks, fountains and a cast of 60 locals, and well deserves a detour.

Elegant Blois

To the north, the town of **Blois** ❿ was a central stage for courtly intrigue. Louis d'Orléans was assassinated in the **Château de Blois**, as was the Catholic Duc de Guise, suspected of plotting against Henry III. His mother, Catherine de Medici, gave up the ghost in the castle after a lifetime of subterfuge and power play; her gorgeous apartments are riddled with secret hidey-holes. Their stories are told in the spectral *son et lumière*. (Château open daily; entrance fee.)

In the clear light of day, Blois is a pleasant, sunny place. The château's monumental octagonal staircase and its sculpted balconies are superb examples of early French Renaissance design. Though the town itself suffered severely during World War II, the reconstruction was all carried out in regional style, with slate roofs and brick chimneys. The pedestrian areas near the castle are paved in colourful stone.

The Loire river at nearby **Chaumont** ⓫ is very wide and the round towers of the **Château de Chaumont** (open daily; entrance fee) look down upon it from the top of a wooded hill. Catherine de Medici acquired it in 1560. At the death of her husband Henry II, she forced his mistress, Diane de Poitiers, to leave her palace of Chenonceau and move here. Visiting the richly furnished rooms, it is hard to relate to Diane's distress.

As you cross the river at Chaumont, the park and the Loire form a lovely

Map on page 166

BELOW: deer in the Chambord Forest.

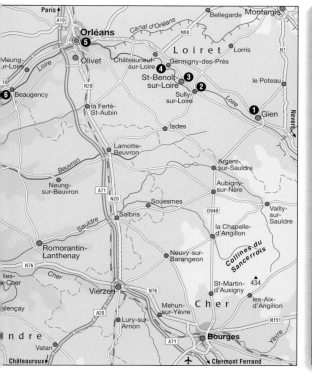

Leornardo da Vinci, born in Tuscany in 1452, died in France in 1519.

picture. Reaching the village of **Onzain**, you are in the **Vallée de la Cisse**, whose winding river flows through pleasant rolling hills, many of which are covered with vineyards for making the local wine, Touraine-Mesland. On the road to **Monteaux**, Owen Watson welcomes visitors to his wood-fired pottery shop. The peacocks, and goats roaming freely in the yard will welcome you, too.

Leonardo's last home

Downstream, the town of **Amboise** ⓬ nestles around its impressive **château** (open daily; entrance fee). Rich in history, Amboise belonged to the Counts of Anjou and Berry before becoming a part of the French throne in 1434. Charles VIII died here of a concussion he inflicted on himself passing through a low doorway. Visitors take note – and duck.

The murderous Amboise Conspiracy of 1560 was no accident, however, and the cursed château fell from royal favour. Napoleon handed it over to politician Roger Duclos, who demolished two-thirds of it, and World War II damaged most of what was left. Only the facade facing the river reveals the original Renaissance charm. Nonetheless, the château is still beautiful and contains several unique features, notably the **Tour des Minimes**, with its spiral ramp for mounted horsemen and the **Chapelle St Hubert**, where Leonardo da Vinci is buried.

The town seems to be a natural extension of the château. The **Rue Nationale** is the colourful main market street, reserved for pedestrians. The essence of a provincial French town is captured in this lively thoroughfare: the sing-song of the merchants, the cafés, the aromas and abundance of fresh produce.

About 500 m (¼ mile) from the château is **Clos Lucé,** where Leonardo spent the last four years of his life, invited to join the royal court by his patron and

BELOW: Loire Valley farmhouse.

Map on page 166

admirer, François I. The house is a museum now, displaying scale models of his precocious inventions, based on the master's drawings. His bedroom and kitchen have been reconstructed and furnished, and a secret tunnel uncovered which linked the house to the château. (Open: daily; entrance fee.)

If you leave the banks of the Loire, and follow instead its tributary, the Cher, you will come to the **Château de Chenonceaux** ⓭. This is perhaps the most elegant of all the Loire valley jewels, renowned for the arches that carry it across the water. The building rests on pillars planted in the river bed, but might as well be floating on air, light and delicate as it is. The interior is worthy of the architecture. (Open daily; entrance fee; tel: 02-47 23 90 07.) At night, a *son et lumière* recounts the story of Diane, Henry II's favourite, and his jealous wife, Catherine de Medici, who couldn't stand to see so much perfection and not own it.

The tumultuous events of this century touched the château, when owner Gaston Menier set up a military hospital in the water gallery during World War I. During World War II, a number of people benefited from the particular situation of Chenonceaux village: the southern exit was in the free zone, while the château entrance was in German occupied territory.

The lily of the valley

Amboise and Chenonceaux are on the eastern edge of the region called **Touraine**. The city of Tours is the centre of this "Garden of France" described by novelist Honoré de Balzac in *The Lily of the Valley*: "Each step in this land of enchantment allows a fresh discovery of a picture, the frame of which is a river or a tranquil pool in whose watery depths are reflected a château and its turrets, parks and fountains."

Tours of Chenonceaux are self-guided, so you can wander at will. Don't miss a visit to the kitchens, housed in the feet of the bridge, with their very effective waste disposal system.

BELOW: Chenonceaux.

Honoré de Balzac (1799–1850), author of the great series of novels and stories called La Comédie Humaine.

As you head towards the centre of Touraine, you pass **Château d'Artigny**, high above the Indre river valley. Designed by the famous perfumer François Coty in pure 18th-century style with spacious lawns and terraces, the château has been converted into a luxury hotel.

Nearby, the 10th-century **Château de Montbazon** is mostly in ruins. The eccentric American painter Lillian Whittaker once lived here and fond tales of "La Dame de Montbazon" may still be heard. A small crêperie at the foot of the ruins is a pleasant place for lunch.

Tours ⑭ is a thriving and lively university town which has at its heart a number of interesting monuments (the **Cathédrale St Gatien**, the shrine of St Martin in the **Nouvelle Basilique St Martin**) and museums (the stunning Renaissance **Hôtel Gouin**), reached through endless ugly industrial suburbs. Nearly every French king, from Saint Louis to François I, spent time in the town. The medieval quarter, centred around **Place Plumereau**, is a showcase of Gothic architecture. One very important event which occurred at Tours was reported in the 6th century by local historian Gregory of Tours. A hundred years earlier, Saint Martin had planted a vineyard around his monastery. One day the monks discovered to their dismay that their errant donkeys had found a way into it and managed to chew off most of the tender young branches. In fact, it must have been heavenly intervention, for the following year's harvest was the best ever. The monks learnt a lesson, and *la taille* (pruning) has been practised as a most important part of viniculture ever since.

The River Indre

Deep in the **Indre valley** lies the river itself, "unravelling like a serpent in a magnificent emerald basin". Honoré de Balzac loved the valley dearly, for there he passed his most prolific days in the **Château de Saché** ⑮ (open Feb–Nov: Thurs–Tues; closed public hols; entrance fee). The corpulent author of *La Comédie Humaine* series of 90 novels worked daily from 2am to 5pm when he stayed at Saché.

Inside, devotees will discover a wonderful collection of Balzac memorabilia, including letters and portraits of his lady loves, his manuscripts (which he edited at such length that typesetters refused to work on them more than one hour a day, and that at double pay) and his room, exactly as it was.

The first-floor salon has also retained its character, in part due to the surprising optical illusion of the handpainted wallpaper. The disposition of the furniture and game tables makes it easy to imagine the drawing-room intrigues so often described in novels of the period. Further along the Indre is **Azay-le-Rideau** ⑯, a small château of exquisite proportions (open daily; closed public hols; entrance fee; tel: 02-47 45 42 04.) The river forms a wide moat around this epitome of Renaissance grace and perfection. The influence of medieval defence architecture is clear, but at Azay all is designed for pleasure. The four turrets are slim and elegant, the crenellations ornamental, and the outlook better for observing clouds reflected in the water than advancing enemies.

BELOW: preparing for customers in Tours.

The *son et lumière,* every evening from May through September, tells the sorry tale of Philippa Lesbahy, who dreamed up Azay and supervised its construction. Her husband, who worked in the shadow of the king's treasurer, had trouble keeping the royal account books and his own separate. Scandal broke out among fellow financiers. He fled and Philippa was forced to relinquish her superb home to François I. During the presentation, visitors walk around the park led by torch-bearers dressed in Renaissance costumes.

Touraine's fourth major river is the Cher, and not far from its banks stand the **Château de Villandry** ⑰ and its famous 16th-century **gardens** (château open: Feb–Nov: daily; gardens open: daily; entrance fee; tel: 02-47 50 02 09). The three tiers of the garden (the pond, the decorative gardens, the kitchen garden) can be viewed at once from the high terrace of the château. The gardens, planted with low boxwood and yew hedges enclosing flowerbeds, represent the four faces of love on one side, music on the other. The kitchen gardens and herb garden were designed according to documents preserved by medieval monks.

The kitchen garden is like something from *Alice Through the Looking Glass.* Each square describes a different geometric design in contrasting colours that change from year to year in the course of crop rotation. The standard red roses sweetening the air represent the monks tending the vegetable plots.

Sleeping beauties

North of Villandry, on the Loire, the **Château de Langeais** ⑱ presents a much more severe image (open daily; entrance fee). Built as a defensive fortress on the site of a 10th-century stronghold, it has never been altered or added to. The last owner, Jacques Siegfried, oversaw the complete furnishing of the cas-

Map on page 166

In Villandry's kitchen garden you will find many vegetables, both exotic and common, but no potatoes: they were not introduced until the 18th century.

BELOW: Fontevraud chimneys.

Effigy of Eleanor of Aquitaine at Fontveraud 'Abbaye.

tle in wonderful period pieces before donating it to the French Institute in 1904. Those who are particularly interested in the transition from medieval to Renaissance life will be enraptured by the authentic interiors, the 15th-century Flemish and Aubusson tapestries, the unequalled collection of wooden furniture, lovingly maintained.

In 1491, Charles VIII married Anne de Bretagne in the Langeais castle. Her dowry was the realm of Brittany, which thus became united with France. Her reputation for piety is unsurpassed, and her humility and strength of character shine through the ages in the handsome wedding portrait of the couple as well as in her motto, which she had inscribed on the walls: "If God is with us, who can be against us?".

Cross the Loire and head down the D7, where the many turrets of a tall white castle loom up against the background of the tenebrous forest of Chinon. This is **Château d'Ussé** ⓲, the castle which inspired Charles Perrault to write *Sleeping Beauty of the Woods*. The furnishings are in poor repair, but children will want to go in to see the wax figures of fairlytale characters (open mid-Mar–mid-Nov: daily; entrance fee).

Rabelaisie

On the other side of the dark forest lies Chinon on the River Vienne, in the heart of **Rabelaisie**, the name given this locality in honour of the 16th-century humanist and author, François Rabelais. His satirical works, *Gargantua* and *Pantagruel*, are recommended for those who would like a less stuffy view of the Renaissance. Particularly juicy passages of *Gargantua* describe rather unholy activities at the imaginary Thelème Abbey, where the entrance gate bore the motto: "Do What You Will!".

BELOW: Saumur leads the world in mushrooms.

You can visit his house, **Maison Rabelais**, in nearby **La Devinière** (open daily; entrance fee). The immaculate town of **Chinon** ⓴ itself has an imposing, though largely ruined, 10th-century **château fort**. The English Plantagenet kings spent much time at Chinon, and Charles VII met Joan of Arc here in 1429. There is a **Musée Animé du Vin** (open Apr–Sept: daily; entrance fee) replete with life-size automatons for kids and wine tasting for adults. Boat trips, carriage rides and steam locomotive excursions are available. These, plus the Vienne river beaches, the *son et lumière* and the medieval market in August make Chinon a fun place to visit.

Now turn back towards the banks of the Loire, passing by **Fontevraud l'Abbaye** ㉑ (open daily; closed public hols; entrance fee). In this restored 12th-century abbey lie the remains of the earliest Plantagenet kings. Four recumbent funeral effigies are the only decoration in the vaulted 90-m (295-ft) long church. Three of the stone sculptures represent Henry II, his wife Eleanor of Aquitaine and their son Richard the Lionheart. Henry was buried here at his request, though English interests would have preferred that he rested closer to the heart of his kingdom. Eleanor had been the abbess and royal protectoress of Fontevraud. Richard, who succeeded his father to the English throne, also chose to be buried here, next to his beloved parents. The three polychrome sculptures lie side by side. The fourth figure is that of Isabelle of Angoulême, wife of King John Lackland (Richard's brother), and the oldest known wooden monument of this type.

Architecturally, the abbey is celebrated for its large Romanesque kitchens in the **Tour Evraud**, with 21 chimneys constructed entirely of stone, though the restoration here was completed with some disregard for historical accuracy.

Just across the street in this restored 12th-century village is a **Musée Régional** with a very interesting collection of bric-à-brac from past centuries. The pot-pourri of objects ranges from neolithic shards to World War II uniforms and a fine collection of traditional tools used in local trades.

The Loir Valley

The River Loir runs to the north of the great Loire, stretching from Ile-de-France to Anjou. The two should not be confused, for the Loir is far more tranquil, flowing slowly through a gentle landscape of deep meadows and lines of poplars. Leaving for a time the mighty river, follow the valley of the Loir along the stretch from La Possonnière to Vendôme, where it is at its loveliest.

The manor of **La Possonnière,** birthplace of the poet Ronsard, is a beautiful Renaissance building of white stone. (Open Apr–Nov; entrance fee.)

All around the Touraine region, cellars, terraces and dwellings have been carved out of the tufa, the chalky white stone used to construct most of the Loire châteaux. The village of **Trôo** is known for its maze of subterranean dwellings, called *habitations troglodytiques.* One or two are open to the curious, and the owners will show you how comfortably and snugly you can live underground.

Vendôme ㉒ is a sophisticated and attractive old town full of elegant shops

Map on page 166

TIP

For a complete change of gear, visit the Musée du Cadillac at Château de Planchoury, St Michel-sur-Loire. It sports the largest collection of gleaming Caddies outside the US.

BELOW: troglodyte interior.

Map
on page
166

and restaurants. Its centrepiece is the abbey church of **La Trinité,** which encompasses architectural styles from the 11th to 16th centuries. The belltower is the earliest part of the building; the most spectacular is the facade, resplendent in Flamboyant Gothic tracery.

At the crossroads

The route from Fontevraud to **Saumur ㉓** (D947) sums up the Loire valley. Besides the numerous châteaux perched above the majestic river, prehistoric dolmens and Roman churches and baths testify to a long history of human community in this region at the crossroads of Anjou, Poitou and Touraine.

The network of tufa limestone caves cut into the high cliffs set back from the river serve to age the fine wines of Saumur, and many of the *grands caves* are open to the public for a tour and a taste. Another use of these cool, dark spaces is the cultivation of mushrooms. The Saumur region is the world's leading mushroom producer; a single cave can produce up to 12 tons in one day. At Saumur itself the **Musée du Champignon** (open Feb–Nov: daily; entrance fee) offers guided visits of the underground galleries where all the various uses of the caves are demonstrated.

RIGHT: calling
the hounds.
BELOW: detail from
the *Apocalypse
Tapestry: The
Whore from
Babylon.*

Saumur is dominated by the romantic white turrets of its **château**, which houses two museums, **Musée des Arts Décoratifs** and **Musée du Cheval** (open Apr–Sept:daily; Oct–Mar Wed–Mon; entrance fee). It is also known for the Cadre Noir Cavalry School. As you continue on towards Angers, (along route D74), notice the distinguished 18th-century **Château de Montgeoffroy ㉔**, and its long, tree-lined drive. The château, resplendent with Louis XIV furnishings, is still inhabited, but visitors are welcomed in summer (open May–Oct: daily; entrance fee).

The Apocalypse Tapestry

Angers ㉕ is the ancient capital of Anjou. The **Château de Foulques** took 100 years to build. The 17 turrets are built in local stone and slate in a striking striped pattern. Formidable from the exterior, the battlements have only a few small openings at the top. From inside the castle, the view of the grassy moat with its deer and flowers softens the image.

Angers is home to an incomparable tapestry collection. Most famous is the **Apocalypse of St John**, displayed inside the château in a specially constructed building. The world's largest tapestry is 107 m (350 ft) long and was commissioned by the dukes of Anjou in the 14th century. It is an astonishing show of complexity, technique and imagination. Each of the 75 wonderfully detailed and coloured panels reveals John, in a small Gothic structure, observing and reacting to his fantastic visions. On the other side of the river, the **Musée Jean Lurçat** holds that artist's reply to the Apocalypse, *Le Chant du Monde* (Song of the World). Woven at the Aubusson studios from 1957 to 1966, the 10 tapestries are on display in the Gothic **Hôpital St Jean**, built by Henry II Plantagenet in repentance for the death of Thomas à Becket at Canterbury Cathedral in 1170. ❑

CHÂTEAU COUNTRY

*"Chambord is truly royal – royal in its great
scale, its grand air, its indifference to common
considerations," wrote Henry James. It's a
verdict that would have pleased French monarchs.*

From the Middle Ages until
the 17th century, the Loire
was the seat of royalty.
Government from the
centre of the kingdom
made good sense. Fine
feudal châteaux and a soft
and sensual landscape also
swayed the balance. Orléans
was France's intellectual capital in the 13th
century, confirmed by the presence of the royal
court. Under the dukes of Anjou and Orléans, the
courts and castles of Angers and Blois took over
Orléans' mantle, attracting artists, poets and
troubadours. The reign of Charles VIII (d. 1498)
heralded a period of sustained château-building.
This tradition was continued by Louis XII and
François I, who transformed Blois into a splendid
palace. Following the royal lead, the Renaissance
élite used their profits from the silk trade and
banking to indulge in château-building. The
lovely Azay-le-Rideau, Chenonceau and
Villandry date from this period. Azay and
Chenonceau, the most romantic of Loire
châteaux, were built by noblewomen whose
husbands were away in battle.

The accession of Henri II in 1547 marked the
apogée of Renaissance excess with Diane de
Poitiers, Henri's mistress, running Chenonceau as
a pleasure palace. Catherine de Médicis, Henri's
wife, plotted Diane's downfall with the aid of her
Italian astrologer in Chaumont. After the creation
of Versailles, the Loire became a pleasant
backwater, providing a racy salon for the literati
and occasional hunting for Louis XIV. The
Loire châteaux did not escape the Revolution
unscathed but, thanks to the popularity
of individual châtelains, many were
spared, including Chenonceau,
Cheverny and Chambord.

▷ **STONE SENTINEL**
Linked to Joan of Arc and Charles VII,
feudal Loches acted as a fortress and
a feared prison.

△ **ORIENTAL FANTASY**
Dove-grey domes and
delicate cupolas mean
Chambord can be likened
to an Oriental town in
miniature.

▷ **HIGH LIFE**
Chambord's vaulted,
coffered chambers were
ballrooms in Renaissance
times but became theatres
and billiards rooms.

ROYAL CHAMBORD

Louis XIV (above) loved hunting at Chambord, a château which began as a mere hunting lodge but finished as a sumptuous palace, with 365 fireplaces. Chambord was François I's bid for immortality, prefiguring Louis XIV's relationship with Versailles. Chambord also foreshadows Versailles in its scale of conception and sheer size. It represents a château in transition: Renaissance quicksilver poured into a Gothic mould. Almost 2,000 craftsmen worked on the site, producing a vast palace containing about 450 rooms, 365 windows and 70 staircases.

As the supreme Renaissance king, François presided over an airy palace partly designed by Leonardo da Vinci. Chambord was conceived of as an escape from an unhappy marriage and the claustrophobia of court life in Blois. François chose the salamander as his enigmatic emblem, accompanied by the inscription: "I cultivate good and extinguish evil." After François' death, the court left for Chenonceau, while Chambord was inhabited fitfully.

◁ **CRISP GEOMETRY**
Villandry has Renaissance gardens, from the geometric *jardins d'amour* (symbolising the faces of love) to kitchen gardens.

▽ **BORED BOAR**
Wild boar roam the vast Chambord estate but keep a low profile, not just in the autumn mating season.

◁ **WOMEN'S CHÂTEAU**
Chenonceau is a sumptuous pleasure palace moulded by a series of female owners.

Map
on page
180

· Paris

*Boat trips operate
along the Charente
as far as Saintes or
Jarnac.*

BELOW: fishing
boats, Ile d'Oléron.

POITOU-CHARENTES

*A strong attachment to traditional ways of cultivating,
of building, of living and of distilling their best known product,
brandy, characterises the people of Poitou-Charentes*

One ancient art that is still practised in **Angoulême** ❶ is paper-making, for which the city was famous in the 16th and 17th centuries. Today, rag paper is still made in the traditional manner in the towns of Puymoyen and Nersac. This "paper connection" no doubt also explains why a museum here is devoted to the comic strip. The **Centre National de la Bande Dessinée et de l'Image** (CNBDI) was founded in 1982. The stories behind favourite characters such as Asterix and Tintin, and the people who created them, are revealed (21 Rue de Bordeaux; open Tues–Sun; entrance fee).

A visit to the *ville haute*, to see the magnificent 12th-century **Cathédrale St Pierre** is recommended: it has an intricately detailed Romanesque facade and 60-m (216-ft) high Romanesque belltower rising from the north transept. The neo-Gothic **Hôtel de Ville** was built in the 19th century in place of the city's château of which only two towers now remain. From the medieval ramparts there is a splendid view of the Charente valley.

Very Superior Old Pale

In **Cognac** ❷ you can enjoy the famous brandy of the same name. Grapes grown in the region are first turned into wine, then distilled to make Cognac. Curiously, Cognac is never "vintage", that is to say, the year it was made does not figure on the label. The age of a Cognac is determined by a series of highly regulated aging "codes": *Trois Etoiles* from 2½ to four years of age; VSOP (Very Superior Old Pale) from four to 10 years; XO, Napoléon, or Royal if over 10 years. Cognac also enters into another speciality of the region, Pineau des Charentes, a fortified wine made by mixing Cognac with grape must. The result is a pleasantly sweet "wine" often served as an apéritif.

A number of private distilleries open their doors to visitors for tours and tasting sessions. One of the most spectacular is the **Château des Valois**, a large part of which was built in the 15th century for Jean de Valois (also called John the Good), but with cellars and a Salle des Casques dating from the 12th and 13th centuries respectively. (Open June–Sept: Wed–Mon; Oct–May: Mon–Fri.) At the back of the château is **Rue Grande** which leads toward the centre of the old town and is lined with gracious 15th- and 16th-century buildings. Also worth a visit is the **Otard** distillery, where the guided tour affords a chance to see the remains of the 13th-century Château de Cognac, in which François I was born in 1494 (open daily; closed public holidays).

Located in the Hôtel de Ville is the **Musée de Cognac** (open Wed–Mon; entrance fee), which not only presents the history of the famous brandy but

houses collections of prehistoric, Gallo-Roman, and more recent local artifacts, as well as paintings from various periods and countries.

Sandy beaches and oyster beds

The region of **Charente-Maritime** begins where the Gironde river empties into the Atlantic on the Avert Peninsula. The traveller will find the coast more spacious and beautiful moving north towards the **Ile d'Oléron ❸**.Famous for its sandy beaches and its oyster farming, Oléron is France's largest Atlantic island, reached by toll bridge from the mainland. At **Le Château**, stop and visit the **Oyster Museum** housed in the 17th-century **Citadelle** built by Vauban (open June–Sept:Wed–Mon; entrance fee).

Returning to the mainland, **Brouage ❹** was once an important fortified port until its harbour silted up in the 18th century. The ramparts of the fortress which Cardinal Richelieu occupied during the Siege of La Rochelle now command a view of the oyster beds below. Most prized of all oysters are those from **Marennes ❺**, recognisable by their greenish tinge. The panoramic view from the belltower of St Pierre-de-Sales is also worth the detour.

Oyster farming is an important industry on the Ile d'Oléron.

White isle

North of Oléron is the **Ile de Ré ❻**, reached by bridge from the mainland. Smaller than Oléron, **Ré La Blanche** is 30 km (18 miles) long. The dunes and beaches are made of white sand, giving Ré its surname: White Isle.

At **St Martin**, remains of Vauban's 17th-century fortifications still surround the town and its 15th-century church. Ré can easily be visited in one day by bicycle, gliding through the vineyards and oyster parks, the cool woods and

ABOVE AND BELOW: oysters for sale.

In 1627 Cardinal Richelieu laid siege to the Huguenot stronghold of La Rochelle. When the siege finally ended, after 15 months, only 5,000 of the original 28,000 inhabitants were still alive.

dunes, on the way to the salt marshes of **Ars-en-Ré**, with its long beaches, complete with German bunkers.

Back over the bridge is **La Rochelle** ❼, one of France's loveliest ports, now a busy yachting centre. In the 10th century it was a fishing village in the middle of the expansive salt marshes, but it grew to become one of the jewels of Eleanor of Aquitaine's dowry and continued to flourish during the medieval period.

Tour St Nicolas and **Tour de la Chaine** face each other over the sheltered 13th-century port where nightly a huge chain was drawn across to keep ships out. The **Tour de la Lanterne** was used as a prison, with graffiti carved there by English soldiers in the 17th and 18th centuries; it makes a good place for an overview of the whole town.

Through the old gate at Place Barentin are many 15th-century houses, with fine vaulted archways. On the main square is the high Gothic **Hôtel de Ville**, the town hall and, on Rue Dupaty, **Maison Henri II**, an intricately sculpted Renaissance residence. Several museums include the **Musée du Nouveau Monde** (open Wed–Mon; closed Sun pm, public hols, entrance fee), dedicated to La Rochelle's connection with the New World.

La Venise Verte

Inland and north of La Rochelle is a mysterious region of swamplands and woods. This remarkable national park, **Le Marais Poitevin** ❽, is better known as *La Venise Verte* – Green Venice. Eleventh-century monks took advantage of coastal dyke-building to dig out 1,450 km (900 miles) of waterways, filled from the Sèvre Niortaise river.

At **La Garette** and **Coulon**, local boatmen await tourists with their long

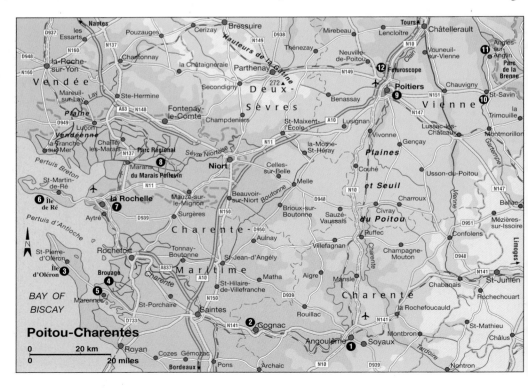

forked poles, *pigouilles*. There are 15,000 hectares (37,000 acres) of green silence to discover, under the dome of poplar and oak, on a carpet of water lilies, iris and reeds.

Map on page 180

Historic city

The regional capital of **Poitiers ❾** is one of the oldest cities in France. It was just north of here that, in 732, Charles Martel stopped the Moorish invasion from Spain, eventually forcing their retreat from France. The architectural richness of Poitiers is rarely equalled elsewhere in France. **Notre-Dame-la-Grande**, with a magnificent, richly sculpted Romanesque facade in the *poitevin* style and 12th-century frescoes decorating the vault of the choir, must be visited, but more important still is the church of **St Hilaire-le-Grand**. The original structure, roofed in wood, was damaged by fire in the 12th century. It was rebuilt in stone and the resulting church, which has seven naves, remains unique in France.

The 11th-century abbey of **St Savin ❿**, roughly 40 km (25 miles) east of Poitiers on the Gartempe river, has been called "the Sistine chapel of France" and is decorated with the oldest and most beautiful frescoes west of the Alps. Dating from the 12th-century, they depict stories from the Old Testament. To the north is the entrancing village of **Angles-sur-Anglin ⓫**, where the traditional craft of fine needlework, which gave its name to a stitch called *jours d'Anglin*, is still practised by local women. Castle ruins, a watermill, willows and waterlilies make it a picture perfect setting.

At Jauney-Clan, 7 km (4 miles) north of Poitiers is the extraordinary **Futuroscope ⓬** theme park, its futuristic architecture a setting for the latest in visual technology (open: daily; entrance fee). ❑

TIP

At Coulon you can hire a punt with or without a boatman, a canoe or a pedalo. If you are happier on dry land, you can hire a bicycle or take the tourist mini-train.

BELOW: coming home in La Venise Verte.

THE NORTH

History is imprinted in the rock and stained on the grass of northern France. Surrounded by prehistoric menhirs and megaliths, speaking their own ancient language and dressing in traditional clothing at festival time, there's a sense that the people of **Brittany** *(pages 203–211)* are still in touch with their past. Theirs is at times a savage homeland, gripped by Atlantic weather, and with its savagery comes dramatic beauty.

Neighbouring and mellower **Normandy** *(pages 191–200)* is one of France's most fertile areas, its prosperous agriculture producing butter, cheese – including the world-renowned Camembert – cream, meat, poultry and fruit. From its apples come Normandy cider and Calvados.

History has also trampled through Normandy – and comparatively recently. Some 200,000 buildings were destroyed and hundreds of thousands of people killed in the battles of World War II. Along the coast, scene of the D-Day landings of 1944, are concrete bunkers and rusting scraps of old tanks. Fortunately the old town centres have been carefully restored.

Yet it is in the northernmost corner of France, **Le Nord** *(pages 186–189)* where the dreadful price of war is most evident: the physical scars of World War I and the brutal battles played out on the poppyfields of Picardy are all but gone, but the immaculately-kept cemeteries remain, a lasting testament to the cruelty and waste.

Northern France is riddled by rivers: the Seine flows through Rouen on its way from Paris to the sea; the Rance hits the Channel at St Malo, the Epte crosses the rich arable land of the Vexin plateau, and the Orne flows through Caen. Not content to be surrounded by 1,200 km (750 miles) of coastline, Brittany also has its own inland sea in the Gulf of Morbihan, with the largest concentration of seabirds on the Atlantic coast.

But perhaps the most significant of the landmarks of the north is Mont-St Michel, once in Brittany and now in Normandy, one of Europe's greatest abbeys, perched on an island just offshore. On either side of this lonely abbey are such smart seaside resorts as Deauville, Honfleur and Dinard, where Parisians come for the weekend, seeking peace from the city. ❐

PRECEDING PAGES: cruising past Brittany's Josselin Castle.
LEFT: windsurfing in the wild.

Map on page 188

LE NORD

The resonance of names such as Flanders and the Somme recall the region's beleaguered past, symbolised by the Vauban fortresses and the poppy-strewn battlefields of World War I

As befits a border region, Le Nord is a cultural crossroads influenced by both France and the Low Countries. The towns are by turns cosy and elegant, with ornate Flemish brickwork interspersed with sober French classicism. The northern spirit is open-minded and entrepreneurial yet home-loving and hearty. At best, there is a Burgundian belief in the good life and a Flemish sense of hospitality and conviviality; this measured way of life is underwritten by French good taste and abiding cultural values. In public, French terraced cafés, chic shops and classical boulevards vie with Flemish gables and vaulted cellars, belfries and carillon concerts, rich tapestries and old masters. In private, Flemish beer, hearty stews and *moules-frites* are as acceptable as French fine wines and gastronomic cuisine.

Boulogne ❶ makes a fitting introduction to the seafaring region. As the most important fishing port in France, Boulogne produces 25 per cent of the national catch. The medieval walled upper town, later fortified by Vauban (1633–1707), is well-preserved, with picturesque cobbled streets and a cluster of historic buildings. Finest of these is the **Château-Musée** (open Wed–Mon; entrance fee), completed in 1231, the first castle to be built without a keep. Apart from strolls along the ramparts, Boulogne offers edible pleasures in the form of a morning fish market or visit to one of the best cheese shops in France, **Philippe Olivier** (43 Rue Thiers). Near the port is **Nausicaa** (open daily; entrance fee), a popular marine centre packed with aquaria and games.

BELOW: a café in Boulogne.

Côte d'Opale ❷ stretches from the Baie de Somme to the Belgian border but is particularly charming around **Cap Gris**, between Boulogne and Calais. The Opal Coast is named after its iridescent light, a challenge to unrelentingly grey northern skies. The rugged promontories have a bluish tint, with chalky cliffs, grassy sand dunes and the occasional prim, slightly faded Edwardian resort.

English ties

Calais ❸, the closest port to England, only escaped the English yoke in 1558 and, given the presence of Channel-shoppers, remains economically in thrall to the old enemy. Devastated between 1939-45, Calais is distinctly shabby and soulless, with a lacklustre modern centre redeemed by the presence of a couple of provincial museums and good restaurants. However, most visitors simply make use of the hypermarkets or the **Cité Europe** shopping centre.

Dunkirk ❹, once one of the great northern sea ports, is forever associated with the evacuation of British and French troops in 1940. The city itself was virtually destroyed by bombardment in the same year. A hulking tobacco warehouse on Quai de la Citadelle is home to the **Musée Portuaire** (open Wed–Mon; entrance fee), dedicated to the port's maritime past, from tug boats to lighthouses and beacons.

Bergues ❺ is a fitting foretaste of French Flanders, a landscape of windmills, Flemish hotpots and small breweries. This fortified, partially moated wool town possesses a Baroque gabled pawnshop, now a museum of Flemish and French treasures, and is crowned by medieval and Vauban fortifications. **Cassel ❻** nearby, is the most appealing small Flemish town, with its whitewashed houses, Gothic church and winding streets. **Castelmeulen**, the working windmill on the hill, is a reminder that in the 19th century there were over a thousand windmills in windswept northern France.

Lille ❼ is the capital of French Flanders and the fourth largest city in France. Set close to the Belgian border, this socialist citadel conveys a welcoming Flemish atmosphere. Indeed, with its youthful population, beguiling bars and richly restored Flemish architecture, Lille belies its lingering reputation as drab and industrial. Like Dijon and Brussels, Lille was a force in the Burgundian empire before becoming part of the Spanish Netherlands. Finally French in 1667, the city retains a Flemish heart and a Franco-Flemish stomach, best appreciated in the *estaminets*, the traditional brasseries in Vieux Lille.

Monument to a World War I battle at Neuville St Vast, west of Lens, Pas-de-Calais.

Vieux Lille

Place Rihour houses the tourist office in a Burgundian palace while Rue Rihour shows Flemish and classical influences. The neighbouring **Grand Place** is lined with café terraces and gabled mansions, notably the **Vieille Bourse**, the former stock exchange. The Flemish flair for illusionistic design means that thin gabled houses can be slotted into narrow passages concealing improbably large

BELOW: Boulogne's famous cheese shop, Philippe Olivier, is a good reason to cross the Channel.

CHANNEL HOPPING

Channel shopping has long held an appeal for cost-concious British day-trippers in search of fine French food and wines. Although duty-free goods were theoretically eliminated by the European Single Market, currency and tax differentials still make French goods advantageous. In particular, the quality and cost of French food and drink draw visitors to numerous coastal hypermarkets and vast out-of-town shopping centres. The combined effect of the Channel Tunnel and the competing ferry companies now means that the region attracts more visitors from Britain than from Belgium.

Eurotunnel provides a shuttle service between the Kent coast and Calais, while the Eurostar train service connects Calais and Lille with Ashford (Kent), London, Paris and Brussels. (Pierre Mauroy, Mayor of Lille, used his influence to add his power base to the Eurostar route.) Hovercraft services link several Kent ports with Boulogne, Calais and Dunkirk while the car and passenger ferries provide similar options. Over 20 million ferry passengers visit the French ports every year, including 12 million day-trippers. The ports depend on these lucrative customers and dread the arrival of July 1999, the date by which the European Union plans to ban duty-free shopping definitively.

Vieux Lille is the ideal place to try hearty Flemish specialities – mostly a cuisine for committed carnivores – such as carbonade flamande *(beef in beer),* waterzooi *(creamy vegetable and fish stew) and* tarte aux maroilles *(rich cheese tart).*

interlocking courtyards. **Rue de la Monnaie** is an elegant street lined by historic mansions converted into chic shops and brasseries. Here too is the atmospheric museum, the **Hospice Comtesse** (open Wed–Mon; entrance fee). This intimate medieval foundation contains the former hospital, framed by an upturned keel roof.

Lille's driverless Métro system is an efficient means of exploring the rest of the city. The newly-restored **Palais des Beaux Arts** (open Wed–Mon; entrance fee) displays a fine collection of Flemish works, from Rubens to Van Dyck. However, the highlight is the mysteriously vaulted cellars containing a collection of Flemish medieval and Renaissance paintings and sculptures. In the northwest of the city is **La Citadelle**, the largest and best-preserved bastion in France. The star-shaped bastion was designed in 1670 by Vauban, Louis XIV's military strategist, as part of France's defence against the Spanish Netherlands. A modern addition to the city is **Eurolille**, a futuristic glass and steel complex encompassing both city stations as well as a shopping centre.

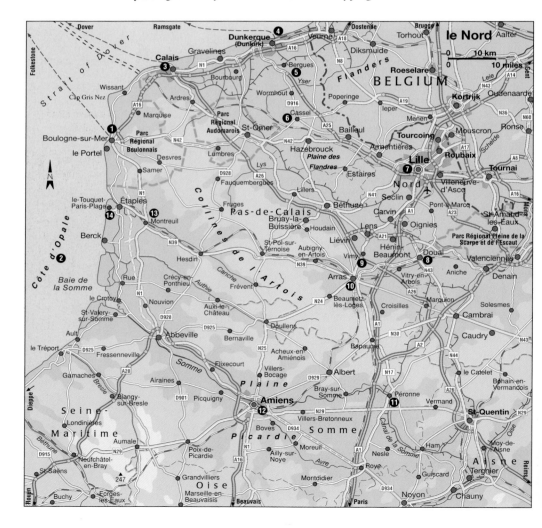

Douai , an historic, sober city south of Lille retains its 18th-century design despite devastation in 1940. Douai's pride and joy is a magnificent Gothic belfry encrusted with turrets and pinnacles, surmounted by the Lion of Flanders. **Vimy** ❾, west of Douai, is the site of a poignant Canadian war memorial to the 66,000 Canadians who lost their lives in the Great War. On the slopes, a number of trenches, dug-outs and tunnels have been preserved. The neighbouring town of **Arras** ❿ also suffered from shelling, given its proximity to the front until 1917. However, civic pride ensured that the capital of Artois embarked on dignified post-war reconstruction. The **Grand Place** is somewhat austere, with its serried ranks of 17th-and 18th-century gabled mansions standing on arcaded sections. On **Place des Héros**, visitors can appreciate the Flamboyant neo-Gothic town hall and belfry before touring *les boves*, the labyrinth of medieval limestone passages that line the city. These provided refuge in times of strife, from the 11th century to the Great War.

Memories of war

Château de la Péronne ⓫, south of Cambrai, is a starting point for the **Circuit de Souvenir**, a tour of the Somme battlefields, scenes of some of the bloodiest slaughter on the Western Front. The **Historial de la Grande Guerre** (open Apr–Sept: daily; Oct–Mar: Tues–Sun; closed mid-Dec–mid-Jan; entrance fee), the challenging war museum, is beside the château.

Northern France became an international graveyard, with the Battle of the Somme, a series of bitter campaigns conducted by the British and French forces against fortified positions held by the Nazis. The lovingly tended cemeteries are the most poignant legacy of World War I, mostly clustered around Albert, Arras and Amiens.

Amiens ⓬, the capital of Picardy, was devastated during both World Wars and retains precious little of its rich past as a wealthy cloth town. The shining exception is the **Cathédrale Notre-Dame**, the largest in the country and the most impressive monument to survive this war-torn corner of France. Twice the size of Notre-Dame in Paris, the cathedral displays a grandiose facade which should be fully restored for the millennium. As a bridgehead, Amiens bore the brunt of attacks in 1918 and was set ablaze in 1940, with 60 percent of the city destroyed. As a result, the only charming quarter is **St Leu**, the renovated millers' area beside the banks of the Somme, dotted with lively bars, brasseries and craft shops.

Further north, inland from Le Touquet, is picturesque **Montreuil** ⓭, a hill-top market town with a medieval citadel and Vauban gate, cosy cottages and half-timbered inns. By contrast, **Le Touquet** ⓮ enjoys the soubriquet of Paris-Plage, promising a touch of city sophistication at the seaside. Once exclusive, the resort has an air of faded gentility and off-season *tristesse*, with prim tea-rooms and villas adorned with Art Deco or Anglo-Norman facades. Like its rivals, Deauville and Biarritz, it has gambling, golf, and horse-riding. However, bounded by the sea, sand dunes and lush pine woods, secretive Le Touquet remains a nostalgic mood rather than a resort. ❑

Map on page 188

BELOW: Amiens cathedral.

NORMANDY

A land of plenty first settled by Viking Norsemen, Normandy has an eventful history and embraces rich, pastoral farmland, a varied coastline, great monuments and thriving cities

Map on page 192

The city of **Caen** represents the powerful, purposive side of Normandy, bustling, businesslike, forever arranging trade fairs and exhibitions, with a lively university and a chamber of commerce that draws attention to itself by flamboyant modern sculpture. Though essentially a practical town, with an excellent bus service and wide variety of shops, Caen has its traditional glories. The **Château de Caen** is the site of the **Musée des Beaux Arts** and **Musée de Normandie** (open Wed–Mon; entrance fee), while the **Abbaye aux Hommes** and **Abbaye aux Dames** (both open daily; entrance fee) were built for William the Conquerer and his wife Matilda respectively.

In Caen one can eat very well and very economically. Those who set a proper value on that nourishing and easily digestible meat – tripe – will naturally want to sample *tripes à la mode de Caen:* down-to-earth Normans are not likely to let a valuable food resource go unappreciated for lack of good preparation. It has a variant, *tripes au Calvados*, prepared with a dash of the nectar that the Normans make from their abundant apples.

Bayeux's comic strip

At the opposite extreme is **Bayeux** ❷, set amid the placid countryside of the northwest, just inland from the Côte de Nacre, and devoted largely to guardianship of the splendours of the past. Of course, the daily worshippers in Bayeux's great cathedral would immediately reject the notion that their religion, rooted in history though it is, belongs to the "past".

The **Cathédrale Notre-Dame** at Bayeux rears up to the sky, austere in outline and extravagantly fanciful in detail, as if every pillar and every stone were leaping passionately towards heaven. For centuries it was the home of the celebrated **Bayeux Tapestry**, which is both an immortal work of art and an invaluable historical source – you might say, the world's most famous comic strip, setting out in continuous form the story of Duke William's invasion of England in 1066, the defeat and death of the Anglo-Saxon Harold, and the subjugation of England by Normandy. It takes, of course, great pains to tell the story from a Norman point of view.

After 900 years, the tapestry is still extraordinarily vivid and evocative, its two colours hardly at all faded, and its cartoon-like figures arresting and, behind the first impression of comicality, deeply moving. Everyone has seen reproductions of one kind or another but, even more than most masterpieces, it is worth taking the trouble to see the work.

Housed nowadays in a special building, **Centre Guillaume-le-Conquérant** (open daily; entrance fee),

LEFT: Caen.
BELOW: the Bayeux tapestry.

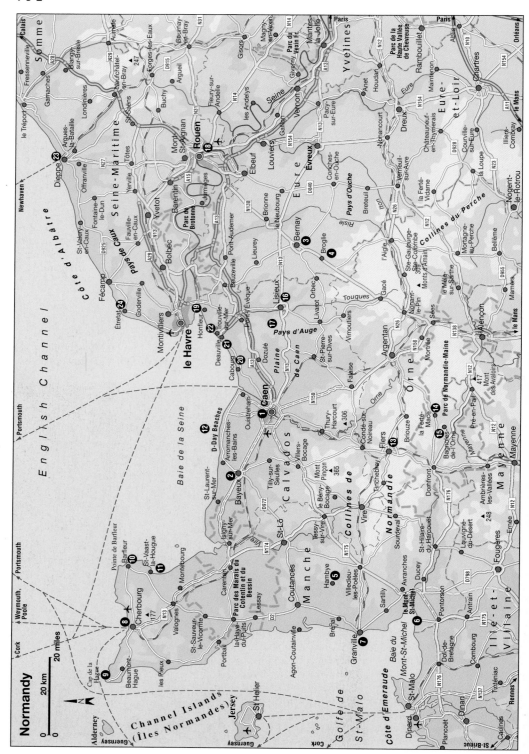

Normandy

the tapestry has to be approached via an exhibition which prepares the visitor with the aid of a detailed audio-visual presentation. Surprisingly, when you get there this seems quite natural, not only because it is done with taste and historical knowledge but because there is an aura of something like show-biz about the tapestry itself, something that can meet this kind of popularisation on its own ground and survive it.

Medieval zoology

Once you get to the tapestry, which is 70 m (230 ft) long, it is best to walk past it twice; once slowly, taking in the detail, and once at a normal walking pace. Above and below the narrative band are friezes depicting animals – some - realistic, some mythological, and some on that intermediate ground between the two, a medieval European notion of what animals probably looked like.

When the parleying and mustering and shipfitting and armouring are at last over and battle is joined near Hastings, the figures in the main band become more and more urgent and elongated. They lean forward over their horses' necks, galloping towards the horrible clash with the foe, spears at the ready. At the height of the battle, horses somersault and men are replaced by the figures of dead warriors. It is as stark a representation as one would find in some antiwar novel of the 1920s.

Bayeux was one of the first towns to be liberated by the Allies in 1944, and it is one of several with museums devoted to the D-Day landings of 1944 (**Musée Mémorial de la Bataille de Normandie**; open daily; entrance fee). Others include St Mère-Eglise, and Cherbourg, and there are British, American and German war cemeteries all along the coast. A peace museum, **Musée pour la Paix**, was opened in Caen in 1988 (open daily; closed Jan; entrance fee).

The Calvados region is full of enchanting riverside towns like **Bernay ❸**, **Broglie ❹** and **Hambye ❺** with its ancient abbey. Their older houses, crookedly aligned along narrow streets or the waterside, are half-timbered, and their atmosphere is rural and peaceful. If you strike one of those towns after about nine o'clock at night, don't expect to find anything open. Not even a café stays awake once people have dispersed for the evening meal.

Mont-St Michel

The coastline of Normandy is as varied and beautiful as everything else about it. Over to the west on the Manche (English Channel) below the Cotentin Peninsula, Normandy has the Breton qualities of wild rockiness, the cry of seabirds and hurrying of the tide-race.

If Carnac represents the furthest point of Breton religious symbolism on one side, then the furthest point on the other is **Mont-St Michel ❻** away to the north and the east, one of the greatest religious buildings in Europe. The first abbey on this site was built after the Archangel Michael appeared to Aubert, Bishop of Avranches. The building that stands now represents some 500 years of work, from the 11th to the 16th centuries, though there are later elements. (Open daily; closed public hols; entrance fee.)

Map on page 192

TIP

A spectacular time to visit "God's pyramid" is when very high tides flood round the island of Mont-St Michel at new and full moon and, even better, during the spring and autumn equinox.

BELOW: a stallholder at market in Dieppe.

Archangel Michael.

Mont-St Michel is a dangerous place. The abbey stands at the summit of a huge lump of granite, 75 m (250 ft) above the sea; when the tide is out there are quicksands. And surely this is no accident. This spot was deliberately chosen: dangerous in itself, and constantly in the presence of the most dangerous element of all, the ungovernable ocean. Since the abbey as we know it was begun in the 11th century, it dates from the heyday of Norman power and influence, the noontide of Normandy's importance in the world; and while this knob of rock has been from time immemorial a place of religious meditation and hermitage, as bleak and wild places tend to be, these same bold, strenuous Normans put themselves under the patronage of Saint Michael.

The cult of the archangel

In the traditional Christian view of the universe, the archangels were the highest order of created beings, and Saint Michael had the qualities among archangels that the Normans saw themselves as having: strength, courage, and leadership, the qualities that enabled him to defeat Satan.

Mont-St Michel makes such a strong impression when seen from a distance, and the heroic cult of the Archangel makes such a strong impression on the mind, that the main problem for the visitor is to keep hold of these great central threads when he or she actually arrives in the place and is confronted, as usual, with rows of bric-à-brac shops selling rubbish to the tourists, all the detritus of the consumer society at its least dignified.

But one can still hear the Atlantic wind, and see the foam crawling in over the quicksands, the grey dots that are the grazing sheep, and the massive sombre pillars within the great brooding structure of the Hall of the Knights.

BELOW:
"God's pyramid".

Coastal towns

Granville 7, the most westerly large coastal town in Normandy, is also almost Breton in its atmosphere. Perhaps its one truly Norman quality is its diversity and practicality, its willingness to have a try at any kind of enterprise. A busy port with docks and warehouses and trucks trundling to and fro, it is also a quiet haven for family holidays, with smooth, golden sands and great stretches of butterscotch-coloured rock dotted with shallow rock pools, where generations of French children have played happily.

Granville's upper town is perched on a great headland staring out at the Channel. The old houses, dominated by the magnificent church of **Notre-Dame,** from which one has a total perspective of the town, are solidly made of heavy blocks of stone, ready for any weather the sea may throw at them. They are roofed with dark grey slates, meticulously laid and firmly fixed, exactly like the houses in the corresponding parts of Brittany and Wales.

These slates tell their own story. They are the one form of roofing that will keep out the most torrential and driving rain, and when you get to a place where grey slates are common – even if you go there in fine sunny weather and never see rainfall – you know that the inhabitants expect rain, a great deal of it and often. And when, as in Granville, you see houses with not only the roof but an entire wall slated, the wall that faces the prevailing wind, you know that there are times in the year when the rain comes blasting in from the sea horizontally.

The Cotentin Peninsula

Moving north up the **Cotentin Peninsula**, jutting out into the Channel and having at its tip the deep-water harbour of **Cherbourg 8**, one still finds a coast as

Map on page 192

BELOW:
Cap de la Hague.

A perfect perch at Cap de la Hague.

wild as Brittany's with high cliffs sheltering fine beaches. Those fascinated by ships find themselves at home in Cherbourg, where the busy port has the authentic smell of oil, rotting seaweed and fish-heads, and where a brief stroll down a couple of streets from the waterside will bring you to a beautiful square dominated by the elegant municipal theatre.

Nor is nature far away among these scenes of maritime industry and urban art. Just to the northwest of the city is the **Cap de la Hague** ❾, a splendid promontory, and a little further south at **Nez de Jobourg**, the cliffs are among the highest in Europe, rearing to an awesome 158 m (520 ft).

Following the coastline eastward from Cherbourg, **Barfleur** ❿ is a hardworking fishing port with great grey stone houses facing the harbour, once the peninsula's chief port, used by the Vikings. A little further along comes **St Vaast-la-Hougue** ⓫ known for its oysters and its Vauban-built fortifications. Watch the brightly painted boats bobbing up and down in the harbour, or treat yourself to a memorable seafood lunch.

From then on eastward, from the Cotentin Peninsula to the bright lights of Deauville and the Côte Fleurie, the cliffs drop down to the low coast and sandy beaches providing the funnel through which the Allied forces poured their men and weapons in 1944.

War in Normandy

The **D-Day Beaches** ⓬, with their museum and memorials, batteries and bunkers, still serve as a reminder of the tremendous Allied operation of 6 June. The wartime code names remain proudly in place: Utah and Omaha taken by the Americans in the west; Gold, Juno and Sword by the British, Canadians and Poles in the east.

BELOW: countryside commentary on World War II.

Every part of France suffered terribly from the deep trauma of World War II, but Normandy underwent more physical damage than any other region. To find anything similar one has to go back to the French and Belgian towns that were shelled into rubble in World War I. In 1944, it was the Allied bombardment that did most of the damage – a terrible prospect, but one that the French accepted in the interest of regaining liberty.

The traveller in Normandy is also forever meeting with startling reminders of the colossal effort that went into the rebuilding of towns destroyed in the fighting. Town after town – Caen, Le Havre, Rouen, Avranches, Dunkerque, Boulogne – had to be built up from rubble. Where the town was ancient and beautiful, its historic buildings were lovingly recreated stone by stone, in replicas which, now that they have had time to become weathered, have become historic in their own right. It was a labour of love and there are few real blemishes.

Indeed, the French have never been given the credit that they deserve for this heroic effort. With all the shortages and difficulties of the immediate post-war years, it would have been so easy and so forgivable to put up cheap, shoddy buildings and get on with life. But the French wanted their country back as it had been, and they planned and worked and reconstructed until they had it back.

Essentially Norman

As quick a way as any of indicating the variety that awaits those who wander through Normandy is to take three towns, all within the **Orne** region and a modest distance from each other, so that with a car, or an intelligent use of the train and bus services, they can all be fitted into a single day. Flers, La Ferté-Macé, and Bagnoles-de-l'Orne are all very different from each other and all offer something essentially French and Norman.

Flers ⑬ is not a tourist town but a pleasant, bustling, workaday place, very much the centre of a large area of countryside. It has the mandatory château, but does not set out to offer historical romance to the visitor, and its wide, handsome streets are lined with well-stocked shops and good cafés and hotels where the traveller gets value for money without frills.

The huge barn-like parish church, obviously a rebuilt job after the devastation of 1944, dominates a market square that, on the days when the country people bring in their produce, is crammed with stalls and the sort of relaxed, joking, basket-carrying crowd of purchasers that you never see in a supermarket.

The produce stalls in Norman country towns seem to extend right across the spectrum, from large farms and co-operatives down to smallholders and even families selling the small surplus of a cottage garden. Sometimes families actually operate without a stall, simply occupying a few feet of pavement, sitting on cane stools and upturned boxes in front of a few kilos of potatoes.

Flers is a historical town, like most French towns, but it lives in the present and much of its history is of recent date. The Rue de la Banque, at the top of the town's sloping main street, has been renamed the Rue de la IIème Division Britannique, Liberatrice de Flers Les 16 et 17 Août 1944. That is the kind of his-

Map on page 192

Bocage normand is the term used to describe the typically Norman rural terrain which lies to the east of Avranches. The best months to visit are July and August, or in the autumn.

BELOW: Norman timbers stuffed with straw.

Farmer's wife Marie Harel, credited with bringing Camembert to the attention of a grateful world.

BELOW: Joan of Arc.

tory they go in for around here. The charm of Flers for the tourist is precisely that it is so normal and not interested in tourists.

La Ferté-Macé ⓮ attracts visitors because part of its atmosphere is made up of a kind of "history" that can be tabulated (it has a castle, a modern church with an 11th-century Romanesque tower and a carillon), and there is a *visite commentée* (a guided tour) of the place every Friday afternoon in the season. Perhaps, however, its greatest attraction lies in the unselfconscious way its sloping streets and leaning houses are so obviously home to a community of ordinary country people, getting on with their lives.

The trickle of visitors does not disturb the town's daily rhythm. The town has also made its contribution to Norman cuisine with a recipe for tripe cooked, this time, on skewers.

Part of the magic of La Ferté-Macé comes from its setting amid verdant and peaceful countryside, with small fields and rolling hills. But a few more miles to the south and you strike a town right in the middle of a national park and on the edge of the **Forêt de l'Andaine** that even this beautiful setting cannot redeem.

A different face

Bagnoles-de-l'Orne ⓯ owes its existence to the discovery, centuries ago, of thermal springs with curative properties. There is naturally a legend about this (in France, there is a legend about everything), to the effect that Hugues, the Seigneur of Tesse, one day turned loose in the forest a horse of his that had become too old for service. A few days later the same horse turned up again, in rampant form. Hugues mounted and indicated that he wished to be taken to wherever the horse had been and this turned out to be the **Source de Bagnoles**. A few dips therein soon put the veteran Hugues in magnificent form, such that he married the Dame de Bonvouloir and begat a numerous second family.

The town in its modern form is not devoted to the renewal of fertility, however, but to the treatment of rheumatic disorders, for which purpose it is dominated by huge Institutes and Residences. Sufferers walk slowly along the carefully levelled gravel paths with their aluminium canes, and the town strives to keep up their spirits, and those of the friends and relatives who accompany them by a determined cheerfulness that extends through every detail of architecture and layout.

An engineered lake winds through the centre of town, on which you can hire a pedalo and squeak slowly back and forth. There is a casino, a "Festival of Sir Lancelot du Lac" during the summer, an oval sandy track where children can have rides in carts pulled by tiny Shetland ponies, and long rows of shops selling tacky souvenirs.

Bagnoles-de-l'Orne is worth visiting simply because one's picture of modern Normandy, and modern France, would be incomplete without it: amid so much beauty and historical dignity, it is another quite different, but equally important, face of the country.

Although not pre-eminent in any of those three

towns, another facet of Normandy, (and one it shares with Brittany, except that it has a different flavour) is its conspicuous preoccupation with shrines and auspicious commemorations.

Shrines and saints

That most lovable and approachable of saints, Saint Theresa, "the Little Flower", has her personal cult, and the museum that houses her relics is in the little Calvados town of **Lisieux** ⑯, which lies in the heart of the **Pays d'Auge** ⑰. Here is Normandy at its most seductive: green meadows, remote half-timbered villages and narrow country lanes which wind through the shady valleys and broad pastures like a roller coaster.

At **Rouen** ⑱ on the River Seine, over towards the eastern boundary of Normandy and upriver from the industrial port of Le Havre, stands the house where that saintly heroine, Joan of Arc was imprisoned and interrogated. In the **Place du Vieux-Marché** Ⓐ they have marked the spot on the pavement where she was mercilessly burnt as a witch on 30 May 1431.

If, after contemplating these vestiges of human error, you need to restore your spirits by contemplating the positives of religious faith, the great late-Gothic **Cathédrale de Notre-Dame** Ⓑ should help you, and so should the medieval church of **St Maclou** Ⓒ, which contains some of the finest wood carving in France. Nearby is something more oppressive however: the **Aître de St Maclou** Ⓓ, a rectangular inner courtyard used as a mortuary during the plagues of the 16th century; carvings on the two-storey gallery display macabre motifs of skulls, crossbones and gravediggers' tools.

St Maclou stands amid streets that match it in age, and they and the golden-

Maps:
Area 192
City 199

TIP

Rouen Cathedral is illuminated every night until 1am and if you are staying nearby it's worth going back into town to view the spectacular silhouette.

BELOW: Rouen's Gros Horloge.

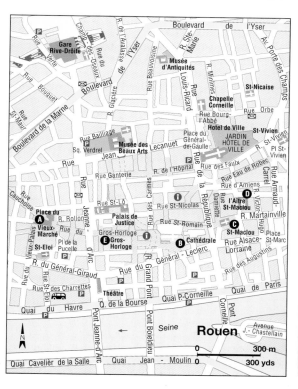

In A La Recherche du Temps Perdu, *Marcel Proust likened the dining room windows of Cabourg's Grand Hotel to a giant aquarium.*

RIGHT:
Deauville's casino.
BELOW: *boules*
by the beach.

faced clock known as the **Gros Horloge** ❺, arched over another ancient street, emphasise the town's historic dimension. Gustave Flaubert was born here in 1821 and this is where he set his most famous novel, *Madame Bovary*.

Rouen is not only the largest city in Normandy, but also an important centre for business and industry, with its own metro and France's fourth largest port.

The Seine was also the place where Impressionism was born. Its main instigator, Claude Monet, grew up in Le Havre at the mouth of the river. But it was at the delightful little port of **Honfleur** ⓳, the prize of Normandy's holiday coast on the opposite bank, where the artists met and developed their style.

Cabourg, Deauville, Trouville and Dieppe

But what of the resorts, famous names that occur again and again in the memoirs of the wealthy and powerful of the world? "Memoirs" is perhaps the operative word. In 1919, German doctors discovered that certain deficiency diseases in children could be alleviated by exposure to sunlight – that the body could, under some circumstances, take in certain vitamins through the skin. Their announcement of this discovery was the shout that started an avalanche. It began the sun-worship that has made holiday resorts out of glaring deserts of the earth and bankrupted the cool and shady places.

Tiny fishing villages in the south of France suddenly began to have visitors not merely in the mild rainy winter but also in the parching summer. And at the same moment the majestic resorts of the northern coasts, with their miles of smooth sand, their casinos and golf courses and theatres, their row upon row of hotels so magnificent and solid that they seemed built to last forever, began to languish like the equally enormous dinosaurs of old.

They are not dead yet. But to take a holiday at any French resort that faces north is to risk cool weather, even rain. No sun-lover will take that risk.

The battle goes on. **Cabourg** ⓴, favoured by Marcel Proust, and described by him in *A La Recherche du Temps Perdu* has decided to stay fashionable and exclusive, hoping that if you exclude the many you automatically get the discerning few. **Deauville** ㉑, convenient to Paris, still draws TV stars and fashion models to have their photographs taken and, to lure them, the town has constructed a board-walk.

With its casino, theatre, racecourse, night clubs, enormous yacht marinas, and phalanx of elite European polo players, this resort can hardly be called conquered. And **Trouville** ㉒, close by but separated by a small river, offers proximity to all these facilities but a quieter atmosphere. Of all the traditional northern resorts, **Dieppe** ㉓ can perhaps be said to have survived best. It deals good-humouredly with a huge volume of English day-trippers and, with its long beach, picturesque 15th-century **château** and lively shops and stalls crowding the streets of the old town, has kept its hold on French families *en vacances*.

Adding to Dieppe's allure is its proximity to the naive **Pays de Caux** and the **Côte d'Albâtre**. The famed sheer cliffs of **Etretat** ㉔, cut with a perfect arch protruding into the sea, might well be the best place along the Channel for sighting *les serpents de mer*. ❏

BRITTANY

The key to the Breton character is that the people are firstly Atlantic dwellers and secondly Celts. Along with endurance, they have a rich imagination and ready recourse to symbol and legend

Map
on page
204

Perhaps the best way to introduce oneself to Brittany is to travel, either by road or rail, from Rennes to Vannes. In **Rennes ❶**, though the city is within Brittany and is its regional capital, you *feel* you are still in hard-working, realistic, practical Normandy. The town has an immensely important place in French history and, among other things, provided the nation with useful experience in the rebuilding of disaster-stricken cities when the medieval town was almost entirely – a few picturesque streets are still standing – consumed by fire in 1720. It was rebuilt in the severe classical style of the time, elegant but too formal for some tastes and, to speed up the process of getting the citizenry housed, the new buildings were sold off in separate flats, two centuries before this practice became usual. The parliament building survived, only to be severely burned during fishermen's riots in 1994.

Today Rennes has two universities, a Citröen car plant and is host to much high-tech industry, notably in electronics and communications. It crackles with energy and sparkles with modernity. In search of Brittany take due note of Rennes – for it, too, is Brittany – and then head southwest to **Vannes ❷**.

At first, you pass through a landscape that, like Normandy, is lush and smiling with plenty. But as mile after mile of westward land slides by, the country becomes rougher and more windblown, the houses lower, the agriculture more basic. Everything combines to remind you that you are penetrating more and more deeply into the westward peninsula of France and that the open Atlantic is around you on three sides.

Vannes is on the coast – almost. It's one of those ports whose maritime importance, partly through silting and partly through the increasing size of ships, is largely historical. But you can still sail there in a small boat; there's a yacht-basin under the fine old ramparts.

LEFT: Brittany is bicycle-friendly.
BELOW: traditional Breton bonnet.

City scenes

Visually, Vannes is delightful. The great **ramparts** are punctuated by fairytale round towers with tall conical slate hats. Beside the Porte Poterne, there is a **laverie**, a place constructed for the communal washing of clothes, such as one sees in every old French town that has a stream or river, but this one has the most delightful curving and overhanging slate roof.

Inside the walls, in the old town, are the usual half-timbered houses, most of them built by making each floor project a little beyond the one below it (for stability), so that in a narrow street the topmost floors are almost touching. There are also some of those obviously phoney half-timberings – modern constructions across which strips of hardboard have been nailed at random, with no serious attempt to make

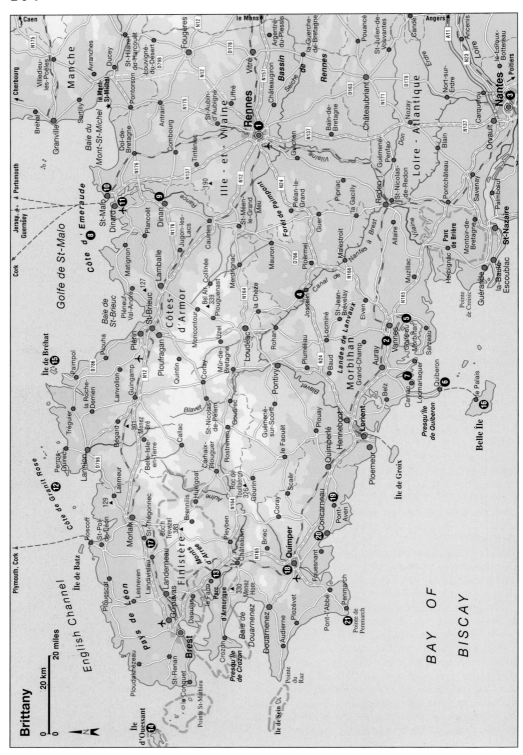

Brittany

them look structural. Other buildings worth looking at are the **Cathédrale de St Pierre** – noble and lofty outside, though rather lowering and forbidding in its interior – and the **Hôtel de Ville**, a striking example of the florid confidence of Western man in the later 19th century, when he assumed that his cultural and material ascendancy would last forever. Beautiful it isn't, but such a bold statement does hold one's attention, and what it must have cost to build is incalculable. In the open space in front is a fine swaggering statue of the Duc de Richemont, a 15th-century worthy who severely trounced the English and thereby put an end to the Hundred Years War.

Certainly there is plenty to see in Brittany without leaving the big cities. Nantes ❸, although officially no longer a part of Brittany following local government re-organisation in 1972, remains emotionally and economically attached to the old duchy. The city is fascinating in the range of what it contains: a large industrial area centred on the docks and shipyard; the beautiful, austere **Cathédrale de St Pierre** whose pale stone, almost luminous in the light from the windows, reminds one of the stone of Canterbury and which does in fact come from the same source; and the wonderful **Château des Ducs de Bretagne** (open Wed–Mon; closed public hols; entrance fee), begun by Duke François II and continued by his daughter, the Duchess Anne, who in its chapel married King Louis XII of France, in 1499, thereby uniting France and Brittany. A fascinating woman, physically slight and frail with a limp, but witty, intelligent and well-read, she acted out her destiny with style.

One cannot, however, stay long in an urban setting if one is to know Brittany for, like Normandy, it is overwhelmingly a rural province. One seems always to be travelling immense distances, chancing across isolated villages that seem like places history has passed by. This Breton countryside, wild and lonely, evidently bred a highly differentiated way of life, so that up to the 20th century the Breton costume was very distinctive (elaborate lace head-dresses for the women, known as *coiffes*, and for the men black jackets and trousers and wide-brimmed black hats). These costumes have not entirely disappeared – they are worn on festive occasions.

Cormorants and spoonbills

Josselin ❹, in the heart of inland Brittany, is a pleasant place to spend a couple of days. This energetic little town, with its one steep street running down to the river bank, its half-timbering, its bustling Saturday morning street market and friendly, crowded local cafés, really speaks the language of rural Brittany.

The river that runs below the town is the **Oust**, or the **Nantes-Brest Canal**, as it has long been canalised to form part of that important artery. Its rippling waters reflected the dream-like **château** of the Rohan family, exactly the kind of castle that a book illustrator would draw to accompany a story of chivalry and enchantment (open Apr–May: Wed, Sat, Sun, public hols, pm only; June–Sept: daily, pm only; Aug: daily; entrance fee). And across the river, perched on the opposite bank, is the unpretentiously lovely **Chapelle de Ste Croix**, which speaks of the other side of the Middle Ages – homely, graceful piety.

Map on page 204

TIP

The best way to approach Josselin is from the south on the D4. As you cross the River Oust there is a superb view of the château with bobbing boats at its foot.

BELOW: memorial in Nantes.

The massive chamber tomb, Table du Marchand, at Locmariaquer. A gallery leads under the great table and a low relief can be made out on one of the support stones.

BELOW:
two Bretonnes in native costumes.

Josselin, like Vannes, is in Morbihan. The name means "Little Sea" and the **Golfe du Morbihan** ❺ is a vast inlet, effectively a seawater lake, fed by various channels from the Atlantic. It is 20 km (12 miles) wide and from the open sea to the inner shore it reaches 15 km (9 miles). It is tidal and dotted with islands, of which the largest are **Arz** and **L'Ile des Moines**, each of which supports a few hundred inhabitants, though most of the multitudinous islands are green lumps of solitude amid the advancing and receding waters, and the human beings who frequent the Gulf do so on those movable man-made islands we call boats. They are there in plenty enough, fishing away, and keeping them company is a vast army of seabirds, usually ranging from 60,000 to 100,000 in the Gulf alone, representing the largest concentration of seabirds on the French Atlantic coast. In a number of places (for example **Groix, Rohellan, Theriec, Belle-Ile, Méaban** and the marsh area of the **Presqu'Ile de Rhuys**) there are bird sanctuaries. There, according to the season of the year, you can see oyster-catchers, crested cormorants, Brent geese, hooded mergansers, sand-pipers, plovers, spoonbills, herons and egrets, not to speak of a whole range of gulls.

Neolithic worship

The connoisseur of coastline can enjoy both wild and stormy, with pounding breakers and rocks hurled far up the beach by the fury of the sea, or alternatively calm, meditative and sheltered. The mouth of the Gulf is guarded by a thin shell of land which makes safe haven for **Locmariaquer** and **Arzon**, and further out there is an even thinner finger of shore, running down from the summer resort of **Quiberon** ❻ with its little harbour and sandy beach, which provides shelter for, among other places, the magical **Carnac** ❼.

Map on page 204

The name Carnac reminds us that the Celtic mind has always been, for want of a better word, "mystical"; the unseen has been as real to the Celt as the seen, the measureless as actual as the measured. This outlook runs seamlessly from Neolithic worship, through the tangled mass of Dark Age legends and myths, to the more ordered but still prodigally rich imaginative landscape of medieval Catholicism.

Carnac is one of the places, perhaps in Brittany *the* place, where one finds this feeling concentrated so strongly that in thousands of years it has not dispersed; the great stone circles and alignments, the raising with frightful labour of those huge everlasting groups of menhirs (single vertical standing stones) and dolmens (hanging stones) by which our ancestors of the Neolithic and Early Bronze Ages marked the places where they enacted their sacred rituals of death and the renewal of life.

The mysterious menhirs

Carnac consists of three groups of menhirs, arranged in patterns of 10 to 13 rows, and also a series of long cairns covering funerary chambers. Time has not left the menhirs intact – it is probable that each row ended in a semi-circle of standing stones which have gone – but still there are nearly 3,000 of them, and the effect is awe-inspiring.

Carnac has, of course, long been carefully investigated and excavated, and many grave goods of fine workmanship have been taken away to museums. These included beautiful polished axes in greenstone – or, more precisely, jadeite, one of the group of related stones to which the general name "greenstone" is given. Objects made from jadeite have also been found in tombs of the

Many terms which describe prehistoric monuments are Breton in origin, e.g. menhir (men = stone, hir = long); cromlech (crom = bend, lech = place); dolmen (dol = table, men = stone).

BELOW:
Alignements
de Kermaria in
Carnac.

Statue of Breton hero Bertrand du Guesclin, who saved Dinan from seige and died in 1380.

BELOW:
fishing by pulley
on the Rance.

ancient Chinese and of the Indians of North America. In such ways did the religious observances of our remote ancestors girdle the earth and unite all human beings in their most solemn moments.

Fishing on stilts

The stretch of coast between Pointe de Grouin and Val André is known as the **Côte d'Emeraude** ❽ and it encompasses sweeping sandy bays, rocky headlands – such as Cap Fréhel with its lighthouse and carpet of spring flowers – secret inlets, meandering estuaries and pretty seaside towns. Take a boat trip up the Rance to visit **Dinan** ❾, a beautiful old town some 10 river-miles inland. The voyage begins with an enforced inspection of the hydro-electric dam built in 1966 across the estuary. It is nothing much to look at, but so technologically advanced that it is the only dam in the world that manages to harness both the ebb and flow of the tide.

Once on the river, simpler pleasures take over. The banks are green and wooded, with fine houses to be glimpsed. The local inhabitants have a quaint method of fishing that involves building small cabins on stilts so as to get right over the tidal flow of the river. On top of these cabins are crossed staves, which, when projected forward, make a square framework for a close-meshed net; this they lower and bring up repeatedly with pulleys. The catch has to be something too small to be fished with a baited hook, but abundant enough to be caught in bulk such as whitebait. The stilted huts give the placid European riverside a curious flavour of Borneo, and one wonders, as one glides by, whether anything has been caught with all that patient plunging.

Dinan, when it comes in sight, dispels these trivial amusements with some-

thing really worth looking at. **Rue du Jezual**, rising steeply up the high bluffs that overlook the river, is lined with fine old half-timbered houses, in many of which artist-craftsmen live and work. And from the Jardin Anglais behind the stately church of **St Sauveur** there is a wonderful view of the river, crossed by a huge viaduct and a reconstructed Gothic bridge.

Map
on page
204

Casinos and beach huts

As for **St Malo ⑩** and Dinard, together they form an attractive holiday centre on the Côte d'Emeraude. **Dinard ⑪** is modern, with the usual paraphernalia of palm-trees and a casino and beach huts; St Malo is august, historic, dignified. Perhaps they are both a little too all-or-nothing; St Malo can be a calmly austere shrine because it can unload its workaday life and its frivolities on to Dinard, and Dinard can have a cheerful spa vulgarity because St Malo, just over the river, will take care of the refined matters of historicity and beauty.

Being unfair to Dinard will hardly cause its prosperous citizens to lose any sleep. The place has been a successful resort ever since resorts came into being. Here, some 80 to 100 years ago, the well-to-do merchants of northern France built their Gothic mansions, with turrets and pillars and buttresses that don't buttress anything, all part of that 19th-century dream of reviving the picturesque side of the Middle Ages, a dream doomed to failure because you can't just skim the picturesqueness off society and sell it as if it were cream – it has to rise up naturally from the beliefs and actions and assumptions that underlie it. These amusing monstrosities are probably quite cheerful to live in, with their large pleasant gardens overlooking the sea (Dinard is a conspicuous beneficiary of the Gulf Stream and its climate is very agreeable), but they strike the onlooker as

Natives of St Malo are Malouins, whose forefathers roamed far and wide. They settled in the Malvinas (Falkland Islands) and landed in Canada in 1534.

BELOW:
souvenir clogs on
sale at St Malo.

Work of the Pont-Aven school.

to use a phrase that George Orwell applied to certain resort hotels in England ("lunatics staring over the asylum wall").

Land's end

Leaving the resorts behind, the coast – between Paimpol and Trébeurden called the **Côte de Granit Rose** ⓬ for its pink-hued cliffs – becomes increasingly wild, rocky and stormy as you move west towards Finistère, the End of the Earth. A good chunk of this weatherbeaten landscape now belongs to the **Parc Régional d'Armorique** ⓭, which extends westward from the granitic moorlands of the Mons d'Arrée, along the Crozon Peninsula and across the sea to Ouessant. This is a wild region of desolate gorse-edged uplands and dense green woodlands, shot through with streams, lakes and rivers littered with huge moss-backed boulders. The peaked crown of its highest point, Roc'h Trévezel juts out of a windswept moorland plateau and gives magnificent views north to the coast and south past the Montagne St Michel to the Montagnes Noir.

Known to the English as Ushant, **Ile d'Ouessant** ⓮ is the most remote of the scores of islands sprinkled around the Breton coast. Of these, 15 are large enough to seduce a permanent population to live on them, and you will not have seen Brittany till you have visited at least one of them. **Bréhat** ⓯, off the Côte de Granit Rose, and **Belle-Ile** ⓰, south of Quiberon, are two of the most accessible and rewarding. The same can be said for *les enclos paroissiaux*, the parish closes of **northern Finistère**, of which perhaps **St Thégonnec** ⓱ is best known (*see page 211*).

Southern Finistère is known as Cornouaille, so named by the Celts who fled here from Cornwall in the 6th century BC. Here Breton culture remains

BELOW: oyster hunters.

most evident. In its capital, **Quimper** ⓲, you can find specialist shops selling Breton-language books, traditional costume, local Quimper pottery and *keltia musique*, while the old streets around the **Cathédrale St Corentin** have some of the region's most enjoyable crêperies. A *galette* (buckwheat pancake) and a cup of cider will seem quite appropriate after visiting the city's recently restored **Musée des Beaux-Arts**, which houses an excellent collection of paintings *sur la thème Bretagne*, including works by Paul Gauguin and the Pont-Aven School (open July–Aug: daily; Sept–Apr: Wed–Mon; closed public hols; entrance fee).

Map on page 204

Secluded coves and shipwrecks

Pont-Aven ⓳ lies 34 km (20 miles) east of Quimper, amid a benign country-side of wooded river valleys and secluded coves that reveals the mellow side of Brittany. A little to the northwest is **Concarneau** ⓴, whose granite-walled citadel, **Ville Close**, is built on a rocky outcrop in the bay, and tethered to the shore by a causeway, but cut off at high tide. This is France's third largest fishing port, which now successfully mixes its long-established trade with tourism.The **Musée de la Pêche** (open Tues–Sun; closed Jan; entrance fee) traces the history of the industry from its earliest days, and a trawler moored alongside can be toured.

Before retiring inland, take a trip out to **Pays Bigouden**, southwest of Quimper. Here the land falls flat to the sea, provoking thoughts of storms, shipwrecks and toiling seaweed gatherers. From the top of the Eckmühl Lighthouse you can survey **Pointe de Penmarch** ㉑ and the immense sweep of the Baie d'Audierne. Such great and majestic stretches of coast look much as they must have done 2,000 years ago. Even today, a primitive Brittany isn't difficult to imagine. ❑

One Breton legend concerns the drowned city of Ys in Douarnenez Bay: it was engulfed by waves because of the debauchery of the king's daughter. The king made his escape on horseback, but his daughter behind him was too late and drowned.

BELOW: Calvaire at Guimiliau.

PARISH CLOSES

Born of an intense faith and spurred by a keen interparish rivalry, Brittany's parish closes (*enclos paroissiaux*) now stand in lichen-covered testimony to the fervour and superstition that once gripped the Breton soul. Begun in the mid-16th century and completed over the next 150 years, these are grandiose religious ensembles adorned with elaborate granite carvings, their churches, calvaries, ossuaries and triumphal arches absurdly large for the small rural communities that created them.

Morlaix is the closest town to the three most interesting parish closes, of which St Thégonnec is the most complete, exhibiting all the traditional elements: triumphal arch, ossuary and superb calvary. Rivalry with neighbouring Guimiliau was intense: theirs is the *grand fromage* of Breton calvaries with more than 200 figures carved between 1581 and 1588. Lampaul-Guimiliau has perhaps the simplest close complex, but its church has a marvellous baldaquin canopy over the font, while in front of the choir, a rood beam spans the central nave. Christ on the cross can be seen on one side, and on both sides groups of figures depict the way of the Cross. To the left of the choir stand three altarpieces depicting St Miliau and the birth of the Virgin, a rare theme in Brittany.

THE NORTHEAST

Hardly any corner of France lacks vines, but vineyards run riot across the eastern provinces of Champagne, Lorraine and Alsace – and then on to Burgundy and the Rhône valley (both covered in the Central France section beginning on page 235).

Champagne (pages *216–219*) is the most northerly wine producing area of France, and in fact used to be known for its red wines before the delicious fizz came into existence in the 17th century, supposedly discovered by monk Dom Pérignon. "Champagne is the only wine which makes a woman more beautiful after drinking it," declared Madame de Pompadour.

Both Champagne and neighbouring **Lorraine** (*pages 220–221*) are celebrated for fine cathedrals, particularly in Reims and Metz. Hugging the western slopes of the crumpled, wooded Vosges hills in the south, Lorraine is a region of tranquil, little-visited countryside. whose major cities of Metz and Nancy and well worth a visit, as well as the deeply moving battlefields of Verdun.

The very existence of **Alsace** (*pages 225–232*) is a tribute to the ability of humankind to sort out territorial disputes; over the centuries it has been torn, like a hare between hounds, by the rival powers of France and Germany. Now Alsace lives in peace, doubly endowed by the cultures of both countries, with its capital city of Strasbourg now the seat of the European parliament. Two-thirds of the population speak their own dialect, Elsassdutch, in their neat, picture-book villages of Hansel-and-Gretel gingerbread houses where geraniums burst from every balcony. The well-trodden Wine Route takes the visitor through a procession of them, amongst a sea of vines producing the distinctive white wines of Alsace. ❑

PRECEDING PAGES: the sign of Hautvilliers Champagne.
LEFT: gathering grapes during the harvest in Hunawihr, Alsace.

Map on page 218

Paris

BELOW: Christian Pol Roger and a double magnum.

CHAMPAGNE

The name of the region has become the generic term for sparkling wine, but genuine champagne comes only from this area with its undulating plains, forests, lakes and lovely towns

A Frenchman once recounted with a mixture of mirth and dismay his discovery that a bottle of "champanya" sold in Spain bore the caveat "not to be confused with foreign imitations". The name of this French province has become a universally accepted term for sparkling wine, and the French insist that true champagne comes only from Champagne.

Surrounded by large fields of wheat and sugarbeet whose uniform colours blanket the countryside, **Reims ❶** marks the start of the royal road through Champagne as far as Vertus, the **Route du Champagne**. The kings of France were crowned in this city's magnificent **Cathédrale Notre-Dame**. We tend to think of Gothic as an affair of pointed arches and needle-like spires; here the striking feature is the decoration of coolly imperturbable draped angels, whose reserved smiles contain a whole new aspect of Gothic architecture.

The present cathedral was begun in 1211, and not completed for 300 years, but there were other buildings before it, dating from 401. Clovis, the first king of the Franks, was baptised here in 496, and the significance of this act was not lost on future kings of France, 26 of whom elected to be crowned in the city. The 1,500-year anniversary of Clovis's baptism was celebrated in Reims in 1996 and many of the city's sights were restored in time for the occasion.

Though badly scarred, the west front is covered in 13th-century carvings – look for the **Smiling Angel** and attendants decorating the north portal. A further surfeit of statuary decorates the interior wall, and richly carved friezes encircle the pillars in the soaring but otherwise simple nave. The stained glass is superb, from the 13th-century **Rose Window** to the 20th-century windows by Chagall in the ambulatory, with their luminous deep blues and purples cut with green and red.

For students of art history, the early Gothic **Basilique de St Remi** is to be compared to the classic forms of the cathedral. The former archbishop's residence, **Palais du Tau** (open daily, closed public hols; entrance fee), with its precious objects and tapestries, was the residence of royalty during their sojourns in Reims. At the **Musée des Beaux-Arts** (8 Rue Chanzy; open Wed–Mon; closed public hols; entrance fee) you can almost relive the coronation rites through the paintings that were hung in the streets in honour of the royal arrival.

It would be fun to imagine the damasked and brocaded guests of these festivities with a flute of champagne in hand, bubbles ascending to heaven like the direct link between the king and God. Alas, champagne as we know it didn't come into existence until the 17th century. Its creation is attributed to Dom Pérignon, who allegedly announced its genesis with the words, "Come quickly, I am seeing stars!".

Méthode champenoise

The *méthode champenoise* consists of starting and controlling a second fermentation in the spring. Once the wine has been assembled from different vines, a sugary liqueur is added that sets off fermentation in the bottle. Despite thick glass and dense corks wired to the bottles, some two to three percent regularly explode, proof of this wine's exuberance.

Extending to Vertus, the champagne vineyards are the northernmost in France, making them susceptible to freezing, but also giving the wine its characteristic light acid taste. **Épernay ❷** is the heart of the grape district. Although it has only one-sixth of the population of Reims, this town produces almost as much champagne. The famed **Moët et Chandon** establishment gives guided tours of its cellars, and the town's museum has a section on champagne production. Otherwise the town is less interesting, having been much rebuilt after World War I. Nearby is **Hautvilliers**, Dom Pérignon's homeland, offering a view of the valley and the rare example of an old town transformed both by military destruction and the reconstruction of prosperous wine growers and merchants.

Statue of Joan of Arc in Reims.

Champagne's great names

Unlike most other wine regions, in Champagne there are "brand names" that are not designations of varietal or territorial origin, but that of the company assembling and manipulating the wine. These large and famous companies buy the grapes from the growers, and after a first pressing at the harvest site, transfer the incipient wine to their cellars, concentrated in Reims and Épernay.

Great underground galleries and caverns provide the necessary constant cool temperature. Apart from the millions of bottles, these cellars are spectacular in

BELOW: church at Châtillon.

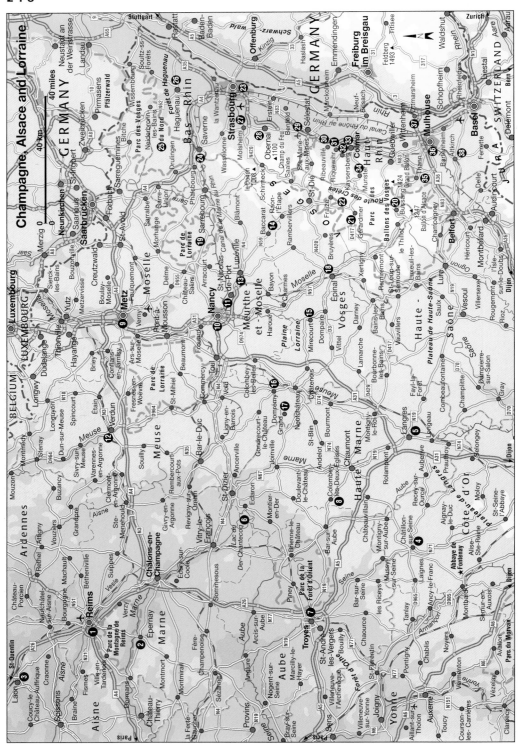

Champagne, Alsace and Lorraine

themselves. Under Epernay alone they cover 100 km (60 miles). Each has its distinctive features; Gallo-Roman quarries (Lanson), statues sculpted into the walls (Pommery and Greno), a tour on a small train (Piper-Heidsieck).

Map on page 218

City on high

In the far north of the region, bordering the Pays du Nord, a high, narrow ridge is occupied by **Laon ❸**, whose historic **Ville Haute** (upper town) is completely separate from the modern Ville Basse and feels very remote from below. In fact the best way to reach it is by the Poma electric train which begins at the station.

The view from the ramparts is best appreciated on a sunny day, but the town's main draw, **Cathédrale Notre-Dame**, is just as spectacular wreathed in mist. An early example of Gothic architecture, built between 1155 and 1235, many of its innovative features were later taken up in the cathedrals of Chartres, Paris and Reims.

Champagne on ice.

The southern part of the province, merging with Burgundy, reaches farther back in history. The **Musée Archéologique** in **Châtillon-sur-Seine ❹** displays the spectacular Vix collection of bronzes, ceramics and gold jewellery found in a pre-Roman burial site (open mid-June–mid-Sept: daily; mid-Sept–mid-June: Wed–Mon; entrance fee). The town's Romanesque church, **St Vorles**, has long been of important religious significance.

On an exposed plateau, **Langres ❺**, birthplace of the encyclopedist Diderot, has intact Roman ramparts that look over a valley where modern highways follow the line of Roman roads. Its Burgundian Romanesque **Cathédrale St Mammès** is a gloomy affair, save for the carved capitals in the apse. To the north, **Montier-en-Der** has a Saxonesque former abbey church constructed in timber, and in the rustic surrounding woods is **Lentilles** whose 16th-century timbered and roughcast plaster **church** with its shingled front is an example of Champagne architecture. Nearby, **Lac Der-Chantecoq ❻** is the largest artificial lake in France, once a vast forest of oak (the name *der* comes from the Celtic for oak).Its creation in 1974 to regulate the flow of the rivers Seine and Marne submerged three villages.

BELOW: memorial to Charles de Gaulle.

Renaissance city, modern monument

Troyes ❼ is a particularly brilliant souvenir of the Renaissance period. The old town has its specific architecture of wood-sided houses whose upper levels jut over the narrow streets. No fewer than nine churches contain marvels of stained-glass, statuary and religious treasures, including the manuscripts saved from the Clairvaux abbey.

To the east of Troyes, off the main road to Chaumont, a 44-m (145-ft) double-barred Cross of Lorraine in pink granite stands on a hilltop, visible from far across the rolling, chalky plain. It beckons the visitor to the village of **Colombey-les-Deux-Églises ❽** where Charles de Gaulle had his country home; he lies buried in the humble churchyard. The house, a creeper-covered manor, is a museum full of fascinating de Gaulle memorabilia. It is a pity about the countless souvenir shops in the village, selling every kind of kitsch to the 500,000 annual visitors. ❑

Map on page 218

Paris

LORRAINE

Industrial towns contrast with unspoilt countryside in Lorraine, which hugs the slopes of the Vosges and extends north to the borders of Germany, Luxembourg and Belgium

orraine's regional capital, **Metz** remains an important industrial centre in an area which has become synonymous with the economic difficulties of steel works and coal mines. In the factory outskirts, trucks laden with beer kegs trundle out of the high brick blocks of breweries. Other prominent industries include printing, and the manufacture of shoes and metal goods.

With the largest stained-glass windows in the world, some of them by Marc Chagall,and a fine Gothic exterior, the **Cathédrale de St Etienne** makes a stop in Metz well worthwhile. The 4th-century **St Pierre-aux-Nonnains**, in the Vieille Ville, has the distinction of being the oldest church in France, and nearby is the 13th-century **Chapelle des Templiers**, its walls covered in frescoes.

The seat of Nancy

The historic heart of the region is **Nancy** ⓾, former seat of the dukes of Lorraine. The hub of this cultural capital is the **Place Stanislas**, named after the deposed king of Poland, who gratefully accepted the Lorraine duchy from his son-in-law Louis XV in 1735. It is extension of the existing city created a modern rectilinear street plan. The chequered stone esplanade is enclosed by gilded wrought-iron grillework linking the indispensable trappings of the 18th century, the town hall, the theatre, and the art museum. In the older town, the renovated houses of the Grande Rue lead to the **Porte de la Craffe**, whose two towers and connecting bastion are impressive reminders of earlier fortifications. Along the way, the **Palais Ducal** is a sober town dwelling. Inside is the **Musée Historique Lorraine** (open Wed–Mon; closed public hols; entrance fee). Housed in a separate museum is the unique **Ecole de Nancy**, the epitome of Art Nouveau or Art 1900, whose flowing lines are applied to a number of buildings in the newer Nancy (open Wed–Mon; closed public hols; entrance fee). A few miles from the city is **St Nicolas-de-Port** ⓫ and its **basilica** dedicated to the patron saint of Lorraine.

Thousands of crosses

In striking contrast are the memories of World War I. From 1914 to 1918, the Marne valley was part of an immense battlefield straddling the northeast from the Ardennes to Lorraine. The name **Verdun** ⓬ remains unforgettable. Surprisingly, a good deal of the historic city has survived. The main battlefields of Verdun, where 800,000 died in 1916–18, are outside the city to its northeast, on the hills above the River Meuse. A visit to the giant forts, the grassy remains of trenches, and the towering ossuary of Douaumont, is an immensely moving experience. Today the theme of Franco-German reconciliation

BELOW: stained glass in Metz by Marc Chagall.

dominates and Verdun has been made World Centre for Peace and Human Rights. Nearby lies the plaque laid by Chancellor Helmut Kohl and President François Mitterrand, pledging their nations to friendship.

Arts and crafts

Traditions of arts and crafts flourish in Lorraine. In **Lunéville** ⑬ Stanislas created the château and formal gardens. **Baccarat** ⑭, from the town of that name, is crystal in all its forms and stages, from workshop to the windows of the modern church. Musicians must not miss **Mirecourt** ⑮ where a museum and workshops demonstrate the infinitely delicate art of violin-making. **Domrémy** ⑯ has the house where Joan of Arc was born, an example of how peasants lived in the 15th century. **Grand** ⑰ is a Gallo-Roman site, with an amphitheatre and the largest mosaic discovered in France.

The image of **Épinal** ⑱ is precisely that: images. These engravings of popular proverbs and homilies were a 19th-century precursor of comics. Printed in thousands, they constituted an infinite rogues' gallery of stereotypes.

A drive towards the **Vosges** hills is enchanting. From the Lorraine side, the slopes rise quietly in dark green forests. Along the northern and lower range, in the **Parc Régional de Lorraine** ⑲ near Sarrebourg, the forest harbours wild boar and roe deer. From Epinal the main highway follows the Moselle river upstream to its source in the high Vosges. **Bussang** ⑳ and **Gérardmer** ㉑ are hill resorts famous for fine skiing and hiking trails that lead to innumerable waterfalls. The high passes, known as *ballons*, make your head spin – taking in the panorama that widens from the Alps in the distance to the impressive **Route de Crêtes** ㉒ that marks the border between Alsace and Lorraine. ❑

BELOW: view of the Vosges.

ALSACE

Nestling between the Rhine and the Vosges, France's smallest province is cosy and compact, with a picture-postcard prettiness, an excellent cuisine and fine wines

Map on page 218

With an Alemannic dialect, a Protestant as well as a Catholic tradition, and a distinctly German-style wine, cuisine, folklore and architecture, Alsace demands some explanation.

Originally, Alsace was integrated into the Alemannic kingdom of Charlemagne's succession, and not until 1648 did it become part of France. Meanwhile, its capital Strasbourg retained the right to levy its own taxes and finance a Protestant university. Then, after the French defeat in 1871, Alsace and part of Lorraine were annexed by Bismarck and not returned to France until 1918.

For all these reasons, Alsace has retained its special religious, social and cultural status, including a local dialect that is commonly heard on the city streets.

From June and its internationally renowned classical music festival to the September Musica featuring contemporary compositions, Strasbourg's cultural life never stops. Meanwhile, a European capital of flagpoles, luxury hotels and conference translators dwells in the city's landscaped parks. Strasbourg is the seat of the Council of Europe, regular host to the European Parliament and site of the futuristic **Palais de l'Europe**.

The crossroads of Europe

Strasbourg ㉓, known as the "Crossroads of Europe", is not actually on the Rhine, but enclosed in a series of basins and canals regulating boat traffic and flood waters. Within the outer rings of modern convention centres and genteel uncramped neighbourhoods is the nutshell of old Strasbourg, a small island formed by the **Ill river**. Numerous bridges cross over the artificial arm of the Ill, channelled in its brick-lined bed. On the facing bank weeping willows droop among a collection of idiosyncratic 19th-century mansions.

From the *quais*, cobbled lanes converge on the **Cathédrale Notre-Dame**. The building, in rosy stone splotched with cream, is like an immense marble cake. When it was finished in the 15th century, the 142-m (465-ft) steeple was the highest in Europe. This is a cathedral laden with decoration, carrying the Gothic idea to its limit. Incessantly modified during its construction, the exterior is layered with lace spires and innumerable statues, as in infinitely reflecting mirrors. Inside, the pulpit and the celebrated **Column of Angels** are flights of a sculptor's fancy. More recent is the **astronomical clock**, a multifaced mechanism tracing hourly, daily and yearly celestial movements. When it strikes at 12.30pm, figures of ancient and biblical mythology execute their ordained rounds.

The **Oeuvre Notre-Dame** was created in the 13th century to supervise the building of the cathedral, and

LEFT: across the Ballon d'Alsace.
BELOW: houses alongside the River Ill, Strasbourg.

*Tucking into La
Choucroute
Alsacienne.*

has been in continuous existence since. Due to this unprecedented life-span, its **museum** (Place du Château; open Tues–Sun; entrance fee) has untold treasures. In a Renaissance mansion of lovingly polished wood, the displays range from a rare series of pre-14th century Jewish epitaphs to a superlative collection of late medieval art, especially paintings of the Lower Rhine school. Most exceptional of all, this museum shows the original master plans for the cathedral. On 2-m(6-ft) scrolls of parchment the artists drew and coloured each section of the facades exactly as they were to appear.

The old city

The old neighbourhood bustles during the weekly flea-market. No two buildings on the evocatively named streets (like Old Fishmarket Street) appear exactly alike. The half-timbered houses seem to have been inflated to giant proportions. Above wide fronts to two or three storeys, the roofs carry up to five gabled windows, one above the other, diminutive in the distance.

Other museums are housed in monuments. The **Grande Boucherie**, or Great Butcher's shop houses the **Musée Historique** (currently closed for refurbishment) and the former Customs House, **Ancienne Douane**, bristling with square masonry spikes like chimneys, is now an exhibition gallery (open daily during exhibitions). The **Musée de l'Art Moderne** is located in Rue Jean Arp (open Wed–Mon; entrance fee).

The **Palais des Rohan** – which includes museums of fine art, decorative art and archaeology – amazes the eye with princely chambers of gilt and velvet (open Wed–Mon; closed public hols; entrance fee). Across the river at the Pont du Corbeau, the **Musée Alsacien** is installed in a typical 16th-century Strasbourg

BELOW: La Petite
France quarter of
Strasbourg.

dwelling. It displays the distinctive objects of traditional Alsace – square ovens of green tiles, splay-legged chairs with f-holed backs rather like violins, armoires with spiralling columns as thick as small trees. (Open Wed–Mon; closed public hols; entrance fee.)

Congregations and their churches

In keeping with its humanist tradition, Strasbourg is noted for prominent Jewish and Protestant minorities that generate an ecumenical spirit. Protestant congregations are numerous, and their properties likewise, as in the twin churches of **St Pierre-le-Jeune** (one for each confession.) The church of **St Thomas** and its cloister, long a revered Protestant sanctuary, contains the splendid mausoleum of the royal Marshal de Saxe.

Beyond the rather bare **Place Gutenberg,** the waterfront affords a view of firemen placidly fishing from a flat-bottomed skiff behind the station. New buildings with long steep roofs and balconies successfully adapt traditional forms. In the picturesque, traffic-free **Petite France** quarter, a central knot of traditional houses is impeccably maintained, with fresh colours and flowers. In fact, it is so picturesque that it seems a little unreal, like a film set or an oversize doll's house. Along the **Rue des Moulins**, where the river is divided into several channels for the running of mills, buildings have doors at water level. The **Ponts Couverts** are no longer covered bridges, but the square towers of the 14th-century fortifications still stand. Just upstream is the **Vauban Dam**, designed to block river traffic, and offering a good view of the old city.

Strasbourg has strong connections with two famous Germans, Johannes Gutenberg and Wolfgang von Goethe. It was during his years in the city,

Map on page 218

TIP

Strasbourg is enjoyable at any time of year, but the Wine Route is best visited in autumn, when the huge volume of tourists and tour buses has died down and the pretty villages are quiet once more.

BELOW: Sundhouse village festival.

1434–48, that Gutenberg evolved the printing press. Goethe spent a year there as a student in 1770–71. And it was in the pretty village of Sessenheim, to the northeast near the Rhine, that he had his love-affair with a pastor's daughter, Frederike, the inspiration of some of his poems.

The Alsatian plain between the Rhine and the Vosges is studded with picturesque villages. The noble Rohan family built an extravagant and ostentatious **château** in **Saverne** ❷ complemented by an immense rose garden. It houses the **Musée de la Ville de Saverne** investigating the town's past (open Mar–mid-Sept: Wed–Mon; Dec–Mar Sun pm; entrance fee).

The surrounding countryside north of Strasbourg is a region of ancestral forests and razed castles. **La Petite-Pierre** is the information centre for the **Parc Régional des Vosges de Nord** ❷, where trails wander among wildlife preserves. The **Forêt de Haguenau** ❷ shelters hamlets of wooden houses, renowned for colourful festivities, the women coiffed with the giant starched bow of Alsatian folklore. At several points along the border with Germany, it is possible to visit some of the Maginot Line's underground forts, built in the 1930s.

La Route du Vin

The famous Upper Alsatian Route du Vin is a 180-km (108-mile) meander through a series of "idyllic wine villages strung out like precious pearls on a necklace", to quote one travel brochure, where typical Alsatian wine and cuisine – *choucroute garnie* and *tarte flambée* – are on offer in countless traditional wine taverns.

The route commences at **Molsheim** ❷ In the walled city typically preserved with traditional houses, the **Metzig** is a favourite stop. This museum and wine-

"I went on horseback to Saverne, where in fine weather the little friendly place seemed to smile at us most charmingly."

– WOLFGANG VON
GOETHE

BELOW:
view of Saverne.

tasting cellar is in a beautiful Renaissance building adorned with a double staircase and sculpted balconies (open Mar–Oct: Sat, Sun; entrance fee).

Obernai ㉘ is the next stop on the wine road. It is distinguished by a central, covered market-place and an elaborate 16th-century fountain equipped with six buckets. A few miles from the town, on a winding road which leads into the Vosges hills, is **Mont Ste Odile.** From pre-Christian times this spot was both sacred and strategically important, as the 10-km (6-mile) long "pagan wall" attests. This presumably defensive installation continues almost without interruption through the forest, with views towards the remnants of surrounding fortresses. Two chapels remain from the 11th and 12th centuries.

Medieval castles

Of all the castles built along the slopes of the Vosges in the Middle Ages, only ruins remain. The European wars following the Reformation, often using the pretext of religious argument to mask simple territorial desires, ran rampage over Alsace. At Nideck and Schirmeck, as at Obernai and Ribeauvillé, desolated towers and fragmented walls stand lost in the forest. At **Haut-Koenigsbourg,** however, the ruined **château** was completely restored at the beginning of the 20th century by Kaiser Wilhelm II who stayed there. The vision of red roofs stands out against the mountain foliage. This renovation is more of a reproduction of 15th-century military architecture than a restoration.(Open daily; closed public hols; entrance fee).

Sélestat ㉙ is one of the old independent cities of Alsace that grouped together as the Decapole to defend the privileges accorded them by the Holy Roman emperor. A traditional market town right in the middle of Alsace, the city has an

Map on page 218

BELOW: hot day on the Route du Vin.

One of the many traditional wrought-iron shop signs for which Riquewihr, on the Wine Route, is known.

old medieval section including two city gates. The church of **Ste Foy** is of dusky yellow-pink stone with a slightly bulging central hexagonal tower. In the same stone is the Gothic **St Georges**. The city is proud of its **Bibliothèque Humaniste** (open July–Aug: daily; Sept–June: Mon–Sat am; closed public hols; entrance fee), one of the most important cultural treasures of Alsace. It houses the library of Beatus Rhenanus, (1485–1547), a friend of Erasmus and leading light in Sélestat's influential humanist school. Illuminated manuscripts and rare tomes dating back to the 7th century are displayed alongside 15th-century carvings and *faience*.

A shelter for the storks

One of Alsace's most cherished symbols is the stork, who in lore and life nested on chimneys or cartwheels set on a pole for them. By the early 1980s storks were dying out, as few returned from their winter migration to Africa. But now they are being specially bred in enclosures such as the Stork Reintroduction Centre in the **Château de Kintzheim** (open Apr–mid-Nov: daily; entrance fee), part of the **Volerie des Aigles**, dedicated to the protection of the great and rare birds of prey.

From the narrow plain the **Vosges** mountains do indeed form a true "blue line", as the saying goes. The foothills are green, the light green of the vineyards shimmering in the sun. The vines touch the walls of **Ribeauvillé** ❸⓪, in the heart of the wine-growing region. The town is stretched in a band along the Grand Rue, rising through the busy new town (18th century) to the tower guarding the medieval city. While cars continually climb up the main street, the few side-streets are calm with their shaded, beamed houses.

About halfway up, the houses pull back a bit from the street, forming a plaza of several Renaissance stone facades. The curve of an enclosed staircase, a dog's head carved on a beam end, a date set in the lintel over the door, are the details to be admired. At the end of the street an ancient fountain provides a few moments' rest. The perspective continues towards a ruined castle. One of three such châteaux is an hour's walk on the marked path from town. From these high points away from the crowds, there are splendid views both of the valley and the misty peaks above.

In the seemingly endless chain of picturesque towns, **Hunawihr** possesses a stork centre and a fortified church of thick crenellated walls overlooking the valley. The signs indicating **Riquewihr** ❸① are intended for hikers, not for drivers. This, a little medieval townlet, is completely enclosed in its protective walls, leaving at least some of the cars outside. The town is a tourist's heaven. Practically every house is a delight of colours, tiles, balconies and flower boxes. Many have cobbled courtyards multiplying the possibilities of little turrets or intricate woodcarvings. Riquewihr's most distinctive trait is its tradition of shop signs of forged iron, old ones as in the **Postal Museum**, and modern ones in the streets. There are also plenty of wine cellars.

The town of **Kaysersberg** ❸② is one of the most seductive in Alsace. Birthplace of Albert Schweitzer, the old part has the frequent narrow form of the

BELOW:
stork watching at
Mittlebergheim.

region, enhanced by the River Weiss. Near the top of the town, the river traverses a circular plaza united by a fortified bridge and a stone altar, in the shadow of the castle keep perched on the mountain above. The 16th-century houses in narrow alleys are served by Renaissance fountains, although the local wisdom is to prefer wine to water. As well as Schweitzer's house, there is a small museum, **Centre Culturel Albert Schweitzer** (open May–mid-Nov: daily; entrance fee).

Map on page 218

The wines of Alsace

Alsace is synonymous with fruity dry white wine, designated by varietals and not by the land it is grown on. Tiny quantities of red (Tokay) and rosé (Pinot Noir) are produced. Of the seven most common Alsace varietals, the most prestigious are Riesling, Gewürztraminer and Tokay, also called Pinot gris.

These wines have a pleasant immediate flavour, but little depth for savouring, as they are generally young. In the informal taverns known as *winstubs* they are served in attractive glasses with long green stems, and are very popular with fish, seafood and Alsatian specialities such as *tarte flambée*, *choucroute*, *foie gras*, and sweet cheese pie. Among the vineyards are orchards of cherries and plums for the famous "white alcohol" fruit brandies.

Business centre for wine professionals, **Colmar** ㉝ is the second tourist centre of Alsace. The sculptor Bartholdi, creator of the Statue of Liberty, was born here, and his works are prominent in the town's parks. The old town is a large pedestrian zone of irregularly shaped plazas connected by short streets that detour around historic buildings and churches. The **Dominican church** is the site of the altarpiece *Madonna with the Rose Bush* (1473), which hangs in the

The hors d'oeuvre tarte flambée is the Alsatian equivalent of pizza, traditionally made with crème fraîche, cheese and onions, and baked in a wood-fired oven.

BELOW: a street in Colmar.

Map
on page
218

choir, an expressive masterpiece by 15th-century artist Martin Schongauer, a native of Colmar.

The **Musée d'Unterlinden**, exceptional overall, is renowned for the works of Schongauer. Its highlight, however, is the phenomenal **Issenheim altarpiece** by Mathias Grünewald. The central tableau is surrounded by double panels, painted on both surfaces and emitting a strange glow rendering the saints' tortures and monsters as livid and fantastic as science fiction. (Open daily; closed public hols; entrance fee).

The stroll through Colmar leads to the quarter called **La Petite Venise**, in honour of the little River Lauch and adjacent canal where tanners once cleaned their pelts. Here, as throughout the city, the balconies are lined with flowers, and each half-timbered house has an individualistic touch, a gabled turret or unusual sculptures such as the heads on the **Maison des Têtes**. The **Ancienne Douanne** is covered in glazed tiles arranged in patterns of green and yellow.

Skyline drive

Leaving Colmar, the wine route merges with the **Route des Crêtes**, a skyline drive through the highest and most beautiful part of the Vosges. **Munster ❸** with its celebrated cheese is the appropriate gateway to a wealth of farmhouse inns proposing hefty snacks of local cuisine. The little towns of the area have a special homogeneity of high-pitched roofs, red-berried trees and pastoral streams that distinguish them from other regions. Into the Vosges the valley is quickly left behind; a few fields on the first slopes, and then all is pine and oak forest. From the **Schlucht** and **Hohneck** passes, to the **Ballon d' Alsace**, the mountains are on all sides, the grass of the worn peaks yellowing at the end of summer. Snow and skiing are abundant in winter. From the **Grand Ballon**, the area's highest summit, many hikes are possible. At its foot, in **Thann ❸**, the rich flamboyant collegiate church of **St Thiébaut** with its beautiful steeple, is set in the pleasant town. In the former market hall a small **museum** contains native paintings on wood depicting events of local memory (open mid-May–mid-Oct: Tues–Sun; entrance fee).

Mulhouse ❸ is an industrial city whose past as an independent republic has been erased by war bombings. To make up for this lack, it is a city of museums. The unique **Musée de l'Impressionisme sur Etoffe** (open daily; entrance fee) is devoted to techniques and arts of printed cloth and wall paperings. Another legacy of industrial wealth is the **Musée de l'Automobile** (open Wed–Mon; entrance fee), with a spectacular array of over 500 antique and rare cars.

At the fascinating open-air **Ecomusée d'Alsace** (open daily; entrance fee) north of the town, traditional timber-framed houses have been regrouped to form an Alsatian village. A few miles east among electrical installations on the Rhine is a Romanesque marvel, the octagonal church of **Ottmarsheim ❸**. South of Mulhouse is the **Sundgau**, marked by the character of neighbouring Switzerland. In contrast to northern Alsace, the old towns such as **Altkirch ❸**, capital of the Sundgau, present a muted chiaroscuro palette against the backdrop of the forests of the Jura. ❑

RIGHT: typical half-timbered Alsatian home, this one in Itterswiller.
BELOW: La Route des Crêtes.

CADET
ROUSSEL

CITOYEN

CENTRAL FRANCE
AND THE ALPS

The region defined as Central France in this book encompasses Burgundy, the Rhône Valley and Auvergne and the Massif Central; we also include in this chapter the French Alps, which rise up to the east of the Rhône Valley.

Burgundy *(pages 236–244)* is the land of wine, food and dukes which saw itself as the heart of Europe in medieval times. Modern Burgundians believe that paradise begins in the kitchen and ends in the wine cellar, and "better a good meal than fine clothes".The Lyonnais love their food no less than the Burgundians, and Lyon, principal city of the **Rhône Valley** *(pages 249–253)* and second city of France, is a gourmet's paradise, awash with fine restaurants, where the daily rhythm of life centres on meals. Never turning its back on its long and fascinating past, it is today a vibrant, modern city of culture and industry. Traditional crafts also thrive in these regions, but they are of course chiefly known for their superb wines. Wherever you go, you can be sure that there will always be a sympathetic *cave* open for a little wine tasting around the next bend.

If wine is synonymous with Burgundy and the Rhône Valley, water is associated with the rugged high plateau of the **Massif Central** *(pages 261–268)*, where the spa towns of Vichy and Volvic produce some of France's finest. Although in the very heart of France, the **Auvergne**, hoisted high on the Massif plateau as it is, has rarely seized centre stage. This is a land of untouched towns, thermal spas, and shepherds, peacefully isolated in their precipitous valleys.

In days gone by, the higher passes of the **French Alps** *(pages 254–259)*, dominated by Mont Blanc, the highest peak in Europe, were almost deserted when the winter weather closed in; now the more remote the valley, the more likely it is to ring with the delighted or despairing shrieks of skiers. Lower down, there are landmarks aplenty: Briançon, highest town in Europe, the monastery of Chartreuse, and of course Geneva and its elegant lake. ❏

PRECEDING PAGES: Alpine bar with a view of the glacier at Chamonix.
LEFT: Auxerre figurine.

Map on page 238

BURGUNDY

The "heart of France" is an opulent province, blessed with glorious architecture, bastions of gastronomy, world-renowned vineyards and a beautiful, lush landscape

Less than an hour from the roar of Paris traffic, the calm, bright Burgundian countryside has come as a welcome surprise to more than one visitor travelling south from the French capital. North of Dijon, where the powerful dukes of Burgundy (Handsome Philippe or Charles the Bold) controlled an immense kingdom, the Yonne river winds its way to Sens through a peaceful valley where ancient glory still clings to the unpretentious Burgundian farmland.

Gothic splendour

Up to 1622 the Archbishop of **Sens ❶** lorded over an area extending all the way to Paris. His palatial lodgings, **Palais Synodal** (open Wed–Mon; closed public hols; entrance fee) are still an impressive site. They now house a museum devoted to local history with rooms showing a variety of *objets* dating from the Bronze Age to 18th-century artwork.

The **Cathédrale St Etienne** was the first in France to be built in the Gothic manner. Construction began in the 12th century and work was not completed until 500 years later. In the course of time, this monumental structure was embellished with intricate sculpture, high arches and an impressive series of stained-glass windows. In the adjoining buildings, the **Trésor de la Cathédrale St Etienne** (open June–Sept: daily; Oct–May: Mon, Thur, Fri pm; closed public hols; entrance fee) is remarkable for rare liturgical garments.

Auxerre ❷, the immemorial capital of northwestern Burgundy, resounds with history, being one of the oldest cities in France. Renaissance houses follow a semi-circular pattern around the 15th-century **Tour de l'Horloge** which once guarded the ramparts. The unusual clock has two dials, one for the time and the other for tracking the movement of the sun and stars. Two churches rival one another for attention. The **Cathédrale St Etienne** is recognised by the sharp slope of its asymmetric facade. The medieval sense of Christianity is vivid in this church, from the tympanum's three-tiered life of Christ, to the red and blue lives of the saints depicted in stained glass. The abbey church dedicated to **St Germain**, also Gothic, is built on an extraordinary hive of underground chapels. Parts of the church date from the time of Charlemagne and the **frescoes of St Stephen** go back to AD 850, the oldest in France.

Southwest of Auxerre, the spires adorning the brick and stone **Château de St Fargeau ❸** (open Apr–Nov; entrance fee) appear like minarets on the horizon. This is where the *Grande Mademoiselle,* Louis XIV's sister, once lived. Dating from the 15th century, the château was renovated in the mid-17th century by Le Vau, the architect of Versailles.

BELOW: bucolic Burgundy countryside.

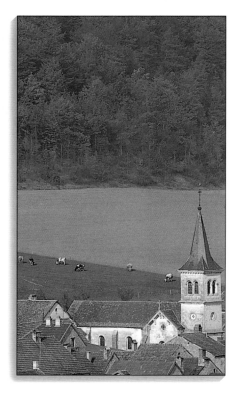

Many of the rooms have been restored to their original splendour and every summer the grounds are the site of historical re-enactments that trace the history of France from the Hundred Years' War to the liberation of Paris in World War II.

La Puisaye

St Fargeau is situated in an area known as **La Puisaye**. This is rural Burgundy at its best. The hills shimmer in the early afternoon heat and tall trees line the banks of rivers such as the Loing. Gentle and watery, it is a perfect region to explore by bicycle or on foot. The area's most famous native daughter is Colette (1873–1953) whose writings remain popular in France and whose birthplace can be seen in Rue des Vignes in the centre of the little town of **St Sauveur-en-Puisaye ❹**.

Through a network of farm towns, each nonchalantly raising its church steeple, the back roads can, with some determination, be made to lead to **Ratilly ❺**. Here the superbly restored 13th-century **Château de Ratilly** (open June–Oct: daily; Oct–June: Mon–Sat; entrance fee) lies hidden in a brambly wood. From the outside it seems like nothing but towers, but just inside the arched entry a cheerful grassy courtyard opens onto a pottery school.

From Pontigny to Montréal, the **Serein** (Serene) **river valley** is a quiet haven that merits its name. A major attraction is the small town of **Chablis ❻** not because it is of any particular architectural interest but because of its world-famous vineyards, stitched like quilts over the hills. Upstream, cradled in a bend of the river, the little town of **Noyers ❼** has preserved all the charm of its history. The rampart wall is guarded by no fewer than 16 towers circling the arcades of the central square.

"A solemn house… that smiled only on its garden side…. Both house and garden are still living, I know; but what of that if the magic has deserted them?"
— COLETTE

BELOW: afternoon on the Burgundy Canal.

Chalis for sale.

Canal country

Beyond the Chablis vineyards is the **Canal du Bourgogne** ❽. Part of a countrywide network of waterways built for freight (*see page 237*), the canal is now increasingly used by houseboats, and barges are rented by vacationers looking for a novel way to visit this part of France. Just the width of a single *péniche* (barge), the narrow channel is equipped with locks and wider basins for crossing traffic. Once on a canal, the rest of the world ceases to exist and one can drift down the tranquil waters visiting châteaux from **Tonnerre** to Bussy-Rabutin.

Named after its 17th-century owner, the **Château de Bussy-Rabutin** is Burgundy's most absorbing stately home. It was rebuilt in 1649 by Roger de Bussy-Rabutin, who was banished to the country by Louis XIV for his satirical commentaries on court affairs. In exile, he decorated the house with contemporary portraits: there are 25 women onlookers in his bedchamber, including Mesdames de Sévigné and Maintenon (open Wed–Mon; entrance fee.)

Passed along the way between Tonnerre and Bussy-Rabutin, the Renaissance

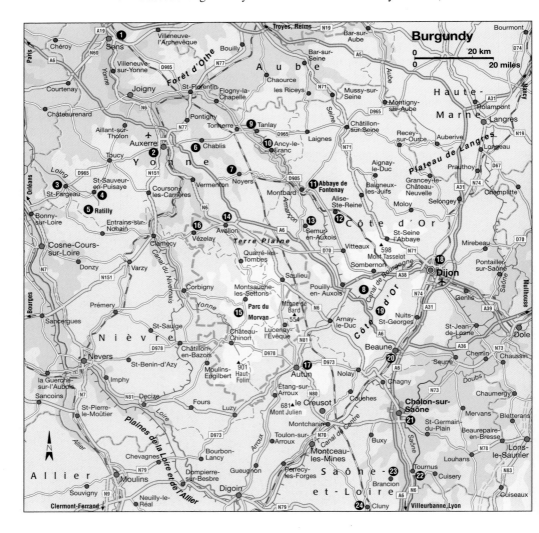

Château de Tanlay ❾ (open Apr–mid-Nov: Wed–Mon; entrance fee) is a magnificent sight ensconced as it is in a series of moats, arcades and iron grilles. Another château gem, **Ancy-le-Franc** ❿ (open Apr–mid-Nov: daily; entrance fee) presents an austerely symmetrical exterior, but the inner courtyard and furnishings are of sumptuous splendour inspired by the Italian Renaissance.

Founded by Saint Bernard, the **Abbaye de Fontenay** ⓫ is Burgundy's most complete ensemble of life in a medieval monastery. Solitary and independent at the bottom of a remote valley, all the buildings used when the abbey housed an active community of monks have been preserved. The church and cloister are examples of Cistercian simplicity; intended to be piously modest, without ornamentation of any kind, the bare paving stones and immaculate columns have acquired, in the course of time, a look of grandeur (open daily; entrance fee).

The defeat of Vercingetorix

Just south of Fontenay is the site of a battle decisive in French history and of which it has been rather dramatically stated "It is here that Gaul died and France was born." Mont Auxois, above the village of **Alise-Ste Reine** ⓬ is generally accepted as the site of the battle of Alésia, where the Gauls under Vercingetorix were defeated by Julius Caesar. A monumental statue of Vercingetorix overlooks the Gallo-Roman city where excavations have been under way since 1906. Among the foundations uncovered are those of an early Christian church dedicated to the martyred Reine. Objects from the site are on display at the **Musée Alésia** (open Apr–Oct: daily; entrance fee).

Travelling west, one arrives in **Semur-en-Auxois** ⓭, which still retains the flavour of a medieval fortress town, guarded by imposing dungeon towers that

Map on page 238

Vercingetorix, immortalised by sculptor Aimé Millet, surveys the battlefield.

BELOW: produce from Burgundy.

BURGUNDIAN CUISINE

The people of Burgundy's near-religious devotion to food is long-established. To prove that the high quality of the region's cuisine is a result of their innate understanding of food, Burgundians will point to ancient culinary inscriptions in the Dijon archaeological museum and tell of their dukes, whose kitchens were vast and whose meals took on the aura of religious ceremonies, with hand-held torches escorting dishes to the duke's table, and pointed allusions to the sacramental properties of bread and wine.

Dijon's two main culinary specialities, mustard and *pain d'épice*, both have long historical associations, as do some of the great cheeses of the region: Chaource and the marc-washed Epoisses were first made in the abbeys of Pontigny and Fontenay, while the delicately-flavoured Cîteaux is still only made in its eponymous monastery. Yet it is not only tradition, but the quality and variety of the local ingredients which shape Burgundian cooking.

Wild produce is prized: crayfish, snails, boar, quail, thrushes and woodland mushrooms, while the famed Bresse chickens are reared on a special diet. Then there are the charcuterie from Morvan, pork dishes such as *jambon persillé*, *gougère* made with cheese, kidneys with mustard, and the great stews, liberally doused in red wine.

Christ in Majesty: detail of the tympanum at Vézélay.

BELOW: a fête in Dijon's Place François Rude.

overlook the peaceful Armançon river and the Pont July which crosses it. The eclectic church of **Notre Dame** (1218) offends purists but delights others. Beyond Semur lies **Epoisses**, less known for its medieval **château** and Renaissance houses than for its cheese. Creamy, pungent and soft, its orange rind is washed with brandy (*marc de Bourgogne*) as it matures in the cellars. It's the region's most famous cheese and *must* be tried with a glass of red Burgundy wine.

The Black Mountains

A town of parks and cosy old houses, **Avallon** ⑭ is the gateway to the **Parc Régional de Morvan** ⑮. These first spurs of the **Massif Central** are covered with dense forests, hence the Celtic name *Morvan*, meaning "Black Mountain". Once an inaccessible back-country derided by its richer neighbours, the **Morvan** is now a favoured weekend retreat. Fast streams churning in narrow gorges provide excellent fishing and canoeing. Although not very high above sea level, the landscape gives an impression of mountains, with sheer drops and clefts.

Set on a high hilltop, **Vézelay** ⑯ offers a splendid view of the countryside and is one of Burgundy's most spectacular monuments. The majestic **Basilique Ste Madeleine** was founded in the 9th century as an abbey, and it was here that Bernard of Clairvaux launched the Second Crusade in 1146. The presence of Mary Magdalene's supposed relics in the basilica made Vézelay a place of pilgrimage. A winding road climbs through the town to the basilica, a spiritual journey. Clustered in the shadowy penumbra of the narthex, medieval pilgrims could ponder the mysteries of the magnificent tympanum before flooding into the uplifting nave, flanked by black and white arches.

From the **Mont Beuvray**, an ancient wooded plateau, there's a splendid view

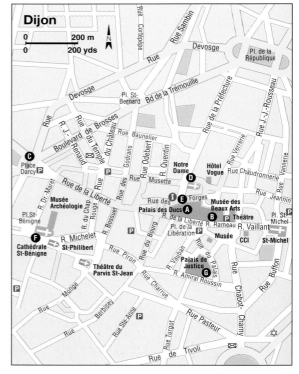

east over the soft contours of the vineyards toward **Autun** ⓱. This town, which celebrated its bi-millennial in 1985, has been an administrative centre ever since Augustus defeated the Gauls. Traces still remain of the Roman roads that led to the town and the quadruple-arched gates of this small provincial city bear witness to its imperial past. The **amphitheatre**, the largest in Roman Gaul, held up to 15,000 spectators. Medieval prosperity left behind the **Cathédrale St Lazare**, whose white sculpted doorway contrasts with the more rustic rock of the church itself. Opposite is the **Musée Rolin** (open Wed–Mon; entrance fee) where it is hard to choose between the seven rooms of Gallo-Roman archaeology and the collections of medieval painting and sculpture. Behind the cathedral the remaining ramparts make a lovely stroll to the ancient Ursulines' keep.

Northeast of Autun is the undisputed capital of Burgundy, **Dijon** ⓲. The many old buildings are in the active city centre, particularly the monumental **Palais des Ducs** Ⓐ. Arched passageways give access to its spacious courtyards where the light colour of the wide, regular paving stones echoes the pale facades.

The **Musée des Beaux Arts** Ⓑ, one of the finest in France, is housed in the oldest part of the palace where French, German and Italian statuary and art from the 14th to 18th centuries are on display. Much of the vast collection, the most significant outside Paris, was acquired during the Revolution from the homes of local nobility, as well as churches and monasteries. The **Salle des Gardes** contains the museum's most famous tombstones, of three members of the ducal dynasty, sculpted in alabaster and black marble. The 14th-century **kitchen** has six gargantuan fireplaces an enduring reminder of the splendour of banquets in times past (open Wed–Mon; closed public hols; entrance fee.)

A circular stroll from the palace to the **Place Darcy** Ⓒ and back takes in the

Maps:
Area 238
City 240

The first recorded mention of mustard in Burgundy was at a banquet for Philip VI, when, according to the account book, 66 gallons were consumed.

BELOW:
Dijon rooftops.

Nicéphore Niepce (1765–1833), who was born in Chalon-sur-Saône, is the much neglected inventor of photography.

BELOW: up to no good.

old quarter with its malls and tiny plazas. **Notre Dame D** is a 13th-century Gothic church full of delightful curiosities, such as the family of figures animated by a clock mechanism. Idiosyncratic old facades line the narrow streets only a few feet from the church walls. Along the pedestrian shopping streets, elegant boutiques and antique shops have taken up residence with lustrous, low-beamed ceilings and sculptures decorating the upper floors. The **Rue des Forges E** was, until the 18th century, the main street of Dijon, named after the goldsmiths, jewellers and knife-makers who had their workshops there. The **Hôtel Chambellan** which houses the tourist office, is the most striking of a series of Renaissance residences which line the street, with elaborate balconies and staircases hidden away in interior courtyards. Further to the west, **Cathédrale St Bénigne F**, which houses the Archaeological Museum, draws the eye with its tall spire and multicoloured octagonal towers. Coming full circle, the **Palais de Justice G** and its neighbourhood are reminiscent of the days when the provincial parliament officiated under the painted and wainscoted ceilings.

Before leaving Dijon, be sure to sample the famous *pain d'épice* (a honey sweetened, anis-flavoured cake/bread) and purchase a jar of the pungent mustard that has been produced here for more than 600 years.

Hills of Gold

What name is more evocative than that of the *département* in which all the great vineyards are located, **Côte d'Or ⑲**, the "Hills of Gold". Some say the name comes from the gold-coloured leaves that cover the hills in autumn, while others maintain that it is from the great wines or "bottled gold" they produce. No matter, the hills are beautiful and the wines excellent.

The vineyards are quite easy to visit since most of them line the western edge of the N74 that runs from Dijon to Chalon-sur-Saône. Here, the names of the towns evoke great vintages: Gevrey Chambertin, Vougeot, Vosne-Romanée, Nuits-St-Georges, Aloxe-Corton, Beaune, Pommard. Sometimes one is invited to stop and sample the wine. You will be expected to buy if you decide to taste.

Map on page 238

Travelling the Wine Route

One of the largest vineyards, the **Clos de Vougeot**, is set back from the road roughly mid-way between Dijon and Beaune. It was nurtured by the Cistercians, who greatly contributed to the development of vineyards on lands bequeathed to the order founded by Saint Bernard in **Cîteaux**, to the southeast. The small **château** of the Clos, built to house wine presses, is also the home of the Chevaliers du Tastevin, a society of connoisseurs whose prizes are coveted.

Directly south of Vougeot is **Beaune ⑳**, where the jewel-like roof of the **Hôtel-Dieu** made of multicoloured tiles can be seen glimmering in the distance as one approaches. Since the 18th century, Beaune has been the heart of the Burgundian wine trade, and the auction of the *Hospices de Beaune* in the Hôtel-Dieu, a charity hospital historically supported by the wine produced on lands donated by benefactors, is still the high point in the local wine calendar.

Under its splendid multicoloured roof, the long ward contains the original sick beds. The halls off the courtyard house a collection of art work and tapestry crowned by a painting of the *Last Judgment* by Roger Van der Weyden so detailed it requires a magnifying glass (open daily; entrance fee).

The wine culture in Beaune is all-pervasive. Every other shop peddles if not wine, then books on wine, cellar equipment or wine glasses; every other café or

Burgundy has a larger concentration of Michelin-starred restaurants than any other part of France except Paris, with no fewer than four ranking three stars.

BELOW: original sick beds in the Hôtel-Dieu, Beaune.

Map on page 238

restaurant proclaims its loyalty to the vinous tradition. The big Beaune *négociants,* dominant here for 300 years, lure tourists into their cellars with offers of free tastings. But what comes out of the bottle may bear little relation to what the label advertises. The **Musée du Vin de Bourgogne** (open daily; entrance fee) can be found in the Hôtels des Ducs de Bourgogne, on Rue d'Enfer.

Beyond Beaune are the villages that produce the Burgundy whites. These humble stone cottages hardly suggest that here are some of the most sought-after vineyards in the world. It is here the Chardonnay grape is at its best and the names of Meursault and Montrachet are synonymous with excellence.

Approaching **Chalon-sur-Saône** ㉑, vineyards are few and far between. Although an industrial centre today, half-timbered houses still crowd around the **Cathédrale St Vincent** in the old quarter of town. Chalon is also the birthplace of Nicéphore Niepce, the inventor of photography, and has a museum dedicated to him and the history of photography.

Small towns and great churches

Further south in the Saône valley, **Tournus** ㉒ is the remarkably quiet site of one of Burgundy's greatest Romanesque churches. **St Philibert** owes its special beauty to the unretouched surface of its small irregular stones. The exterior, with a square tower and almost no decoration, has a forbidding military appearance. Inside, massive columns of the same yellow stone carry three parallel systems of arches. This austerity is the hallmark of the church, cloister and surrounding monastery buildings (11th–12th century). Old streets lead to the river and from the bridge there's a splendid view of the church and its buildings.

Perched on a narrow crest of rock, **Brancion** ㉓ is a feudal burg delightful to visit. Above the old quarter of the church and marketplace is the crumbling but proud château, one of the few such examples in Burgundy where the dukes' power countered individual fiefdoms.

The Burgundy of the Middle Ages was marked by the great monastic orders whose fervour and ramified organisation revived a spiritual life while greatly affecting the politics of Christian Europe. The Benedictine rule radiated from **Cluny** ㉔, where the abbots were on equal footing with the Pope until, in the 12th century, the monk Bernard launched a purifying reform, the Cistercian order, named after its headquarters in Cîteaux.

The remains of the Cluny monastery, the **Ancienne Abbaye St Pierre et St Paul**, founded in 910, only faintly suggest the secular and spiritual power of this order, whose abbots reigned for life. Five of 15 guard towers remain. The church that was for five centuries the largest of all Christendom was almost entirely destroyed after the French Revolution, leaving a small group of chapels and spires. The cloister, built in the 18th century, was luckier, and the whole immense ensemble can be admired from the central gardens (open daily; closed public hols; entrance fee).

The town's museum, **Musée Ochier** (Palais Jean de Bourbon; open daily; closed public hols; entrance fee) offers an overall view of the dramatic rise and fall of Cluny. ❑

RIGHT: glass pageantry from St Seine l'Abbaye.
BELOW: the south tower at Cluny.

SANCTUS : EGIDIUS

THE GOLDEN AGE OF CANALS

The commercial heyday of the canals was the 19th century. Since then, working barges have given way to pleasure boats.

The French network of canals began during the reign of Plantagenet Henry II. Later, Henri IV (1589–1610) created a canal system which linked the Loire with the Seine and the Saone with the Rhone, to provide a flowing highway from the Channel to the Mediterranean. The Canal de Briare, created 1604–42, was one of the first in the kingdom, and work continued during Louis XIV's reign. The canals represent notable technical achievements of their day: the Canal du Midi passes 115 locks and the first canal tunnel ever built; at Agen a flight of four locks signals a dramatic 23-arched aqueduct crossing the Garonne. At Pouilly-en-Auxois in Burgundy, the canal disappears underground for 3 km (5 miles), an engineering feat that pre-dates Brunel.

CROSSING THE LANDSCAPE

Although the initial climatic contrast is between the lush northern canals and sun-baked southern ones, more subtle regional variations can be seen across the network. In Aquitaine, canal banks are planted with poplars and willows, in Languedoc, with pines and mulberries. In the south, oaks, elms and limes were planted to prevent the banks drying out; in the Mediterranean cypress and olive trees thrive. The Canal du Nivernais crosses cheese and wine country and is the least spoilt canal in northern France. The Canal du Midi embraces Cathar country and the Camargue. It forms part of the Canal des Deux Mers, linking the Atlantic and the Mediterranean, and has been a UNESCO world heritage site since 1996.

▷ **GOLD COAST**
Canal de Bourgogne, Curgey, on Burgundy's Côte d'Or. Acting as a watery crossroads, Burgundian canals link northern and southern France.

△ **BRIDGEWORK**
Pont Paul Bert, in Auxerre, a Burgundian backwater. The successful advent of the railways in the 19th century spelt the end of commercial river navigation all over the country.

△ **BARGING IN**
Commercial barges have priority. Locks can be manual, automatic or operated by lock-keepers.

◁ **AQUATIC FLIGHT**
The canal and locks at Rogny-les-Sept-Ecluses, overlooking Briare's flight of seven locks.

CANAL CRUISING

The French waterways offer an array of possibilities, from narrow boats to cabin cruisers and floating hotels. Apart from the famous *bateaux-mouches* along the Seine in Paris, there are short city cruises in Strasbourg and Colmar in Alsace. Real canal-lovers can choose between houseboats (*bateaux habitables*), *péniches* and *pénichettes* (narrow boats). *Péniches* act as floating hotels with attentive crews and dinner on board. As well as standard narrow boats, the Canal du Midi offers short pleasure cruises in a *gabarre*, a replica of the traditional canal boat that once plied the waterways. For those still enamoured of boats, canoing, sailing and water-skiing can be enjoyed in lakes and rivers close to many canals.

There are canal-cruising opportunities in Alsace, Champagne, Burgundy, the Loire, Poitou-Charente, Ardeche, the Dordogne, Aquitaine, the Midi-Pyrenees and Languedoc. Cruises along canals in the Loire, Burgundy, Bordeaux and the Midi can be combined with wine-tasting tours. Cruises from Avignon to Chateauneuf-du-Pape, for example, include visits to vineyards. For land-lovers, cycle routes often run parallel to the canals.

◁ **EIFFEL TOUR**
The Briare canal aqueduct (1897) across the Loire is a 610-metre (2,000-ft) Art Nouveau construction designed by Gustave Eiffel of tower fame. It is open to cyclists, pedestrians, pleasure boats and yachts.

▷ **ALL ABOARD**
Now almost commercially redundant, the future of the French waterways is pleasure cruising.

◁ **CAPITAL HIGHWAY**
Canal de Bourgogne, designed to link Paris and Dijon, was begun in 1775 but only completed in 1833.

▷ **LOCKED IN**
A lock-keeper's cottage, Canal du Nivernais. Those on the Canal du Midi are generally older, dating from the 17th century.

THE RHONE VALLEY

*On its journey from the Alps to the Mediterranean,
the mighty Rhône flows through Lyon, France's vibrant second city,
a modern metropolis with a long history*

Map on page 250

Mâcon ❶ marks a transition. Straddling the borderline between Burgundy and the Lyonnais, it is the frontier between northern pointed roofs of slate, and the southern, red, rounded Roman tile. Just outside the city are the Pouilly-Fuissé vineyards. This celebrated white Burgundy wine has a bouquet combining a smoky, dry sensation with a rich taste, making it a sought-after delicacy.

The massive **Roche de Solutré** rears above the wavy line of hills like a listing ocean liner, giving its name to Solutrean Stone Age civilisations. Prehistoric man used this cliff as a hunting ground, herding deer and wild horses towards the summit and then frightening them into jumping over the edge. The bone yard below extends over 4,000 sq. m (almost an acre). The panorama, as one walks up the slope, encompasses the black and yellow patchwork of surrounding hills.

Beaujolais Nouveau

Like taciturn troops guarding the vineyards, the **Monts du Beaujolais** are covered with sombre chestnut and pine forests, and there is a local wood industry. The bell-shaped vines reach high up the slopes, as do the typical farmhouses, with living quarters over the cellar. Technically part of the Burgundy wine region – the ten *crus* have the right to use "Burgundy" on their label – all Beaujolais is made from the Gamay grape as distinct from Burgundy's Pinot Noir. Only Beaujolais Nouveau is produced by accelerated fermentation, and should be drunk within a few months. Normally fermented Beaujolais, produced in 35 villages, is best after two years.

The grapes are harvested in October and the first tastings take place before the end of the month. In **Juliénas** the wine cellar is in a long disused church. At the **Château de Corcelles** the former guard room is now a tasting room. **Belleville** ❷ is the commercial centre of an area where the most serious wine-makers work at improving the quality of the traditional Beaujolais. The Beaujolais Nouveau "season" opens with a media bang in mid-November – the third Thursday of the month, to be precise – just a few weeks after the grapes have been harvested. At midnight preceding the date set for the first sale, luxury sports cars and private planes rev their engines for the race to be the first to bring the year's vintage to London, Dublin, or New York.

On the opposite bank of the Saône is a land of solid farm traditions, whose products are the basis of the city-dweller's cuisine. **La Ferme de la Forêt** in **Courtes** (open July–mid-Sept: daily; Easter–June, mid-Sept–Oct: Sat, Sun, public hols) is a farm museum, where all activities were concentrated in a

LEFT: poet from Pérouges.
BELOW: sample ware from Pérouges.

Sample some regional products along the way.

single building combining stable, tool shed and dwelling. The "Saracen" chimney topped by a cowl is just one of the signs of the **Bresse** region. The rustic building materials and wood furniture used by generations of the same family are now relics, emblems of a lifestyle that died out in the 1950s.

Poultry specialists

Bourg-en-Bresse ❸ is the capital of a region with a thriving speciality in farm-fattened chickens and capons. At the weekly poultry market thousands, specially prepared in a milk bath after slaughtering, are snapped up by professional buyers. On the outskirts of town the church of **Brou** is a splendid jewel of the Flamboyant Gothic style. It was commissioned by Archduchess Marguerite of Savoy, as a memorial to her husband, who died in 1504, aged 24. Inside, the triple-arched rood screen, one of the few left in France, which separates the nave from the choir, is famous for its beautiful stone lattice-work. Seventy-four monks' stalls intricately carved in dark oak line the entry to the choir. Finest of all the marble sculptures are those of the three royal tombs in the

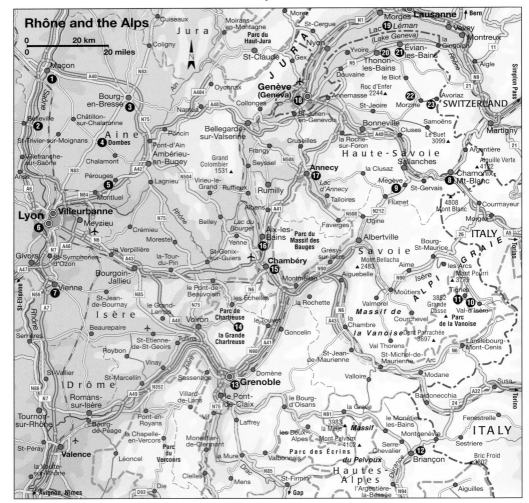

choir itself, exquisitely carved with small statuettes and life-size figures of the noble family. Southwest of Bourg-en-Bresse is the **Dombes** ❹, a marshy plateau with more than 100 lakes, most artificial. Large sectors are private hunting grounds, with waterfowl and fish. A system of channels and sluices drains water from one lake to another, for the traditional land use rotating fish to grain crop.

After the sparse waterscape, **Pérouges** ❺ is a return to urban bustle, that of the Middle Ages. The entire town is medieval in character, and thrives on its past. Saved from destruction in the early 20th century, the houses and ramparts have been conscientiously restored and marvellously adapted to modern ideas of space and light. The stone-paved streets encourage a snail's pace ideal for looking into a crooked passageway or window shopping in the boutiques devoted to traditional Bresse crafts, such as blue Meillonas ceramics.

Lyon

The high-speed TGV arrives at the central Perrache station, a unique causeway of ramps and escalators leading directly into **Lyon** ❻. Central Lyon, with the Rhône on one side and the Saône on the other, is compact and ideal for visiting on foot.

Perhaps the most unusual of Lyon's many museums is the **Musée Historique des Tissus** Ⓐ which covers the development of textile techniques in all ages and from all over the world, and displays some of the rarest and most beautiful materials ever made (34 Rue de la Charité; open Tues–Sun; closed public hols; entrance fee). The **Musée des Arts Décoratifs** Ⓑ is close by (30 Rue de la Charité; open Tues–Sun; closed public hols; entrance fee). The newly restored **Musée des Beaux Arts** Ⓒ ranks next in importance to the Louvre with a col-

| Maps: |
| Area 250 |
| City 253 |

TIP

Much Beaujolais Nouveau is poor quality. When buying, steer clear of all but the most reliable *négociants* (Pierre Ferraud, Louis Tête, Georges Duboeuf).

BELOW:
Brou church.

A transport and communications hub, and host city for many conventions and exhibitions, Lyon is a mere two hours' journey from Paris by TGV (Train à Grand Vitesse).

lection of French and European paintings (Palais St Pierre, 20 Place des Terreaux; open Wed–Sun; closed public hols; entrance fee). Lyon was the first town to have a stock exchange and first to issue a cheque and the **Musée de l'Imprimerie** (13 Rue de la Poulaillerie; open Wed–Sun; closed public hols; entrance fee) outlines the history of European commerce, as well as holding a collection of rare books. A new **Musée d'Art Contemporain** has opened in the **Internationale Cité** on Quai Charles de Gaulle (open daily; entrance fee).

Gastronomic capital

Lyon is the undisputed gastronomic capital of France. As in Burgundy (*see page 239*) food is a science and an art, even a religion. The city is stuffed with fine restaurants, and regional specialities abound: *rosette* and *Jésus* salamis, pâté cooked in pastry, *quenelles de brochet* (poached mousse of pike), *coq au vin* (using *poulet de Bresse*), freshwater crayfish. The daily rhythm of life centres on meals, and where food is concerned the Lyonnais housewife does not mess around. The mid-morning *mâchon*, specifically Lyonnais, is no snack but a meal of *charcuterie,* which might include sausages and *rosette* salamis as well as stuffed hocks and hams. Traditional meal times are strictly observed, and after these hours nothing is left in the kitchen. In a city renowned for hearty home cooking, a missed meal is a real loss.

Along the Saône, a tree-lined *quai* extends a view over the wide water, with some bridges painted red. On the opposite bank lies the city's oldest quarter, **Vieux Lyon** . The restoration of the medieval and Renaissance quarters started some years ago. Typically the Renaissance houses were built round a courtyard, reached from the street through a vaulted passage beneath a house. In each street a few courtyards had another vaulted passage at the back leading into the next street. These public passages, still in use, are called *traboules*.

A walk offers many discoveries. From the Rue Saint Jean to the Place du Change, and on to the Place du St Paul, back down the Rue Juiverie and then the Rue Gadagne, is less than a kilometre altogether. The **Hôtel de Gadagne** is the finest Renaissance mansion in Lyon. It now houses the **Musée Historique de Lyon** and the **Musée de la Marionnette**, a special collection of puppets from all over the world (open Wed–Mon; closed public hols; entrance fee). The **Cathédrale St Jean** dates from the 11th to the 14th centuries. It contains a remarkable 14th-century astronomical clock, still in working order. At midday, one, two and three pm bells ring, cocks crow, doors open and puppet figures come out and mime the Annunciation. The clock was designed to mark religious feast days right up until the year 2019.

Above Lyon

The **Fourvière Hill** is reachable on foot by steep *montées,* or by funicular cable cars. It is topped by a rococo **Basilique de Notre-Dame** and a terrace overlooking the city. On the southern slope, the **Musée de la Civilisation Gallo-Romaine** (open Wed–Sun; closed public hols; entrance fee) is an orig-

BELOW: a proud chef with some local delicacies.

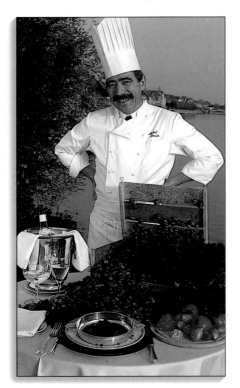

inal building eminently well-conceived. Built into the hill, from the upper entry a spiral ramp glides gently down through artifacts such as a chariot wheel, or a bronze Neptune. Windows look out onto two **Théâtres Romains** ❾ still used for performances.

The other hill rising between the two rivers is **La Croix Rousse,** bastion of the *Canuts,* skilled workers in silk-weaving for generations. From the 15th century to the Industrial Revolution thousands of small workshops painstakingly produced the richly coloured silks. A handful of stubborn craftsmen have maintained the tradition, furnishing the museums and palaces of Europe with the brocades of a bygone era. **La Maison des Canuts** ❿ (10–12 Rue d'Ivry; open Mon–Sat;Aug: Tues–Sat; closed public hols; entrance fee) gives demonstrations on different types of looms and patterns. From the **Place Bellevue,** a maze of passages and courtyards winds down to the **Hôtel de Ville** ⓛ. Behind is the dramatic modern steel-and-glass addition to the **Opéra de Lyon** ⓜ.

Gateway to Provence

The Rhône valley, gateway to Provence, is best seen off the main routes. **Vienne** ❼ is full of the echo of its distant glory as a Roman and then episcopal city. Its restored **Théâtre Romain** is used for performances in summer. The **Temple d'Auguste et Livie** is, with the Maison Carrée at Nîmes, the best example of a Roman temple surviving in France. The **Cathédrale de St Maurice,** built from the 11th to the 16th centuries, has a facade with three portals carved in the Flamboyant style, still remarkable though its statues were removed during the Wars of Religion. Across the river at **St Roman-en-Gal** a Roman suburb of Vienne has been excavated. Mosaics are shown in a small museum. ❑

Maps:
Area 250
Lyon 253

Lyon's first residents, who settled on Fourvière hill, arrived 600 years before the Roman occupation. The medieval city grew up alongside the Saône.

BELOW: mushroom gatherer, Rhône Valley.

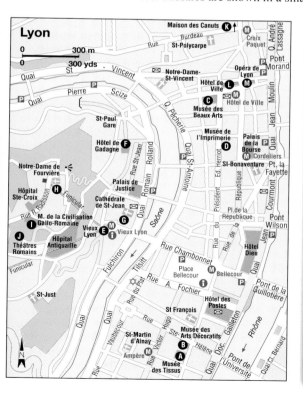

Map on page 250

THE FRENCH ALPS

A paradise for skiers and walkers, the old regions of Savoie and Dauphiné roll south from Geneva and its elegant lake across snow-capped mountains, including magnificent Mont Blanc

Any account of the French Alps should start with **Mont Blanc**, the highest mountain in Europe at 4,800 m (15,780 ft), which rises above the border town of **Chamonix** ❽. Regarded from any viewpoint, with its notable broad shoulders, the mountain is deservedly famous.

At the top, the great chains of the Alps, stretching from Italy to Austria, seem like tiny mountain ridges far below. In the spring, accomplished climbers and guides, with a bit of luck, climb the mountain during two days on their skis and spend their final night two hours from the summit. Then they go to sleep just as new snow begins to fall. The next morning they climb to the summit in the very early hours, and then spend the entire day skiing all the way back down to Chamonix in fresh deep powder snow.

Mont Blanc comes down upon Chamonix in the form of the **Bossons Glacier**, which may be seen quite closely at the entrance to the **Mont Blanc Tunnel**. At 11.5 km (7 miles), it was the longest road tunnel in the world until 1978, and at its highest point, the tunnel's roof reaches nearly 2,470 m (8,100 ft) in altitude. The tunnel links Chamonix to the Italian resort of **Courmayeur**, which is now less than 20 km (12 miles) away.

The tourist can take the same trip to Italy and return via the spectacular cable-car network which goes up from Chamonix to the **Aiguille de Midi** (3,800 km/12,500 ft), traverses the top of the famous **Vallée Blanche** spring ski run and the **Géant Glacier** to the **Pointe Helbronner** where hundreds of year-round skiers may be found, and then descends to the village of **Entrèves**, near Courmayeur. The trip is one of the most spectacular, if somewhat harrowing, voyages of its kind in the world. For the more sedentary, a train goes up from Chamonix to **Montenvers** with a view onto the end of the Vallée Blanche and the **Mer de Glace** (Sea of Ice).

In truth, cowbells are heard no more in the Chamonix region. The town has become a fully-fledged tourist resort year round, and the pastures and herds of cattle have been replaced by hotels, swimming pools and restaurants. In its centre, however, like most Alpine resorts, it remains an old-fashioned mountain town, with a sophisticated international clientele.

St Tropez of the Alps

Not far from Chamonix is **Megève** ❾, the "St Tropez of the Alps". Like Gstaad in Switzerland, Megève is frequented by the rich and famous. It is also a summer resort set in pine forests, with foothills and mountain streams, that has retained its alpine charm. This old village with turreted houses has a very famous ski school.

The hometown of famed French skier Jean-Claude

BELOW: Alpine splendour.

Killy, **Val-d'Isère** ❿ constitutes for many the finest ski area in all of Europe, together with the more recently developed **Tignes** ⓫. The trails go up to 3,750 m (12,300 ft) and, as in Chamonix, skiing continues all year long. From both Megève and Val-d'Isère are splendid views of the French and Italian faces of Mont Blanc. It is said that in Val-d'Isère-Tignes you can ski for a week without taking the same lift twice.

In the summer, Val-d'Isère is a tourist centre near the **Parc National de la Vanoise**, one of the more important reserves of Alpine flora and fauna, well worth the visit by cablecar up to **Mont Bochor** (2,070 m/6,650 ft). Footpaths for properly equipped hikers lead through wild and spectacular domains.

Further to the south is **Briançon** ⓬, a military town and home of the *Chasseur Alpin,* the French army's mountain brigade. At 1,320 m (4,334 ft) it is the highest town in Europe. Another ancient Alpine place, with narrow streets and wooden balconies, it is the gateway to the valley of **La Vallouise** and the **Parc National des Écrins**, the largest of the six French national parks. Dominated by its fortress, the old part of town remains much as it was in the time of Louis XIV. Narrow streets make automobile traffic virtually (blessedly!) impossible.

The fauna in Vanoise includes chamoix, marmot, blue hare and the splendidly horned Alpine ibex, once almost extinct but now numbering over 500.

Grenoble

The big city of the French Alps is **Grenoble** ⓭, birthplace of Stendhal, author of *The Red and the Black.* It is a many-faceted city, with chemical, computer and microchip industries, and all the noise and rush of modern traffic. It is also an old and respected university town, though the complex is now in the suburbs.

The Winter Olympic Games of 1968 gave Grenoble a boost into the modern age that has marked it forever. A superb view may be had from the **Fort de la**

BELOW LEFT: between runs at Val de Thorens.
BELOW: Megéve.

The philosopher Jean-Jacques Rousseau (1712–78).

Bastille. The **Musées de Grenoble**, **Dauphinois** and **Stendhal** all testify to a rich cultural heritage, as do the library and the modern sculptures that have been erected in the huge patio of the Hôtel de Ville.

The monks' liqueur

To this day the monks of the **Monastère de La Grande Chartreuse** ⓮ distill a rather well-known liqueur. In 1084 the bishop of Grenoble dreamed of seven stars announcing the arrival of seven travellers, led by Saint Bruno, who had decided to live in complete isolation from the vexatious world. The good bishop then led them to the mountain chain of La Chartreuse, which gave its name to the Carthusian Order of monks. They built their famous monastery there, well-removed from all other human habitation.

The Carthusians live in solitude and engage in religious devotion, study and manual labour. They meet only three times each day in the chapel. They eat together only once a week, on Sunday in the refectory. The monastery was completely destroyed by an avalanche in 1132 and has been nearly destroyed by fire on eight different occasions. The present buildings date from 1688.

The monastery, of course, is closed to visitors. But there is a museum depicting the Order's history and the monks' daily life at its entrance, the **Musée de la Correrie** (open Easter–Oct: daily; entrance fee). Of particular interest are the representations of the monks passing their solitary lives in prayer.

Nearby **Chambéry** ⓯ brings the visitor back down to earth. The town became the capital city of the dukes of Savoy in 1232. To this day it remains a largish town, defended by its fortress. Its best-known monument is the **Fontaine des Eléphants**, built in 1838 as a memorial to a town benefactor, the Count de Boigne, and his rollicking adventures in colonial India. The **Château des Ducs de Savoie** was erected as the home of the first rulers of Chambery and then the Savoie dukes. From the **Place du Château** there is a fine view of the old town centre.

Chambéry is associated with perhaps the most famous French romantic, the creator of the revolutionary social contract, Jean-Jacques Rousseau. In 1728, at the age of 16, Rousseau, then an apprentice engraver who had been badly treated by his employer, ran away from his Calvinist home in Geneva. On the outskirts of Chambéry is **Les Charmettes**, the cottage, completely restored as it was in his day, which he shared for six years with his mistress, 28-year-old landlady Madame de Warens. She had been converted back to Catholicism from Calvinism and was working to reconvert others. As indicated in his *Confessions*, Rousseau was converted to Madame Warens, if nothing else (892 Chemin des Charmettes; open Wed–Mon; closed public hols; entrance fee).

Resort spas and Roman baths

The neighbouring spa of **Aix-les-Bains** ⓰ is known for rheumatism treatment, and the remains of Roman baths testify to past fame and elegance, as does its name, derived from *aquae Gratianae* (Baths of Emperor Gratian). After the fall of the Roman Empire the baths fell into disuse but were rebuilt in 1779–83.

BELOW: reaching the heights.

Today's resort has as its centre the **Thermes Nationaux** (National Thermal Baths), also the **Parc Municipal**, the **Palais de Savoie** and the more recent **casino**. It also has a superb small museum, **Musée Faure** (10 Bd des Côtes; open Wed–Mon; closed public hols; entrance fee), with works by Bonnard, Pissaro, Degas, Renoir and other Impressionists. During the summer, there is much activity around the two ports and the beach on **Lac du Bourget**. The hot baths are open all year, with sulfuric waters and hot pools for the cure of rheumatism.

The lake and small city of **Annecy** ⓱ are both associated with Jean-Jacques Rousseau. It was here, soon after his flight from Geneva, that he first met Madame de Warens. Like most cities around Lake Geneva (Lac Léman) on both the French and Swiss sides, Annecy was a lake-dweller town in prehistoric times, and derives its name from an ancient Roman estate, the *Villa Aniciaca*. Annecy developed in the 12th century, when its fortress was constructed. Its most famous citizen, Rousseau aside, was Saint François de Sales, who became a priest in 1593 and entered into the wars of Reformation with the Calvinists.

In the 1990s Annecy is a small industrial city involved in the manufacturing of ballpoint pens, razor blades and fashionable jewellery. The main street, the **Rue Ste Claire**, is lined with ancient arcaded buildings intersected by canals. Cars are forbidden in parts. The 17th-century church of **St François**, the **Palais de l'Isle** (12th century), the 16th-century **château** and the **Cathédrale St François de Sales**, constitute the major landmarks.

Geneva, the frontier town

Nearby **Geneva** ⓲ is no longer part of France – strictly speaking. But the city is the main aircraft entry point to the French Alps and figures prominently in the

Map on page 250

TIP

The entire 38-km (23-mile) circuit of Lac d'Annecy can be driven, walked or cycled (bicycles available from the SNCF station); or you could see the lake by taking a cruise. Details from the Annecy tourist office.

BELOW: Annecy's old prison.

Mountain goat.

area's history and activities. People who live in Geneva tend to ski and go for excursions in France and the offices of the busy city are filled with *frontaliers,* French citizens who cross the borders daily.

The two famous French spas on the shores of **Lake Geneva** (Lac Léman, between France and Switzerland, the largest entirely inland body of water in Europe), are Thonon and Evian-les-Bains. The road along the lake from Geneva passes by the picturesque French village of **Yvoire**, which juts out into the lake and is famous for its restaurants and its narrow gabled streets. Part of the 14th-century ramparts still stand, as do many medieval houses bedecked with flowers. Here visitors must park their cars at the gates of the fortress wall and make their way down to the port on foot.

Thonon-les-Bains ⑳ specialises in waters with a high mineral content and as an ailment and cure of intestinal disorders. On the **Place du Château** stood a fortress of the dukes of Savoy (from whom, of course, the entire province takes its historical name) which was destroyed by the French in 1589. The **Musée Chablais** (open July–Sept: Mon–Sat; entrance fee) is devoted to the folklore of the region. At the church of **St Hippolyte** (12th to 17th centuries), Saint François de Sales also preached the return to Catholicism to the wavering believers in the area.

Évian-les-Bains ㉑, with its casino, is internationally famous. Much of the construction along the lakeside dates from 1865, when the city fathers decided to develop "Evian Water" and turn the small fortified city into a spa. The baths are open all year and Evian produces 40 million bottles a month on average. The **Jardin Anglais** (English garden) fronts the lake near the port, where the Lake Geneva paddle-wheel steamers carry tourists to the famous towns all around the

BELOW: the summer green of Les Praz-de-Chamonix.

lake and make repeated journeys from Evian to **Lausanne** (on the Swiss side) to provide transport for French people who come to work daily in Switzerland.

In summer it is possible to make a complete tour of Lake Geneva from Evian. The steamers of the *Compagnie Générale de Navigation* link up a total of 42 ports on both French and Swiss sides of the lake. In season there is a night crossing from Evian to Lausanne, enlivened by an orchestra for dancing.

Ski resorts

The Lake Geneva area of the French Alps is called **Le Chablais**. The Swiss border, at **St Gingolph**, is the gateway to **Les Portes du Soleil**, or the Gateway to the Sun, a ski area involving eight French and six Italian resorts, most notably Morzine and Avoriaz, and several other more recently developed ski towns on both French and Swiss (Champéry, Les Crozet) sides of the Alps.

Developed over the past 20 years, Les Portes du Soleil is now a vast series of sun and snow bowls where the downhill skier may hiss from one lovely ski area to another, the cross-country skier may trek to his heart's content, staying the night in different towns, and the mountain climber and hiker consider himself in an outdoorsman's paradise. **Morzine** ㉒ is in a particularly well-placed situation where six beautifully wooded valleys come together. **Avoriaz** ㉓ is an example of a modern French town constructed purely for tourism – winter and summer. Its architecture of high-rise wood does not please everybody, but the skier on holiday in Avoriaz can put on his skis in front of his apartment building, ski away, and return right to the doorstep.

From hundreds of look-out points in the Portes du Soleil area, tourists will have still another glimpse at one of Europe's lovliest mountains, Mont Blanc. ❑

Map on page 250

"Mont Blanc yet gleams on high"
– PERCY BYSSHE SHELLEY

BELOW:
hardy Savoyard.

AUVERGNE AND THE MASSIF CENTRAL

The Massif Central is the remote core of France, a huge, rugged plateau of granite and rock. It embraces the Auvergne, whose volcanic landscape is dramatic yet serenely peaceful

Map on page 262

or centuries the **Massif Central** was largely cut off from the rest of France, whose history took place along its perimeter. It was a self-contained, mountainous region of isolated valleys, and its principal common denominator was its remoteness.

But the map shows that numerous rivers, like the fingers of a hand, radiate out from the Massif Central's craggy heights and develop into mighty waterways that snake their way to the Atlantic or the Mediterranean.

The River Lot is one of these. As you travel upstream into the Massif Central, its slow-moving waters are increasingly hemmed in by steeply-rising wooded hills. Just a few kilometres up one of its tributaries lies the charming village of **Conques ❶** and its magnificent church, the 11th- and 12th-century **Ste Foy**, which was one of the most important shrines on the medieval pilgrimage route to Santiago de Compostela in Spain. The Romanesque church and its treasure are one of the marvels of Christian Europe.

Of Romanesque construction, Ste Foy's simple barrel-vaulting is given the lofty proportions of a Gothic cathedral. The extraordinary weight of the building has caused the ground beneath it to subside and necessitated sophisticated prosthetic restoration. Unusually, the **tympanum** radiates an almost irreverent mirth. In the semicircle above the west door, Christ the King presides over the Last Judgment. Of the 117 figures, the grimacing devils and tortured souls are far more amusing than the happy few elected to Paradise. The **treasury** (open daily; entrance fee), amongst many rare and precious objects, contains a magnificent, largely 10th-century **reliquary of Ste Foy**, a primitive statue covered with successive plaques of gold and decorated with precious stones and intaglios, some of which date from Greek and Roman times.

Volcanic hills

Formed by volcanic activity, most recently only 8,000 years ago, the **Monts du Cantal** – massive, bare hills rather than mountains – seem to bulge skywards as though subjected to huge repressed forces. At their southwest extremity lies **Aurillac ❷**, whose **Maison des Volcans** (open Tues–Sat; entrance fee) is a source of exhaustive information about the area's geological history and its natural park, the **Parc Régional des Volcans ❸**. Extending from Aurillac to Clermont-Ferrand, this vast reserve of volcanic origin is crisscrossed by a network of signposted hiking paths (including one along the Compostela pilgrimage

LEFT: young Auvergnat.
BELOW: shadows and arches in Salers.

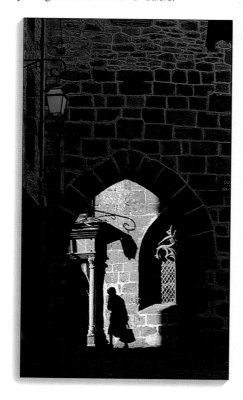

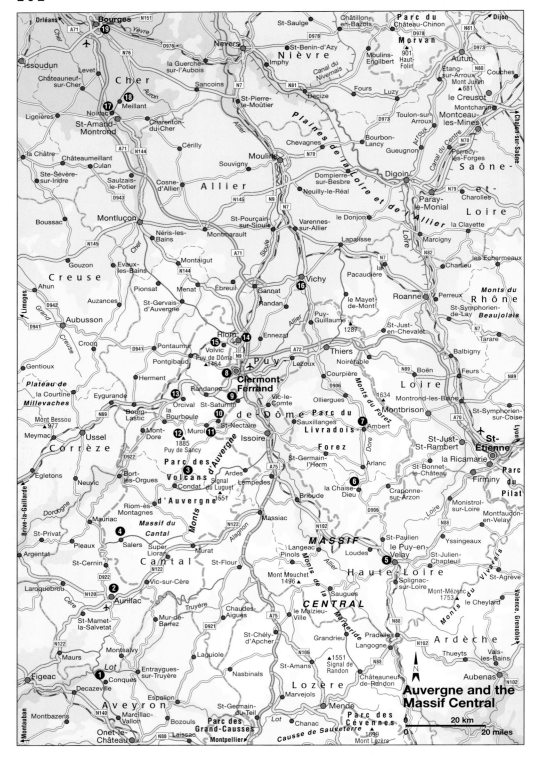

Auvergne and the Massif Central

route) that wend their way through forests, grassy meadows dotted with wild flowers, and banks of heather and blueberry. These expanses of unspoilt natural beauty are still used as summer pastures for cows whose milk goes into the making of Cantal cheese and its higher-grade version, Salers. In the old days, a lone cowherd would stay up in the hills for the entire season. The low-slung stone huts called *burons* that dot the slopes would serve as bedroom, dairy and cellar for maturing the 40-kilo (88-lb) cheeses. The cowherd's tasks covered every phase of cheese-making, from gathering firewood to boil the water for sterilising the cheesecloths, to filtering the milk and pressing the curd.

Cows, cheese, and an apéritif

Perched above the scenic valley that runs westwards from the Puy Mary, one of the highest Cantal mountains, is the striking little town of **Salers ④**, which has given its name to a breed of cow, a cheese and an apéritif made from the wild gentian that grows on the surrounding mountains. Significantly, the largely Renaissance town has no château. A long-standing conflict between the towns-people and the local lord culminated in 1666 with a royal order to raze the castle. The lovely houses, notable for their *bartizans* (turrets), spiral staircases and stone window sashes, reflect the prestige the town earned by becoming a bailiwick in the 15th century.

A few kilometres from Salers is the village of **Tournemire** and its remarkable 15th-century **Château d'Anjony** (open daily Feb–Nov; entrance fee), overlooking a valley that was once administered by no fewer than four feudal lords, each with his respective castle. It has survived almost intact and been tastefully restored, its most interesting feature being its murals. A miniature chapel

Map on page 262

In the third week of September, Le Puy holds the "Roi de l'Oiseau", a masked and costumed carnival which had its origins in the 16th century as a display of archery skills.

BELOW:
Notre-Dame Cathedral, Le Puy.

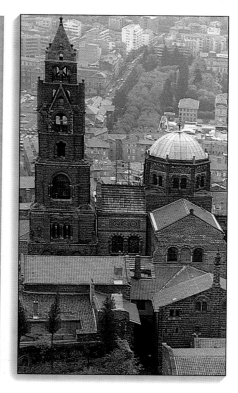

ROMANESQUE CHURCHES

The Auvergne is remarkable for its own brand of Romanesque (11th and 12th century) churches. They comprise some of the most original, simple and moving architecture in France. Beautifully proportioned, uncompromising in their severity, they are built of local rugged materials — sandstone or volcanic lava — and are characterised by a prominent apse, a narrow ambulatory around the choir and a nave flanked by sturdy pillars, with galleries above the side aisles. The capitals are often intricately carved with biblical subjects. The most interesting examples can be seen in the following places: Brioude; Clermont-Ferrand (Notre-Dame du-Port); Issoire, Orcival, Le Puy, St Nectaire, and St Saturnin.

The strong sense of religion in the Auvergne manifested itself in a way peculiar to the region: processions in which the patron saint of the parish is worshipped by means of a relic or revered statue being carried through the village and into the surrounding countryside. In Orcival, for example, on Ascension Day, the Virgin of Orcival is taken around at night. Also peculiar to the Auvergne are the Black Virgins, dark wood statues which appeared under the Byzantine influence of the Crusaders. Another famous Black Virgin can be found at Rocamadour (*see pages 285–6, 287*).

tucked into one of the castle's four towers is frescoed from ceiling to floor with a vast anthology of biblical lore in deep reds and sombre blues. In the Salle des Chevaliers the walls tell the tale of the nine knights of legend, the Neuf Preux. The banner identifying King Arthur has been effaced, perhaps indicating disapproval of the English, who ravaged the region during the Hundred Years War. The ninth knight disappeared when a new window was opened in the wall during the Renaissance.

Lace and spindles

The town of **Le Puy ❺**, in the heart of the **Velay** region, makes a spectacular sight with its two huge, almost vertical pillars of volcanic rock rising above its roofs. It was an important staging post for pilgrims on their way to Santiago de Compostela. Its steep streets rise to the **Cathédrale Notre-Dame**, whose west facade, reached by a broad flight of steps, is a Romanesque mosaic of yellow, black and reddish stone that seems to float surreally against the sky. The lively geometric patterns of naturally-coloured stone in the outstandingly beautiful, Arabic-inspired cloister make this a less solemn place than might be expected.

Lace-making is a traditional craft in Le Puy, and in many of its lace shops *dentellières* can be seen manipulating dozens of small spindles with incredible speed and dexterity. Work on an intricate tablecloth can take up to a year, so the mind boggles at the number of hours' work that must have gone into some of the lace collection in the **Musée Crozatier** (open Wed–Mon; entrance fee).

Perched on top of the largest lava pillar, looking indeed as if it has grown out of it, is **Chapelle St Michel Aiguilhe** (open mid-Feb–mid-Nov, 21 Dec–5 Jan: daily; entrance fee). The name Aiguilhe refers to the "needle" of rock, which is

BELOW: picking jonquils in Cantal.

reached by a climb of 268 steps. The original sanctuary, the shape of a three-leafed clover, was just large enough for an altar. It was later enlarged by an asymmetrical ambulatory. The intricacy and expressiveness of the tableau of saints sculpted over the doorway contrasts with the touching simplicity of the rough-hewn interior.

Map on page 262

Remote and rugged

The road north from Le Puy climbs through uninterrupted colonnades of pine forest to **La Chaise-Dieu** ❻, where even in August a slight drizzle can begin to turn to sleet. This is the remote and rugged site of a grand 11th-century monastery, and the venue of a prestigious classical music festival at the end of August.

In the **choir** of the abbey church of **St Robert**, the marvellously carved monks' stalls are surmounted by an incomparably rich series of 16th-century tapestries. Contemplating this succession of 11 tableaux, miraculously restored to their original luminous colours, is like walking straight into an illuminated manuscript. Each tapestry, a triptych representing scenes from the Old and New Testaments, is alive with a rich cast of vigorously and naturalistically portrayed characters, from urchins to executioners, who could have come out of a passion play. Another drama is depicted in the Danse Macabre fresco on the outer side of one of the stalls, a grim picture in which Death invites a succession of elongated figures, contorted into all the shapes the popular imagination could find, to dance with him.

Ambert ❼ was the cradle of the paper industry in Europe. Paper-making techniques, which were thought to have been brought by Crusaders from the Middle East, had, by the 16th century, spawned some 300 paper mills (*moulins*), fed by the many streams and rivers in the Ambert region. The surviving **Moulin Richard-de-Bas** (open daily; entrance fee), still makes paper the traditional way, sheet by sheet, from a paste of strong cotton fibres. The result, a de luxe article often incorporating fragments of wild flowers, is much sought after by printers of limited editions.

Two towns into one

Clermont-Ferrand ❽, the regional capital, originally consisted of two rival towns, Clermont and Montferrand, which merged in the 18th century. There is a startling contrast in Montferrand between the elegant Renaissance architecture of its old quarter and the sprawling Michelin tyre factory. Clermont's **Basilique de Notre-Dame-du-Port** is one of a group of specifically Auvergnat Romanesque churches that are the pride of the Puy-de-Dôme *département* (*see page 263*). Hemmed in on all sides by the houses and narrow streets of the old quarter, the 11th- and 12th-century church takes one by surprise. Steps lead down into a dim nave formed by semicircular arches with fine capitals. Round chapels are arranged like lobes round the apse, and the theme of roundness is repeated in the semicircular tiles of their almost flat roofs.

St Saturnin ❾ is a well-preserved village. Its

The Michelin tyre factory, which still dominates Clermont-Ferrand and is famous for its rubbery trademark Michelin Man, was founded here in 1830.

BELOW: tuning up in the kitchen.

Auvergnat farmer.

12th-century Romanesque **church** of pale yellow stone bears carved figures of almost casual spontaneity on the outside. The interior is lit from above by pairs of windows whose semicircular arches repeat the pattern of the nave.

On the square in front of St Saturnin's medieval **château** is a remarkable Renaissance fountain, a large sculpted stone basin into which water flows from a central column. The château itself was restored in the 16th century, when it was given a remarkable roof of grey stone tiles (*lauzes*) that protected its main structural elements. But many other features suffered from the gradual encroachment of the town; a jumble of shacks and sheds were built along its moat wall; and its formal gardens were used by farmers. Restoration by volunteers, however, has gradually succeeded in recreating the illustrious past of a castle that was visited by Catherine de Medici and Marguerite de Valois. (Open June–Sept: daily; entrance fee.)

Water worship

The sleepy little town of **St Nectaire** ❿ nestles in a hollow of greenery. It has numerous typically Auvergnat attributes. Its nutty-flavoured eponymous cheese is renowned all over France. The mineral water from its 40 springs, which inspired the Gauls' water worship, run along conduits deep below the streets. Today, turn-of-the-century hotels cater for families looking for peace and retired people coming to take the waters.

Majestically set on a promontory overlooking the town is the church of **St Nectaire** whose building stone ranges in colour from a deep mossy green to a violet-tinged black. Its nave and choir contain 103 lively **capitals**, which evoke the miracles worked by St Nectaire.

BELOW:
the sleepy village
of St Nectaire.

The partly ruined 13th-century **Château de Murol** (open June–Sept: daily; entrance fee) overlooking the village of **Murol ⓫**, near **Lac Chambon**, is an imposing construction. Its thick, copper-coloured walls enclose a complex of cellars, courtyards, staircases, two chapels and living quarters. Only those with a head for heights are advised to visit the rampart walk and watchtower. The château makes a perfect setting for the historical plays, recreating life under the feudal lords of medieval France, that are performed there in summer.

Map on page 262

Highest point

Not far to the west, on the other side of a high pass that is closed by snow in winter, is the highest point in the Massif Central, the **Puy de Sancy ⓬**, on whose slopes the River Dordogne rises. In winter, skiers from the nearby resorts of **Le Mont-Dore** and **La Bourboule** have an exhilarating time on the Puy de Sancy, while in summer it is visited for the unparalleled view it offers from the summit, encompassing the Monts du Cantal, the Puy de Dôme and, on a very clear day, the Alps. There is a cable car for those who don't want to walk.

A spectacular drive through mountainous terrain leads to **Orcival ⓭**, whose 12th-century **Basilique de Notre-Dame** is another fine and remarkably homogeneous example of Auvergnat Romanesque architecture. Behind the altar there is a striking Virgin and Child in Majesty. Made of wood covered with silver and gold plaques, the sculpture shows the figures in a stiff, front-facing, almost hieratic pose. It is the object of several pilgrimages.

Riom ⓮ was for centuries Clermont's fierce rival as administrative capital of the region. Its erstwhile importance can be judged from its numerous Renaissance townhouses built of dark volcanic stone. **Sainte Chapelle**, all that re-

BELOW: Auvergne landscape.

Map on page 262

In the third week of April, Bourges plays host to an excellent festival of music and dance, with a varied programme.

RIGHT: the needle-top abbey of St Michel Aiguilhe.
BELOW: country character.

mains of Duc de Berry's château, contains remarkable stained-glass windows (open Mon–Fri; closed public hols; entrance fee). The main attraction of the church of **Notre-Dame du Marthuret** is its superb 14th-century Gothic statue, *Virgin with Bird*. The little town of **Volvic ⓕ** is best known for its mineral water, but it also gives its name to a very resistant grey volcanic rock which has been used locally as a building material since the 13th century. The **Maison de la Pierre**, next to the spring, organises guided tours of the lava quarry and a slide-show (open Mar–Nov: Wed–Mon; entrance fee).

Just to the north of Volvic, the half-ruined **Château de Tournoël** (open Easter–Oct: Wed–Mon; entrance fee) provides a fascinating insight into how people lived in centuries gone by. From the medieval keep to the *châtelaine*'s chambers with their secret entrance, all its elements evoke a precise period and activity. **Vichy ⓖ** won a bad name when it was chosen as the seat of the government that collaborated with the Nazi occupation forces. But today it is a pleasant town that has kept up with the times, unlike some of Auvergne's other spas, whose faded salmon-pink hotels are only a shadow of their former glory.

The last section of rugged terrain in the Massif Central driving northwards comes with the canyons of the River Sioule. They are succeeded by the rolling country of the Bourbonnais, which in turns flattens into a vast agricultural plain approaching the invisible frontier between northern and southern France.

The centre of France

Abbaye de Noirlac ⓗ, located almost at the geographical centre of France, is that great rarity, a perfectly intact Cistercian abbey. Its 12th-century church of light-coloured stone conveys a powerful simplicity through its total lack of decoration, which the monks regarded as frivolous and distracting. For that reason it is an ideal setting for the summer concerts.(Open daily; entrance fee.)

Located in the lordly seclusion of its wooded grounds near St Amand-Montrond, the splendidly maintained **Château de Meillant ⓘ** is an example of how successfully the sophisticated Renaissance style could be grafted on to a medieval castle complete with moat. Its courtyard is quintessential Renaissance, with its free-standing chapel. (Open Feb–Dec; entrance fee.)

In the far north of the region, and close to the Loire Valley lies **Bourges ⓙ**, an architectural gem, and seat of the duchy of Berry. The city displays northern artistic influences. Visible for miles around, its flower-girt 13th-century **Cathédrale de St Etienne** is indisputably one of the finest Gothic buildings in Europe. Supported by majestic flying buttresses placed at regular intervals, its high, narrow nave is a symphony of vertical lines culminating in superb stained glass.

The finest example of the city's Renaissance domestic architecture is the 15th-century Gothic **Palais Jacques Coeur**, named for its first occupant, a wealthy merchant and royal treasurer to Charles VII (Rue Jacques Coeur; open daily; closed public hols; entrance fee). More fine Renaissance houses line **Rue Bourbonnoux**, including **Hôtel Lallemant** (open Tues–Sun; closed Sun am; entrance fee.). Nearby is Place Gourdaine, with its half-timbered medieval houses. ❑

THE SOUTHWEST

Southwest France spans the country from the Atlantic coast to the Mediterranean encompassing not just widely differing coastlines, but the wildest reaches of the Pyrenees and the gentlest curve of ancient rivers.

North of the Pyrenees, the landscape is essentially pastoral. **Bordeaux** (*pages 274–276*), on the Gironde estuary, is both an important port and a key wine-producing region. At its back, the Dordogne flows gently through the heart of **Limousin and Périgord** (*pages 279–286*) and some of France's most lovely countryside, which has proved particularly popular with the British holidaymaker. In fact, this has always been a popular place to live; the cave paintings at Lascaux suggest that artistically-gifted hunters were resident here more than 30,000 years ago. More recent aristocrats have liked it too, and the Dordogne *département* has more châteaux than any other in Périgord.

The southwest is a region of specialities. Périgord is famous for its walnuts, truffles and *foie gras*, the liver paté that results from the controversial force-feeding of geese. Limoges is best known for its porcelain. South of the Garonne, Armagnac is the pride of **Gascony** (*pages 288–289*), a gentle region of medieval *bastide* towns, undulating hills and lazy rivers.

The Atlantic coast has wonderful long sandy beaches flanked by the huge pine forests of the Landes, and culminating in the fashionable resorts of Biarritz and St Jean-de-Luz. Beyond, the snow-capped peaks of **The Pyrenees** (*pages 290–298*) stretch all the way to the Mediterranean coast. It is possible to follow the GR10, France's most famous footpath, all the way across, traversing widely varying terrain from high plateau pastures to craggy river valleys, and encompassing a remarkably wide variety of activities from skiing to spa visiting, mountain-climbing to caving. ❑

PRECEDING PAGES: skiing in the Pyrenees.
LEFT: early artwork at Lascaux caves in Périgord.

Maps:
Area 280
City 275

BORDEAUX

Many of the greatest wines of France are produced from Bordeaux, a region which stretches from the prosperous maritime city of the same name to the great forest of the Landes

rance's fifth largest city and sixth largest port, **Bordeaux ①** has the appearance of long-standing prosperity. In addition to the wine trade, its merchant marine was active in the slave trade, and later in commerce with French colonies in Africa. Since the 1960s it has also become an industrial centre (aeronautics, etc), thanks partly to the dynamic policies of its former mayor, Gaullist Jacques Dulmas. (In 1998, Alain Juppé is the mayor.)

The urban architecture is cool and spacious, dominated by the regularity of 18th-century construction. The one exception to this pattern is the Romanesque church **Ste Croix ④**, whose elaborately sculpted tympanum is topped by a curiously asymmetric tower added later. Restored and immaculate, Ste Croix gives onto a wide cobbled square typical of Bordeaux's modern street lines.

The essence of Bordeaux is to be found along the avenue **Allées de Tourny ⑤**. At one end is the **Grand Théâtre ⑥**, a purely Neo-Classical monument of symmetric columns and arches. On the river side opens the gravelled **Esplanade des Quinconces ⑦**, the name referring to the arrangement of the trees. In between is the **Maison du Vin ⑧**, an indispensable stop for documentation on the different Bordelais vineyards, and in particular those estates open to the public. Just across the street is the well-organised tourist office, which arranges bus tours to a different wine region each afternoon. A foretaste comes without delay in the neighbouring wine stores; the clerks are very knowledgeable about Bordeaux wines. Since medieval times, Bordeaux has exported much of its wine to England, and the rich merchant families still have close British links.

Fittingly, the Bordeaux vineyards begin right on the edge of the city, with **Château Haut-Brion**. Like most of the Bordeaux châteaux, the building in question is not a genuine castle, but rather a stately mansion dating from the 19th-century. The use of the word "château" to designate a wine-producing property is a Bordelais convention. Also specific to Bordeaux wines is their official classification in multiple categories by *cru* (growth). The original classification of 1855 (amended in 1973) was based on land qualities, price and prestige, and concerned only the Médoc and Sauternes wines. Although technically a Graves wine, Château Haut-Brion was included – it was too good to be left out.

The Graves region

The name "Graves" refers to the gravelly nature of the soil, producing both red and white wines, sometimes from the same vines. A visit to the **Graves region ②** starts with **La Brède**, not a wine-producing château but home of the 18th-century philosopher Montesquieu. The baron's castle, dating from the 15th

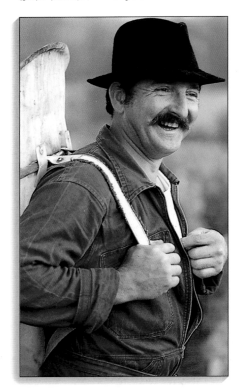

BELOW: *vendangeur* (grape-picker).

century, is surrounded by a functioning moat, complete with carp. Not overly large, the interior is partially furnished, and crowned by a vast library (open June–Sept: Wed–Mon; Apr–June, Oct–Nov: Sat, Sun; entrance fee.)

The famous **Château d'Yquem** can be visited with prior reservation, and the nearby **Château Filhot** offers wine tasting and a friendly welcome.

A little farther is **Roquetaillade**, the best preserved of a series of medieval fortresses built by Pope Clement V (open July–Sept: daily; Oct–June: Sun; entrance fee). An unusual line of four great towers form the facade, surprisingly austere in the sunny and placid vineyards. Another such fortress, in **Villandraut**, is the backdrop for the Uzestes music festival in late August. This is the **Sauternais region ❸**, producing sweet white Sauternes and Barsac wines. Their intensity is caused by "noble rot": that is, allowing the grapes to ripen until attacked by a fungus which causes the grape to shrivel, but the sugar content to increase.

Celebrated Médoc

The **Médoc ❹** is the most celebrated of the Bordeaux wine regions, and for many these wines represent the definition and incarnation of the Bordeaux wine that continues to improve over decades. This narrow band of vineyards, stretching northwest from Bordeaux along the coastline of the Gironde estuary, numbers 180 châteaux. Here, the vines are all grown on slight heights where the soil is more plentiful and less water-logged. At points along the coast are sluice-gates; not to irrigate the land but to drain off excess water, and prevent the tide from moving up the channels. (Tides exist all along the 80-km/50-mile Gironde.)

Most of the Médoc châteaux can be visited, although calling ahead is always recommended. Appointments are needed for the most famous, such as **Mouton-**

Bordeaux, city of wine, is "dedicated to Bacchus in the most discreet form" according to Henry James. One in six Bordelais work in the wine industry.

BELOW: the proprietor of Clos Haut Peyraguey in Sauternes.

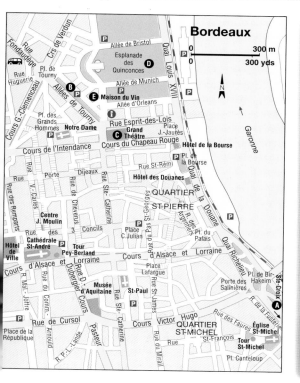

Map on page 280

A true connoisseur.

RIGHT: Bacchus tells all at Mouton-Rothschild.
BELOW: Château Margaux welcomes tasters.

Rothschild, with its excessively ornate mansion, and an art museum with paintings, sculptures, glass and ceramics, celebrating the subject of wine.

The **Château de la Tour de By** (near Lesparre) gives the visitor a particularly warm welcome. After a walk through the vineyards to the lone tower overlooking the estuary, the visit includes a tour of the cellar. "Raising" wine requires many delicate procedures, such as settling the oak casks on chocs and maintaining the same alignment and distribution. These operations are explained by a qualified personnel member, sometimes the wine master himself, who remains available for questions during the sampling. The towns of **Margaux** ❺, **Pauillac** ❻, **St Estèphe** and **Lesparre** ❼ each have wine centres with exhibits and information on their respective wines.

Doves and dunes

If anything can lure a winegrower away from his assembly tanks and glass pipettes, it is the wood pigeon hunting season. The path of these migratory birds is clearly indicated by a sudden array of crude hunters' cabins on stilts, fabricated out of any spare pieces of plywood available. Some locals recount that it is impossible to get a plumber or carpenter when the wood pigeons come over.

Where the vineyards give out the beach takes over. From the mouth of the estuary along the 207-km (140-mile) coast to the **Bassin d'Arcachon** ❽, sandy dunes held down by scrub pine alternate with large inland lakes. While swimming is limited in the high surf, resort towns offer horseback-riding and cycling in the pine forest that is the beginning of the Landes. Arcachon and its bay are renowned for oysters and pleasure boating. An immense fine-sand beach is circled by some of Europe's highest dunes. **Les Landes** ❾, sweeping south for 240 km (150 miles), is the largest forest in France and entirely artificial, created to retain invading coastal sands in the 19th century.

East of Bordeaux, the small town of **St Emilion** ❿ gives its name to yet another wine district. Honoured by the English as the "King of Wines", the quality has been supervised for eight centuries by an elected council of peers, known as *Jurats*. The deliberations of this brotherhood take place with red-robed ceremony in one of the town's Gothic cloisters. With two monasteries, St Emilion offers a wealth of religious architecture. The most spectacular is a unique monolithic church. Tunnelled into the hillside in the 11th century, the steeple emerges full-blown at street level on the hill top. The remains of a cloister mingle with untended greenery.

Not far is the superb Roman villa discovered in **Montcaret** (near Lamothe-Ravel on the road to Bergerac). Extensive foundations of this small community are visible, including ducts for a warm-air heating system, the baths, and several complete mosaic floors.

The novelist François Mauriac (1895–1970) adored his native Bordeaux and the country of the Landes and the Garonne valley. His former country home, Malagar, near the village of Verdelais, above the Garonne, is now a **museum** full of his souvenirs (open Wed–Mon; entrance fee). His masterpiece *Thérèse Desqueyroux* (1927) is set in the Landes forest. ❑

LIMOUSIN AND PERIGORD

*Passing ruined castles and mellow villages, the lovely
Dordogne and Lot rivers flow through idyllic countryside where
man has lived at one with the land since prehistoric times*

Map
on page
280

Limousin is a centre for the arts of fire – porcelain and enamel; and a land of water – rain and lakes. Still relatively unknown to tourists, the lovely region was neglected until the opening of railways in the late 19th century. **Limoges** ⓫, however, is a household word. Many a bridal trousseau has been graced by its delicate china, and there are more than 30 porcelain workshops of all sizes, many offering guided tours. The **Musée National Adrien Dubouché** (open Wed–Mon; closed public holidays; entrance fee) has a collection of 10,000 pieces from all periods.

If china is not your cup of tea, the city abounds in historic sights. Simple and graceful, the eight arches of the 13th-century stone **Pont St Etienne** over the Vienne river marry civil engineering with aesthetic qualities. The **Cathédrale de St Etienne** is a Gothic masterpiece, begun in the 13th century and continued in the Flamboyant style. The church of **St Michel-de-Lions**, is noted for its stained-glass. The **Musée de l'Evêché**, housed in a former episcopal palace, includes a collection of enamel work (open July–Sept: daily; Oct–June: Wed–Mon; closed public holidays; entrance fee). In the summer the city hosts porcelain and enamel expositions.

From porcelain to tapestry

About 86 km (54 miles) to the east, **Aubusson** ⓬ is to tapestry what Limoges is to porcelain. The **Centre Culturel Jean Lurçat**, named after the artist who revitalised the art of tapestry-making from the 1930s onward, includes a **Musée de la Tapisserie** (open Wed–Mon; entrance fee) which has a permanent exhibition of both contemporary and traditional tapestry work.

For a change of element, the artificial **Lac de Vassivière** ⓭ offers a wide range of outdoor activities, while horseback riding is also a favourite activity in the region. One of France's many national (as distinct from private) stud-farms is in **Arnac-Pompadour** ⓮, whose **château** evokes the Marquise de Pompadour, mistress of Louis XV (open daily; entrance fee). Horse races are held from the beginning of July to the end of September.

Sheltered under an impressive array of grey slate roofs and towers, **Uzerche** ⓯ is set on a crag above a loop in the river Vézère, crowned by its Romanesque church of **St Pierre**. There are fine views across the valley from the Esplanade de la Lunarde. One of the region's most spectacular castles is perched above the town of **Coussac-Bonneval** ⓰. The exterior is that of a forbidding feudal fortress; one entire wall has no opening whatsoever. Inside the Renaissance courtyard is the reverse, with decoration

LEFT: famous stud-farm at Arnac-Pompadour.
BELOW: walnut picker.

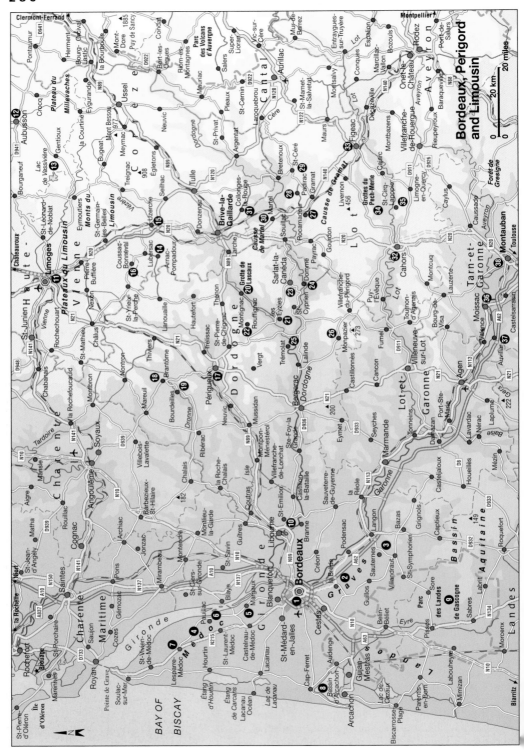

Bordeaux, Perigord
and Limousin

Map on page 280

intended to please, not subdue. And the interior is splendidly furnished (open Mar–Oct: daily, pm only; entrance fee).

In **Périgueux** ⑰, the regional capital, **Cathédrale de St Front** was originally built in the 12th century but suffered a total reconstruction in the 19th century which completely altered its character. The former building was virtually razed – only the great bell tower was spared. The domed roof (not uncommon in the southwest of France) was rebuilt with five domes and 17 new towers and turrets. The result has a rather oriental look about it, more like a large mosque than a Christian church.

The surrounding *quartier*, **Puy St Front**, is now a conservation area. The cobbled streets are lined with Renaissance facades, here a doorway topped by a pointed stone arch, there a majestic staircase giving onto a tiny courtyard-foyer. Many buildings have been recently and elegantly restored, housing chic boutiques. Despite these signs of cosy times the modern-day city is not as prosperous as was the Gallo-Roman agglomeration, some say. The **Musée du Périgord** (22 Cours Tourny; open Wed–Mon; closed public hols; entrance fee) has extensive collections covering all periods.

North of Périgueux on the Dronne river, **Brantôme** ⑱ has an exceptional charm enhanced by human ingenuity. For pleasure, and the creation of a mill-race, a 16th-century abbot undertook the construction of an elbow-shaped canal that hugs the town in the crook of its arm. The slow green water seems entranced by the long tresses of its own vegetation. The quiet old houses pursue their existence without excessive attention to tourists. On one of the banks is a green park with Renaissance gazebos, formerly the monks' garden. Leading to the grounds of the former abbey is a right-angled stone bridge, designed to resist the weight of the water arriving from two directions at once. The abbey buildings include a cave chapel. The bell tower, separate from the church, is a superb 11th-century construction.

Downstream on the Dronne is the superb **Château de Bourdeilles** ⑲. In fact two castles, one feudal, the other Renaissance, the ensemble is bordered by terraces overlooking the cliff edge. The square and crenellated silhouette is dominated by an octagonal keep. The elegance of the 16th-century facades, the regular spacing of the stone-sashed windows, is complemented by lush interior furnishings and tapestries. At the foot of the château is the lord's mill (open Feb–June, Sept–Dec: Wed–Mon; July–Aug: daily; entrance fee.)

Prehistoric art

In a short stretch of the Vézère valley between Montignac and Les Eyzies can be found the world's most astonishing collection of prehistoric art. The paintings and engravings of the **Grotte de Lascaux** ⑳ are breathtaking. Between 13,000 and 30,000 years old, perhaps associated with magical rites, the three-colour friezes (black, yellow, red) representing a variety of animals, use a whole range of techniques to obtain perspective, texture and movement.

Unlike other sites, Lascaux has been saved from the irreversible destruction caused by exposure to the

Bourdeilles lies in the region called Périgord Vert, where walnut trees abound, as well as the special kind of oak tree under which the elusive truffle is found. These, along with the sumptuous foie gras, make Périgord a gastronomic heaven.

BELOW:
the Dromme river at Brântome.

Wild mushrooms are one of the delicacies of the region, and mushroom hunting is a favourite pastime. Pictured here are glorious cèpes (boletus edulis).

BELOW:
force-feeding ducks to make their livers swell for *foie gras.*

air. Closed off in prehistoric times, the cave was not rediscovered until 1940. Due to the preoccupations of the war and ensuing hardships, crowds only started flocking to the site some years later. When an astute official learned in 1963 that a green fungus was growing over the paintings the cave was immediately closed while restoration was still possible. In compensation a partial copy, called **Lascaux II**, has been created with great care and skill in the adjacent quarry, and is open to the public. Most of the paintings are reproduced, including a rare human figure visible only with difficulty in the cave itself because it is inside a well. (Tickets for the site must be obtained in advance from the office in Montignac; open Feb–June, Sept–Dec: Tues–Sun; July–Aug: daily; entrance fee.)

Ancient centre

In **Les Eyzies ㉑**, where prehistoric skeletons were discovered, a statue of Cro-Magnon man looks out, somewhat bewilderedly, from a ledge over the town's roofs. The **Musée National de Préhistoire** (open Wed–Mon; entrance fee) presenting archaeological discoveries, is located in a feudal fortress half built into a cliff that shows traces where beams were inserted. The **church**, with its defensive towers and narrow windows is an example of the fortified churches found throughout Périgord.

Literally dozens of important sites are clustered around Les Eyzies. The tourist office organises day-long excursions to many of these sites which avoids long waits in queues, and also rents bicycles. Just down the road is **Font-de-Gaume** (open Wed–Mon; appointment advised; closed public hols; entrance fee), decorated with both paintings and engravings almost as stunning as Lascaux, despite deterioration; the nearby **Grotte des Combarelles** (open

Thur–Tues; appointment advised; closed public hols; entrance fee) contain engravings. In the same direction, the **Abri du Cap Blanc** (open Mar–Nov: daily; entrance fee) is a prehistoric shelter (*abri*) which contains a 13-m (42-ft) bas relief which includes six horses, a bull, a bison and other animals.

The **Grottes de Rouffignac** ㉒ are the channels of an ancient underground river that dug 10 km (6 miles) of tunnels. An electric train takes visitors through the dimly lit galleries, the walls dotted with knobs of hard rock that resisted erosion, and furrowed by prehistoric bears' claws. Although the caverns have been known for centuries, the drawings inside were not identified as prehistoric until 1956. Mammoths are the speciality, in a sequence depicting the confrontation of two groups. Sadly, the drawings on the "great ceiling" must compete with 19th-century graffiti done in candle smoke.

Along the Dordogne

From Sarlat to Bergerac the **Dordogne valley** combines magnificent views with lovely castles. **Sarlat** ㉓ is a bustling market town that could be the stage for a film set in the Renaissance, the church and episcopal palace creating a breathing space among the interlacing streets that run between the sculpted facades. At **Montfort** begins the almost full-circle bends in the river called *cingles*. From **Domme** ㉔ the road plunges down to the river, and across the bridge, a few kilometres west, the village of **La Roque-Gageac** is lodged on the steep slope between the river bank and the cliff edge. A walk through the streets, which alternate between staircase and sidewalk, provides an intimate view of local architecture. At the highest point metal bars jut from the cliff where once a staircase climbed to the plateau above.

Map on page 280

TIP

To be sure of a ticket to any of the caves around Les Eyzies, plan to make an early start: they sell out fast, especially in the high season.

BELOW: troglodyte caves at La Roque-St-Christophe.

*A pensive moment
in the country.*

At **Beynac-et-Cazenac**, the 13th-century **château** (open Mar–Nov: daily; Dec–Feb: pm only; entrance fee) perched above the town is a vision straight out of a medieval chronicle; the dizzying blank face of the tower keep is softened by the perspective of the surrounding towers and lower buildings.

Leaving the river for a moment, the **Abbaye de Cadouin** (open Wed–Mon; entrance fee), on the road from Le Buisson, is an ensemble of sober architecture in an unusual style. The church of yellow stone presents a wide and sternly undecorated facade, the interior a flat transept. The 16th-century cloisters are rich with elaborately sculpted biblical characters. An excavated Romanesque chapter hall displays the coffer that contained the relic of the Holy Shroud that was Cadouin's glory – and source of considerable income – until it was proved a fake in 1934.

The Bastides' circuit

Between **Limeuil** and **Trémolat** ㉕, from the confluent of the Vézère and the Dordogne to the **Cingle de Trémolat**, the Dordogne, placidly immobile in summer, seems to be on all sides at once, the sun penetrating easily to the shallow bed. This picturesque tableau is the setting for comfortable country manor houses; low and large, the red tiled roofs rise to central dovecote tower. Far more than the religious architecture, even more than the military, it is the civil architecture that characterises Périgord.

Of the numerous fortified cities along the **Circuit des Bastides** between the Dordogne and Lot rivers, **Monpazier** ㉖ is the best preserved. The *bastide* is characterised by a rectilinear street plan around a central square faced by arcades. In Monpazier these arcades are not unified, but vary with each house. Of

BELOW: château on the Dordogne opposite Beynac.

Map
on page
280

disparate heights and depths, at the corners the openings for the street are curious lopsided triangles, like a dunce's cap. Monpazier has not only the central *halle* complete with grain measures, but also three of the six original fortified gateways. The church was defaced during the Revolution, the tympanum replaced by an inscription of the official ideology "The people recognise the existence of the Supreme Being and the immortality of the soul."

Some *bastides* were founded by the English, and some by the French. Monpazier was founded on 7 January 1284, by the English. Both sides sought to win support by granting favours such as the independent, non-feudal status of the *bastides*. These "new towns" of the Middle Ages were often attacked and some changed hands as often as six times during the course of the war. The landscape of Périgord is also characterised by the many fortresses built in the early part of the Hundred Years War.

Rocamadour

Since the body of St Amadour was found uncorrupted in its grave in 1166, **Rocamadour** ㉗ has been a focus for Christian devotion. This pilgrims' paradise is an accretion of crypts, chapels and shrines clustered like the cells of a beehive against the cliff. The essential constructions remain, particularly the chapels using the flank of the cliff as a wall. A path of the Stations of the Cross leads up to a château whose terraces overlooking the valley are practically built in thin air. The **museum** (open daily; entrance fee) has an important collection of 12th–14th century treasures, while the Black Madonna on the altar of the **Chapelle de Notre-Dame** (open daily) is the object of veneration for the pilgrims (as opposed to the swarming tourists) who still journey here.

TIP

The best view of Rocamadour is from the village of L'Hospitalet, across the Alzou gorge, and the best time to see it is in the early morning light.

BELOW: an aerial view of Monpazier.

Map on page 280

There are few more delightful pastimes than to take a picnic and a canoe on the River Célé – children can go too. Details from the tourist office in Cahors.

RIGHT: Rocamadour.
BELOW: outside the abbey at Moissac.

Fifteen kilometres (9 miles) from Rocamadour, the **Gouffre de Padirac** ㉘ is an enormous circular chasm or pot-hole, 99 m (325 ft) across and 103 m (338 ft) deep. Lifts and staircases take the visitor down to a remarkable system of underground rivers and lakes. The tour takes 1½ hours and covers 2 km (1¼ miles) including 1 km by boat across a spectacular lake (open Apr–mid-Oct: daily; entrance fee).

St-Céré ㉙, a charming old riverside town, holds a classical music festival throughout August. Much of the festival takes place at the **Château de Castelnau-Bretenoux**, 9 km (5 miles) away (open June–Sept: daily; closed public hols; entrance fee). This château of bright red, rusty rock betraying iron ore is not as recent as its name "newcastle" suggests, but is remarkably conserved. The long facade dominates the village from steep and unassailable foundations. From the massive wooden portal of the entry to the opposite tower commanding the valley, the evolution of architecture is visible in the different types of windows, roofs, and so on. The interior furnishings are equally splendid. Further east, on the plateau (*causse*) above the Dordogne, **Martel** ㉚, a centre for nuts and truffles, is a delightful town with many medieval buildings. Continuing north towards Brive and the Limousin, the whimsical **Collonges-la-Rouge** ㉛ is an entire village constructed of red sandstone, making it a picturesque site favoured by local artisans.

The Lot and the Célé

Originally the "Olt", the Lot river received its present name when visiting northerners misunderstood the regional language, *occitan*. Between **Cahors** ㉜ (famed for its **Pont Valentré,** one of the rare fortified bridges in Europe) and **Figeac** ㉝ the **Lot valley** is relatively wide, producing rich tobacco fields clasped between the sheer white cliffs that lead up to the surrounding plateaux. To the north flows its lovely tributary, the **Célé**.

Further east, near Cabrerets, the **Grottes du Pech-Merle** ㉞ (open Mar–Nov: daily; entrance fee) combine brilliant rock formations with prehistoric paintings, including enigmatic dots, a negative image of a prehistoric hand outlined in red paint, and a prehistoric footprint.

Continue up the same side of the valley for the best view of **St Cirq-Lapopie** ㉟ from afar. Riding forward like a ship's prow, the church in this village leads the group of warm ochre-walled houses, now mostly shops serving the tourist trade.

In the far south of the region, on the border with Gascony, stands the **Abbaye de Moissac** ㊱, whose superbly carved early 12th-century **south portal** and **cloisters** are a crowning achievement of Romanesque sculpture, bearing witness to the abbey's supremacy at that time in southwest France.

Not far away are **Auvillar** ㊲, an exceptionally beautiful hilltop village with an arcaded market building at its centre, and pink-hued **Montauban** ㊳. This was the birthplace of Ingres, whose bequest of paintings and drawings can be seen at **Musée Ingres** (open Jan–June, Sept–Dec: Tues–Sun; July, Aug: daily; closed public hols; entrance fee). ❑

Map on page 292

GASCONY

Between the river Garonne and the Pyrenees lies a mellow landscape of rivers and rolling hills strewn with sleepy medieval towns and crumbling castles

I n the heart of Gascony (which is the preferred but no longer the official name for the region) lies its compact, friendly capital, **Auch ❶**. Leaving the modern town, make for the old part which stands on a hill overlooking the river Gers. The **Cathédrale de St Marie** is chiefly remarkable for what it contains. The vivid stained glass, depicting some 360 individual figures, both mythical and biblical, and dating from around 1513, is attributed to Gascon painter Arnaud de Moles. Equally exuberant are the oak choir stalls, vigorously and occasionally immodestly carved with over 1,500 figures. To see them to best effect, it's a good idea to bring a torch with you.

Outside the cathedral, the **Escalier Monumental**, a staircase of 232 stone steps, runs down to the river. Here too is a statue of d'Artagnan, the swashbuckling hero of Alexandre Dumas's *The Three Musketeers* (1844). The character was based on the memoirs of a real Gascon, Charles de Batz. Another fictional Gascon was Edmond Rostand's creation, *Cyrano de Bergerac*, brought compellingly to life by Gérard Depardieu in the film of the same name. He was typical of the Gascon character: roistering, passionate, brave, yet tinged with dissatisfaction and regret.

West of the cathedral lies the pedestrianised shopping street, Rue Dessoles, and some fine buildings dating from the 18th century, including the former Archbishop's residence, now the **Préfecture**. As befits the capital of a gastronomic province, Auch takes its Wednesday and Saturday markets seriously, when the town comes to life. There is no shortage of good restaurants.

To the north of Auch is the cheerful market town and centre of Armagnac production, **Condom ❷**. Both places make good bases for exploring Gascony. At the town's heart, surrounded by narrow streets, is the **Cathédrale de St Pierre**, rebuilt in the 16th century in its original late-Gothic style. Close by is the musty **Musée d'Armagnac** (2 Rue Ferry; open June–mid-Sept: daily; mid-Sept–June: Mon–Sat by request at tourist office; closed public hols; entrance fee). What is the difference between Armagnac and Cognac? The former is distilled once, the latter twice.

Castles and bastides

The château at **Lavardens ❸**, between Auch and Condom, cleverly hugs the limestone outcrop on which it is built. Of the 146 castles recorded in the Gers *département*, this is one of the most massive and imposing. Nearby **Barran** is a picturesque *bastide* with moat, covered market, arcades, overhanging houses and a large church with an eye-catching spiral bell tower. Of the 300 or so *bastides* in southwest France, dozens can be found in Armagnac. **Mirande ❹**, due

BELOW: Barran's spiral bell tower.

south of Condom, is a typical example, with grid-patterned streets and central arcaded square. Mirande stands on the Grande Baise, one of the many rivers that flow through the valleys between the hills. They have strangely assonant names: Aulouste, Auloue, Auroue, Auzoue, Lauze, Douze, Ousse, Osse. Nearby is tiny **Tillac**, even older than the *bastides*, which consists of just one street, guarded at either end by fortified gates.

The road by which you enter the *bastide* of **Bassoues ❺**, bordered on either side by medieval half-timbered houses, cuts straight through the covered market hall which straddles it. The church was built on the spot where – local legend has it – the perfectly preserved body of a brave knight called Fris was discovered centuries after his death in a battle against the Saracens. But it is a soaring tower at the end of the main street which draws attention – a splendid 14th-century four-storey keep, from the top of which are wide views of the countryside. To the north, near Condom, **Fourcès** is a *bastide* with a difference: its layout is not in a grid, but circular, with a thick clump of trees in its central circle and an almost Spanish air to its white arcaded houses.

West of Fourcès, where the pastoral Gascon landscape meets the great dark, man-made forest of the Landes, **Labastide d'Armagnac** is a *bastide* founded in 1291 by Bernard IV, Count of Armagnac for the English monarch, Edward I. Place Royal, its lovely central square, has been substituted for Places des Vosges in Paris for more than one period film. Even more enchanting is the tiddler-sized village of **Laressingle ❻**, whose 13th-century fortified walls are still intact. Here you can buy Gascon produce and the local Armagnac. The Cistercian abbey at **Flaran ❼**, with 12th-century church and 14th-century cloisters, is now a cultural centre, with an excellent permanent exhibition on local architecture. ❑

Statue of d'Artagnan in Auch.

BELOW:
the tiny hamlet
of Laressingle.

Map on page 292

THE PYRENEES

The wild and beautiful Pyrenean mountains stretch from the Basque coast of the Atlantic, with its own distinctive culture, cuisine and language, all the way to the Mediterranean

Nearly everyone who heads for the beaches of the Basque coast will find themselves driving through **Bayonne** ❽. Some may curse its traffic jams, or the industrial zone, but once on the beaches, most will barely remember having passed the city.

More's the pity. Since it is not located directly on the coast, Bayonne has largely escaped the tourist onslaught, and thus retained a very traditional Basque character. The town is the capital of the **Pays Basque**, the French part of the Basque country which lies mainly in Spain, home of some 90 percent of Basques. Links across this border are today very close – cultural, social, economic, and alas less desirable. Terrorists of the Spanish Basque militant group ETA have tended to use the French Basque country as a refuge and a base. Spanish Basques are strongly nationalist: but those on the French side, while keen to keep their own culture and traditions, are happy to remain part of France. Many still speak their strange language, all "x"s and "z"s.

Located on the south bank of the River Adour, around the imposing **Cathédrale de Ste Marie**, is old Bayonne. Its narrow streets erupt into wild ecstasy in early August for the city's two-week festival, which includes bullfights.

BELOW: opting for the pool in Biarritz.

Discreet resort

"Discovered" in the mid-19th century by the Empress Eugénie and Napoleon III, who became enchanted with the town, **Biarritz** ❾ has long been a charming, luxurious and discreet resort that attracted many famous personalities. And it is still an elegant city of large houses and *salons de thé* (tea rooms).

The beaches of Biarritz extend past the two advances of cliffs, the **Pointe St Martin** and the **Plateau de l'Atalaye**, to the northern beach of **Chambre d'Amour** (love room), famous for its outrageous waves. Hundreds of surfers congregate here, where many of Europe's important surfing competitions take place.

In the heart of Biarritz are the **Promenades**, where steep cliffs fall to the ocean. The romantic alleys shaded by tamarisk trees lead the traveller to the **Rocher de la Vierge** (Rock of the Virgin), linked to the mainland by a frail footbridge. The sea rages among the jagged rocks below, but the white Virgin Mary remains unperturbed. The entire Basque coast can be admired from this point.

The coastal road winds up and down cliffs before descending into **St Jean-de-Luz** ❿. Set in the only bay on the coast, St Jean-de-Luz is a harmonious amalgamation of an accommodating beach resort, a lively Basque town, and an important, elegant fishing port.

The heart of St Jean is extremely Basque in its architecture and spirit. The narrow houses, covered by an over-hanging roof of red tiles, all have the traditional visible beams and cross-beams painted in brown-red. Halfway down the **Rue Gambetta**, a bustling commercial street, stands the church of **St Jean-Baptiste**. It is the largest and the most famous of Basque churches. Externally quite severe with high walls and a massive tower, the splendid interior, with its three tiers of galleries, creates a very striking contrast.

The Rue Gambetta pours onto the **Place Louis XIV**, centre of nightlife. On the left is **Maison Louis XIV** (open June–Sept: daily), where the king sojourned in 1660 before marrying Marie-Thérèse, "l'Infante", the daughter of the king of Spain. The **Maison de l'Infante** is a block away, facing the fishing port, a beautiful chaos of fishing boats, masts and nets. It is, in fact, France's most important tuna port.

Aquatic playground

The beaches all around the bay of St Jean are well-protected from the unpredictable and often raging Atlantic. Three massive jetties at the entrance of the bay break most of the incoming waves.

On the opposite end of the bay lies **Socoa**, a small village with more discreet beaches, behind which looms the **Fort de Socoa**, that once acted as protector of the bay entrance. The last 10 km (6 miles) of coastal road before reaching Spain are by far the most spectacular. Atop high cliffs, the road ventures precariously near the edge and the view is splendid.

The last French Basque town is **Hendaye ⓫**. The gigantic beach, where the tide moves up and down several hundred metres, is virtually unprotected.

The Sun King and his bride married in the church of St Jean-Baptiste, now entered by a diminutive doorway to the left of the great portal which was immediately walled up after the wedding; a plaque marks the place.

BELOW: *pelota* is a favourite Basque sport.

Proudly presenting the famous Basque speciality, Jambon de Bayonne. *Traditionally it is cured simply by rubbing with salt.*

Dominating the entire Côte Basque is an enormous symmetrical mountain called **La Rhune**. The road to the base of the mountain is a mere 4 km (6 miles) from St Jean-de-Luz. One can either begin the climb from **Ascain** ⑫ or from the pass of **St Ignace**, 3 km (2 miles) up the road. For the less ambitious there is a cogwheel train leaving from the pass. The view from La Rhune's summit, at 890 m (2,952 ft) reveals the entire Côte Basque as well as the hills of the backcountry. On a clear day you can also see the endless beaches of the Landes, north of Biarritz, a marvellous mix of white surf and golden sand.

Basque backcountry

Further inland, at the end of a small road, is the adorable Basque village of **Ainhoa** ⑬. Its characteristic main street is lined with asymmetrical overhanging roofs, and shutters and beams painted with Basque inscriptions.

Deep in the heart of the Basque country, **St Jean-Pied-de-Port** ⑭ once was the capital of the province Basse-Navarre. Rich with a heritage dating back to the Middle Ages, St Jean was a traditional stop on the pilgrimage route to Santiago de Compostela. The *haute ville,* on the right bank of the Nive, is where the pilgrims paraded into the town that always received them with joy. All the houses along that street are built with the unique red sandstone of Basse-Navarre.

To leave the gift shops and crowds behind, take a scenic road leading westward to **St Etienne-de-Baïgorry** ⑮, 11 km (7 miles) away. A perfectly charming little village encased in the surrounding, deep green mountains, St Etienne exemplifies the calm and romantic atmosphere of Basque backcountry. A Roman arched foot-bridge straddles a torrent that separates the town into two distinct quarters, once vicious rivals.

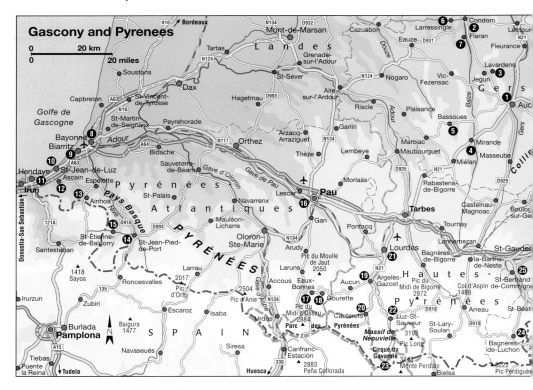

Pau **⓰**, situated above the valley of the Gave, provides the best perspective on the central section of the Pyrenees. On an elevation, slightly away from the mountains, Pau's **Boulevard des Pyrénées** offers the most panoramic view of the entire chain. On the balustrade along the edge of the boulevard are little notches, which, if aligned with the lighting rod of the tram factory below, will enable you to pick out each peak, and learn its name and elevation.

Historically, Pau is the birthplace of Henry IV, venerated king of France who during his reign (1589–1610) managed to put an end to the horribly bloody Wars of Religion. The **Château de Pau** (open daily; closed public hols; entrance fee), located at the end of the Boulevard des Pyrénées, is a charming Renaissance palace, rare for the region, inside which hang close to 100 Flanders and Gobelins tapestries.

Traversing the mountains

Extending from the Atlantic Ocean to the Mediterranean Sea, the **Pyrenees** form a massive and continuous chain along the Spanish border, with an extraordinarily varied physiognomy. Due to the deep and forbidding transversal valleys that slice through the range, several distinct cultures and ways of life dwell in its various provinces.

Its ski resorts and year-round spas, along with the endless mountain trails throughout the range, bring visitors of all kinds to the Pyrenees. Though the relatively warm climate tends to shorten the ski season, it also provides less adverse weather conditions. The Pyrenees are also renowned for the numerous spas which are scattered throughout the range, where one can bathe in various types of spring water that will cure a multitude of ailments.

Map on page 292

Colourful stories about Henry IV abound, from his idyllic childhood (he was given Jurançon wine and garlic to taste at his baptism, and his tortoiseshell cradle is on display at Pau's Château) to his rumbustuous love life. He was the king who wanted "a chicken in every pot".

BELOW: a window in the mountains.

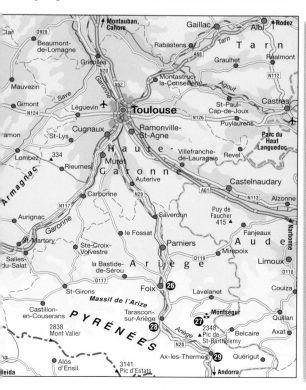

*Choice red peppers,
ready to flavour
local dishes such
as pipérade.*

There are three basic routes into the chain. The most rewarding method is by foot. One main trail, **GR10**, links the Atlantic Ocean to the Mediterranean. To hike the entire trail could take two months, but GR10 offers several shorter ideal trips into the highest mountains.

Another popular way to discover the Pyrenees is by bicycle. The entire chain can be traversed in a gruelling week and a unique experience. The landscape is no less spectacular by car. **La Route des Pyrénées**, D918/D618, begins on the Atlantic coast in St Jean-de-Luz and winds through the magnificent mountains to the Mediterranean.

The ascent

Leaving St Jean-de-Luz, the route soon leaves behind the bustling crowds of the coast. The Atlantic Pyrenees have dense, green forests and gentle terrain. Soon, however, the road enters the Basque province of **Soule**, where it will become slightly steeper. At the wide **Col** (pass) **d'Osquich**, the Basques catch hundreds of ring-doves by stretching large nets between trees.

The road then descends into the **Vallée d'Aspe,** crosses it and climbs again into the thick forest of **Bois du Bager**. It is not until the road re-emerges from the forest in the midst of high mountains, that you are hit by the beauty. If coming from Pau, the surprise is replaced with anticipation, since the road plunges straight into the mountains.

The magnificent **Vallée d'Ossau** begins in **Izeste**. The landscape becomes more and more splendid with each mile as the peaks of the high Pyrenees appear one by one. One can choose to continue along this road (D943) in the direction of the Spanish border. The road climbs steadily nearer to the **Pic du Midi**

BELOW:
along the Route
des Pyrénées.

d'Ossau, an isolated peak which plunges spectacularly into its surrounding lakes. In **Gabas**, one can take the 15-km (9-mile) footpath, or the cog train, up to the **Lac d'Artouste**, a lovely mountain lake above tree level, at an elevation of 1,989 m (6,524 ft). From the lake, the Pic du Midi can be admired.

If one sticks to D918, the journey is no less rewarding. The road climbs eastward, passing **Eaux-Bonnes** ⓱, a popular spa, with a 12th-century Romanesque church and marked paths for mountain walks in summer, and **Gourette** ⓲, an important ski resort at 1,400 m (4,600 ft). Above Gourette the road opens onto fields where flocks of sheep graze in the summertime. Finally at the top of the pass, the **Col d'Aubisque**, one is surrounded by rocky peaks and grassy slopes.

After the pass, the road continues precariously suspended on a cliffside until it reaches the **Col de Soulor**. It then winds slowly down towards the town of **Argelès-Gazost** ⓳, deep in the valley. South of Argelès is the large, elegant thermal resort of **Cauterets** ⓴ whose springs since Roman times have been thought to benefit sterile women. Aptly, it has also been fertile in literary romance. Victor Hugo womanised there; Georges Sand discovered the thrills of adultery; Chateaubriand, in a visit in 1829 to soothe his rheumatism, met the elusive young Occitan girl who was to haunt his life. Rabelais, Talleyrand and the great turn-of-the-century actress Sarah Bernhardt were also visitors.

The shrine

One of the most important Catholic shrines in the modern world, **Lourdes** ㉑, lies 13 km (8 miles) north of Argelès. Nestled in a valley at the foot of the highest Pyrenees, Lourdes is a place of contrast. On the one hand, the magnificent surroundings and picturesque old town contribute to the climate of unrelenting

Map on page 292

The climb up the Col d'Aubisque is one of the most gruelling and challenging ascents facing cyclists in the Tour de France.

BELOW: bird hunters.

A life spent in the Pyrenees.

hope and spiritual devotion. On the other hand, the thousands who crowd the streets each year in search of miracles and healings, physical or emotional, create a grim atmosphere of despair.

The origins of Lourdes as a shrine date back to 1858, when the 14-year-old Bernadette Soubirons first saw the apparition of the "beautiful lady" in a cave, the **Grotte Massabielle**, on her way to catechism. That year, the Virgin Mary was to appear before Bernadette 18 times. The miracle drew crowds at once, and in 1864 a sanctuary, along with a statue of Notre Dame de Lourdes, was built at the entrance of the cave. In 1871, a splendid neo-Gothic basilica was built above it.

Natural amphitheatre

At **Luz-St Sauveur** ㉒, leave the D918 on your left and plunge into the deep, harsh **Gorges de St Sauveur**: they will lead you straight to the world-famous natural wonder of the **Cirque de Gavarnie** ㉓. A mysteriously unreal "monument", Gavarnie has awed countless writers and painters. From the town of **Gavarnie** one can reach the cirque by horse or by foot in one hour.

From the Hôtel du Cirque, 5 km (3 miles) up the trail, one is already blessed with a dazzling view of the mountain. Glacial erosion swept out the magnificent natural amphitheatre, which is is actually made up of three semicircular superimposed shelves, the top shelf being a succession of peaks, all above 3,000 metres (10,000 ft).

Waterfalls tumble from shelf to shelf. It is possible to walk to the bottom of the largest, the **Grande Cascade**, which, at 240 m (790 ft) is the longest in Europe. To its right, a vertical breach, the *Brèche de Roland* slashes into the

BELOW: the faithful at Lourdes.

wall, said to have been carved by Durandal, the magic sword of Paladin Roland, one of Charlemagne's 12 legendary knights.

The highest pass

The **Col de Tourmalet** at 2,114 m (6,934 ft) is the highest of the French Pyrenees. The jagged terrain is memorable, and above the pass, the **Pic du Midi de Bigorre** (accessible by car) at 2,865 m (9,397 ft) dominates the entire chain. You can take a cable car to the summit, which is in the course of being developed as a major tourist site.

The route then continues down and up over two splendid passes, **Col d'Aspin** and **Col de Peyresourde**, before winding down to Bagnères (meaning baths) de Luchon. Tired hikers and bikers will be especially rewarded.

Bagnères de Luchon ㉔ is the spa par excellence, by far the most important of the Pyrenees. The Romans already exploited the springs of Luchon in the 2nd to 4th centuries AD. Excavations have led to the discovery of three large swimming pools with marble floors. The 80-odd springs that feed Luchon yield a water particularly appropriate for the treatment of respiratory ailments. Hence Luchon has drawn its celebrities from actors, singers and politicians. The ski resort of **Superbagnères**, above the valley of the Lys, will give you a magnificent view. From Luchon, a detour to the north is well worthwhile. The attractive village of **St Bertrand-de-Commignes ㉕** is the site of the **Cathédrale de St Marie-de-Commignes**, a man-made highlight of the Pyrenees. The pale facade is adorned by a beautifully sculpted portal, while the High Renaissance choir stalls are masterpieces of wood carving: hounds, monkeys, cherubs and slathering grotesques clamber around the misericordes and arm rests.

Map on page 292

TIP

Time your visit to the Cirque to Gavarnie for early morning or late afternoon, preferably on a weekday rather than a weekend, in order to avoid the overburdened mule trains which take tourists to the site.

BELOW:
Basque shepherd.

Map on page 292

The road travels north of Luchon, then east again towards St Girons. There one meets the River Salat, a stream favoured by kayakers. The road winds through the gorges of Ribanto and then climbs towards the **Col de Port.** From the pass, or better yet from the **Pic d'Estibat** (1,663 m/5,455 ft) a couple of miles away, the division of Central to Eastern Pyrenees is evident. To the west extend the high, majestic peaks that surround Luchon, smooth and even. To the east begins the rocky and rugged terrain of the Eastern Pyrenees.

Cathar country

On the easy descent towards **Foix** ㉖, the landscape changes significantly. Rich, tall trees become scarce, giving space to the short, bristly bushes that grow in between the rocks. The valleys are obstructed by rocky stumps. In Foix, the three towers of the medieval castle dominate the city from atop a rocky peak.

The area where the most spectacular and renowned Cathar castles still stand is along the road between Foix and **Quillan**. Beyond the **Pain de Sucre** (sugar loaf), the ruins of **Roquefixade** can soon be discerned atop a natural wall of rocks. Ahead looms the silhouette of the *roc* of **Montségur** ㉗, symbol of the annihilation of the Cathars (*see page 297*).

Built in 1204, Montségur was a haven for a community of the purest members of the Cathar faith. It soon became a prestigious site of pilgrimage and thereby a challenge and potential danger to the Catholic church and French crown. In July 1243, the *roc* was besieged. By the spring of the following year, the inhabitants of the fortress, weakened by repeated attacks and lack of food, decided to surrender after obtaining the promise that they would remain unharmed. However, the Cathars of the village refused to take part in the negotiations or to deny their faith.

RIGHT: St Martin-de-Canigou.
BELOW: mountain homes.

They opted for martyrdom; on 16 March 1244, 207 Cathars descended from Montségur onto the gigantic burning stake of the **Prats des Cramats** (field of the cremated), in *occitan* language. This was a fearful blow to Catharism.

Yet in some upland villages the heresy lingered on into the 14th century – as related by social historian Emmanuel Le Roy Ladurie in his best-selling book *Montaillou* (1978), the vivid account of medieval life in one such village, on a plateau southeast of Foix. The village still possesses the crumbling ruins of its feudal château.

The descent

The road from Foix into the high peaks of the Eastern Pyrenees follows the course of the **River Ariège**. First it crosses **Tarascon-sur-Ariège** ㉘, supposed site of the hidden grail of the Cathars. Next is **Ax-les-Thermes** ㉙, a serious spa which has its roots in Roman times.

After Ax-les-Thermes the road follows the Ariège, now a torrent, until the valley widens above the tree line. Cattle graze on the barren slopes, and often wander onto the road in search of grass. Here, finally, is the **Col de Puymorens** (1,915 m/6,281 ft), gateway to Roussillon and last major obstacle before the mountains fall away to the Mediterranean. ❑

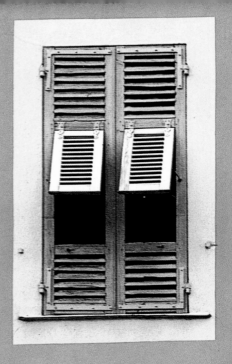
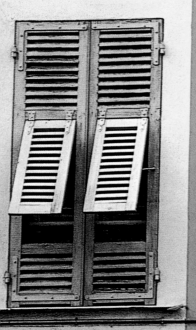

THE SOUTH

The Mediterranean coast of France stretches from Italy to the Pyrenees and the border with Spain. The coast of **Languedoc-Roussillon** (*pages 305–312*) offers charming fishing ports like Collioure, another lure for artists, as well as a string of spanking new resorts distinguished by their golden beaches and modernistic architecture.

Inland, Languedoc is Cathar country, its ruined castles and defensive villages marked by years of religious struggle in the Middle Ages. Most distinguished of these is the medieval theme park of Carcassonne, its familiar walls and turrets so controversially restored. Toulouse is the hub, a lively city built of the rosy red brick typical of the region, and combining pride in the past and innovative plans for the future, typical of this rapidly developing part of France.

Today **Provence** (*pages 315–322*) has acquired almost as mythic a status as the coast, and during the summer months it can seem almost as popular; vast crowds flock to the theatre festival in Avignon, the bullfight *feria* in Nîmes and the gypsy pilgrimage to Saintes Maries-de-la-Mer. But there is more – some of France's finest Roman remains are here, including the amphitheatre in Arles, the theatre in Orange and the extraordinary Pont du Gard.

Always in the background are the windswept mountain plateaux, river gorges and lavender terraces of Provence. The South is famous for its *villages perchés*, hamlets that cling to inaccessible mountain crags like an organic part of the landscape. The region provides wonderful walking country whether you choose to clamber over the dry maquis and sunbleached rocks of the Luberon, or explore the many verdant river gorges of tumbling streams and rushing waterfalls.

The South of France has been a glamorous holiday destination, both winter and summer, for more than a century and its enduring popularity accounts for millions of visitors every year. Along the southeast coast of the Mediterranean the star-studded names of the **Côte d'Azur** (*pages 327–338*) are strung like a glittering necklace; Cannes, Nice, Monte-Carlo, Antibes and St Tropez.

Their plentiful pleasures include not only sun and sea but magnificent modern art museums and medieval architecture, glorious perfumes and exotic flower gardens, world class yachts, casinos, and film and jazz festivals. It is a region best appreciated through the eyes of the many artists inspired by its luminous light and dazzling colours; Picasso's nymphs and sea urchins, Matisse's balcony views of Nice, Dufy's triangles of white sails on a blue sea. ❏

PRECEDING PAGES: living behind shutters in Provence.
LEFT: tropical gardens at Eze-sur-Mer.

LANGUEDOC AND ROUSSILLON

This region offers wide river valleys and rugged gorges as well as popular coastal resorts and regenerated cities which are centres of artistic activity and architectural innovation

Map on page 306

Although half of the Languedoc-Roussillon administrative French region, **Roussillon** is most distinguished by its Catalonian identity. Local architecture, landscapes and lifestyles all have a largely Spanish flavour, and the language of Catalan is widely spoken here. Indeed, some of Roussillon's older inhabitants still stubbornly refer to the city of Barcelona as their capital.

Coming from the Pyrenees and the Col de Puymorens, the road winds down steeply, passing the ski resort of **Font-Romeu** ❶, into a very wide valley that separates France and Spain, and gives the impression of being already near sea level. Yet at the fortified town of **Mont-Louis** ❷, the road suddenly plunges into the steep and narrow **Gorges de Carança**, and does not level off until it reaches the town of Prades.

Prades ❸ and its surrounding villages are built at the foot of the **Pic du Canigou** and provide some of the best scenic and cultural treats of all the region. The favoured town of the cellist Pablo Casals, who died in 1973 aged 97, Prades holds a commemorative music festival from late July to early August in the magnificent surrounding of the 11th-century abbey of **St Michel-de-Cuxa** ❹.

Up the road, at the foot of the Pic's wooded heights, the spa **Vernet-les-Bains** is cooled by a vociferous mountain torrent. From the nearby village of **Casteil** is the steep ascent (on foot) to the spectacularly sited monastery of **St Martin-de-Canigou** ❺ (open daily; entrance fee), superbly restored and one of the finest examples of Romanesque architecture in the region.

The forbidding road to the Pic du Canigou leaves from the **Col** (pass) **de Millières**. It's 16 km (10 miles) to the **Chalet-Hôtel des Cortalets** where one must leave the car for the two-hour walk to the top of the Pic. The panorama is worth the effort. At 2,784 m (9,132 ft), the Canigou looks out over the Pyrenees and towards the Mediterranean, sometimes as far as Montpellier.

A French Catalonia

Anyone falling from the sky and landing in Perpignan's **Place Arago**, paved with marble, lined with palm trees, and straddling the flowered canal, would be sure that he had dropped in on Spain. For a long time the second city of Catalonia, **Perpignan** ❻, has fully kept its Spanish flavour. A city of moderate size (pop. 120,000) and only moderate touristic appeal, its streets are always lively.

The best way to reach the heart of the city is through the **Castillet**, along the canal. This medieval gate sided by two massive brick towers is the emblem

LEFT: Perpignan has kept its Spanish flavour. **BELOW:** the beach at Collioure.

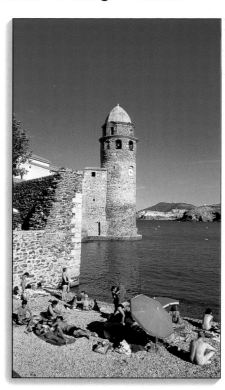

*A corner of the
harbour at Collioure.*

of Perpignan, and opens onto its oldest streets. Straight ahead, the **Loge de Mer**, **Hôtel de Ville** (city hall) and the **Palais de Députation** are three adjacent 15th-century facades of extraordinary beauty, whose inner courtyards have the delicacy and ornate splendour of Spanish palaces. The **Place de la Loge**, paved with pink marble, is reserved for pedestrians and captures the lively and festive nightlife.

The gem of the Catalonian coast, the chosen paradise of kings past, the inspiration of great 20th-century painters like Matisse, Braque and Picasso, is **Collioure ❼**, the goddess of Roussillon. Encased in a small, rocky bay, the Albères mountains practically pushing the town into the sea, Collioure has escaped the development that has devoured the coast of Roussillon down to **Argelès-sur-Mer**, 10 km (6 miles) away. The horseshoe-shaped bay is separated in two halves by the 13th-century **Château Royal** (open daily; closed public hols; entrance fee) of the king of Mallorca.

The rocky coast south of Collioure is particularly scenic and refreshing, but beware of July and August traffic jams. The narrow road winds up and

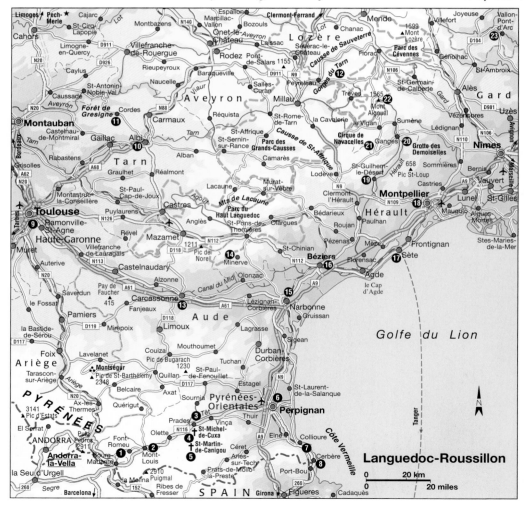

down across Port-Vendres and Banyuls, all the way to charming **Cerbère** ❽, the last port before Spain.

Land of Oc

Although it no longer has definite boundaries, the ancient region of **Languedoc** extends basically from the Rhône valley to the Garonne at Toulouse. The area benefited from the Roman occupation of the 1st to 4th centuries. Its early cultural and intellectual development, led by cities like Toulouse and Montpellier in the Middle Ages, gave Languedoc a sense of pride and independence from the French crown. The apogee came in the 13th century when Catharism, the movement aimed at Christian reform (*see page 297*), gained popularity and power throughout Languedoc. The crushing of the Cathars weakened and destroyed much of the region, assuring its allegiance to the kingdom of France.

The only material yielded by the plain of the Garonne, the red brick, has given **Toulouse** ❾ its trademark rose-red buildings. From the 9th to 13th centuries, the city enjoyed complete autonomy, and the Toulousians lived a life of prosperity and leisure. Today Toulouse is the fastest developing city in France, boasting an extremely advanced technological and intellectual community. Concorde, for example, was created here, and the university established in 1229 is the second largest in France.

Entering Toulouse from the south, stop a quarter of the way across the modern **Pont St Michel** ❹ to admire the perspective of old Toulouse. The churches are easily recognisable, and at sunset reflect a deep red or mauve.

The centre of Toulouse is at the Place du Capitole. The vast **Capitole** ❷, Toulouse's city hall, also houses a theatre and opera house. Nearby is the Rue

Maps:
Area 306
City 308

"Pink city at dawn, red in the raw sun, mauve at dusk." This popular phrase describing Toulouse is amazingly close to the truth.

BELOW: Toulouse's red-brick is its special trademark.

La Goulue et
Valentin-le-Dessose
by Henri Toulouse-
Lautrec (1891), in
the Musée Toulouse-
Lautrec, Albi.

du Taur, which leads to both the 11th-century Roman basilica **St Sernin** , the largest Romanesque church in Europe, with a magnificent bell tower, and **Notre-Dame-de-Taur** . Taur is the Latin word for bull and Notre Dame de Taur was erected in the spot where martyr Saint Sernin (of the Basilica) was buried after being dragged about Toulouse by one of those brutal beasts. Two blocks from the Capitole towards the river stands **Les Jacobins** , a complex of church, convent and cloister. The imposing brick walls suggest a fortress, but the interior displays the Flamboyant Gothic style, celebrated by palm-tree vaulting.

Off to the right of the Capitole is the pedestrian street of **Rue St Rome** . Along with the noisier **Rue d'Alsace-Lorraine** running parallel, these streets have the liveliest shopping. Beyond the Place Esquiro 1 which connects the two streets, begins the hushed **Vieux Quartier** , the medieval core. Nightlife centres about **Place du Président Wilson** and the **Allée Roosevelt** that emanates from it. Parisian-style cafés line the pavements while outdoor musicians provide entertainment.

Toulouse-Lautrec's home town

Albi "*la rouge*" is situated on the banks of the River Tarn, which meanders through the region to which it gives its name. Albi, the birthplace of Henri de Toulouse-Lautrec, is a city with a rich historical and artistic heritage.

Because in the 12th and 13th centuries Albi was a haven for the Cathars, religious heretics are often referred to as *Albigeois*. It was not until 1282, after most Cathars had been massacred, that the Catholic bishop of Castanet started building the **Cathédrale de Ste Cécile**. As a show of force to any who might aspire to heresy, it was conceived externally as a fortress, a style that charac-

BELOW: vegetable
seller, Carcassonne.

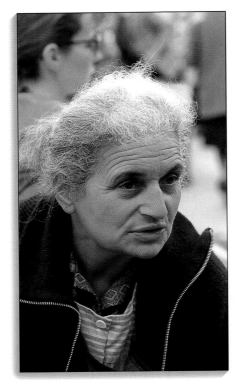

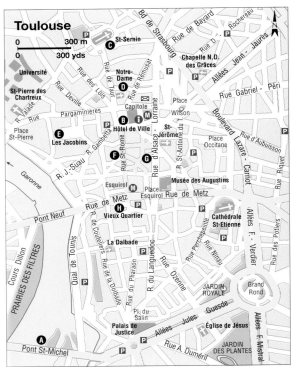

terised many Gothic cathedrals in Languedoc. Its giant, barren walls of bright red brick dwarf the old town. But while the exterior is as plain and austere as a cathedral could be, the decoration of the interior is exquisite. The walls are all painted with religious scenes or intricate patterns. Most celebrated are the 15th century frescoes of the *Last Judgment*. A wall of arches, in Flamboyant Gothic style, encloses the choir in the middle of the nave.

Adjacent to the cathedral is the old episcopal palace that now houses the **Musée Henri de Toulouse-Lautrec** (open Apr–Sept: daily; Oct–Mar: Wed–Mon; closed public hols; entrance fee) which contains the most complete collection of his work, as well as some of the famous portraits.

Northwest of Albi, wrapped around a conical hill in a cloak of steep cobbled streets, mellow stone and mossy Roman tiles stands **Cordes** ⓫. With a rough history of excommunication during the crusade against the Cathars and later plague, the restored town is now a bustling centre for arts and crafts and tourism.

While the Tarn at Albi is wide and majestic as it meanders westward, 100 km (60 miles) to the east the magnificent **Gorges du Tarn** ⓬ begin, the river carving extraordinary canyons through steep limestone cliffs. Les Detroits (the straits), the most impressive section of the gorges, start from the town of Le Rozier. Here the river is but a few metres wide with the cliffs towering more than 300 m (1,000 ft) above. Just a few kilometres upstream of the town of Les Vignes, where the river widens, is the **Point Sublime**.

Victory with a pig

Halfway between Toulouse and the Mediterranean sea along what was once the border with Spain, **Carcassonne** ⓭ is without question the only medieval monument of its kind in Europe. Built on a hill of 50 m (160 ft), the fortified town dominates the plain.

Legend has it that after Charlemagne had besieged the city for five years, one Dame Carcas gathered all the last bits of grain remaining in the starved-out city, fed them to a stray pig, and ordered the animal to be thrown over the ramparts. On landing, the stuffed beast burst, scattering grain at the feet of Charlemagne's army. Amazed at the apparent abundance of food, Charlemagne called for negotiations, and Dame Carcas answered with victorious trumpet blasts: whence the name *"Carcas sonne!"* (Carcas rings).

Aside from its romance, the uniqueness of Carcassonne lies in its two sets of intact fortifications, which surround a tiny town of 350 inhabitants overlooking the modern city. The first ramparts were built by the Romans in the 3rd and 4th centuries AD. They were later improved upon in the 13th century under St Louis, for fear of a Spanish invasion.

During the Middle Ages, the town housed 4,000 inhabitants, and in periods of siege, up to 10,000 would take refuge inside the fortifications. The two sets of walls rendered the city absolutely impregnable; if a group of enemy soldiers managed to climb over the first set, they would only find themselves trapped between the two ramparts.

Early detection of Carcassonne's beauty in the 19th century by the author Prosper Merimée led to its

Maps: Area 306 City 308

TIP

A stroll outside the Toulouse-Lautrec museum will take you around the dungeon and into the flower gardens below, allowing you a magnificent view over the Tarn.

BELOW: the medieval city of Carcassonne.

A modern pilgrim following the famous medieval route to Santiago de Compostela in Spain. The scallop is the symbol of St James (Santiago).

BELOW:
playing *boules*.

restoration by the controversial 19th-century architect Viollet-le-Duc, who rebuilt it in what he considered to be medieval style, complete with dubious pepperpot towers.

After crossing the drawbridge, or **Porte Narbonnaise**, and passing a few tourist shops, you reach the heart of the bustling little town, filled with cafés and restaurants, bakeries and antique shops. A nocturnal visit to the medieval **Château Comtal** (open daily; closed public hols; entrance fee) is particularly impressive, and during June and July a cultural festival is held here, using its fabulous outdoor amphitheatre for a stage. Walking between the ramparts, one can follow the entire perimeter of Carcassonne and admire the combination of Roman and medieval construction methods.

The plains

The journey between Carcassonne and Montpellier is a pleasant one, through fields of grapevines, along the banks of slow rivers and roads lined with plane trees. This is the growing region for the abundant Corbières and Minervois wines, robust reds that are becoming increasingly popular. Surrounded by a sea of vines, **Minerve ⓮** is proud of its defiant past, when the Cathar town held out against Simon de Montfort in a siege that lasted seven weeks; 140 citizens were burned at the stake when they refused to renounce their faith.

The roads in this region are often accompanied by the friendly **Canal du Midi**, which links the Mediterranean with the Atlantic via the Garonne river, and is a favourite playground for vacationers on rented houseboats. **Narbonne ⓯**, once the capital of the Roman region of *Narbonensis Prima*, is today a shadow version of its former self. However it is worth visiting for its well restored medieval quarter, the excellent archaeological collection housed in the Archbishop's Palace, and next to it, the remarkable **Cathédrale St Just**, with its beautiful stained glass and tapestries and 14th-century cloisters. Note that despite its vast size, the cathedral today is only the choir of the gigantic structure originally planned.

The city of **Béziers ⓰**, 80 km (50 miles) from Montpellier, prospered under the Roman occupation. However, the crusade against the Cathars in 1209 reduced the city to ruins. Since the 19th century, thanks to the growing wine market, Béziers has regained its vitality, and is today a quiet city typical of the Midi. Life is taken at an unhurried pace along the plane-tree shaded esplanades where the *Biterrois* (inhabitants of Béziers) play *pétanque*, or sip pastis over lively talk about rugby.

The Coast

In the 1960s a major development programme on the Languedoc-Roussillon coast created a string of new and highly popular resorts. Some, like Cap d'Agde and La Grande-Motte, came complete with dramatic (if controversial) modern architecture – but all, fortunately, were still interspersed with miles of wind-swept, beaches.

Sète ⓱ stands out as the most authentic town along this coast, its bridges and canals reminiscent of

Venice, and its seafood restaurants unsurpassed anywhere, particularly popular with the fishermen who still frequent the port.

Set a few kilometres inland from the Mediterranean, **Montpellier** is the capital of the Languedoc-Roussillon region and one of the liveliest and youngest cities in the Midi. It has been revitalised by a dynamic mayor and a programme of avant-garde, public architectural developments, such as the Antigone project. The city has one of France's largest universities, but most important is its medical school, the oldest in France, dating back to the early 13th century.

The old town of Montpellier is confined to the very centre of the city, which embraces all the active student and social life. The best starting point into this section is the **Place de la Comédie**, a large oval, often known as l'Oeuf, in front of the opera house. From here, the **Rue de la Loge** leads to the **Place Jean-Jaurès**, perhaps the liveliest square of the city. During the day, a market of fresh fruit and meat, clothes and jewellery bustles until early afternoon. Once cleared, the square is filled with tables and chairs from the surrounding cafés. In the evening, it becomes a popular meeting place for students and for the well-heeled.

Rue de la Loge soon meets up with the **Rue Foch** that, in turn, climbs to the **Promenade du Peyrou** at the top of the hill. The Promenade consists of wide alleys lined by tall trees and flowerbeds, with an imposing statue of Louis XIV at its centre. From here, the sunset over the Cévennes mountains is splendid.

Across the boulevard from the 14th-century **Cathédrale de St Pierre** is the **Jardin des Plantes**, the oldest garden in France, founded in 1593 by Henry IV. And don't miss the **Musée Fabre**, a beautiful building with an excellent collection of French paintings (open Wed–Sun; entrance fee).

Map on page 306

TIP

Although the facades lining the side streets around Montpelier's Rue de la Loge are quite austere, the curious visitor who pushes open some of the heavy doors will step into magnificently elaborate courtyards.

BELOW: Château le Champ in the Cévennes.

The novelist Robert Louis Stevenson recalled his sojourn in the Cévennes in his 1879 book Travels with a Donkey in the Cévennes.

RIGHT: Pont d'Arc.
BELOW: Café chat.

Map on page 306

Secretive mountains

The distant mountains of **Cévennes** offer some spectacular natural formations, along with the solitary peace of mountain trails. Amongst the large *massifs* are several *causses*, which are the elevated, extremely dry plateaux, divided by very deep gorges, through which flow some of the major rivers of Languedoc.

The Cévennes rise abruptly about 60 km (36 miles) north of the Mediterranean. Considering the proximity to the sea, the climate is drastically cool, with temperatures of 18–21°C (65–70°F) in the summer, and chilly winds constantly blowing over the more elevated points. The winters can be harsh, with freezing winds and regular snowfalls. Now protected as a national park, the Cévennes provide an ideal break, in the summer, from the torrid heat of lower Languedoc. They could still be classified as virtually undiscovered by European vacationers.

En route from Montpellier is the once remote Romanesque abbey of **St Guilhem-le-Désert** ⓲, tucked into the head of a ravine overlooking the gorge of the Hérault river. Close by, the caverns of the **Grotte des Clamouses** can be explored. At the foot of the Cévennes the **Grotte des Demoiselles** ⓴, (open daily; entrance fee) are reputedly the most spectacular caves in the region. The central chamber, dubbed the cathedral, is 120 by 80 by 50 m (395 ft long, 262 ft wide and 164 ft high). Following the flow of the **River Hérault** northward will lead to the looming **Cirque de Navacelles** ㉑, an immense natural amphitheatre 300 m (1,000 ft) deep and 1.6 km (1 mile) in diameter created by the **River Vis**. Continuing along the course of the Hérault, the pretty road ultimately leads to the highest peak of the Cévennes, **Mont Aigoual** ㉒ (1,567 m/5,140 ft). From here the view is magnificent. On a clear day one can see the Alps to the east, the Mediterranean to the south, and the Pyrenees to the southwest.

The entire region surrounding the Mont Aigoual is full of foot trails, marked by the code GR, followed by a number. These trails are well-travelled in the summer and have mountain lodges along the way. Still further north, however, in the area known as **Lozère**, one can easily lose oneself on deserted paths.

Adjacent to the Cévennes on the eastern side, 100 km (60 miles) northeast of Montpellier, lies the region known as the **Ardèche**. Situated on high plateaux that resemble the *causses*, and are given to abrupt descents, this area marks the eastern edge of Languedoc. The Ardèche river, which gives its name to the region, follows a particularly picturesque course to the Rhône.

While canoeing and kayaking are prevalent throughout all of Languedoc, the Ardèche is most ideal. The section beyond the village of **Vallon Pont d'Arc** ㉓ is especially scenic and challenging. The river has dug incredibly deep and large gorges that are equally spectacular when viewed from the river or from the road 400 m (1,300 ft) above. At **Pont d'Arc** the river has pierced a passage through the rock, which has grown into a beautifully symmetrical arch.

For canoeists, the river runs at a reasonable speed with challenging rapids. It's best to descend before mid-July, after which the water level is too low. Canoes can be rented at many places around Vallon Pont d'Arc. ❑

PROVENCE

This is the magical, light-infused world of the Mediterranean, where black cypresses bend in the breeze under an azure blue sky, and the scent of pine and lavender hangs on the air

Provence is a place where the myth of the French people comes alive: open-hearted, relaxed and full of *joie de vivre*. There is plenty of laughter here, good wine, late hours and warm smiles. The passionate Provençal people have witnessed civilisation succeed civilisation over thousands of years and, although independent in character, have learned the advantage of accepting the influence of Italy, Spain and the Arab world. Vestiges of this turbulent past are scattered liberally across the region. Stretching from the marshy Camargue to the Alpine foothills, most of Provence is a dry but fertile land whose austere pine forests are in constant danger of sweeping fires.

Bullfights and Romans

The 2,000-year-old Roman amphitheatres at Arles, Nîmes and Orange still echo with thundering hooves and desperate cries, when summer bullfights draw enormous crowds to these former gladiatorial arenas. Nîmes is home to France's top bullfighting school and each May hosts the **Feria de Pentecôte** series of bullfights, the best attended festival in Europe. In Arles the noble bull is not killed. Instead 10 white-suited matadors attempt to snatch a red ribbon from its tossing horns; a far more skilful and exciting contest.

In addition to the bulls, the arena at **Nîmes ❶** is a summer venue for rock concerts and sporting events. Nearby, the ancient temple of the **Maison Carrée** (open Tues–Sun) is a fine example of Roman architectural flair with its delicate Corinthian columns. Opposite, the new arts complex, the **Carré d'Art** (open Tues–Sun; entrance fee), is a modern tribute in glass and steel by British architect Norman Foster. This is only one of many new buildings in Nîmes, a far-sighted city which successfully combines the old with the avant-garde. Amongst the old is the lovely **Jardin de la Fontaine** (open daily), an 18th-century network of terraces, bridges and water pools.

Nîmes is also the spiritual home of blue jeans. Blue durable cloth was imported from Egypt by Nîmois tailors as early as the 17th century. In 1848 Levi-Strauss, a Californian, discovered the cloth in America, and used it to make work clothes for farmers. The cloth he used had the mark "de Nîmes", and "Denim" was born.

Twenty kilometres (12 miles) northeast of Nîmes is the spectacular **Pont du Gard ❷**, one of the finest remaining Roman aqueducts in the world. Spanning half a mile over the river Gardon, its massive stones have stood intact for more than 2,000 years. The view from the top tier of arches is breathtaking.

North of the Pont du Gard, in the dusty, scrub-covered hills of the *garrigue*, the town of **Uzès ❸**

LEFT: the regal fountains of Aix-en-Provence.
BELOW: Provençale in native costume.

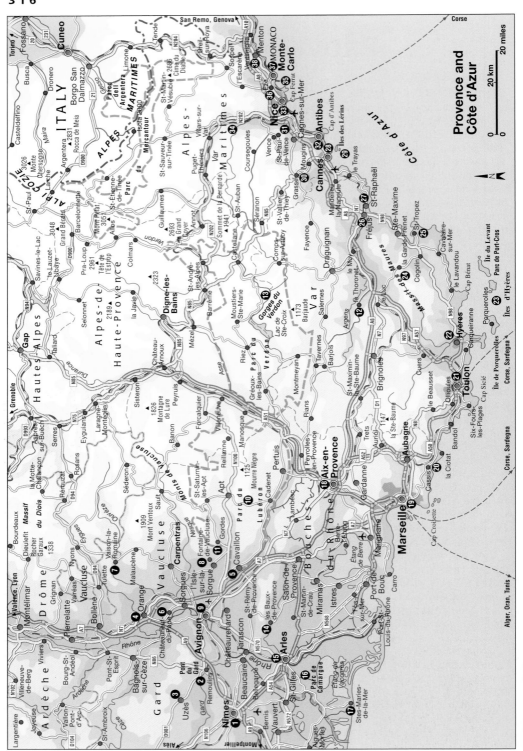

Provence and
Côte d'Azur

Map on page 316

announces itself with a flourish of medieval towers. Its focal point is the central Place aux Herbes, with its arcaded buildings and colourful Saturday morning market laid out under the trees.

Orange ❹, at the northern tip of Provence, was also a thriving Roman settlement and possesses a majestic amphitheatre complete with 3-m (10-ft) high statue of Emperor Augustus and the original **Arc de Triomphe**, built in AD 26. Surrounding Orange, the area of the **Vaucluse** is richly fertile. In May the sweet melons of **Cavaillon** ❺ are carried up to Paris for the French president's delectation. In early summer wild morel mushrooms, sweet tomatoes and peppers colour the fields. In October the grape and olive harvests begin. This is also home to the Provençal truffle: furtive figures roam the hills in early spring seeking its priceless flesh. The dark, earthy vegetable has a strong smell attractive to pigs. The rich earth also nourishes some of France's most famous vineyards, in particular those at **Châteauneuf-du-Pape** ❻ which are famous for their strong red and flavourful white wines.

Northern Provence

This is a beautiful land of hills and woods much of which has national park status. Nature rules this barren countryside – the violent Mistral wind roars down the Rhône bending street-lights and tearing the ears off unsuspecting donkeys. **Vaison-la-Romaine** ❼ suffered a tragic flood in 1992 in which 30 people drowned. The area is recovering and proceeds from tourists visiting the Roman ruins are helping to restore the village. **Fontaine-de-Vaucluse** ❽, where poet Petrarch spent 16 years composing ballads for Laura, is Europe's largest natural spring with a 400-m (1,300-ft) deep pool. Jacques Cousteau almost

Cavaillon is famous for its melons.

BELOW: Dentelles de Montmirail – the barren landscape of northern Provence.

drowned here and nobody has yet plunged to the bottom of the spring's secret.

Capital of this region, **Avignon** ❾ is a walled city of history, refinement and culture. The Popes moved here from Rome in 1309 at the behest of King Philippe the Handsome. For 70 years Avignon was the centre of European religion, art and prostitution. The clerics and brothels are long gone, but the palace remains the most breathtaking sight in Provence. The **Palais des Papes** (open daily; entrance fee) is superb inside and out with its silent cloisters, cavernous halls and imposing ramparts. Leading from the palace, **Place de l'Horloge** is the place to sip a *pastis* and wonder why the Popes ever left. The famous "Pont d'Avignon", **Pont St Bénézet**, on which the nursery rhyme dances, is a disappointing four-arch ruin tumbling into the Rhône.

Le Lubéron

To the east of Avignon lies **Le Lubéron** ❿, the region made famous by Peter Mayle's international best-seller *A Year in Provence*. Still relatively untarnished, the Lubéron retains a mystic attraction. Mayle lived in **Ménerbes**, but the small villages of **Oppède-le-Vieux** and **Gordes** ⓫ have far more charm. Here too is the moonscape of **Roussillon** and its incredible rock formations of red ochre. In the 1990s the Lubéron is one of the most fashionable places to live in France: Brigitte Bardot and Sean Connery have houses here, along with the *crème* of Parisian society.

For fewer crowds and more countryside, head north to the sleepy vine-fringed villages of the **Haut-Var** with their legends of flying donkeys and fire-breathing dragons. The **Abbaye du Thoronet** ⓬ is a beautiful 12th-century monastery hidden in the hills on the way to the **Gorges du Verdon** ⓭, France's

Grand Canyon. The Verdon cuts through limestone cliffs which plunge to the torrent 600 m (2,000 ft) below. From here stretch the **Alpes de Haute Provence**, a wild, barren landscape leading up into the French Alps.

South of Avignon the land flattens, punctuated only by the rock outcrop of **Les Baux-de-Provence ⓮**. This medieval citadel inspired Dante's view of hell in *Inferno*. Today the wind tears at the twisted rock from which bauxite was first mined in 1822. Its desolate summit provides an unforgettable panorama over the **Crau Plain** to the flower-clad slopes of **Les Alpilles**.

Soul cities

The soul of Provence lies in **Arles ⓯**. In among the pretty nests of red roofs and soft stone the splendid church of **St Trophime** chimes out its relaxed charm each hour, while the statue of Frédéric Mistral, poet of Provence, and the man responsible for reviving the Provençal language and traditions at the turn of the century, gazes down benignly. Above all, this is a place to wander and sit, following in the footsteps of Van Gogh who lost his sanity in the sun-dappled cafés and neighbouring heat-swirled fields. The Saturday market, when gypsies gather from surrounding villages with their guitars, is eternally lively.

Arles is the gateway to **La Camargue ⓰**, a wild place of lagoons, rice fields and cowboys. The *gardians* ride white horses and tend to the herds of black bulls that roam the marshes. In summer, thousands of flamingos congregate on the lagoons, turning the water pink. Today the best way to experience the Camargue is still on horseback (organised excursions). **Saintes-Maries-de-la-Mer ⓱** is the gypsy capital of the world. In late May thousands of travellers flock to the village for the festival of the black Madonna, when a statue of the Virgin is

Map on page 316

In Les Baux-de-Provence, if you can afford it , seek shelter from the wind and the tourists at Jean-André Charial's famous restaurant l'Oustau de Baumanière (tel: 04-90 97 33 07).

BELOW: Camargue symbol.

The Fontaine des Quatres Dauphins, surrounded by four dolphins, lies at the heart of the Quartier Mazarin. This aristocratic area, with its chequerboard street plan, was named after an archbishop of Aix, the brother of the famous cardinal.

BELOW: Marseille's Vieux Port.

carried into the sea surrounded by white horses. The statue is kept in the crypt of the village church, along with a terrifying effigy of a woman whose stare follows you around. The beach here is one of the longest in Provence: kilometres of white sand and shallow water. To the east, the salt works at **Salins-de-Provence** turn sea into mountains of salt.

Intellectual heart

Handsome, aristocratic **Aix-en-Provence** ⑱, city of fountains and tree-lined avenues, is the intellectual heart of Provence. Between 1487 and the Revolution the Supreme Court of France sat here, and today Aix still possesses one of Europe's most prestigious universities. Its ancient streets, 17th-century residences and numerous squares are reminiscent of Paris and, like the capital, Aix adores its "beautiful people". A Sunday afternoon in a café on the **Cours Mirabeau** ❶ is a lesson in crafted chic. Adjust your sunglasses, pout, and watch the world and his poodle go by.

Aix derives its name from the Latin for water, *aqua*. Water is everywhere and fountains trickle in every corner. The **Fontaine des Quatre Dauphins** is one of the most beautiful in a small square of 17th-century hotels. During the 19th century, novelist Emile Zola's father was the engineer responsible for building aqueducts to improve Aix's water circulation. Zola grew up in the city along with his friend, painter Paul Cézanne (*see pages 324–325*). One of the best ways to see Aix is by taking the **Cézanne Trail**, following a free leaflet from the tourist office. Bronze plaques mark sites from the painter's life. North of the cathedral on Avenue Paul Cézanne, **L'Atelier Paul Cézanne** (open daily; entrance fee) preserves the artist's studio and house – his cape and beret hang

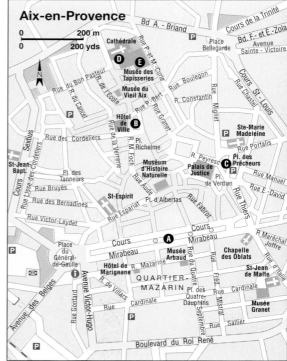

where he left them. Modern art is found at the **Fondation Vasarely** (4 km/2 miles west; bus from Boulevard de la République; open daily; entrance fee).

Aix is the place for markets, and on Saturdays **Place de l'Hôtel de Ville** and **Place des Prêcheurs** ● are filled with stalls of garlic, tomatoes, beans, olive oil, spicy sausage and riotous flowers. To the north of the city centre is the **Cathédrale de St Sauveur** ● and behind is the **Musée des Tapisseries** ● (open Wed–Mon; closed public hols; entrance fee).

Dominating Aix, the **Montagne Ste Victoire** was depicted by Cézanne in over 60 of his paintings. Strikingly triangular when viewed from the picturesque hamlet of **Le Tholonet**, the mountain is a naked contortion of white rock. Cézanne collapsed on one of the paths leading to the mountain, and died in Aix in 1906. The magical light of Ste Victoire attracted numerous other artists – Picasso himself is buried under the shadow of the rock, at his former château in **Vauvenargues**.

Gateway to the Mediterranean

South of Aix, **Marseille** ⓭ is France's oldest and second biggest city. Founded by Greek traders in 600 BC, the gateway to the Mediterranean, the Orient and beyond has been a bustling port for centuries. Marseille's reputation as the "Chicago of France" was built on tales of Mafia, financial corruption and drugs. In the 1960s and '70s this was the infamous "French Connection" providing drugs for the United States.

More recently Marseille has done much to clean up its image. The Mafia has moved down the coast and today the city is a vibrant, spicy concoction, worthy of its most famous dish, the thick fish stew *bouillabaisse.*

Maps:
Area 316
City 320

Some years ago the Marseille police seized 40 fruit machines in a clampdown on illegal gambling, storing them overnight in the main police station. Next morning, they found that 36 of the machines had been meticulously stripped down, the parts removed for use elsewhere.

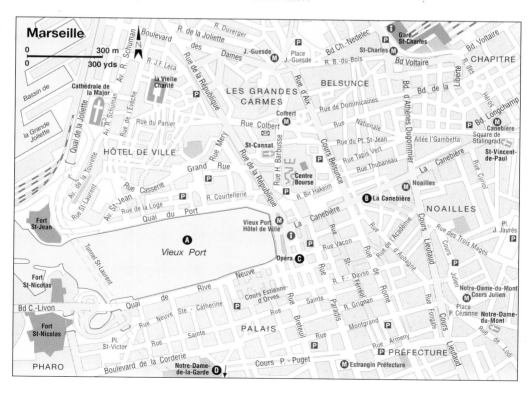

Maps:
Area 316
City 321

"The breeze is deliciously sweet, the sun is already warming the earth, and yet the air remains sharp and dry, like the taste of wine. Everywhere are the fragrances of honey, thyme, lavender, all the herbs of the nearby hills."

— PAUL CEZANNE

RIGHT: Marseille port bustles with life.
BELOW: Paul Fouque, famed crèchemaker.

Today the **Vieux Port** has a colourful fishmarket and many seafood restaurants. (Beware – most of the seafood has been cargoed down from Scandinavia, and unfrozen that morning.) Running from the port is **La Canebière** , or "Can o'beer" as it was to British sailors of the 19th century. Marseille's most famous street, the boulevard is a human tide of different nationalities by day and an empty wasteland at night. The streets around the Canebière are lively, with the **Opéra** a focal point for music-lovers and prostitutes. On nights when the American navy is in town this area becomes a farcical stage as fur-wrapped opera buffs weave their way daintily through crowds of drunken, singing, whoring sailors.

Whilst commonsense is required in the city at night, Marseille's nightlife is surprisingly quiet. The good and the bad head to the nightclubs in Aix, whilst the rest of them are in bed by 10 o'clock. When the football team, Olympique de Marseille, is playing at home the city is a ghost town until the final whistle of the match when, if the team has won, the streets erupt into a noisy party.

Marseille is still a great port, and as such has welcomed immigrants from all round the Mediterranean basin. Tales of racism are not without foundation, but Marseille deals successfully with its urban tensions. North Marseille is a concrete land of megalithic apartment blocks hastily constructed in the 1960s to house immigrants after the Algerian War. To the south are elegant 17th-century townhouses. Climb to **Notre-Dame-de-la-Garde** , the white church which is the spiritual home of the city. A golden Virgin looks seaward, and at sunset time stops and Marseille appears the most beautiful place on earth.

To the east is **Aubagne** whose rough white rock hills were home to Marcel Pagnol and his stories of Provençal lust and revenge: Jean de Florette prayed in vain for water in the parched fields, and Manon des Sources stalked the herb-scented ravines.

Dramatic coastline

The least developed of a much-abused coastline lies between Marseille and Toulon. Here the shore is distinguished by **Les Calanques**, steep-sided fjords carved out of cliffs, best viewed by boat from Cassis.

Cassis ⑳ is a charming little port, today a chic resort of restored village houses with a popular golden beach. It is famous for its fragrant white wine which tantalises the palate with savours of rosemary, gorse and myrtle – the herbs which cover these hills. A little further down the coast is **Bandol**, home to another of the finest wines in Provence.

To the north, the high ridge of Le Gros-Cerveau (Big Brain) overlooks vineyards, orchards and fields of flowers – and on clear days, the distant harbour of Toulon. By the D11, around Gros Cerveau, one proceeds into wilder country, through the **Gorge d'Ollioules**, a hill village with ruinous basalt houses holding fast to the side of a long-extinct volcano.

Down the road is **Mont Caume** whose panorama extends from Cap Bénat in the east to La Ciotat in the west. Returning to the coast, there is another great view from Cap Canaille, just east of Cassis. The highest sea cliff in Europe (350-m/1,000-ft) offers vistas across Cassis, the Calanques and the Mediterranean. ❑

POST-IMPRESSIONISTS IN PROVENCE

"The whole future of art is to be found in the South of France," declared Vincent van Gogh, a northern artist with a southern sensibility.

While impressionism emerged in Paris Provence was the creative melting pot between 1875 and 1920. Monet and Renoir, two leading lights, were entranced by the seductive landscape and intoxicating southern light. In their footsteps came French and foreign post-impressionists, from Van Gogh and Gauguin to Cézanne, the greatest of them all. It was in the south that Van Gogh (1853–90) abandoned the illusion of painting as an imitation of nature. The wave of avant-garde artists continued, from Picasso and Braque in their Cubist incarnations, to Chagall, Matisse and Dufy. Van Gogh and Gauguin are associated with Arles, Cézanne with Aix, while Signac and Matisse are linked to Saint Tropez and Nice. The Nabis were post-impressionists who styled themselves as followers of Gauguin. Bonnard (1867–1947), the painter of sensations, lived in a hillside villa above Cannes. His was a seductive Mediterranean idyll of dreamy southern interiors and sun-dappled light. Les Fauves, founded by Matisse (1869–1954) in 1905, were dubbed "wild beasts" for their fondness for lurid colours. Picasso (1881–1973) lived on the Côte d'Azur, notably in Antibes and Juan les Pins, and worked on Cubism with Braque (1882–1963) in Céret in 1911. Picasso dismissed Bonnard as painting in "a pot pourri of indecision" and failing to "go beyond his own sensibility".

▷ **VINCENT VAN GOGH'S** *SELF-PORTRAIT* (1890)
Van Gogh adored the olive groves close to Aix but died a tragic death in the north in the same year.

▷ **CÉZANNE'S** *MONT-STE-VICTOIRE* (1882–85)
Cézanne wished to turn "impressionism into something solid and enduring, like the art of museums." Art-lovers can look for his landmarks in the Aix landscape.

△ **TOULOUSE-LAUTREC** *AT HIS DESK* (1898)
When southern painters went north they took the southern spirit with them. The aristocrat from Albi (1864–1901) led a raffish life in Paris. Albi's Toulouse-Lautrec museum also has paintings by Gauguin, Dufy, Bonnard, and Matisse.

△ **PAUL GAUGUIN'S** *ALLÉE DES ALYSCAMPS, ARLES* (1888)
Van Gogh persuaded Gauguin (1848–1903) to join him in Arles but then attacked him, resulting in Gauguin fleeing to Paris. Gauguin believed in intensity of feeling and the pre-eminence of colour.

▽ **PICASSO'S** *LE PAYSAGE À MOUGINS*
The artist's cubism did not find favour with Marc Chagall (1887–1985): "To me, cubism seemed to limit pictorial expression unduly".

CÉZANNE COUNTRY

Paul Cézanne (1839–1906), self-portrait above, is considered the founder of modern painting. Yet, as a painter born and bred in Provence, he was also a southern spirit. His credo was: "Colour can move, can make mountains." Cézanne country consists of blue quarries and red clay, darkly green pine trees and geometric, sun-baked rocks. His sacred themes were the primeval limestone mountain, the darkly romantic castle. In his Provençal landscapes, Cézanne strove for order, serenity and solidity in a scene bathed in light.

Cézanne's ambition was 'to re-do Poussin from nature," to remake pastoral idylls of the old masters in a modern way. According to the British art critic Brian Sewell, Cézanne broke the mould, anticipating "cubism, expressionism, Picasso, Matisse, Utrillo, Modigliani and even Lucien Freud." Cézanne's bathers are heir to Renaissance nudes while his later landscapes led to cubism. A fascinating Cézanne trail can be followed in and around Aix-en-Provence, visiting areas that were immortalised by the painter, from the Chateau-Noir estate to Mont-Ste-Victoire.

▷ HENRI MATISSE'S *PLACE DE LICES, ST TROPEZ*
Matisse (1869–1954) loved the Catalan landscape but whereas Bonnard painted in his studio, Matisse luxuriated in the outdoors.

▷ RAOUL DUFY'S *ANTIBES – LE CHEMIN DE FER*
In Fauvist style, Raoul Dufy (1877–1953) used broad brushstrokes and vivid colours.

THE COTE D'AZUR

Map on page 316

Despite its popularity, the Côte d'Azur maintains its allure and remains the classic image of a summer holiday, whilst a rich artistic legacy and unspoilt hinterland only add to the heady mix

Paris

Debate as to the precise definition of the Côte d'Azur continues to rage, especially among property developers anxious to claim some of the magic. This chapter follows the coast from Toulon to the Italian border, and samples the secrets of the interior.

The prefecture of the *département* of the Var, **Toulon** ㉑ has been France's most important naval base since the royal navy was established. An amphitheatre of limestone hills, covered with pine, screens its deep natural harbour, one of the Mediterranean's most attractive. The surrounding hills are crowned by the star-shaped forts built by Vauban, Louis XIV's great military architect and engineer. Toulon was badly damaged in World War II and much of the post-war building is ugly, especially along Quai Stalingrad, where boats depart for tours of the harbour and nearby islands. Toulon is famous for the work of 17th-century sculptor Pierre Puget, who began his career carving ships' figureheads, and two of his best works, the *Atlantes*, can be seen on the *quai*. Works by his followers can be seen in the **Musée de la Marine** (open Wed–Mon; entrance fee), along with models of the many ships once made in Toulon.

Quai Stalingrad separates the port from the old town of Toulon which is at least as louche and authentic as Marseille, with plenty of sleazy bars and cheap hotels in streets like Place Puget and Rue d'Alger. The best time to visit is during morning market hours, especially the fish market on Place de la Poissonnerie.

Islands of gold

Modern **Hyères** ㉒, northeast of Toulon along the coast, is made up of a *vieille ville* and a newer area with modern villas and boulevards lined with date palms. This was an ancient and medieval port, but it is now 4 km (2 miles) from the sea. Hyères was the first "climatic" resort on the Côte d'Azur.

Hyères has long been a centre for seriously *sportif* French as well, its sub-tropical climate encouraging sailing, scuba-diving, wind-surfing and water-skiing. The busy atmosphere of a modern town combines charmingly with its backdrop of faded *belle époque* grandeur. The 14th-century château is built on the Casteou hill, above the old town's twisting medieval streets. Nearby is the 13th-century church of **St Louis**, a marriage of Italian Romanesque and Provençal Gothic. Within the old town, entered via its 13th-century gate, is the **Place Massillon**, where there is a food market every day, especially good for Arab and Provençal delicacies.

Presqu'Ile de Giens, which was once one of the **Iles d'Hyères** ㉓, is connected to the mainland by sand bars. The **Salins des Pesquiers** is the only salt marsh still worked on the Côte.

LEFT: the yachts of Monaco.
BELOW: cool in Cannes.

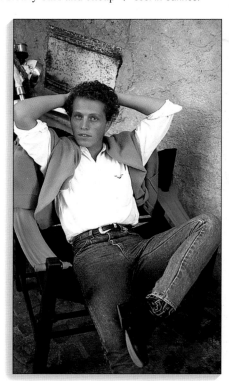

A travel guide from the 1800s.

Most of the forest on **Porquerolles**, the largest of the three islands, and **Port-Cros** next to it burned in the 1890s so that they now resemble rugged hilltops lushly planted with semitropical vegetation – which is, in fact, what they are; part of the very old mountain system to which the Maures and Esterel massifs belong. The Iles d'Hyères and Massif des Maures are schistous rock, while the colourful Massif de l'Esterel is famous for its blood-red porphyry. Sunlight reflected by mica in the rock is the origin of the name bestowed long ago, *Iles d'Or* or golden islands.

The navy bought **Ile du Levant**, the easternmost island, in 1892 for a firing range. Comparatively barren, it is now an aircraft engine testing centre. Sharing Ile du Levant is the well-known nudist colony, **Héliopolis**. Today, when facilities for nudists are all over France and topless sunbathing has become normal on the Riviera, Héliopolis is less sensational than when it was founded in 1931.

Massif des Maures

In the Middle Ages these islands and their tiny islets belonged to monks who were constantly at risk from pirate raids and until the 18th century the shore opposite, the wild, wooded, hilly region called the **Massif des Maures ㉔**, was almost deserted for fear of pirates. Only well-fortified hill and fishing villages like St Tropez and its upland neighbours were inhabited.

BELOW:
the plunging
coastline of the
Massif des Maures.

The demand for sea-and-sunbathing accommodation transformed the Maures coast into a lively strip of resorts – some, so far, less spoiled than others – and traditional local industries like bottle-cork and briar pipe manufacturing took second place to tourism.

The Maures's uncrowded inland roads pass through charming villages, ravines

Map on page 316

with waterfalls, and forests of carefully cultivated cork-oak and chestnut. Visitors are rewarded with glimpses of the sea; an abandoned 18th-century monastery, **Chartreuse de la Verne**; a medieval town, **La Garde-Freinet**, built around ruins of a Saracen castle with gardens designed by André Le Nôtre, and a market town, **Draguignan**, formerly the prefecture and now the centre of commercial wine production in the Maures (reds and rosé).

The damage from forest fires, a serious problem here, is very noticeable from the **Corniche des Maures**, the spectacular coastal road from **Le Lavandou** (a pleasant fishing village protected by Cap Bénat – although, like the others, overdeveloped – whose name evokes its fields of lavender) to **La Croix Valmer**, a resort that grows one of the better Côte-de-Provence wines.

The ultimate resort

At the eastern end of the Maures, **St Tropez** ㉕ looks north across the Golfe de St Tropez. Thus the quayside cafés receive the golden evening light and the bay's stunning sunsets. Today this once tiny fishing village receives up to 10,000 visitors in summer, becoming a sort of Mediterranean extension of the Left Bank of Paris, with all that this implies for parking and prices.

The writer Colette and other Parisians complained as early as the 1920s that "S'trop" was too crowded. Today even the yachts number in the thousands. French painters and writers had discovered it by the late 19th century and kindly recorded their findings. Paintings by these artists, some showing the village in its unspoiled state, have been collected in the **Musée de l'Annonciade** (open Wed–Mon; closed public hols; entrance fee), a converted 16th-century chapel.

It is still possible to head for the hills to get away from holidaymakers who

St Tropez is a barometer of style, and designers such as Jean-Paul Gaultier and Joseph Ettedgui still make a point of hanging out at the fashionable Sennequier café by the port to see who's wearing what.

BELOW:
in the evening sun at St Tropez.

Bikinis struck the beaches of St Tropez at the end of World War II. In 1957, director Roger Vadim filmed his then unknown wife Brigitte Bardot, wearing even less on the beach, starting the national craze for her and for St Tropez.

BELOW: capturing the Café des Arts, St Tropez.

assemble every summer to watch celebrities and each other. Several villages in the Maures have their own elaborate way of preparing *marrons glacés,* the delicious sugary chestnut that comes foil-wrapped. A tour could be built around them or, since this is the place for it, squeeze into discos and onto the beaches (**Tahiti** and **Pampelonne** are still the best-known), shop in designer boutiques, admire the eclectic Hôtel Byblos, try to get a table somewhere and order a white Cassis, the best Côte white wine, or one of M. Ricard's anisettes, and watch the mob. There are motorboat tours of the port and of Port-Grimaud.

Port-Grimaud is a recent resort built in the style of a Provençal village, except that each house has its own waterfront and boat mooring. Built by architect François Spoerry in 1966, this Provençal Venice has its detractors, but has nevertheless proved popular, contributing to the purported future of the Var as the "Florida of Europe".

Roman remains and forest fires

Fréjus ㉖ and **St Raphaël** ㉗, grown together, divide the Massif des Maures from the Massif de l'Esterel. Fashionable St Raphaël has a casino and a **Musée Archéologique** (open Wed–Mon; entrance fee), where the substantial collection of amphora has mostly been collected by diving teams from the sea. The plateau of Fréjus, like Hyères, used to lie on the sea. Its name derives from *Forum Julius;* it was founded by Julius Caesar as one of the important trading centres of Transalpine Gaul. At Fréjus, Augustus built the galleys that won the Battle of Actium. Here there are important Roman ruins, including the 10,000-seat arena where Picasso liked to watch bullfights. Hour-long tours are available of the Roman city and the episcopal city with its outstanding 5th-century

baptistry, cloisters dating back to the 12th century, and cathedral with parts as early as the 10th century.

The Romans built with porphyry taken from the Massif de l'Esterel that lies between the Golfe de Fréjus and Golfe de Napoule, where strata of yellow, green, blue and purple run together with the famous red. Ragged red cliffs, occasional red beaches, lichen-covered rocks and islets contrast with the intense blue of sea and sky. The **Corniche de l'Esterel** follows the promontories and long, deep indentations of the coast, linking beach resorts and isolated panoramic view points. The **pic du Cap Roux**, a 452-m (1,483-ft) peak visible 48 km (30 miles) out to sea, and **pic de l'Ours** inland provide highly-rated views.

The Aurelian Way (*Via Aurelia*) that connected Gaul to Rome, one of the triumphs of civil engineering in which southern France abounds, passed through the Esterel. Early on, escapees from galleys and other criminals hid in its gorges and dense forest. Smaller in area than the Massif des Maures, the Esterel is even wilder and more rugged. Highwaymen and a weird, unwelcoming landscape discouraged visitors until the 19th century, when Charles Lenthéric, an engineer, wrote: "To the geologist and the botanist it is a most remarkable upheaval of eruptive rocks, whose mineral wealth and remarkable flora call for minutest investigation. To the traveller and the artist it is a piece of nature's most wonderful scene painting."

The hills above Fréjus contain moving reminders of the last days of French colonialism and World War I: a mosque built by Sudanese soldiers and a cemetery with a Buddhist shrine where 5,000 Annamite (Vietnamese) soldiers are buried.

Cannes and its islands

Lord Brougham discovered **Cannes** ㉘ at the eastern end of the Esterel in 1834 when it was among the least important fishing villages on the coast; in his wake arrived wintering British and Russian royals and aristocrats and a few rich Americans, attracted by the constant climate and lovely setting.

Competition for the *palme d'or* at the international film festival, begun in the late 1940s to rival the competition held in Venice, consolidated its reputation for glamour. One of the most fashion-conscious seaside promenades in the world, palm-lined **Boulevard de la Croisette**, divides a long row of luxury hotels, galleries, boutiques and other expensive speciality shops from the sweep of beach. Nowadays people come to Cannes just to see who else is there.

Cannes should be viewed from the **Pointe de la Croisette** at the eastern end of the promenade (where the original "Palm-Beach" is located) and from the *vieille ville,* known as **Le Suquet**, just west of it. One of the most spectacular views is that from the **Observatoire de Super-Cannes**, north of the point.

The **Iles des Lérins** ㉙ off Cannes are called **St Honorat** and **Ste Marguerite** after the 4th-century monk and his sister who founded a monastery and a nunnery on each. The monastery declined due to pirate depredations and by the 18th century had become a "monks' galley" for disgraced priests.

Cardinal Richelieu built a fort on Ste Marguerite, which was improved by Vauban. It is a melancholy place where the mysterious "Man in the Iron Mask", whose story was told by Alexandre Dumas, was imprisoned from 1687 to 1698.

BELOW:
the Carlton's strip in Cannes.

A 1920s poster the new fashion for sea bathing and sunny seaside resorts.

Picasso country

Two of the 20th century's most important artists spent their last years above Cannes (*see page 331*): Pierre Bonnard (1867–1947), at Le Cannet and Pablo Picasso (1881–1973) at **Mougins**. From Mougins, in 1937, Picasso first visited nearby **Vallauris**. Returning in 1947, he combined his gifts for painting and sculpture in fashioning thousands of ceramics at the Madoura Pottery, where copies are still sold.

Ancient Gaul had sent ceramics to Rome, and the potters of Vallauris had long practiced their craft. Picasso revitalised the village industry, living there until the mid-1950s. He gave one of three bronze castings of his *Man with a Sheep* to Vallauris on the condition that it be placed in the square. It was.

In the barrel-vaulted, deconsecrated 12th-century chapel where the ceramicists gave Picasso a 70th birthday banquet, he painted the *War and Peace* with War on one wall and Peace opposite, a controversial work conceived during the war in Korea. In order to complete it, Picasso isolated himself in his studio on **Rue de Fournas** in Vallauris, formerly a perfumery, for two months.

The artists who painted on the Côte d'Azur during the past century have responded strongly to the earlier art of southern France – from naive *sandos* and ex-votos reminiscent of Mexico to the remains of the Romans and Greeks, and much earlier primitive art. Thus Picasso's suggestion, not acted on, that his chapel be visited by torchlight like the paleolithic cave paintings at Lascaux.

Just outside the little walled village of **Biot** to the north, also famous for its glassworks, is the **Musée Fernand Léger** (open Wed–Mon; entrance fee), with its gigantic ceramic panels and mosaics exhibited on the exterior walls of the building, a spectacularly colourful sight burnished by the strong sun of the Midi.

BELOW:
"nose" at work.

THE PERFUMES OF GRASSE

The gentle climate, rich soil and cradle of mountains that protect it from the north wind make Grasse ideal for flower production almost all year round. Golden mimosa blooms in March. By early summer, there are many acres of fragrant roses, ready to be picked. Jasmine appears in the autumn. And, high above the town, the mountains are terraced with row upon row of lavender.

The perfume industry in Grasse originated from immigrant Italian glovemakers in the 16th century. They discovered the wonderful scents in the area and began perfuming their soft leather gloves at a time when the odour of the populace definitely required masking.

Today, Grasse is better known for improving raw materials imported from other countries. Nonetheless, you can still see heaps of flowers waiting to be processed each morning. The flowers must be picked early, when the oil is most concentrated, and delivered immediately. It takes enormous quantities of the blooms to produce even the tiniest amounts of "absolute" perfume: about 750 kilos of roses for just one kilo of rose "absolute", about 4,000 kilos to produce one kilo of "essential oil". The highly trained "noses" of Grasse can identify and classify hundreds of fragrances.

Beyond is the plain of Valbonne, the vast **Sophia-Antiopolis** technology park, and above it, **Grasse** ㉚, a sheltered retreat of pink villas and palm trees. This was the home of another important artist, Jean-Honoré Fragonard. Here he lived in the 17th-century country house that is today the **Villa-Musée Fragonard** (open June–Sept: daily; Oct–May: Wed–Sun; closed public holidays; entrance fee).

Grasse has had perfume distilleries since the 16th century (*see page 332*). Two of them, Fragonard and Molinard, give tours that explain the difference between *enfleurage,* extraction and distillation, methods of obtaining the essences that are sent to Paris. At the **Musée International de la Parfumerie**, (open June–Sept: daily; Oct–May: Wed–Sun; closed public hols; entrance fee), housed in an elegant 18th-century mansion, you can observe the entire history of perfume manufacture, see a remarkable collection of perfume bottles and best of all, smell the perfumed plants themselves in a rooftop greenhouse.

Matisse's masterpiece

"Au fond," Picasso said about one of his neighbours on the Côte d'Azur, *"il n'y a que Matisse."* ("After all is said and done, there is only Matisse.") Matisse (1869–1954) may have been the greatest 20th-century artist and he considered his **Chapelle du Rosaire** (open Tues, Thur, Sat, Sun; entrance fee), painted for the Dominican nuns at **Vence**, northeast of Grasse by D2210, his masterpiece. He gave to it much of his time between 1948 and 1951.

Matisse's chapel is a finely tuned synthesis of architectural elements, the most important being stained glass and the white walls on which their coloured light falls. In his villa nearby, the bedridden artist was in the habit of making

The Fragonard museum, surrounded by a charming formal garden, contains copies of his masterpiece – The Progress of Love panels painted for Mme du Barry, now in the Frick Collection, New York. Notice the cascades of flowers.

BELOW:
one of Vence's tree-shaded squares.

large wall drawings with a thick, longhandled brush and india ink. These became the chapel's mural-sized black line drawings on white tile.

In another mode, the invalid at Villa La Rêve had also begun to make gouache-painted *papiers découpés* (paper cut-outs). He called this "drawing in colour" with his scissors, and it is the method he used to design the windows and vestments. Picasso so admired the chasubles, designed at Nice where Matisse had worked intermittently since 1916, he was inspired to attempt a bullfighter's cape. Green, red, violet, rose, black and white chasubles were worn by the priest according to the liturgical calendar. The nuns' habits were black and white. It is only during Mass, therefore, that the success of Matisse's scheme can be correctly judged. His designs are in a gallery next to the chapel.

St Paul-de-Vence to Antibes

It has often been pointed out that the modern artists who worked along the Mediterranean, from Claude Monet to those of the present *(see page 324-325)*, were attracted by the quality of the light. This will vary from one fishing or hill village to the next. It has, by all accounts, always been especially fine at **St Paul-de-Vence** ❸❶ directly south of Vence. A walled town with 16th-century ramparts almost intact, St Paul was discovered by artists (among them, Signac and Bonnard) in the 1920s.

La Colombe d'Or at the entrance to the village, an exclusive hotel and restaurant patronised by famous entertainers, has developed from the café where pre-war painters met to enjoy each others' company, the view of the Mediterranean or the Alps over terraced hillsides, the healing warmth and fresh air. Today the hotel has a priceless collection of works originally donated by visiting artists; in the garden are Léger mosaics, a Calder mobile and an exquisite Braque dove (best seen by visiting the restaurant, an expensive but memorable experience).

St Paul itself is a perfectly formed hill village complete with walls ideal for strolling round and admiring the vista of swimming pools, villas and cypresses as far as the eye can see. It is however extremely popular and its narrow winding main street becomes jammed with visitors. Just outside the village **The Fondation Maeght** (open daily; entrance fee) occupies a white concrete and rose brick structure designed by Spanish architect J.L. Sert. In addition to the 20th-century paintings and space for temporary exhibitions in the building itself, there are several outdoor sculpture areas among the pines with works by Giacometti, Calder, Miró, Arp and others. Inside you can see works by Braque, Bonnard, Kandinsky and Chagall, whose huge, colourful *La Vie* expresses joy in all aspects of life.

Auguste Renoir spent the last 12 years of his life at **Cagnes-sur-Mer** where his home, **Maison Les Colettes** (open Wed–Mon; closed public hols; entrance fee), remains almost exactly as it was when he died. The old town, **Haut-de-Cagnes**, is squeezed tightly into its walls and is crowned by its 14th-century **château**.

Antibes ❸❷ and **Cap d'Antibes** face Nice and St Jean-Cap-Ferrat across the Baie des Anges (Bay of

BELOW:
flower seller in the Nice flower market.

Map on page 316

Angels). Here sandy French beach turns into Italian shingle. The "Antiopolis" of the Greeks, Antibes was a Roman arsenal and, until 1860, the first French port west of the Var. Today **Port-Vauban** is the centre of Mediterranean yachting, sheltering some of the world's most expensive yachts. Remains of the Vauban-built ramparts now constitute the seawall and the imposing Fort Carré can still be seen to the north. On a terrace overlooking the sea is the Grimaldi château, originally a 12th-century building, reconstructed in the 16th-century and now home to the magnificent **Musée Picasso** (open Tues–Sun; closed public hols; entrance fee). It contains a remarkably unified collection of more than 50 works Picasso painted here in 1946 when offered the château to use as a studio. The light and intense colour of the south and the antiquity of the Mediterranean inspired many of his major works like *La Joie de Vivre* and the *Antipolis Suite*.

Juan-les-Pins, south of Antibes, has an active nightlife: many clubs close with the Riviera casinos at 4am. The very expensive villas and hotels are hidden by high walls and vegetation; but take D2559 around **Cap d'Antibes** for the coastal views, the sailor's offerings at the **Sanctuaire de la Garoupe**, and the **Jardin Thuret** (open Mon–Fri) named after the horticulturist who acclimatised a number of the tropical plants that give the Côte what the French call its "African" appearance. At the southern tip, visit the bar or swim in the pool at the glamorous **Hôtel du Cap Eden Roc** ("Hôtel des Etrangers" in F. Scott Fitzgerald's novel *Tender is the Night*).

Nice, capital of the Côte

Prefecture of the Alpes-Maritimes, and France's fifth largest city, **Nice** ⓧ was a resort by the mid-18th century. The style of its architecture, from medieval to

Juan-les-Pins was practically invented by the American millionaire Frank Jay Gould, who made it a sought-after resort between the wars. Here was the "bright tan prayer rug of a beach" that F. Scott Fitzgerald spoke of in his novel Tender is the Night.

BELOW: the Picasso Museum, Antibes.

Writer Graham Greene, who lived in Antibes, criticised the corruption of Nice in J'Accuse: The Dark Side of Nice *in 1982, anticipating the scandal surrounding the downfall of the flamboyant mayor, Jacques Médecin, in 1990.*

BELOW: running the Promenade des Anglais, Nice.

early 20th-century, is Genoese but it was the British who created the **Promenade des Anglais**. Today the promenade is like a 3-km freeway leading to the **Quai des Etats-Unis**.

Nice is divided by what remains of the Paillon river, now a mere trickle and covered over with promenades and hanging gardens, dominated by the **Acropolis** convention centre and the **Musée d'Art Contemporain** (open Wed–Mon; entrance fee) with its collection of modern works, especially the Nice school of Yves Klein, Martial Raysse, Caesar and Arman. To the east is the **vieille ville** of Nice, a charming, bustling maze of winding streets and pastel houses. The Cours Saleya is the promenade between the old city and the sea.

Cimiez to the north has recently excavated Roman ruins, including baths and an amphitheatre often used for festivals. Here also is the **Musée Matisse** (open Wed–Mon; entrance fee), which contains many of his drawings, all his bronzes, and was specially designed to house his masterpiece, *Messages Bibliques*. It also has the biggest single collection of his work.

The Riviera Corniches

Until 1860, when France annexed Nice, the Var river was the French border. The **Var Corniche** (Avenue Auguste-Renoir from Cagnes) follows the west bank of the river, tamed since the 19th century. A once controversial motorway (the A8), completed in 1980, runs along the opposite bank a few miles north from Nice before turning east to tunnel through several mountains.

The **Alpes-Maritimes** ❸❹ between Nice and Menton, on the Italian border, plummet to the sea, producing some of the most spectacular scenery along the coast. For the adventurous prepared to explore beyond the coast a whole new

world awaits in the hinterland of the Alpes-Maritimes; high mountain peaks, plunging gorges, clear sparkling rivers and crowning the most inaccessible craggy peaks, the famous *villages perchés* (perched villages).

Three *corniches,* one above the other, traverse the 30 km (20 miles) from Nice to Italy. The *grande corniche,* highest and most breathtaking, follows the military road built by Napoleon in 1806. After Nice the coastline changes dramatically, wide bays giving way to towering craggy cliffs. Here, **Villefranche** is a surprisingly unspoilt little town, built round its harbour, one of the deepest in the world, and until recently home to the American sixth fleet. It is well restored with a huge 16th-century citadel, and lovely pastel-painted Italianate houses along the seafront. Here there are lots of lively bars, and on the Quai Courbet is the 14th-century **Chapelle St-Pierre** (open Tues–Sun; closed Nov; entrance fee) with a candy-coloured facade and an interior decorated by Jean Cocteau who spent his childhood in Villefranche.

Luxurious enclave

Beyond Villefranche is the refuge of the seriously rich, **Cap Ferrat** ❸❺, though the 10-km (6-mile) drive around the perimeter offers only glimpses of celebrity villas and glorious gardens secreted behind security systems. The **Fondation Ephrussi de Rothschild** (open daily; entrance fee) gives a hint of the lifestyle, with 7 hectares (17 acres) of whimsical garden spread right along the crest of the Cap with views on all sides. The pink and white *belle époque* villa was built to house the art collection of the Baroness Ephrussi de Rothschild and includes a magnificent variety of 18th-century furniture, porcelain, carpets, and paintings, with ceilings specifically designed to accommodate her Tiepolo paintings.

Map on page 316

TIP

Visiting the lovely *villages perchés* in the hills behind Nice provides a refreshing contrast to the crowded and urbanised coast, and some, like Ste Agnès, Gorbio, Peille and Peillon, are only a few miles inland, making them perfect places for lunch.

BELOW: painting perfumed soaps in Eze.

Map on page 316

In the 1920s, Sir Frederick Treves, in the Riviera of the Corniche Road, described Eze thus: "It is a silent town and desolate. On the occasion of a certain visit the only occupant I came upon was a half-demented beggar who gibbered in an unknown tongue".

RIGHT: Menton's lemon festival.
BELOW: Monte-Carlo's casino.

Just the other side of the Cap is **Beaulieu-sur-Mer**, which lays claim to the best climate on the coast, protected from the north wind by a great rock face. It is thus a popular retirement town, with many elegant rest homes and genteel hotels, surrounded by softly waving palm trees. It also boasts some of the best hotels on the Riviera, and was where the British and Russian gentry used to spend their winters. Worth a visit is the **Villa Kerylos** (open Dec–Oct: Tues–Fri, pm only: Tues–Sun; entrance fee), a complete reconstruction of a Greek villa with marble columns and cool courtyards open to the sea and sky, and housing a large collection of mosaics, frescoes and furniture.

The tiny village of **Eze** ㊱, perched high above the sea, is today restored to the last stone; a bijou museum of medieval detail, with charming features to be seen at every turn; medieval chimneys, Romanesque windows and tiny rooftop gardens. But its current prosperity belies its troubled past. For most of its history Éze has been nothing but a charred ruin, razed successively over several centuries, enslaved by Saracens, its citizens regularly tortured and burned. Today what little remains of the château is surrounded by the **Jardin Exotique** (open daily; entrance fee), a fine collection of cacti and succulents.

High up on the *grande corniche* beyond Eze there is a dramatic view of Monaco from the Roman monument at **La Turbie**. The name La Turbie comes from the Latin, *tropaea*, meaning trophy, and the village is named after the vast monument which was erected to commemorate the conquest of the 45 Alpine tribes who had been attacking Romanised Gaul.

It was built between 13 and 5 BC probably using enslaved tribes as labour. The names of the tribes are inscribed on the monument, the longest intact Roman inscription to have survived.

High rollers

Between the 1870s and 1930s, changing laws and fashions made **Monte-Carlo** ㊲ the roulette capital of Europe, and the wintering place of the very rich and of mothers with eligible daughters. Prince Rainier III has diversified his economic base by turning the tiny country of **Monaco** into the Miami of the Mediterranean. Nonetheless some pleasure-seekers still hesitate before entering this strange principality (that some accuse of being filled with thieves).

Sea, skyscrapers and mountains form concentric circles around the tiny headland that is Monaco. Like many Americans in 1956, Mrs Kelly is said to have believed her daughter was engaged to the Prince of Morocco. Tourism in Monaco doubled within a few years of Grace Kelly's televised wedding in **Cathédrale St Nicholas** on Le Rocher, alongside the **Musée Océanographique** (open daily; entrance fee) and the **Palais des Princes**, Prince Rainier's official residence. From the Palace, where a daily changing of the guard is still performed, a stroll through the old quarter leads to the cathedral and **Jardin Exotique** (open daily).

A little further along the coast, **Menton** ㊳, pretty and well-protected, was the home of a large British colony until 1914 and remains more reserved than its Côte neighbours. Each February, on Shrove Tuesday, it hosts the famous lemon festival. ❑

Map
on page
340

CORSICA

The least populated but perhaps the loveliest of the larger Mediterranean islands has a flavour as much Italian as French, a proud people and an astonishingly varied landscape

The rugged island of Corsica, with a turbulent history to match, looks like a mountain thrust from the sea, pointing an accusatory and gnarled northern finger, Cap Corse, towards the Genoan Riviera. Its wild and often surprising scenery is its chief glory, ringed by a 960-km (600-mile) coastline of world-class sandy beaches, quiet coves, fishing villages, jagged headlands and tumbling rocks. The interior comprises an extraordinary variety of landscapes. There are snow-capped mountains, rocky peaks and clear pools and streams, forests of chestnut and *laricio* pine (used by the Romans for masts), vineyards, olive and orange groves, tropical palms, even a region of arid desert.

Almost two-thirds of the interior is covered with the thick tangle of scented shrubs and wild flowers known as *maquis,* renowned for concealing bandits, and the name given to World War II French Resistance fighters. Though friendly and welcoming to tourists, traditionally Corsicans are fiery and hot-blooded – the word "vendetta" is theirs.

Evidence of Corsica's earliest occupation by man can be seen in the mystical, majestic granite menhirs at **Filitosa ❶** (open Apr–mid-Oct: daily; entrance fee) carved into warriors by megalithic man around 4,000 years ago. Since then, centuries of oppression have dogged the island. Excavations have uncovered

BELOW: the rocky coast of Bonifacio.

Roman remains at **Aléria** ❷ (museum open daily; entrance fee) where Greek invaders before them had established a prosperous trading port. Between the 11th and 13th centuries, Corsica was ruled by the Italian city state of Pisa, resulting in a crop of small, perfectly proportioned Tuscan Romanesque churches. One lies outside the sophisticated yachting centre of **St Florent** ❸: the **Cathédrale de Santa Maria Assunta**, only remaining vestige of the ancient city of Nebbio; the other is **St Michele** at nearby **Murato**, whose swirling green and white walls dazzle the eye. West of St Florent, the parched landscape of the **Désert des Agriates** stretches along the coast.

Brief independence

In 1284 the Genoese finally crushed their Pisan enemies in a decisive sea battle, and took Corsica. They were to rule for 484 years: many of their coastal watchtowers can still be seen today, such as the one on the promontory at Porto (see below), a wonderful place to watch the sunset. For 15 short, but deeply felt years in the 18th century, Corsica tasted independence under the leadership of Pasquale Paoli. He was born in the **Castagniccia** ❹, a beautiful region of rocky crests and valleys covered in chestnut groves which was once the island's most prosperous part, but is now all but deserted (tourists outnumber Corsicans by six to one in high season; many seek work in France, particularly in government service jobs, such as the police force).

In 1769, Corsica was annexed by Louis XV and has belonged to France, without ever becoming quite French, ever since. Militant separatist groups continue to plague the island with sporadic violent attacks against the authorities. Most prominent is the Front Libéral National Corse (FLNC), but it was apparently

TIP

A wonderful way to see the island is by taking the narrow-gauge railway between Ajaccio and Bastia by way of Corte.

BELOW: goat milking in Venaco.

Map
on page
340

Bust of Napoleon.

BELOW:
Capod d'Orto.
RIGHT: typical
Corsican interior.
OVERLEAF: a TGV
in the French Alps.

an obscure breakaway group which ordered the assassination, in early 1998, of the chief French government official on the island.

An island of contrasts

Visitors who want to explore Corsica are hard-put to do so without a car, and one which will easily negotiate the many narrrow and twisting inland roads.

Ajaccio ⑤ with palm-lined boulevards and a wonderful morning market, is Corsica's capital and the birthplace of Napoleon Bonaparte, who had to learn French when he went to military school on the mainland (the Corsican dialect is a variation of Italian). Visit his baptismal font in the **Cathédrale Notre-Dame-de la-Miséricorde** and his childhood home, **Maison Bonaparte** (Rue Saint Charles; open daily; entrance fee). Most interesting though, is the **Palais Fesch,** built by Napoleon's uncle, Cardinal Fesch, who swept up a notable collection of early Italian paintings during the Italian campaign and displayed them here (50 rue Fesch; open Tues–Sun; closed public hols; entrance fee).

Ajaccio heralds the island's southern *département*, Corse-du-Sud, whose coastline is studded with sandy bays and long white beaches, **Plage de Palombaggia** and **Plage de Pinarello** near the busy port and holiday resort of **Porto-Vecchio ⑥**. At the southernmost tip is **Bonifacio ⑦**, with superb seaward views as far as Sardinia, a fortified old town crowning the hilltop, and a bustling harbour, where you can dine at one of the many seafood restaurants which line the quay. Inland, **Sartène ⑧** is an austere medieval town of grey granite where each Good Friday a moving re-enactment of Christ's walk to Calvary takes place in a procession called Catenacciu. **Quenza ⑨** is a typically attractive hill village with a fine church and excellent auberge, Sole e Monti; nearby is the well-known beauty spot, **Col de Bavella.**

From **Porto ⑩** to Bastia, the coastline is at its wildest and loveliest, no more so than at the **Golfe de Porto,** where the famous red cliffs of the **Calanche** plunge a sheer 300 m (1000 ft) into the sea below. The Porto river, calm where it reaches the sea, can be followed inland to the point where several mountain torrents form the **Gorges de Spelunca.** The old mule track to the mountain village of **Evisa** passes through these gorges, and a walk in the lowest part gives a good idea of what the island's former 'road system' used to be like. Further inland is the island's highest mountain, the 754-m (2,475-ft) **Monte Cinto ⑪**, on the slopes of which, at **Haut-Asco,** you can ski. This is the **Niolo** region, the one part of Corsica where the husbandry of sheep and goats still provides the main income. At the island's centre is **Corte ⑫**, Paoli's capital during independence, and the seat of Corsica's university.

To the west are the impressive gorges of the **Restonica** and **Tavignano**. **Bastia ⑬** is the principal town of Haut-Corse, the island's northern *département*, and an important commercial port. It has a colourful, Mediterranean flavour, with a lively main square and **Vieux Port,** and a 16th-century **citadel**. From there you should head north and explore remote **Cap Corse ⑭**, particularly the west coast, where the charming port of **Centuri** lies near the tip. Leave plenty of time: the road is narrow and wildly twisting. ❑

INSIGHT GUIDES

Travel Tips

Simply travelling safely

American Express Travellers Cheques

- are recognised as one of the safest and most convenient ways to protect your money when travelling abroad

- are more widely accepted than any other travellers cheque brand

- are available in eleven currencies

- are supported by a 24 hour worldwide refund service and

- a 24 hour Express Helpline service provides assistance and information when travelling abroad

- are accepted in millions of shops, hotels and restaurants throughout the world

Travellers Cheques

CONTENTS

Getting Acquainted

The Place

Area 543,965 sq. km (210,026 sq. miles).

Population Around 58 million.

Language Everyone in France speaks French, but regional languages still exist in Brittany (Breton), Alsace (Alsatian), the western Pyrénées (Basque) and the eastern Pyrénées (Catalan).

Time Zone For most of the year, France is one hour ahead of Greenwich Mean Time. When it is noon in France, it is 6am in New York.
Note that France uses the 24hr clock.

Currency French franc (FF). 8–10FF = £1 and 5–7FF = $1.

Electricity Generally 220/230 volts, but still 110 in a few areas. Visitors from the US will need a transformer for shavers, hairdryers and other equipment; visitors from the UK just need an adaptor plug.

Weights & Measures France is metric for all weights and measures, although old-fashioned terms such as *livre* (about 1 lb or 500 g) are still used by many shopkeepers. For quick and easy conversion: 2.5 cm is about 1 inch, 1metre is about a yard, 100g is just over 4 oz and 1 kg is just over 2 lb. A kilometre is five-eighths of a mile, so 80 km is 50 miles and 80 kpm is 50 mph.

Direct Dialling Dialling from the UK 00 (international code) + 33 (France) + area code (1 for Paris, for example) + an eight figure number.

The People

With a population approaching 58 million, France is predominantly a white Christian (Roman Catholic) country. The French are proud of their rural roots, and to be called a peasant (*paysan*) here does not have the same demeaning connotation that it does elsewhere. The biggest influx of immigrants has come from French North Africa. Unfortunately, the French have a reputation for being chauvinistic and are not always as tolerant of these newcomers as they might be.

Each region enjoys its own culture and customs, which have survived over a long history. France does not have a "national dress" as such, but traditional costumes are often worn during local pageants and festivals.

Some of the best examples can be seen in Brittany, during the regular *pardons*, when the women can be seen in their finest lace. Pardons are religious festivals, but many of the local events in France are a celebration of local produce, such as wine festivals and apple fairs in the autumn; flower festivals in the spring and summer. Local tourist offices give information about these, as well as municipal museums (too numerous to list in this guide) which often give a fascinating insight into the history of an area.

The Economy

France is an important industrial nation in terms of EU and world markets, with over 30 percent of the working population employed in industry: primarily in car production, steel, textile and aircraft industries. Its stake in the area of information technology is also growing. Agriculture is still extremely important, although now only around six percent of the country's workforce is involved in farming; many farms are still very small-scale affairs, with dairy produce, wine and wheat being the main exports. Another continuing growth area of the economy is tourism and indeed, many areas of the country rely heavily on this trade.

Government

France is made up of 22 regions, including Corsica (covered fully in *Insight Guide: Corsica*) and overseas territories such as Guadeloupe, Martinique, Réunion and New Caledonia. Each region comprises several *départements* or counties. French *départements* are identified by an individual number which is used as a reference for administrative purposes, for example it forms the first two digits of the postcode in any address and the last two figures on vehicle licence plates. The *département* numbers are in alphabetical order, so Ain is 01; Aisne, 02.

Each *département* is divided into a number of disparately-sized communes whose district councils control a town, village or group of

The Climate

The French climate is varied and seasonal.

In the north, it is similar to that of southern England and springtime is often suggested as the best time to see the capital, but be prepared for showers. In the autumn, mornings can be quite sharp, but by midday the skies are usually clear and bright.

In the south, summer temperatures can frequently rise to over 30°C (86°F). Watch out for very heavy thunder and hailstorms.

Many areas of France have quite distinct micro-climates and the weather can change rapidly. The Midi has its own particular *bête noire*, the fierce wind known as the Mistral which mostly appears in winter and spring, but which may blow up at other times, and is known to have a very depressing effect on the local population.

villages under the direction of the local mayor. Communes are responsible for most local planning and environmental matters. Decisions on tourism and culture are mostly dealt with at regional level, while the state controls education, the health service and security.

France first became a republic in 1792 after the abolition of the monarchy. Constitutional change resulted in the establishment of the Second, Third, Fourth and the current Fifth Republic, which was instituted when General de Gaulle became Prime Minister in 1958. The President, who holds a powerful office, is elected for seven years. He appoints the Prime Minister as head of government. Parliament is made up of two houses, the National Assembly and the Senate.

In recent history France has been ruled by a centralised form of government, but under the socialists (1981–86) the Paris-appointed *préfets* lost much of their power as the individual *départements* gained their own directly elected assemblies for the first time, giving them more financial and administrative autonomy. Each *département* still has a préfet, but the role is now much more advisory. The *préfecture* is based in the county town of each *département*.

Planning the Trip

Clothing

Be prepared for seasonal differences; in summer only light clothes will be needed except in coastal and mountainous areas where a warmer outer layer will be required for evenings.

Maps

A first essential in touring any part of France is a good map. The Institut Géographique National is the French equivalent of the British Ordnance Survey and their maps are excellent. For route planning, IGN 901 is ideal at a scale of 1:1,000,000 or 1" = 16 imiles (1 cm:10 kms); the Michelin M911 at the same scale shows just motorways and main roads which is a good clear presentation if you do not plan to go off the beaten track.

For more detailed maps, the **IGN Red Series** (1:250,000, 1 cm:2.5 km) covers the country on 16 sheets at a good scale for touring. Michelin also produces regional maps at a similar scale (1:200,000, or 1" = 3 miles approx.). These sheets are also available bound as a *Motoring Atlas* including route planning maps, Paris area map and several town plans. Collins also produces a good atlas based on the IGN's regional maps.

Another particularly good series for touring are the **Telegraph** (Recta Foldex) maps which cover France on four maps: northwest, northeast, southwest and southeast.

The IGN **Green Series** (1:100,000, 1" = 1.6 miles or 1 cm:1 km) are more detailed local maps which cover the whole of France on 74 sheets. These are useful for travellers with a single main destination, and also quite good for walking. Serious walkers though will need IGN's highly detailed 1:50,000 and 1:25,000 scales (Blue Series). Other specialist maps for walkers and climbers are produced by **Didier Richard** (Alpine maps), while the IGN produces detailed maps of the Pyrenees and the national parks.

Michelin publishes town plans, but local tourist offices often give away their own town plans free.

Shopping for maps and books

In France, most good bookshops and **Maisons de la Presse** should have a range of maps, but they can often be bought more cheaply in **supermarkets** or service stations. Motorway maps can often be picked up free of charge at rest areas.

Stockists in London are:

• **Stanfords International Map Centre**, 12–14 Long Acre, Covent Garden, WC2E 9LP, tel: (0171) 836 1321.

• **The Travel Bookshop**, 13 Blenheim Crescent, London W11 2EE, tel: (0171) 229 5260.

• **World Leisure Marketing**, 9 Downing Road, West Meadows Industrial Estate, Derby DE21 6HA, tel: freephone 0800 83 80 80, fax: 01332 340 464, is the agent for IGN and offers a mail order service.

• **France Magasin**, France House, Digbeth Street, Stow-on-the-Wold, Gloucester GL54 1BN, tel: (01451) 870 920, fax: (01451) 831 367, carries the most comprehensive stock of French publications in the UK. A new French Travel Centre for information, books and guides has opened at the French Government Tourist Office, 178 Piccadilly, London W1V 0AL. Tel: 0171 491 9996, fax: 0171 491 0600.

Entry Regulations

All visitors to France require a valid passport and a visa except for citizens of EU countries, Andorra, Monaco, the USA, Canada and

Switzerland. If in any doubt, check with the French consulate in your country, as the situation may change from time to time. If you intend to stay in France for more than 90 days, then you should have a *carte de séjour* (again from the French consulate) – this also applies to EU citizens until restrictions are relaxed.

Customs Regulations

All personal effects may be imported into France without formality (including bicycles and sports equipment). It is forbidden to bring into the country any narcotics, pirated books, weapons and alcoholic liquors that do not conform to French legislation.

Certain items (such as alcoholic drinks, tobacco, perfume) are limited as to the amounts you can take in or out duty-free, and these amounts differ depending on whether you are coming from another EU country, a non-EU European country, or outside Europe. From 1 January 1993, customs barriers within Europe for alcoholic drinks and tobacco (bought and duty paid in France) practically ceased to exist, but the old regulations still apply for goods bought at duty-free shops on the ferry or aeroplane, although these can be exceeded if you prove the goods are for personal consumption (such as a family wedding) and not for resale. EU allowances are due to be reviewed in 1999. For information contact HM Customs and Excise, Dorset House, Stamford Street, London SE1 9NG, tel: (0171) 928 3344 or any Excise office.

The current allowances for persons over 18 years old are shown below, with on-board duty-free shop allowances (until duty free is abolished, that is) in brackets:
• **10 litres** (1 litre) of spirits or liqueurs over 22 percent alcohol by volume
• **20 litres** (2 litres) of fortified wine
• **90 litres** (2 litres) of wine (no more than 60 litres of it may be sparkling wine)
• **200 cigars** (50 cigars) or **400**

Animal Quarantine

No animal under three months of age may be taken into France. It is not advisable to take animals to France from the UK because of the six-months' quarantine required by the British authorities on the animal's return. However, if you do wish to take a pet you need to have either a vaccination certificate for rabies or a certificate to show that your country has been free of the disease for three years. For further information contact your local vet or the French consulate in your country.

cigarillos (100 cigarillos) or **800 cigarettes** (200 cigarettes).

Healthcare

The International Association for Medical Assistance to Travellers (IAMAT) is a non-profit-making organization which anyone can join free of charge. Benefits include a membership card (entitling the bearer to services at fixed IAMAT rates by participating physicians) and a traveller clinical record (a passport-sized record completed by the member's own doctor prior to travel). A directory of English-speaking IAMAT doctors on call 24 hours a day is published for members.

EU nationals should check before leaving that they qualify for subsidised treatment in France under EU rules. Most British nationals do – check with the Department of Health and ask for the form E111. The E111 does not cover the full cost of treatment, so you may find it worthwhile to take out private insurance as well.

IAMAT Offices
US: 417 Center Street, Lewiston, NY 14092, tel: (716) 754 4883. **Canada**: 1287 St Claire Ave., W. Toronto, M6E 1B9, tel: (416) 652 0137 or 40 Regal Road, Guelph, Ontario, N1K 1B5, tel: (519) 836 0102. **New Zealand**: PO Box 5049, Christchurch 5.

Money

The French Franc is divided into 100 centimes. A 5-centime piece is the smallest coin and the F500 note the highest denomination bill.

Changing money: Banks displaying the *Change* sign will exchange foreign currency and, in general, give the best rates; you will need to produce your passport in any transaction. If possible, avoid hotel or other independent *bureaux de change* which may charge a high commission.

Credit cards are widely accepted, but Barclaycard is the most common. Access (MasterCard/ Eurocard) and Diners Club are also widely accepted, as well as American Express in many places.

Credit cards and cash cards from many European banks can be used in French cash machines. Check the validity of your card with your bank before departure. You will need to know your PIN number. Note that French credit cards often have a chip (or *puce*) rather than the more common magnetic strip, and this is not always easily read by French card reading machines.

Cheques Travellers' cheques are a popular way to take money on holiday. Also, UK tourists may consider using Eurocheques, which can be used in conjunction with a cheque card to draw cash from your own bank account, but many French banks do not accept them. You should apply for a book of Eurocheques from your own bank a couple of weeks before you leave.

Getting There

BY AIR
Several airlines operate to France from the UK, and deregulation means the choice is constantly changing.

Air France is the main carrier, with flights to Lyon, Toulouse, Paris, Nice and Strasbourg. **British Airways** flies from various destinations in the UK to Marseilles, Bordeaux, Toulouse, Nice, Lyons and Montpellier. **British Midland** also flies to Paris and

Nice. **Ryanair** flies to Carcassonne and St-Etienne, and **Easyjet, AB Airlines** and **Debonair** to Nice.

Travellers from North America and elsewhere can get direct flights to Paris and major destinations, such as Nice and Lyon, via Air France and most national airlines. American Airlines, United Airlines, TWA and Delta also fly to France.

Internal flights are operated by Air France, Air Littoral, Air Liberté and AOM.

Paris Airports

Paris has two airports:
Roissy–Charles de Gaulle, 23 km (15 miles) north of the city via the A1 or RN2, tel: 01 48 62 12 12
Orly, 14 km (9 miles) south of the centre via the A6 or RN7, tel: 01 49 75 15 15.

See *Getting Around* for information on travelling to and from (as well as between) the two airports.

Rail Packages

Air France operates a rail package with flights available from 15 airports around the UK and Ireland (not Heathrow) to Paris, then onward by train to one of 3,000 stations. These inclusive tickets can also be combined with a 15-day France Vacances rail pass (see *By Train*). Air France also has offices abroad offering advice and information on holidays in France.

Students

Students and young people can normally obtain discounted charter fares through specialist travel agencies in their own countries. In the UK, try: **Campus Travel**, 52 Grosvenor Gardens, London SW1W 0AG, tel: (0171) 730 3402 for your nearest branch. Campus is part of the international group usit, whose main US address is the New York Student Centre, 895 Amsterdam Avenue, New York, NY 10025, tel: (212) 663 5435.

Useful numbers

IN THE UK
Air France
Tel: 0181 742 6600

Air UK.
Tel: 0990 074074
British Airways
Tel: 0345 222111
British Midland
Tel: 0345 554554
Easyjet
Tel: 0990 292929
Ryanair
Tel: 0171 4357101

IN FRANCE
Air France
Tel: 01 41 56 78 00
Air Littoral.
Tel: 04 67 20 67 20
Air Liberté
Tel: 01 49 79 23 00
AOM.
Tel: 01 49 79 10 00

IN THE US & CANADA
Air France New York.
Tel: (212) 838 7800
Air France Los Angeles.
Tel: (310) 271 66 65
Air France Montréal.
Tel: (514) 288 42 64

BY SEA

There are several ferry services operating from the UK, the Republic of Ireland and the Channel Islands to the northern ports of France. All of them carry cars as well as foot passengers. Hovercraft crossings are fast, but more dependent on good weather than the ferries. The Seacat catamaran service offers the quickest crossing but, like the

hovercraft, can only carry a limited number of cars. The ports of Boulogne, Calais and Le Havre offer direct access by motorway to Paris; there is almost direct motorway access also via Dunkerque and Caen.

Brittany Ferries sails from Portsmouth to Saint-Malo and Caen, Plymouth to Roscoff, Cork (Eire) to St Malo and Roscoff, and a cheaper Les Routiers service from Poole to Cherbourg (summer only). Contact The Brittany Centre, Wharf Rd Portsmouth PO2 8RU, tel: 0990 360 360, fax: 01705 873237 or Millbay Docks, Plymouth PLI 3EW, tel: 01752 600698.

Hoverspeed operates hovercraft from Dover to Calais and Boulogne (crossing time about 30 minutes). The *Seacat* catamaran runs between Boulogne and Folkestone. Details of all services from International Hoverport, Marine Parade, Dover CT17 9TG, tel: 0990 240 241.

North Sea Ferries connects travellers from the north of England and Scotland to France, via their Hull-Zeebrugge route. Situated 56 km (35 miles) from the French border, Zeebrugge gives good motorway access to the Paris region. The overnight services offer entertainment; a five-course dinner and breakfast are included in the fare. Contact the company at King George Dock, Hedon Road, Hull HU9 5QA, tel: (01482) 377177.

Public Holidays

It is common practice, if a public holiday falls on a Thursday or Tuesday for French business to *faire le pont* (literally, bridge the gap) and have the Friday or Monday as a holiday too. Details of closures should be posted outside banks and other major institutions a few days before, but it is easy to be caught out, especially on Assumption day in August, which is not a UK holiday. Major public holidays are:
• **1 January** (New Year's Day)

• **Easter Monday** (but not Good Friday)
• **Labour Day** (Monday closest to 1 May)
• **Ascension Day**
• **8 May** (to commemorate the end of World War I)
• **Whit Monday** (Pentecost)
• **14 July** (Bastille Day)
•**15 August** (Assumption Day)
•**1 November** (All Saints Day)
•**11 November** (Armistice Day)
•**25 December** (Christmas Day, but not Boxing Day)

The Channel Tunnel

The Channel Tunnel offers fast, frequent rail services between London (Waterloo), Lille (2 hours) and Paris (Gare du Nord – 3 hours) for connections to other destinations. Rail passenger services are by a consortium of the French, British and Belgian railway companies, and tickets are bookable through French or British railway companies (*see Rail*).The Eurostar service offers high speed connections via Lille or Paris. Eurostar also operates high speed trains direct from London and Ashford to Disneyland Paris.

Le Shuttle is the name of the service that takes cars and their passengers from Folkestone to Calais on a simple drive-on-drive-off system. The journey time through the tunnel is about 35 minutes. Reservations are not needed – you just turn up and take the next service. Le Shuttle runs 24 hours a day, all year round, with a service at least once an hour through the night. Enquiries in UK, tel: 0990 353535.

P & O European Ferries operates the short sea routes from Dover to Calais, as well as Portsmouth to Le Havre and Cherbourg. Fares and schedules from P & O, Channel House, Channel View Road, Dover CT17 9TJ, tel: 0990 980980.

Holyman Sally Ferries uses the smaller ports of Ramsgate and Dunkerque. Contact Argyle Centre, York Street, Ramsgate, Kent CT11 9DS, tel: 0990 595522.

Stena Line Ferries operates from Dover to Calais (the fastest shipping route at 90 minutes), Southampton to Cherbourg, and Newhaven to Dieppe. Details and reservations for all services are available from Charter House, PO Box 121, Park Street, Ashford, Kent TN24 8EX, tel: 0990 707070.

Irish Ferries offers a service from Rosslare to Le Havre and Cherbourg, with ferries leaving daily

from 1 April to mid-September to one of the two ports. It currently runs a service once weekly from Cork to Le Havre and Cherbourg from June–August. Contact them at 50 West Northland Street, Dublin 2, tel: (353)16 610511.

BY RAIL

France has a fast efficient rail network operated by the SNCF (Société Nationale des Chemins de Fer de France.) Its much praised TGV programme is developing all the time, offering comfortable express services via Paris and Lille to many destinations. For visitors travelling from Paris, the train is a comfortable way to reach any major destination in France, with most express services offering refreshments (and even play areas for young children). There are five main stations serving the provinces from Paris, so check which one you need before setting off. Getting across country by rail is less easy. Car and bicycle hire is available at most main stations – as a package with your rail ticket if you prefer (details from French Railways).

Tickets and Information

Tickets may be booked for through journeys from outside France.

In the UK, tickets can be booked from any British Rail Station, including ferry travel. British Rail travel centres can supply details of continental services or contact British Rail International Enquiries, International Rail Centre, Victoria Station, London SW1, tel: (0990) 848 848. If you are a student , under 26 years old or retired don't forget to ask about discounts. For details of Eurostar + TGV or Motorail contact your local travel agent or the Rail Shop – a new telephone booking service opened in London by French Railways. Be warned that the lines are usually very busy and a little patience is required.

Rail Shop can arrange ferry bookings, discounted tickets for young people, a *Carte Vermeil* for senior citizens, which gives a

generous discount on tickets and Eurodomino rail passes (*see Rail Passes*). Lines are open Monday to Friday from 8am–8pm and Saturdays from 9am–4pm.

Tel: 0990 300 003 for information and reservations.

SNCF has a central reservation office in Paris, tel: 08 36 35 35 35 (national info.) or 01 53 90 20 20 (Paris info).

Most French railway stations accept Visa and American Express cards.

Rail Passes

There are several rail passes available to foreign visitors. These must be purchased before leaving for France.

In the UK, a Eurodomino Pass offers unlimited rail travel in France on any 3, 5, or 10 days within a month. This can also be bought in conjunction with an Air France Rail Ticket (see *By Air*).

In the US, visitors have a wider choice of passes, including Eurailpass, Flexipass and Saver Pass. Call (212) 308 3103 (for information) and 800 223 636 (for reservations). The France Rail 'n' Drive pass offers a flexible rail and car-rental package,

Similar passes are available in other countries, but the names of the tickets and conditions may vary slightly.

Motorail

Motorail takes the strain out of driving long distances to your holiday destination while allowing you the freedom of being able to drive your own car once you arrive.

Some services operate during the summer only from the channel ports e.g. Boulogne to Biarritz, Brive, Bordeaux, Toulouse, Narbonne; Calais to Nice; Dieppe to Avignon and Fréjus. Also useful for ferry users are the routes from Lille to Avignon, Brive and Narbonne. There are over 30 motorail routes out of Paris, some of which depart daily all year round. Tickets can be booked to include cross-channel ferries with Stena, P & O or Hoverspeed.

BY BUS

Eurolines is a consortium of almost 30 coach companies, operating in France and throughout Europe. They operate services from London (Victoria) to many major French destinations. Some (such as Paris) are daily, others are seasonal and some have services several times a week throughout the year.

This is one of the cheapest ways of reaching France, and there are discounts available for young people and senior citizens. The ticket includes the ferry crossing (via Dover). National Express coaches have connections from most major towns in the UK that link up with the London departures.

For details contact Eurolines UK, 52 Grosvenor Gardens, Victoria, London SW1W 0AU, tel: 01582 404511 (enquiries) or tel: 0990 143219 (telesales); or in France at 28, Avenue du Générale de Gaulle, 93541 Bagnolet, tel: 01 49 72 51 51.

BY CAR

Almost all the motorways in France are privately owned and subject to tolls (credit cards are usually acceptable). The trip from the northern ports to the south of France costs around £50 (US$84) in tolls one-way. The benefits of paying for the use of the motorway can be seen in the high standards of maintenance of the roads and the frequent rest areas, picnic sites and catering facilities.

Free motorway maps are often available at motorway service stations/cafeterias and are useful as they mark the position and facilities of all the rest areas on the route.

If speed is not of the essence and you intend to make the drive part of your holiday, follow the green holiday route signs (bis) to your destination – these form part of a national network of bison futé routes to avoid traffic congestion at peak periods. You will discover parts of France you never knew existed and are more likely to arrive relaxed. The first and last (rentrée) weekend in August and the public holiday on 15 August are usually the worst times to travel, so avoid them if you can. (For further details about driving in France, see Getting Around.)

STUDENT TRAVEL

Students and young people under the age of 26 can benefit from cut-price travel to France and rail cards for getting around the country (for details see Getting There).

If you wish a prolonged stay in the region, it may be worth finding out about an exchange visit or study holiday. Several organizations provide information or arrange such visits.

In the UK, you can contact the **Central Bureau for Educational Visits and Exchanges**, 10 Spring Gardens, London SW1A 2BN, tel: 0171 389 4004, or the French Tourist Office and ask for the free information booklet France Youth Travel.

Another option, for those with decent French, is to approach one of the UK-based camping holiday operators who often employ students as site couriers during the vacation (see Where to Stay).

Organizations in the US include:
• **American Council for International Studies Inc.**, I9 Bay State Road, Boston, Massachussets 02215, tel: (617) 236 2051.

Start Them Young – France for Children

Restaurants: in France generally, children are treated as people, not just nuisances. It is pleasant to be able to take them out for a meal (even in the evening) without heads being turned in horror at the invasion. It has to be said, however, that French children, being accustomed to eating out from an early age, are on the whole well behaved in restaurants, so it helps if one's own offspring are able to understand that they can't run wild.

Many restaurants offer a children's menu; if not they will often split a prix-fixe menu between two children. If travelling with very young children, you may find it practical to order nothing specific at all for them but just to request an extra plate and give them tasty morsels to try from your own dish. It is a good introduction to foreign food for them, without too much waste. French meals are generally generous enough (nouvelle cuisine excepted) to allow you to do this without going hungry yourself, and you are unlikely to encounter any hostility from le patron (or la patronne).

Another option is to order a single simple, inexpensive dish such as an omelette, which most children will happily eat.

Hotels: most hotels have family rooms so children do not have to be separated from parents, and another bed or cot (lit bébé) can often be provided for a small charge, although it is a good idea to check availability if you are booking in advance.

Holiday Centres: it is possible to organize activities for unaccompanied children, including stays in gîtes d'enfants or on farms, or activity holidays. Naturally, children would only be happy to be left if they have a reasonable command of French, but it is quite common in France, as in the United States, for children to spend a part of their summer vacation at a holiday centre.

For more information, contact Loisirs Accueil in individual départements (see Useful Addresses). Loisirs de France Jeunes is a national organization which offers good-value activity holidays (including winter sports) for young people. Contact them at 30 Rue Godot de Mauroy, 75009 Paris, tel: 01 47 42 51 81.

- **Youth for Understanding International Exchange**, 3501 Newark Street NW, Washington DC 20016, tel: (202) 966 6800.

Volunteers are welcome at the camps organized on several of the archaeological sites in Burgundy (mainly in the summer). For information on individual sites contact the Direction Régionale des Affaires Culturelles, 39 Rue Vannerie, 21000 Dijon, tel: 03 80 72 53 53. Although unpaid, this is a good way to meet other young people of all nationalities and to learn the language.

Once in France, students will find a valid student ID card is useful in obtaining discounts on all sorts of activities, including admission to museums, cinemas, etc. If you do not happen to have your ID card with you, reductions may sometimes be allowed by proving your status with a passport.

The Centre d'Information et Documentation de Jeunesse (CIDJ), based at 101 Quai Branly, 75740 Paris, Cedex 15, tel: 01 44 49 12 26, fax: 01 40 65 02 61, is a national organization which issues information about youth and student activities. The noticeboard in the Paris office is a mine of useful information regarding accommodation and events.

For individual holidays, the cheapest option is to sleep under canvas, or in a hostel.

TRAVELLERS WITH SPECIAL NEEDS

An information sheet aimed at travellers with disabilities is published by the French Government Tourist Office: for a copy send a stamped addressed envelope.

The **Royal Association for Disability and Rehabilitation** (RADAR), 12 City Forum, 250 City Rd. London EC1V 8AF, tel: 0171 250 3222, provides useful information for tourists, and France's sister organisation to RADAR, the **Comité National Français de Liaison pour la Réadaptation des Handicapés** (CNFLRH) is based at 236 bis Rue de Tolbiac. 75013 Paris, tel: 01 53 80 66 85 (Veronique Claude - Service International), fax: 01 53 80 66 67. It offers a good information service for visitors with special needs travelling to France, although it does not have any specific information about the regions of France.

In the US, the following offer services to travellers with disabilities:

Travel Information Service, Moss Rehabilitation Hospital, 1200 West Tabor Road, Philadelphia, PA 19141–3099, tel: (215) 456 9600. General information for would-be travellers.

Society for the Advancement of Travel for the Handicapped (SATH), 347 5th Ave. Suite 610. New York, tel: (212) 447 0027, fax: (212) 725 8253. Web site: http://www.sath.org/index.html

Mobility International USA. PO

Disabled Youth

Centre d'Information et de Documentation Jeunesse, 101 Quai Branly, 75740 Paris Cedex 15, provides information on services for young travellers with disabilities. It publishes *Vacances Personnes Handicapées* and annual leaflets on activity and sports holidays for young disabled people. Parents may also find the following organization helpful: Union Nationale des Associations de Parents d'enfants Inadaptés (UNAPEI), 15 Rue Coysevox, 75018 Paris, tel: 01 44 85 50 50.

Box 10767. Eugene. OR 97440, tel: (514) 343 1284, fax: (514) 343 6812. E mail: info@miusa.org

NARIC (National Rehabilitation Information Center) Suite 935. 8455 Colesville Rd. Silver Spring. MD 20910-3319, tel: 800 346 2742 (free call), fax: (301) 587 1967.Web site: http://www.cais.com/

Finding Accommodation

Most disabled travellers will be keen to book accommodation in advance. Most of the official list of hotels (available from the FGTO or the regional tourist office – see *Useful Addresses*) include a symbol to denote wheelchair access, but it is always advisable to check directly with the chosen hotel as to exactly what facilities are available.

Balladins runs a chain of budget hotels throughout France which all have at least one room designed for disabled guests. Restaurants and all other public areas are wheelchair accessible. For a complete list contact Hotels Balladins, 20 Rue du Pont des Halles, 94656 Rungis Cedex, tel: 01 49 78 24 61, fax: 01 69 28 24 02.

There is a guide – *Où Ferons Nous Etape?* (in French only) – which lists accommodation in France that is suitable for people with disabilities. It is available by post from the **Association des Paralysés**, Service Information, 17

Public Holidays

Several French tour operators organize study tours and language courses. The best include:

APEC (Association pour la Promotion des Echanges Culturels): 11 Rue Tronchet, 75008 Paris, tel: 01 42 68 17 09, fax: 01 42 68 17 02; and at 12 Rue St Anne, 75001 Paris, tel: 01 40 20 40 08, fax: 01 40 20 07 37.

Souffle is an organisation created in 1991 which embraces 11 centres which specialise in teaching French as a foreign language, and have all signed a

quality charter. Contact Souffle at BP 133, 83957 La Garde Cedex, tel: 04 94 21 20 92, fax: 04 94 21 22 17.

Union National des Organizations de Séjours Linguistiques (UNOSEL), 19 Rue Mathurins, 75009 Paris, tel: 01 49 24 03 61, fax: 01 42 65 39 38.

A complete list of private language schools is obtainable from regional tourist offices (*see Useful Addresses*).

Practical Tips

Boulevard August Blanqui, 75013 Paris, tel: 01 40 78 69 00. This organization may also be able to deal direct with specific enquiries and can provide addresses of their branches throughout France.

The *Rousseau H Comme Handicapé* guide may also prove useful. It is available from Hachette bookshops or at SCOP, 4 Rue Gustave-Rouanet, 75018 Paris, tel: 01 42 52 97 00.

Michelin's Red Guide *France* for hotels and its *Camping-Caravanning – France* both include symbols for disabled welcome.

The **Holiday Care Service** offers free information on travel accommodation and counterpart associations in France. Send a large stamped addressed envelope to 2 Old Bank Chambers, Station Road, Horley, Surrey RH6 9HW, tel: (01293) 774 535, fax: (01293) 784 647, Minicom (for the hearing impaired): (01293) 776 943.

Getting Around

The **Comité de Liaisons pour le transport des personnes handicapées, Conseil National des Transports**, 34 avenue Marceau, 75008. Paris, tel: 01 47 23 01 25, fax: 01 47 29 39 22, publishes a booklet called *Guide des Transports à l'usage des Personnes à Mobilité Réduite*. This gives brief information on the accessibility and arrange-ments for less able passengers on all forms of public transport and contacts for special transport schemes throughout France.

In the UK, some concessionary ferry fares are available for members of the following organisations: The Disabled Drivers' Association, Disabled Drivers' Motor Club, The Disabled Motorists' Federation.

More information about air and sea travel is given in a guide entitled *Door-to-Door*, available free from the Department of Transport, Door-to-Door Guide, Freepost, Victoria Road, South Ruislip, Middlesex HA4 0NZ. There are also copies available on audio cassette for the vision impaired.

Security and Crime

Sensible precautions with personal possessions are all that should really be necessary when visiting France. Theft and other crime exists here as elsewhere.

Drivers should follow the rules of the road and always drive sensibly (see *Getting Around*). Heavy on-the-spot fines are given for traffic offences, such as speeding, and drivers can be stopped and breathalysed during spot checks. The minimum fine for speeding is FF1,300 and immediate fines of up to FF30,000 can be levied for drink-driving offences (if you do not have enough cash, you will be required to pay a deposit). Police are fairly visible on the main roads of France during summer.

Lost Property

If you lose something on a bus or the métro, first try the terminus to see if it has been handed in. In Paris, after 48 hours, you can go to the Bureau des Objets Trouvés, 36 Rue des Morillons, 75015 Paris, tel: 01 55 76 20 00 You must pay 4 percent of the value of any item reclaimed.

To report a crime or loss of belongings, visit the local gendarmerie or commissariat de police. Telephone numbers are given at the front of local directories, or in an emergency, dial 17. If you lose a passport, report first to the police, then to the nearest consulate.

If you are detained by the police for any reason, ask to telephone your consulate, which should be able to offer advice or assistance.

Tipping

Most restaurant bills include a service charge, and this is generally indicated at the foot of the menu. If in doubt, ask: *Est-ce que le service est compris?* In any case it is common to leave a small additional tip for the waiter if the service has been good. Remember to address waiters as *Monsieur*, never as *garçon*; waitresses are *Mademoiselle* or *Madame* according to age.

It is customary to tip taxi drivers 10 percent, though this is not obligatory.

Medical Services

For minor ailments it may be worth consulting a pharmacy (recognisable by its green cross sign), which have wider "prescribing" powers than chemists in the UK or US. They are also helpful in cases of snake or insect bites and identifying fungi.

If you need to see a doctor, expect to pay around FF110 for a simple consultation, plus a pharmacist's fee for whatever prescription is issued. For EU citizens, the doctor will provide a *feuille des soins* which you need to keep to claim back the majority of the cost (around 75 percent) under the EU agreement. The pharmacist will attach to the feuille the little sticker (*vignette*) from any medicine prescribed to enable you to claim for that too. Refunds have to be obtained from the local Caisse Primaire (ask the doctor or pharmacist for the address).

Lost Credit Cards

For lost credit cards, it is important to notify the auth-orities right away on the following numbers.
Visa/Carte Bleue, tel: 01 42 77 11 90. Out of Paris, tel: 02 54 42 12 12.
Diner's Club, tel: 01 49 06 17 50.
American Express, tel: 01 47 77 72 00.

In cases of medical emergency, either dial 15 for an ambulance or call the Service d'Aide Médicale d'Urgence (SAMU) which exists in most large towns and cities – numbers are given at the front of telephone directories.

The standard of treatment in French hospitals is generally high, and you should be able to find someone who speaks English to help you. You may prefer to try to get to either the American Hospital at 63 Boulevard Victor-Hugo, 92292 Neuilly, tel: 01 46 41 25 25; or the British Hospital Hortford, 3 Rue Barbes, 92300 Levallois, tel: 01 46 39 22 22, both just outside Paris. Show the hospital doctor your E111 (*see page 350*) and you will be billed (once you are back home usually), for about 25 percent of the cost of treatment.

Business Hours

Office workers normally start early – 8.30am is not uncommon – and often stay at their desks until 6pm or later. This is partly to make up for the long lunch hours (from noon or 12.30pm for two hours) which are still traditional in banks, shops and other public offices. Many companies are beginning to change to shorter lunch breaks as employees appreciate the advantages of getting home earlier to families in the evening.

Banks are normally open Monday–Friday 9am–noon and 2pm–5pm, but these hours may vary slightly.

Media

NEWSPAPERS

Regional newspapers, as in the US, contain national and international as well as local news, and are often read in preference to the national press. The main national dailies are *Le Monde* (good for a liberal overview of political and economic news), the more conservative *Le Figaro* and the left-wing papers, *Libération* and *L'Humanité*. *Le Point* and *L'Express* are the major weekly news publications. British and American dailies – *The Times*, *The European* and the *International Herald Tribune* – are widely available in major towns and cities.

TELEVISION

There are two main national channels: TF1 (commercial) and antenne 2 (state-owned but largely financed by advertising); as well as FR3 which offers regional programmes. 5-Arté is a Franco-German channel showing cartoons in the day and arts programmes and documentaries in the evening. M6 shows mainly American films and serials (overdubbed into French).

RADIO

France Inter is the main national radio station (I892m long wave); it broadcasts English-language news twice a day in summer (usually 9am and 4pm). During the peak holiday period, other local stations sometimes put out English bulletins. On the Mediterranean, Riviera Radio (106.3 and 106.5 kHZ) broadcasts 24 hours a day in English. In some areas the BBC's Radio 4 can be received on longwave (198 kHZ). The BBC World service broadcasts in English on various wavelengths during the day and evening.

Postal Services

Provincial post offices – Postes or PTTS (pronounced *pay-tay-tay*) are generally open Monday–Friday 9am–noon and 2–5pm, Saturday 9am–noon (opening hours are posted outside); in Paris and other large cities they are generally open continuously from 8am–7pm. Exceptionally, the main post office in Paris is open 24 hours every day, at 52 Rue du Louvre, 75001 Paris.

Inside major post offices, individual counters may be marked for different requirements. If you just need stamps, go to the window marked *Timbres*. If you need to send an urgent letter overseas, ask for it to be sent *priorité* or by *Chronopost*, which is faster, but expensive.

Stamps are available at tobacconists (*bureaux de tabacs*) and sometimes at other shops selling postcards and greetings cards. Letters within France and most of the EU go for FF3 for up to 20g; FF4.40 for airmail to Ireland, the US and Canada; and FF5.20 for Australia.

Telegrams (cables) can be sent during post office hours or by telephone (24-hours); to send a telegram abroad dial 0800 33 44 11. For a small fee you can arrange for mail to be kept poste restante at any post office, addressed to *Poste Restante, Poste Centrale* main post office), then the town's post code and name, e.g. 16000 Angoulême. A passport is required as proof of identity when collecting mail.

Many post offices have coin-in-slot photocopying machines.

Telephone

The French telephone system, once quirky, is now one of the most efficient in the world. That is not to say that you can be guaranteed to find telephone boxes (*cabines publiques*) that are always operational, but most are.

Telephone numbers have been rationalised to ten figures, given in sets of two: 01 23 45 67 89. Note that numbers will be given in pairs of figures, unless you ask for them to be given *chiffre par chiffre* (singly). The only additional codes necessary are for dialling overseas.

Regional Codes

The French telephone system was overhauled in 1996. Eight-digit numbers were extended to 10 digits and the following regional telephone numbers gained a prefix: **Paris, Ile de France**: 01; **Northwest** 02; **Northeast** 03; **Southeast and Corsica** 04, and **Southwest** 05.

When dialling from outside the country, omit the 0.

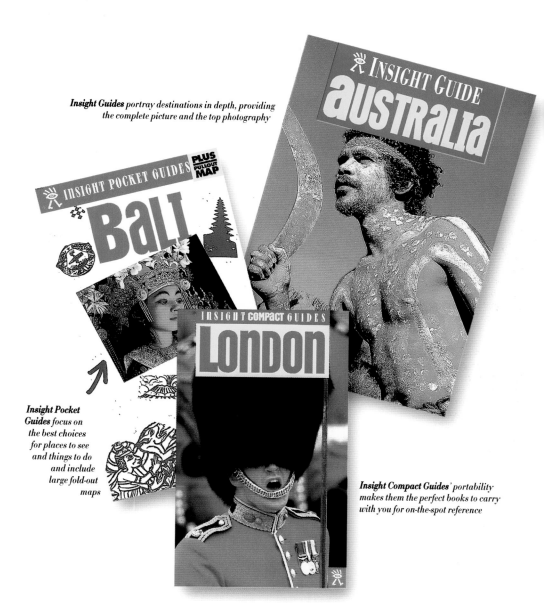

Insight Guides portray destinations in depth, providing the complete picture and the top photography

Insight Pocket Guides focus on the best choices for places to see and things to do and include large fold-out maps

Insight Compact Guides' portability makes them the perfect books to carry with you for on-the-spot reference

Three types of guide for all types of travel

INSIGHT GUIDES Different people need different kinds of information. Some want *background information* to help them prepare for the trip. Others seek *personal recommendations* from someone who knows the destination well. And others look for *compactly presented data* for on-the-spot reference. With three carefully designed series, Insight Guides offer readers the perfect choice. Insight Guides will turn your visit into an experience.

The world's largest collection of visual travel guides

When you're
bitten by the travel bug,
make sure you're protected.

Check into a British Airways Travel Clinic.

British Airways Travel Clinics provide travellers with:

- A complete vaccination service and essential travel health-care items
- Up-dated travel health information and advice

Call **01276 685040** for details of your nearest Travel Clinic.

BRITISH AIRWAYS
TRAVEL CLINICS

Telephoning Abroad

To make an international call, lift the receiver, insert the money (if necessary), dial 00, then dial the country code, followed by the area code (omitting the area code prefix 0) and the number.

International calls can be made from most public booths, but it is often easier to use a booth in a post office – ask at the counter to use the phone, then go back to settle the bill – you have no record of the cost of the call until the end but this is the most convenient way to make a long call if you don't have a lot of small change.

If you use a phone (not a public call box) in a café, shop or restaurant you are likely to be surcharged. Some hotels and cafés now have computerised public telephones whereby the caller receives a printed statement of the details of his call on payment of the bill at the bar – a useful asset for business travellers.

Public phones

Coin-operated telephones take 50-centime, 1-, 2- and 5-franc pieces, but many have been converted to card or card/cash phones. These are simple to use, and it is worth purchasing a phone card (*une télécarte* – around F50 or F100) if you are likely to use a public call box several times. Cards are available from post offices, stationers, railway stations and tobacconists.

Several main post offices now also have telephones that can be used with credit cards. If using a US credit phone card, dial the company's access number.
- **Sprint** tel: 00 00 87
- **AT&T** tel: 00 00 11
- **MCI** tel: 00 00 19

Cheap Rates

The cheapest times to call are weekdays 7.30pm to 8am and at weekends after 1.30pm on Saturday.

International dialling codes:
Australia 61   UK 44
Canada 1   US 1
Ireland 353

Operator services and directory enquiries 12.

Information

Post offices in most major towns and cities in France have replaced their traditional telephone directories with the computerised Minitel system. You can use this free of charge to look up any number in the country. The instructions (in French) are easy to understand, and you simply tap in the name of the town, *département* and person (or company) whose number you are looking for: it will be displayed on the small screen, connected to the telephone.

The Minitel system can also be used in the same way as yellow pages to find, for example, all the dry-cleaners listed in a particular town.

Reverse Charge Calls

You cannot reverse the charges (call collect) for calls within France, but you can to countries which will accept such calls. Call the operator and ask to make a PCV (pronounced *pay-say-vay*) call.

Reverse-charge calls can be received only at call boxes displaying the blue bell sign.

Doing Business

Business travel now accounts for roughly a third of French tourism revenue. This important market has lead to the creation of a special Conference and Incentive Department in the French Government Tourist Office in both London and New York to deal solely with business travel enquiries. They will help organize hotels, conferences and incentive deals for groups.

Paris is a world leader for conferences, exhibitions and trade fairs and its facilities are impressive; many châteaux offer luxurious accommodation for smaller groups – and you can even organize a congress at Disneyland Paris.

For anyone putting on a major business event in Paris, the first line of contact is the **Bureau des Congrès et des Salons de Paris**, (BCSP) 5 av. de l'Opera, 75001 Paris, tel: 01 47 03 16 16, fax: 01 47 03 16 18.

Other posible sources of information are:
- **Convergences**, 120 Avenue Gambetta, 75020 Paris, tel: 01 43 64 77 77, fax: 01 40 31 01 65.
- **SOCFI**, 14 Rue Mandar, 75002 Paris, tel: 01 42 33 89 94, fax: 01 40 26 04 44.
- **Connexions Voyages Hamelin**, 126 Avenue Georges Clemenceau, BP 805, 92008 Nanterre Cedex, tel: 01 46 69 64 64, fax: 01 46 69 64 53.
- **Wagonlits Travel Production**, 50 Rue de Londres, 75008 Paris, tel: 01 44 90 33 10, fax: 01 44 90 33 15.

For general information about business travel and facilities around the country contact the regional tourist offices (*see overleaf*). Another good source of information and assistance on a local level are the *Chambres de Commerce et d'Industrie* in the individual *départements*. These can supply information about local companies, interpretation and translation agencies and conference centres, as well as advice on the technicalities of export and import. Indeed, most chambers of commerce have conference facilities of some kind themselves.

A calendar of trade fairs in France is published every year and this is available in August, for the following year, from the Chambre de Commerce et d'Industrie de Paris, 7 Rue Beaujon, 75008 Paris, tel: 01 45 08 35 00, fax: (1) 42 89 77 18.

Useful Addresses

United Kingdom and Ireland
Air France
• *UK*: 10 Warwick St, London W1R
5RA, tel: 0181 742 6600
(reservations).
• *Ireland*: 29–30 Dawson Street,
Dublin 2, tel: 77 8272, or 77 8899
(for reservations).
French Government Tourist Office
178 Piccadilly, London W1V 0AL;
tel: (0891) 244 123, fax: (0171)
493 6594;
E-mail: piccadilly@mdlf.demon.co.uk
Web site:
http://www.franceguide.com
French Consulate
• *London*: 21 Cromwell Road,
London SW7 2EN, tel: (0171) 838
2000, fax: (0171) 838 2001. *Visa
section*: 6a Cromwell Place, London
SW7 2EN, tel: 0891 887733.
• *Edinburgh*: 11 Randolph
Crescent, Edinburgh EH3 7TT,
tel: (0131) 225 7954,
fax: (0131) 225 8975.
French Embassy
Commercial Department: 21–24
Grosvenor Place, London SW1X
7HU, tel: (0171) 235 7080,
fax: (0171) 235 8598. Cultural
department: 23 Cromwell Road,
London SW7 2EL, tel: (0171) 838
2055, fax: (0171) 838 2088.
**Monaco Government Tourist and
Convention Office**
3–18 Chelsea Garden Market,
Chelsea Harbour, London SW10
0XE, tel: (0171) 352 9962, fax:
(0171) 352 2103.
Rail Shop (SNCF)
179 Piccadilly, London W1, tel:
0990 300 003.
For train information and
reservations.
There is also an International
Rail Centre at Victoria Railway

Entente Cordiale

There is a French Chamber
of Commerce in London at
5th Floor, Knightsbridge
House, 197 Knightsbridge,
London SW7 1RB,
tel: (0171) 304 4040,
fax: (0171) 304 7034.

Station open Mon–Wed 9am to
5.30pm and Thurs–Fri 9am to
6.30pm.

US and Canada
Air France
• *New York*: 666 Fifth Avenue, NY
10019, tel: (212) 315 1122 (toll-
free reservations tel: 800 237
2747).
• *Los Angeles*: 8501 Wilshire
Boulevard, Beverly Hills, CA 90211,
tel: (213) 688 9220.
• *Montreal*: 979 Ouest Boulevard
de Maisonneuve, Québec H3A 1M4,
tel: (514) 284 2825.
• *Toronto*: 151 Bloor Street West,
Suite 600, Ontario M5S 1S4, tel:
(416) 922 3344.
French Government Tourist Office
• *New York*: 444 Madison Ave, NY
10022, tel: (212) 838 7800, fax:
(212) 838 7855.
• *Chicago*: 676 North Michigan
Avenue, Suite 3360, Chicago IL
0611-2819, tel: (312) 751 7500,
fax: (312) 337 6339.
• *Texas*: Cedar Maple Plaza, 2305
Cedar Springs Road, Suite 205,
Dallas, Texas 75201, tel: (214)
720 4010, fax: (214) 702 0250.
• *Montreal*: 1981 Avenue McGill
Collège, Tour Esso, Suite 490,
Montreal PQ, H3A 2W9, tel: (514)
288 4264,
fax: (514) 845 4868.
• *Toronto*: 30 St Patrick Street,
Suite 700, M5T 3A3 Ontario, tel:
(416) 593 4723.

France
Air France
119 Champs Elysées, 75384
Cedex 08, tel: 01 44 08 24 24;
Central Reservations: tel: 01 44 08
22 22.
**Maison de la France (French
Government Tourist Office)**
8 Avenue de l'Opéra, 75001 Paris,
tel: 01 42 96 10 23, fax: 01 42 60
75 12.
Office National des Forêts (Forestry
Commission), 217 Rue Grande,
77300 Fontainebleau, tel: 01 60
74 92 10.

Reservations

Many *départements* now offer
a central booking facility for
accommodation (sometimes
including *gîtes*) and for activity
holidays and other services.
Contact:
• the relevant Comité Regional
du Tourisme (CRT);
• your local French Government
Tourist Office;
• Loisirs Accueil, 289 blvd St
Germain, 75007 Paris, tel: 01
44 11 10 44; or
• Gîtes de France, 35 rue
Godot-de-Moroy, 75009 Paris.
tel: 01 49 70 75 75.

REGIONAL TOURIST OFFICES
In many towns and cities, tourist
information is available from the
office of the *Syndicat d'Initiative*,
often attached to the Town Hall
(Hôtel de Ville) in smaller places.
There are also regional tourist
offices (called Comité Regional du
Tourisme, or CRT), which you may
want to contact before leaving
home.
The following list of regional
offices is in alphabetical order and
gives the individual *départements*
for which information can be
obtained.

Alsace
6 Avenue de la Marseillaise, 67000
Strasbourg, tel: 03 88 25 01 66,
fax: 03 88 52 17 06. For: Bas-Rhin
and Haut-Rhin.

Auvergne
43 Avenue Julien, BP 395, 63011
Clermont-Ferrand Cedex, tel: 04 73
29 49 49,
fax: 04 73 34 11 11.
For: Allier, Cantal, Haute-Loire and
Puy-de-Dôme.

Aquitaine
23 Parvis de Chartrons, 33074
Bordeaux Cedex, tel: 05 50 01 70
00, fax: 05 56 01 70 07.
For: Dordogne, Gironde, Landes,
Lot-et-Garonne and Pyrénées-
Atlantiques.

Brittany (Bretagne)
74 B Rue de Paris, 35069 Rennes Cedex, tel: 02 99 28 44 30, fax: 02 99 28 44 40. For: Côtes d'Armor (formerly Côtes du Nord), Finistère, Ille-et-Vilaine and Morbihan.

Burgundy (Bourgogne)
12 Boulevard Brosse, BP 1602, 21000 Dijon, tel: 03 80 50 90 00, fax: 03 80 30 59 45. For: Côte-d'Or, Nièvre, Saône-et-Loire and Yonne.

Champagne-Ardennes
5 Rue de Jéricho, 51037 Châlons-sur-Marne Cedex, tel: 03 26 70 31 28. fax: 03 26 70 31 61. For: Ardennes, Aube, Marne and Haute-Marne.

Corsica
17 Boulevard du Roi Jérome, BP 19, 20181 Ajaccio Cedex 1 tel: 04 95 51 77 77 fax: 04 95 51 14 40.

Franche-Comté
9 Rue de Pontarlier, 25044 Besançon Cedex, tel: 03 81 83 50 47, fax: 03 81 83 35 82. For Doubs, Jura, Haute-Saône and Territoire-de-Belfort.

Ile-de-France
26 Avenue de l'Opéra, 75001 Paris, tel: 01 42 60 28 62, fax: 01 42 60 20 23. For: Seine-et-Marne, Yvelines, Essone, Hauts- de-Seine, Seine-St-Denis, Val-de-Marne and Val-d'Oise.

Consulates in France

Australia: 4 Rue Jean-Rey, 75015 Paris, tel: 01 40 59 33 00.
Canada: 35 Avenue Montaigne, 75008 Paris, tel: 01 44 43 29 00.
Ireland: 4 rue Rude 75016 Paris. tel: 01 44 17 67 00.
UK: 16 rue d'Anjou. BP111-08, 75353 Paris Cedex 08, tel: 01 44 51 31 00.
US: 2 Rue St-Florentin, 75001 Paris, tel: 01 42 96 14 88.

Languedoc-Roussillon
20 Rue de la République, 34000 Montpellier, tel: 04 67 22 81 00, fax: 04 67 58 06 10. For: Aude, Gard, Hérault, Lozère and the Pyrénées-Orientales.

Limousin
Ensemble Administratif Régional, 27 Boulevard de la Corderie, 87031 Limoges Cedex, tel: 05 55 45 18 80, fax: 05 55 45 18 18. For: Corrèze, Haute-Vienne and Creuse.

Loire Valley
Centre-Val de Loire: 8 rue d'Escures. 45000 Orléans, tel: 02 38 78 04 04. For: Cher, Eure-et-Loir, Indre, Indre-et-Loire, Loir-et-Cher and Loiret.
Pays de la Loire: 2 Rue de la Loire, BP 2412, 44204 Nantes, tel: 02 40 48 24 20, fax: 02 40 08 07 10. For: Loire-Atlantique, Maine-et-Loire, Mayenne, Sarthe and Vendée.

Lorraine
1 Place Gabriel-Hocquard, BP 1004, 57036 Metz Cedex 1, tel: 03 87 37 02 16, fax: 03 87 37 02 19. For: Meurthe-et-Moselle, Moselle, Meuse and Vosges.

Nord/Pas-de-Calais
6 Place Mendès-France, 59800 Lille, tel: 03 20 14 57 57, fax: 03 20 14 57 58. For: Nord and Pas-de-Calais.

Normandy
14 Rue Charles-Corbeau, 27000 Evreux, tel: 02 32 33 79 00, fax: 02 32 31 19 04. For: Calvados, Eure, Manche, Orne and Seine-Maritime.

Picardie
3 Rue Vincent Auriole, BP 2616, 80000 Amiens Cedex, tel: 03 22 91 10 15, fax: 03 2 97 92 96. For: Somme, Aisne and Oise.

Poitou-Charentes
62 Rue Jean-Jaurès, BP 56, 86002 Poitiers Cedex, tel: 05 49 50 10 50, fax: 05 49 41 37 28. For:

Charente, Charente-Maritime, Deux-Sèvres and Vienne.

Provence (Alpes/Côte-d'Azur)
Immeuble CMCI, 2 Rue Henri-Barbusse, 13241 Marseille Cedex 01, tel: 04 91 39 38 00, fax: 04 91 56 66 61.
For: Alpes de Haute Provence, Hautes Alpes, Bouches du Rhône, Var and Vaucluse.

Pyrenees (Midi-Pyrénées)
54 Boulevard de l'Embouchure, BP 2166, 31022 Toulouse Cedex, tel: 05 61 13 55 55, fax: 05 61 47 17 16. For: Ariège, Aveyron, Haute-Garonne, Gers, Lot, Hautes-Pyrénées, Tarn and Tarn-et-Garonne.

Rhône-Alpes
La Combe de Charbonnières, 104 Route de Paris, BP 19, 69260 Charbonnières-les-Bains, tel: 04 72 38 11 11, fax: 04 72 38 44 94.
For: Ain, Ardèche, Drôme, Isère, Loire, Rhône, Savoie and Haute-Savoie.

Riviera/Côte d'Azur
55 Promenade des Anglais, BP 602, 06011 Nice Cedex, tel: 04 93 37 78 78, fax: 04 93 86 01 06. For: Alpes-Maritimes.

Getting Around

FROM CHARLES DE GAULLE AIRPORT

Rail

Take the free shuttle bus *navette* to the Roissy train station. From there take the RER to Métro station Gare du Nord or Chatelet. The RER runs every 15 minutes from 5am–11.59pm. The journey time is on average 35 minutes.

Validating Tickets

Rail tickets bought in France must be validated using the orange automatic date-stamping machine at the entrance to the platform. Failure to do so incurs a fine. These machines are marked *compostez votre billet*.

Bus

Roissy Bus runs to Opéra Garnier (by the American Express office) from terminals 1 gate 30, 2A gate 10, 2D gate 12. Buses run every 15 minutes 6am–11pm, journey time 45 minutes.
Air France Bus (to Métro Porte Maillot or Charles de Gaulle Etoile) leaves from terminals 2A and 2B or terminal 1 arrival-level gate 34. The bus runs every 20 minutes 5.40am–11pm; the journey takes about 40 minutes.

Taxi

By far the most expensive but unquestionably the easiest solution, especially for those laden with bags or children. The cost will be clearly indicated on the meter,

although a supplement of FF5 is charged for each large piece of luggage, pushchairs, and pets.

It is customary, though not required, to tip the driver – usually about 10 percent of the fare.

FROM ORLY AIRPORT

Rail

Take the shuttle from gate H (Orly Sud) or from arrival-level gate F (Orly Ouest) to the Orly train station. The RER stops at Austerlitz, Pont St Michel, and the Quai d'Orsay. It runs every 15 minutes from 5.50am– 10.50pm. The journey takes about 50 minutes.

Bus

Orlybus goes to Place Denfert-Rochereau and leaves from Orly Sud gate F, or Orly Ouest arrival-level gate D. This bus runs every 15 minutes from 6.30am–11.30pm.
Orlyval is an automatic train which runs between Antony (the nearest RER to Orly) and Paris about every 5 minutes from 6.30am–9.15pm (Sunday 7am–10.55pm). This isn't the quickest or easiest way of reaching Paris. The journey takes about 30 minutes.
Air France Bus goes to Invalides and Gare Montparnasse, leaving from Orly Sud gate J, or Orly Ouest arrival-level gate E. It runs every 12 minutes from 6am–11pm. The journey takes about 30 minutes.

BETWEEN AIRPORTS

In addition to the above services, an Air France bus links Charles de Gaulle and Orly leaving each airport every 20 minutes 6am–11pm.

By Bus

Details of bus routes and timetables are generally available free either from bus stations (*gare routière*), which are often situated close to railway stations, or from tourist offices. They will also give details of coach tours and sightseeing excursions which are widely available in many parts of France.

By Train

Information on services is available from stations (Gare SNCF). If you intend to travel extensively by train it may be worth obtaining a rail pass before leaving home (see *Getting There*). These tickets can be used on any journey, otherwise individual tickets need to be purchased, but check on any discounts available, e.g. the *Carte Couple* for married couples travelling together on off-peak services. Children under 4 travel free, from 4 to 12 years for half-fare. People travelling in groups of six or more can also obtain discounts (of 20–40 percent depending on numbers).

Paris Métro and RER

The Paris métro is one of the world's oldest subway systems and some of its stations are almost historic monuments. Despite that, it is quick and efficient. The métro operates 5.30am–12.30am; its comprehensive map and signage make it virtually impossible to get lost; the lines are identified by number and the names of their terminals. It operates in conjunction with the RER, suburban regional express trains, which operate on four lines, identified as A–D.

Flat fare tickets are valid for both the subway and the bus, but a book (*carnet*) of 10 gives a considerable saving. Buy them at bus or métro stations and some *tabacs*.

Another option is the Paris-visite card which is valid for three or five consecutive days on the métro, bus and railway in the Paris/Ile de France region. It also gives dis-counted entry to various tourist sites; available from main métro and SNCF stations and the airports. For shorter stays, buy the Formule 1 card, which allows an unlimited number of trips in any one day on the métro, bus and suburban trains and the night buses (it extends as far as Disneyland Paris). Buy it from métro offices or the Central Tourist Office in the Champs Elysées.

There is also the Carte Orange

which covers all your journeys on the metro for a specified number of days, and can be purchased at the ticket office.

Taxis

Taxis are most readily available at airports and railway stations. In Paris there are almost 500 taxi ranks, but be careful in the capital to hail only a genuine taxi (with a light on the roof); other operators may charge exorbitant fares.

Taxi drivers in Paris operate on three tariffs:
• **Tariff A** 7am–7pm
• **Tariff B** 7pm–7am
• **Tariff C** at night in the suburbs and during the day in the outlying districts of Hauts-de-Seine, Seine Saint-Denis and Val-de-Marne, when the taxi has no client for the return journey.

A 10 percent tip to the driver is usual. Any complaints about Paris taxis should be addressed to the Service des Taxis, Préfecture de Police, 36 Rue des Morillons, 75015 Paris, tel: 01 55 76 20 00.

Driving

Licences

British, US, Canadian and Australian licences are all valid in France. Foreigners are not permitted to drive on a provisional licence.

Insurance

You should always carry your vehicle's registration document and valid insurance – third party is the absolute minimum and a green card from your insurance company is strongly recommended.

Additional insurance cover, which can include a get-you-home service, is offered by several organisations including the British and American Automobile Associations and Europ-Assistance, Sussex House, Perrymount Road, Haywards Heath, West Sussex RH16 1DN, tel: 01444 442211, fax: 01444 455026.

Information

The **Automobile Club National** is the umbrella organisation of France's 40-odd motoring clubs. It will assist any motorist whose own club has an agreement with it. Contact it at 9 Rue Anatole-de-la-Forge, 75017 Paris, tel: 01 43 80 94 63, fax: 01 40 54 00 15.

For information about road conditions, call the **Inter Service Route** line on 01 48 94 33 33 (a recorded message in French) or tune into the local radio stations

Priorité à la Droite – Drive on the Right

Until recently priority on French roads was always given to vehicles approaching from the right, except where otherwise indicated. Nowadays, on main roads, traffic on the major road normally has priority, with traffic being halted on minor approach roads with one of the following signs.
• *Cédez le passage* – give way
• *Vous n'avez pas la priorité* – you do not have right of way
• *Passage protégé* – no right of way.

But care should be taken in smaller towns, and in rural areas where there may not be any road markings (watch out for farm vehicles), in which case you will be expected to give way to traffic coming from the right.

If an oncoming driver flashes their headlights it is to indicate that he or she has priority – not the other way around.

Priority is always given to emergency services and also to vehicles from public utility (e.g. gas, electric and water) companies. A yellow diamond sign indicates that you have priority, the diamond sign with a diagonal black line indicates you do not have priority.

Roads in France

Motorways (*Autoroutes*) are designated "A" roads, National Highways (*Routes Nationales*) "N" or "RN" roads. Local roads are known as "D" routes.

(frequencies often indicated on signs beside roads and Autoroutes).

Petrol

Unleaded petrol (*essence sans plomb*) is now widely available in France.

CAR HIRE

Hiring a car is expensive, partly because of the high sales tax (TVA) – 33 percent on luxury items. Some fly/drive deals work out well if you're only going for a short visit. French Railways offers a good deal on its combined train/car rental bookings. Weekly rates work out better than a daily hire and it can be cheaper to arrange hire through an agent in your own country before leaving for France. The minimum age to hire a car is 21. Some companies will not rent to people under 26 or over 60. The hirer must have held a full licence for at least three years

The central offices of the major car hire companies are listed below. Car hire in France can be arranged through them or via their agencies abroad or through your airline at the same time as you book your ticket. To hire a car locally, check in telephone directories or ask at tourist offices.
Avis, tel: 01 46 10 60 60.
Budget/Milleville, tel: 01 46 86 65 65, fax: 01 46 86 22 17.
Hertz, tel: 01 47 88 51 51.

RULES OF THE ROAD

• The **minimum age** for driving in France is 18.
• Britons must remember to drive on the right: extra care should be taken when crossing the carriage-

way or when emerging from a junction – when it is easy to end up on the left side without thinking.

• Full or dipped **headlights** must be used in poor visibility and at night; sidelights are not sufficient unless the car is stationary. Beams must be adjusted for right-hand-drive vehicles, but yellow tints are not compulsory.

• The use of **seat belts** (front and rear if fitted) in cars and crash helmets on motorcycles is compulsory. Children under 10 are not permitted to ride in the front seat unless fitted with a rear-facing safety seat or if the car has no rear seat.

• The French **drink-driving limit** is 50 mg alcohol per 100 ml of blood. This can mean that just one glass of beer can take you up to the limit.

Speed Limits

Speed limits are as follows, unless otherwise indicated: 130 kph (80 mph) on toll motorways; 110 kph (68 mph) on other motorways and dual carriageways; 90 kph (56 mph) on other roads except in towns where the limit is 50 kph (30 mph). There is also a minimum speed limit of 80 kph (50 mph) on the outside lane of motorways during the day and on level ground. Speed limits are reduced in wet weather as follows: toll motorways 110 kph

(68 mph), dual carriageways 100 kph (62 mph), other roads 80 kph (50 mph).

Fines may be levied for speeding: on toll roads the time is printed on your ticket when you enter and can be checked on exit.

If you can pay 'on the spot' then the fine will be cheaper than if you delay payment, when a surcharge will be added. Nearly all *autoroutes* (motorways) are toll roads.

Accidents and Emergencies

Carry a red triangle to place 50 metres (55 yards) behind the car in case of breakdown or accident (strongly advised and compulsory if towing a caravan).

In an emergency, call the police (tel: 17) or use the free emergency telephones that are every 2 kilometres (1 mile) on motorways. If another driver is involved, lock your car and go together to call the police.

It is useful to carry a European Accident Statement Form (obtainable from your insurance company) which will simplify matters in case of an accident.

Motorbikes & Mopeds

Rules of the road are largely the same as for car drivers. The minimum age for driving machines

over 80cc is 18. GB plates must be shown and crash helmets are compulsory. Dipped headlights must be used at all times. Children under 14 years are not permitted to be carried as passengers.

Hiring Bikes

Car hire is expensive if rentals are organized locally, but bikes (*vélos*) are fairly readily available for hire, often from cycle shops. Local tourist offices keep information on hire facilities. French Railways has them for hire at several stations in the region; they do not necessarily have to be returned to the same station. Bikes can be carried free of charge on buses and on some trains (*Autotrains*). On other, faster, services you will have to pay.

Travelling by a combination of bike and bus or train can be an excellent way of touring and relieves you of some of the legwork. (For further information see *Sports*).

On Foot

There are countless opportunities for exploring France on foot; given the time you could cross the whole of France north-south or west-east by following footpaths. All the main footpaths in France form part of the national network of long-distance footpaths (*Sentiers de Grandes Randonnées* or GR). The routes are numbered for easy identification, e.g. the GR1 takes you around Paris and the Ile de France, covering 395 miles (630 km).

The French Ramblers' Association, Fédération Française de la Randonnée Pédestre (FFRP) publishes Topoguides (guidebooks incorporating IGN I:50,000 scale maps) to all France's footpaths but they are available only in French. For information contact the FFRP, Centre d'Information Sentiers et Randonnées, 14 Rue Riquet, 75019 Paris, tel: 01 44 89 93 90, fax: 01 40 35 85 67. These guides are available in good bookshops in France, as well as abroad. The IGN Blue series maps, at a scale of 1:25,000, are ideal for walkers.

Scenic Routes through France

Following a designated tourist route is a sure way of getting to see the major sights of a region. Tourist offices will help with suggestions.

The **Caisse Nationale des Monuments Historiques et des Sites** (Hotel de Sully, 62 Rue Saint-Antoine, 75186 Paris Cedex 04, tel: 01 44 61 21 50) can suggest historic routes throughout France. Some of these are long – such as the one which takes in the greatest cathedrals of France (including Chartres, Strasbourg and Rouen), and one covering the parks and gardens of the Beauce, Berry and Loire Valley – but they can also suggest many shorter

circuits which take just a day or two, such as the route des Ducs de Normandie or the Quercy Marches road.

You can travel southeast from Paris all the way as far as Lyon, following the Route Historique Buissonière, taking in such sites as Auxerre, Vézelay and Château Chinon among others. Another suggestion is following the William the Conqueror trail, mostly around Normandy, which can be picked up at either Caen or Le Havre.

Another source of is **Demeure Historique**, 57 Quai de la Tournelle, 75005 Paris, tel: 01 55 42 60 00, fax: 01 43 29 36 44.

Walking by the Book

A good basic guide book for serious walkers is Rob Hunter's book **Walking in France**, while **Classic Walks in France,** by Hunter and Wickers, suggests 20 tours in the most beautiful areas of the country. Both published by Oxford University Press. A series of regional walking guides based on the French Topoguides include **Walks in the Dordogne, Coastal Walks in Normandy and Brittany** and **Walks in Corsica**. All of these are published by Robertson McCarta.

WALKING TOURS AND HOLIDAYS

Each *département* has its own ramblers' organization (operating under the FFRP umbrella) which arranges a variety of activities throughout the year: guided walks taking a day, a weekend or more, as well as walks with a particular theme, flora, or wildlife, for example. For more information, contact La Maison de la Randonnée, 1 Rue Voltaire, 75011 Paris, tel: 01 43 71 10 93, fax: 01 46 29 59 72. Tourist offices will also give information about local clubs.

Various walking holidays with accommodation either in hotels or under canvas are available. Some are organized through tour operators in the UK, others are bookable through the French tourist offices and local organisations.

Independent travellers can take advantage of low-priced accommodation offered in *gîtes d'étapes*, hostels offering basic facilities which are to be found on many of the GR routes and in mountain regions. For more information contact the Gîtes de France organization (*see above and Where to Stay*).

The Service Loisirs Accueil in several *départements* (see *Useful Addresses*) offers walking holidays, and a selection of the main operators follows.

France
Les Quatre Chemins, 19 Rue de l'Arquebuse, 71400 Autun, no telephone, fax: 03 85 86 27 19. Walking and activity holidays in the Morvan.

Britain
Headwater Holidays, 146 London Road, Northwich CW9 5HH, tel: (01606) 42220. Holidays in the Creuse, Dordogne, Provence, and other areas.
Ramblers Holidays, Box 43, Welwyn Garden City, Herts AL8 6PQ, tel: (01707) 331133. Wide range of tours, including the Cévennes, Alps, Pyrénées and Corsica.
Sherpa Expeditions, 131a Heston Road, Hounslow TW5 0RD, tel: (0181) 577 2717. Independent guided walks for a fortnight or just a weekend.

Hitchhiking

Hitchhiking is not generally recommended, but if you take sensible precautions it is an interesting and inexpensive way to get around France. Would-be hitchhikers may be discouraged by the difficulty of getting a lift out of the Channel ports, so it may be worth taking a bus or train for the first leg of your journey. Hitching is forbidden on motorways, but you can wait on slip roads or at toll booths. Allostop Provoya is a nationwide organization which aims to connect hikers with drivers (you pay a registration fee and a contribution towards the petrol), tel: 01 42 46 00 66.

Inland Waterways

One of the most pleasant ways of exploring a small corner of France is on board a narrowboat or one of the other craft that can be hired on many of the country's navigable canals and rivers.

Holidays on inland waterways have become extremely popular in recent years and choices range from a simple day or half-day cruise to piloting your own hired boat, or enjoying the luxury of the so-called hotel barges, where you just sit back and relax while the navigation and catering is all taken care of for you.

Even if you have never navigated before, you will feel confident after a minimum of instruction (foreigners require no permit or licence). Several companies offer "package" holidays afloat including travel arrangements. A selection follows.

In the United Kingdom
Abercrombie and Kent
Sloane Square House, Holbein

Discovering France by Boat

Burgundy is particularly favoured by internal waterways; the longest is the **Canal de Bourgogne** which connects the river **Yonne** in the north to the **Saône** in the south.

Devotees of canal architecture can use the aqueduct at **Briare**. This masterpiece of engineering, whose foundations were laid by the engineer Eiffel's company, was built in 1896 to connect the **Briare** and the **Loire lateral canals,** to enable freight to be carried all the way from the Channel to the Mediterranean. The Briare canal itself was built by Sully in the early 17th century and served as a prototype for all France's later canal-building.

Other popular options for boating holidays are the **canal du Midi**, the **Nantes-Brest canal** in the southwest and the little **Rhône-Sète canal** which finishes on the Mediterranean coast. The mysterious green waterways of the **Marais Poitevin**, in the area known as "Green Venice" just inland from **La Rochelle**, have their own particular charm and are ideal for day trips.

Place, London SW1W 8NS, tel: (0171) 730 9600.

Canal and river barges in Alsace, Burgundy and the Rhône; hotel barges in Burgundy and the Loire.

Blakes Holidays
Wroxham, Norwich NR12 8DH, tel: (01603) 784131, fax: (01603) 782871.

The widest choice of boats, operating in all areas.

Crown Blue Line
8 Ber Street, Norwich, Norfolk NR1 3EJ, tel: (01603) 630513, fax: (01603) 664298.

Offers a wide range of cruisers on all the main waterways.

Eurocamp
28 Princess Street, Knutsford, Cheshire. WA16 6BU, tel: (01565) 626262.

European Waterways
35 Wharf Road, Wraysbury, Middx TW19 5JQ, tel: 01784 482439, fax: 01784 483072.

Hoseasons Holidays Abroad,
Sunway House, Lowestoft NR32 3LT, tel: (01502) 500555, fax: (01502) 501501. Operates on the canals in Burgundy, Brittany, Alsace as well as on the Mediterranean.

In the United States
Abercrombie and Kent
1520 Kinsington Road, Oak Brook, Illinois 60523-2106, tel: 800 323 7308 (freephone within US and Canada).

French Country Waterways
PO Box 2195, Duxbury, Massachusetts 02331, tel: 800 222 1236 (freephone within US and Canada).

Booking Direct
If you prefer to book direct in France, try the Service Loisirs Accueil in the individual *départements* (*see Useful Addresses*) or contact one of the following companies (this is just a selection of the many operators).

Bateaux de Bourgogne
SRLA Yonne, 1–2 Quai de la République, 89000 Auxerre.
Tel: 03 86 72 92 10.

This company acts as an agent for many smaller operators.

Crown Blue Line
Le Grand Bassin, BP 1201, 11492 Castelnaudary.
Tel: 04 68 23 17 51, fax: 04 68 23 33 92.

Locaboat Plaisance
BP 150, Quai du Port-au-Bois, 89300 Joigny.
Tel: 03 86 91 72 72.

The following operators offer holidays on luxury hotel barges. These trips are not cheap but you are pampered and the cuisine is usually excellent.

**Continentale de Croisières,
Promenade du Rhin**
21000 Dijon.
Tel: 03 80 53 15 45, fax: 03 80 41 67 73.

Quiztour, Bassin de la Vilette, 19–21 Quai de la Loire, 75019 Paris, tel: 01 42 41 50 01, fax: 01 42 41 55 56.

SONAFHO
Château La Chassagne, 21410 Pont-de-Pany, tel: 03 80 49 76 00, fax: 03 80 49 76 19.

If you are navigating for yourself, a map or guide to the waterway is essential. These are often provided as part of a package deal, otherwise you will need to take your own. Crown Blue Line produces large format map-guides for their own clients, which are now available to the general public; ECM map-guides are well-produced strip maps with all navigation aids, boating services and tourist information. Vagnon map-guides are also very good, with some colour photography.

Where to Stay

Booking Hotels

Hotels are plentiful in the main towns of France and along the main highways, but those in the smaller country villages can be the best. All hotels in France conform to national standards and carry star ratings, set down by the Ministry of Tourism, according to their degree of comfort and amenities. Prices are charged per room, rather than per person.

Hotels are required to display their menus outside and details of room prices should be visible either outside or in reception, as well as on the back of bedroom doors. It is possible for a hotel to have a one-star rating, with a two-star restaurant. This is ideal if you are on a budget and more interested in food than fading wallpaper or eccentric plumbing.

Lists of hotels can be obtained from the French Government Tourist office in your country or from regional or local tourist offices in France. It is also worth buying the guide **Logis et Auberges de France** from your local French Tourist Office. This is an invaluable guide to a very good and reasonably priced network of family-run hotels who aim to offer a friendly welcome and good local cuisine. The guide can be bought in bookshops in France but it is more expensive. It can be used to book hotels before travelling (for the central reservation office in Paris, tel: 01 45 84 83 84). Some tourist offices will make hotel bookings for you, for a small fee.

Central Booking Facilities
Several hotel chains and associations offer central booking facilities. These range from the very

cheap and simple groups such as the Balladins chain, which has almost 100 very modern one-star hotels, to the Concorde group of 28 four-star and de-luxe hotels. A list of central booking offices is given below, with UK and US booking offices mentioned where available.

• **Mercure**, 25 cour Blaise Pascal, 91025 Evry, tel: 01 60 77 27 27, fax: 01 60 87 92 30.
UK office, Resinter, tel: (0181) 283 4500 or 4580, fax: 0181 283 4650.

• **Balladins**, 20 Rue du Pont-des-Halles, 94656 Rungis Cedex, tel: 01 49 78 01 45, fax: 01 46 86 50 18. One-star budget-priced hotels.

• **Campanile**, 31 Avenue Jean-Moulin, 77200 Torcy, tel: 01 64 62 46 46, fax: 01 64 62 46 61. 225 Two-star to four star hotels.
UK office, Red Lion Court, Alexandra Road, Hounslow TW3 1JS, tel: (0181) 569 6969, fax: (0181) 569 4888.

• **Climat de France**, 5 Avenue du Cap-Horn, ZAC de Courtaboeuf, BP 93, 91943 Les Ulis, tel: 01 64 46 01 23 or 05 11 22 11 (toll-free in France), fax: 01 69 28 24 02. 150 Two-star hotels.
UK office, Voyages Vacances Int., 34 Savile Row, London W1X 1AG, tel: (0171) 287 3181.

• **Concorde Hotels**, 35-37 Grosvenor Gardens, London SW1W 0BS, tel: 0800 181 591 or (0171) 630 1704, fax: (0171) 630 0391.

• **Formule 1**, 11 Avenue Aristide Briand 93163, Noisy-le-Grand, tel: 01 43 04 01 00, fax: 01 43 04 68 57. 178. One star budget-priced hotels, offering a booking service from one hotel to another in the chain.

• **Ibis**, 6–8 Rue du Bois-Briard, 91021 Evry Cedex, tel: 01 60 77 27 27, fax: 01 60 77 22 83. 170. Two star hotels.
UK office, Resinter, 1 Shortlands, London W6 8DR, tel: (0181) 283 4500, fax: (0181) 283 4650.

• **Minotel France Accueil**, 163 Avenue d'Italie, 75013 Paris, tel: 01 45 83 04 22, fax: 01 45 86 49 82. 150. Two-star and four-star hotels.
UK office, Minotel Great Britain, 37 Springfield Road, Blackpool FY1 IPZ, tel: (01253) 292 000, fax: (01253) 291 111.
US office, Minotel Europe, 683 South Collier Boulevard, Marco Island, Florida 33037, tel: 800 336 4668 (freephone within the States and Canada).
Canada office, Tours Chanteclerc, 152 Notre Dame Est, 8éme étage, Montréal H2Y 3PC, tel: (514) 398 0990.

The following list shows hotel groups which do not have central booking facilities. However, most of these groups offer something other than the average hotel.

Each group produces its own brochure or list of hotels, available from the addresses below, but bookings have to be made with the individual establishments.

• **Moulin Etape**, Moulin de Chameron, 18210 Bannegon, tel: 02 48 61 83 80, fax: 02 48 61 84 92.

Forty-eight former mills offering one-star to four-star accommodation.

• **Les Nids de France**, 15 Rue Verdun, 78800 Houilles, tel: 01 39 68 95 41. Group of 42 two-star and four-star family-owned hotels.

• **Relais et Châteaux**, 15 rue Galvani, 75017 Paris, tel: 01 45 72 96 50, fax: 01 45 72 96 50. Group of 153 independently-owned hotels and restaurants in former castles and other historic buildings (guide available from French Government Tourist Offices abroad).
UK office, 35-37 Grosvenor Gardens, London SW1W 0BS, tel: 0171 828 9497.

• **Les Relais du Silence**, 17 rue Ouessant, 75015 Paris, tel: 01 44 49 90 00, fax: 01 44 49 79 01. Over 200 two-star to four-star hotels in particularly tranquil settings.

Bed & Breakfast

Bed and breakfast accommodation is available in much of France (mostly in rural areas) in private houses and often on working farms, whose owners are members of the Fédération Nationale des Gîtes Ruraux de France.

This means that the accommodation is inspected by a local representative of the Fédération to ensure that standards are maintained in accordance with its "P" rating (which is shown by ears of corn on a scale of one to four). They can be booked for an overnight stop or a longer stay. The price (from around FF120 for one person, FF180 for a couple) includes breakfast. Evening meals – usually made with local produce and extremely good value – are often available.

Staying with a family in this way provides an ideal opportunity really to get to know the local area and its people. A brochure of all recognised *Gîtes-Chambres d'hôtes* is available from regional tourist offices and some are bookable through the Gîtes de France office at **The Brittany Centre**, Wharf Road,

Portsmouth, PO2 8RU,
tel: 0990 360360.

B&B Abroad offers a bed and breakfast service which can include ferry bookings if desired. It will book accommodation at your chosen destination and overnight stops en route. Contact: 5 Worlds End Lane, Green St Green, Orpington, Kent BR6 6AA, tel: (01689) 857838, fax: (01689) 850931.

B& B (France) publishes *Le B&B* (with l'Association Francaise B&B France). Write to 94–96 Bell Street, Henley on Thames, Oxon RG9 1XS, tel: (01491) 578803, fax: (01491) 410806).

For B&B on a slightly grander scale, try **Château Accueil**. This is a group of owners of some 70 private châteaux who offer luxury accommodation and usually evening meals in their own homes. Information from Marquis de Chénerilles, Président, Château de Gerfaut, 37190 Azay-le-Rideau, tel: 02 47 45 40 16, fax: 02 47 45 20 15. Reservations are made through Concept Service, 6 Rue du Général-Leclerc, 93310 Saint-Ouen-L'Aumone, tel: 01 34 64 51 30, fax: 01 34 64 63 32.

They can also be booked in the UK through **Château Welcome**, PO Box 66, 94-96 Bell Street, Henley on Thames RG9 1XS, tel: (01491) 578803; or in Canada through Tours Chanteclerc, 152 Notre Dame Est, 8éme étage, Montréal H2Y 3PC, tel: (514) 398 9009, fax: (514) 398 9860.

Chambres d'Hôtel de Prestige is a fully illustrated guide to superior homes in rural France offering B&B. Available by post from the Gîtes de France office. (*see Self Catering*).

Also operating just in the Loire Valley and western France is **Bienvenue au Château**, for information contact CRT, 2 Rue de la Loire, BP 20411, 44204 Nantes Cedex 02, tel: 02 40 48 24 20, fax: 02 40 08 07 10.

If you do not wish to book in advance, just look out for signs along the road (usually in the country) offering *chambres-d'hôtes*. You will be taking pot luck, but you may be delighted by the simple farm food and accommodation on offer.

Self Catering

France has what is probably Europe's best network of self-catering holiday cottages. The properties are all inspected by the **Relais Départemental des Gîtes Ruraux de France** (the county office of the national federation) and given an *épi* (ear of corn) classification.

Gîtes can get heavily booked in high season, so reserve well in advance. If you wish to deal directly with France, contact the **Maison des Gîtes de France**, 35 Rue Godot-de-Mauroy, 75009 Paris, tel: 01 49 70 75 75, fax: 01 49 70 75 76. They will provide addresses of the individual *Relais Départementaux* who each produce a list of all the *gîtes* in their *département*. Alternatively, you can book through the **Brittany Centre** booking office: (*see above*).

The main ferry companies also offer *gîte* holidays in association with the *Gîtes de France* office – apply to the ferry companies for their brochures (*see Getting There*). Many other tour operators and private individuals also offer self-catering accommodation, ranging from a simple farm cottage to an apartment in a luxurious château.

What is a Gîte?

The **Fédération des Gîtes Ruraux de France** was set up around 40 years ago with the aim of restoring rural properties for the purpose of letting them as affordable holiday homes.

These *gîtes* (literally: a place to lay one's head) are extremely popular – with the British in particular – as an inexpensive way of enjoying a holiday in rural France. The properties range from very simple farm cottages to grand manor houses and even include the odd château.

Many *gîtes* are off the beaten track and a car, or at least a

Sometimes these properties are official *gîtes* and so have to conform to the Féderation's standards, but others are not subject to any form of inspection at all.

Camping

There is a good choice of campsites in France, many of them near lakes or rivers. The Regional tourist offices (*see Useful Addresses*) each produce their own lists of all recognised sites, with details of one-star rating and facilities.

As with other types of holiday accommodation, the sites can get booked up in high season, so do consider advance booking. Members of the Camping Club or Camping and Caravanning Club of Great Britain may make use of their booking services. The Michelin *Camping/Caravanning Guide* lists sites which accept (or insist on) pre-booking.

The **Caravan and Camping Service**, tel: (0171) 792 1944, fax: (0171) 792 1956 can book sites either from their brochure of three star and four star sites or certain others and will also book ferries. A camping carnet is useful (some sites will not accept a booking without one).

Campsites, like hotels, have official classifications from one star (minimal comfort, water points,

bicycle, is usually essential. Bicycles can often be hired locally or sometimes from *gîte* owners. Car hire is expensive – a fly/drive packages is probably the cheapest option.

Gîtes are completely self-catering (in many cases expect to supply your own bed linen), but most have owners living nearby who will tell you where to buy local produce.

One salutary note: though clean and well-maintained, many *gîtes* are on farms. If you get squeamish about the odd mouse in the kitchen, stay in a hotel.

showers and sinks) tfour star luxury sites with more space to each pitch, and offering above-average facilities, often including a restaurant or takeaway food, games areas and swimming-pools. The majority of sites nationwide are two-star.

Some farms offer "official" sites under the auspices of the Fédération Nationale des Gîtes Ruraux (see *Self-Catering*) – these are designated *camping à la ferme*; again facilities are usually limited but farmers are only allowed to have six pitches and if you are lucky you will get to know the farm and some of its produce.

Packaged camping holidays are now very popular with British holidaymakers and ideal for other overseas visitors too, as all the camping paraphernalia is provided on the site – you only have to take your personal luggage. Many companies now offer this type of holiday, mostly with ferry travel included in the all-in price. Like other package tours, the companies have representatives on the sites to help with any problems.

It is interesting to note that where such companies have taken over sections of existing sites, facilities have improved to meet the demands of their customers and so benefit all campers. Many companies offer good opportunities for sports and leisure, such as wind-surfing or surfing; often the equipment, and sometimes instruction is covered by the cost of the package.Some of the sites are very large, however and might not suit those who wish to get away from it all.

Some tour operators include:
Canvas Holidays, 12 Abbey Park Place, Dunfermline, Fife KY12 7PD, tel: (01383) 644000, fax : (01383) 620075. Pioneers in the field; offers a nanny service.
Eurocamp Travel, 28 Princess St. Knutsford, Cheshire WA16 6BU, tel: (01565) 626 262.
Keycamp Holidays, Ellerman House, 92-96 Lind Road, Sutton SM1 4PL, tel: (0181) 395 4000, fax (0181) 395 8868.

Back to Nature

If you really like to get back to nature, and are unimpressed by the modern trappings of hot water and electric power, look out for camp-sites designated *"Aire naturelle de camping"* where facilities will be absolutely minimal and prices to match. These have a maximum of 25 pitches so they offer the opportunity to stay away from some of the more commercial sites (which can be huge).

The **FFCC Guide** (*see Useful Publications & Addresses*) lists over 2,000 sites nationwide.

Campervan Hire

Motorhomes and camper vans can be hired and picked up in France at many locations. Contact the Caravan and Camping Service, 69 Westbourne Grove, London W2 4UJ, tel: (0171) 792 1944. Some Hertz hire offices also have them available.

Useful Books & Addresses
The French Federation of Camping and Caravanning Guide (FFCC), lists 11,600 sites nationwide, and also shows which have facilities for disabled campers. Available from Deneway Guides, Chesil Lodge, West Bexington, Dorchester DT2 9DG, tel: (01308) 897 809. Price £8.95.
Michelin Green Guide – Camping/Caravanning France. Very informative and also lists sites with facilities for the disabled. Published annually in March, £7.45.
Camping and Caravanning Club, Greenfields House, Westwood Way, Coventry CV4 8JH, tel: (01203) 422 024.
Caravan Club, East Grinstead House, East Grinstead, West Sussex RH19 1UA, tel: (01342) 316101.

Youth Hostels

Holders of accredited Youth Hostel Association cards may stay in any

French hostels which are run by two separate organizations; **Fédération Unie des Auberges de Jeunesse** (FUAJ), 27 Rue Pajol, 75018 Paris, tel: 01 44 89 87 27, fax: 01 44 89 87 10, which is affiliated to the International Youth Hostel Federation; and the **Ligue Française pour les Auberges de Jeunesse** (LFAJ), 38 Boulevard Raspail, 75007 Paris, tel: 01 45 48 69 84, fax: 01 45 44 57 47. Expect to pay around FF60 per night.

The British YHA publishes the **International Youth Hostel Handbook, Vol. I** (revised each March), which includes all the hostels in France, available by post from **Youth Hostel Association**, 8 St Stephen's Hill, St Albans, Herts AL1 2DY, tel: (01727) 845 047, or in person from 14 Southampton Street, London WC2E 7HY, tel: (0171) 836 8541, and from 174 High Street, Kensington, London W8 7RG. The London office also handles membership queries, tel: (0171) 836 1036.

In the US apply to the **American Youth Hostels Inc**, P.O. Box 37613, Dept USA, Washington DC 20013-7613, tel: (202) 783 6161.

Gîtes d'Etapes offer hostel accommodation and are popular with ramblers, climbers and horse riders (some offer stabling). All official *Gîtes d'Étapes* come under the auspices of the Relais Départementaux des Gîtes Ruraux. These are a popular form of cheap accommodation particularly in the national parks. Prices are similar to youth hostels – around FF50 per night for basic accommodation, but up to FF110 or more in the more luxurious establishments which may be on farms offering riding facilities and/or stabling. You do not have to be a member of any organization to use them.

Hotels by Region

France has a huge number of hotels and the following is a selection of good hotels in each region of France (for more inexpensive accomodation, consult the previous section). Category ratings are based on the price of an average double room, including tax and service, so that:

$ = Budget (under FF350)
$$ = Moderate (FF400–750)
$$$ = Expensive FF800+

CC means credit cards accepted, (specified as Amex, American Express; DC, Diners Club; MC, MasterCard; EU, Eurocard, and Visa).

The hotels are listed alphabetically by region and then alphabetically by town.

AUVERGNE & MASSIF CENTRAL

Aurillac
Grand Hôtel St-Pierre
Promenade du Gravier
Aurillac 15000
tel: 04 71 48 00 24
fax: 04 71 64 81 83
Classic town hotel with Beaux-Arts classified wood panelling and a pleasant restaurant.
CC: Amex, DC, Visa **$$**

Conques
Hôtel Sainte-Foy
Rue Principale
Conques 12320
tel: 05 65 69 84 03
fax: 05 65 72 81 04
Restored village hotel of stone and timber, furnished with antiques. Spacious bedrooms and courtyard for warm weather dining. Close to the abbey.
CC: Amex, Visa **$$$**

Creuse
Château de la Cazine
23300 La Souterraine
tel: 05 55 89 61 11
fax: 05 55 63 71 85
Gracious pink brick chateau near Guéret in its own vast grounds of forest and lagoons. Sumptuous salon and dining room. Swimming pool.
Closed Dec–Feb
CC: DC, MC, Visa **$$**

Moudeyres
Le Pré Bossu
43150 Moudeyres

tel: 04 71 05 10 70
fax: 04 71 05 10 21
Remote, rustic and tranquil; a beautifully rebuilt stone house in tiny village in the high volcanic massif near Le Puy (25km SE of Le Puy).
Closed Nov–Easter
No smoking
CC: Amex, MC, Visa **$$**

Moulins
Hotel de Paris-Jacquemart
21 Rue de Paris
Moulins 03000
tel: 04 70 44 00 58
fax: 04 70 34 05 39
Attractive central hotel with a good restaurant, swimming pool and garden.
CC: Amex, DC, Visa **$$**

St-Jean-de-Bruel
Hotel du Midi-Papillon
12230 St-Jean-du-Bruel
40km SE of Millau
tel: 05 65 62 26 04
fax: 05 65 62 12 97
Delightful riverside village inn, with garden and pool. Home cooking with own garden vegetables, poultry and home-made jams and croissants.
Closed: Nov–Easter
CC: MC, Visa **$**

Target
Château de Boussac
03140 Target
tel: 04 70 40 63 20
fax: 04 70 40 60 03
Turretted and moated château between Vichy and Moulins with huge terrace, lake and gardens. Truly *la vie en château*, antiques, chandeliers and formal dinner *en famille*.
Closed: Nov–Feb
CC: Amex, MC, Visa **$$$**

Uzerche
Hôtel Teyssier
Rue Pont Turgot
Uzerche 19140
tel: 05 55 73 10 05
fax: 05 55 73 10 05
Charming hotel on the banks of the river Vézère; superb cooking; dining on the terrace in summer.
CC: Amex, MC, Visa **$**

Vichy
Hôtel Regina
4 Avenue Thermale
Vichy 03200
tel: 04 70 97 53 77
fax: 04 70 98 60 05
Comfortable old hotel with garden close to the Parc des Sources.
CC: Amex, Visa **$**

BRITTANY & NORMANDY

Bayeux: Calvados
Grand Hôtel du Luxembourg
25 Rue des Bouchers
14400 Bayeux, Calvados
tel: 02 31 92 00 04
fax: 02 31 92 54 26
Situated close to the pedestrian area and town centre, a comfortably grand hotel with a four-star restaurant, Les Quatre Saisons, and an American bar.
CC: Amex, EU, MC, Visa **$$**

Brest
Hôtel de la Corniche
1 Rue Amiral Nicol, 29200 Brest, Finistére
tel: 02 98 45 12 42
fax: 02 98 49 01 53
New hotel built entirely in the traditional Brest style using local stone, on the outskirts of the town, ideal for coastal walks.
CC: Amex, MC, Visa **$$**

Cherbourg
Hôtel du Louvre
28 Rue de la Paix/2 Rue Henri-Dunant, 50100 Cherbourg
tel: 02 33 53 02 28
fax: 02 33 53 43 88
A member of the Inter group, a central hotel, close to the port and town hall and within easy access of La Hague.
CC: Amex, DC, EU, Visa **$**

Dieppe
La Présidence
Boulevard de Verdun
76200 Dieppe, Seine-Maritime
tel: 02 35 84 31 31
fax: 02 35 84 86 70
Modern, spacious hotel, close to the port ,with large dining room and bar.
CC: Amex, DC, EU, Visa **$$**

Dinan
Hôtel d'Avaugour
1 Place du Champ Clos, Dinan,
22100 Cotes-du-Nord
tel: 02 96 39 07 49
fax: 02 96 85 43 04
Situated on the ramparts with the medieval city behind. There is a brasserie in the 15th-century former guards room and a good restaurant. Breakfast and afternoon tea are served in the private garden.
CC: Amex, DC, Visa **$$**

Dinard
Reine Hortense et Castel Eugénie,
19 Rue de la Malouine
35800 Dinard, Ille-et-Vilaine
tel: 02 99 46 54 31
fax: 02 99 88 15 88
An elegant villa from the Belle Epoque; attractively situated with terraces and views over the sea and beaches. No restaurant.
Closed: mid-November–Easter.
CC: Amex, DC, EU, Visa **$$$**

Le Havre
Hôtel Foch
4 Rue de Caligny,
76600 Le Havre,
Seine-Maritime
tel: 02 35 42 50 69
fax: 02 35 43 40 17
A large town house in a quiet area by St-Joseph's church.
CC: Amex, DC, Visa **$$**

Honfleur
Le Cheval Blanc
2 Quai des Passagers,
14600 Honfleur, Calvados
tel: 02 31 81 65 00
fax: 02 31 89 52 80
A 15th-century hotel at the foot of the Lieutenance, overlooking the fishing port; a popular rendezvous for artists. All rooms have sea views.
CC: MasterCard, Visa **$$**

Mont-St-Michel
Les Terrasses Poulard
Grande Rue, 50116 Le Mont St-Michel, Manche
tel: 02 33 60 14 09
fax: 02 33 60 37 31
Modern and offering all comforts. Two large dining rooms with panoramic views, open all day with seafood specialities.
CC: Amex, DC, Visa **$$**

Quimper
La Tour d'Auvergne
13 Rue des Réguaires, 29000 Quimper, Finistère
tel: 02 98 95 08 70
fax: 02 98 95 17 31
A friendly inn that has been completely and comfortably modernised. There is a flowery courtyard.
CC: Amex, MC, EU, Visa **$$**

Rennes
Hôtel Lecoq-Gadby
156 Rue d'Antrain, 35000 Rennes, Ille-et-Vilaine
tel: 02 99 38 05 05
fax: 02 99 38 53 40
A small, smart, well equipped hotel with a flowery terrace
CC: Amex, DC, EU, MC, Visa **$$**

Hotel Prices

$ = Budget under FF350
$$ = Moderate FF400–750
$$$ = Expensive FF800+
Prices are per double room.

Rouen
Hôtel De Dieppe
Place Bernard-Tissot, 76000 Rouen, Seine-Maritime
tel: 02 35 71 96 00
fax: 02 35 89 65 21
Tall, central hotel with cosy, quiet rooms. Bar and a good restaurant offering Rouennaise specialities.
CC: Amex, DC, Visa **$$**

St-Brieuc
Hôtel Ker Izel
20 Rue du Gouët, 22000 St-Brieuc, Côtes-du-Nord
tel: 02 96 33 46 29
fax: 02 96 61 86 12
Modest, central hotel with peaceful rooms.
CC: Visa **$**

St-Malo
Hôtel Elisabeth
2 Rue des Cordiers, 35400 St-Malo, Ille-et-Vilaine
tel: 02 99 56 24 98
fax: 02 99 56 39 24
A member of the Independant Châteaux et Hôtels group, the hotel, with its late 16th century façade, is within the ramparts of the old city. 13 small apartments and 4 rooms. No restaurant
CC: Amex, DC, Visa. **$$**

Vannes
Hôtel Manche-Océan
31 Rue Colonel-Maury,
56000 Vannes, Morbihan
tel: 02 97 47 26 46
fax: 02 97 47 30 86
A large, modern, centrally located hotel of the Inter-Hôtel chain. Convenient for the old town, theatre and museums. CC: Amex, DC, Visa **$**

BURGUNDY

Autun, Saône-et-Loire
Hôtel Saint-Louis et de la Poste
6 Rue de l'Arbalète,
71400 Autun, Saône-et-Loire
tel: 03 85 52 01 01
fax: 03 85 86 32 54
Elegant old coaching inn with airy bedrooms and a lovely dining room. Napoleon stayed here.
CC: Amex, MC, Visa, **$$**

Auxerre: Yonne
Hôtel Normandie
41 Boulevard Vauban,
89000 Auxerre, Yonne
tel: 03 86 52 57 80
fax: 03 86 51 54 33
Attractive 19th-century country house with quiet rooms overlooking garden or terrace.
CC: Amex, DC, MC, Visa, **$$**

Beaune: Côte-d'Or
Hôtel Central
2 Rue Victor Millot,
21200 Beaune, Côte-d'Or
tel: 03 80 24 77 24
fax: 03 80 22 30 40
Comfortable central hotel with character. Traditional and modern decor. Modern bedrooms and a good restaurant.
CC: Amex,Visa, MC **$$**

Bourg-en-Bresse: Ain
Hôtel Terminus
19 Rue A. Baudin,
01000 Bourg-en-Bresse, Ain
tel: 74 21 01 21
fax: 74 21 36 47
A grand and elegant hotel with a large, beautiful garden hidden behind. The interior is decorated in Napoléon III style and most of the rooms face out onto the park. There is no restaurant.
CC: Amex, DC, Visa, MC **$$**

Chablis: Yonne
Hostellerie des Clos
18 Rue Jules Rathier,
89800 Chablis, Yonne
tel: 03 86 42 10 63
fax: 03 86 42 17 11
A peaceful, entirely renovated hostelry, formerly part of the Chablis Hospices, with comfortable modern rooms. There is an excellent restaurant.
CC: Amex, Visa, MC **$$**

Dijon: Côte-d'Or
Le Jacquemart
32 Rue Verrerie,
21000 Dijon, Côte-d'Or
tel: 03 80 73 39 74
fax: 03 80 73 20 99
Friendly, inviting hotel in the old quarter. There is no restaurant.
CC: Visa, MC **$$**

Nuits-St-Georges: Côte-d'Or
Hostellerie la Gentilhommière
13 Vallée de la Serrée,
21700 Nuits-St-Georges,
Côte-d'Or
tel: 03 80 61 12 06
fax: 03 80 61 30 33
A 16th-century former hunting lodge in a large park with a river. Beautiful, solid rooms all with garden views; a summer pool, tennis courts and optional dining under the pergola. Excellent restaurant.
CC: Amex, DC, Visa, MC **$$**

Sens: Yonne
Hôtel de Paris et de la Poste
97 Rue de la République,
89103 Sens, Yonne
tel: 03 86 65 17 43
fax: 03 86 64 48 45

Close to the cathedral, a hotel with charming public areas and comfortable, modern bedrooms. There is a large terrace, a pretty garden and a good restaurant.
CC: Amex, DC, Visa, MC **$$**

CHAMPAGNE, LORRAINE & ALSACE

Châlons-sur Marne
Hôtel D'Angleterre
19 Place Mgr Tissier, 51000
Châlons-sur-Marne, Marne
tel: 03 26 68 21 51
fax: 03 26 70 51 67
Small, elegant hotel close to church of Notre Dame-en-Vaux, with four-star restaurant.
CC: Amex, MC, Visa **$$**

Hotel Prices

$ = Budget under FF350
$$ = Moderate FF400–750
$$$ = Expensive FF800+
Prices are per double room.

Charleville-Mézières
Abbaye de Sept Fontaines
08000 Charleville-Méziéres,
Ardennes
tel: 03 2437 38 24
fax: 03 24 37 58 75
On the A4 from Reims, direction Fagnon. Peaceful,ancient château in a large park in the Ardennes countryside.
CC: Amex, DC,Visa **$$**

Colmar
Grand Hôtel Bristol
7 Place de la Gare,
68000 Colmar, Haut-Rhin
tel: 03 89 23 59 59
fax: 03 89 23 92 26
Grand traditional hotel with two restaurants specialising in Alsatian food and fish and game.
CC: Amex, DC, Visa **$$**

Colombey-les-Deux Eglises
Motel Les Dhuits
(on the RN 19), 52330 Colombey-les-Deux-Eglises,
Haute-Marne
tel: 03 25 01 50 10

fax: 03 25 01 56 22
Modern hotel conveniently located for pilgrims to de Gaulle's burial place.
CC: Amex, MC, Visa **$**

Gérardmer
Hostellerie des Bas-Rupts
(outside town on the D486)
88400 Gerardmer, Vosges
tel: 03 29 63 09 25
fax: 03 29 63 00 40
Popular large hotel, with swimming pool, in a peaceful mountain setting. Part of the Relais du Silence chain. (Demi-pension only in high season.)
CC: Amex, DC, Visa **$$**

Langres
Grand Hôtel de l'Europe
23–25 Rue Diderot, 52200
Langres, Haute-Marne
tel: 03 25 87 10 88
fax: 03 25 87 60 65
Charming old hotel with good traditional restaurant.
CC: Amex, DC, Visa **$**

Luxeuil-les-Bains
Hôtel Beau Site
18 Rue Georges-Moulinard, 70302
Luxeuil-les-Bains, Haute-Saône
tel: 03 84 40 14 67
fax: 03 84 40 50 25
Peaceful spa hotel with garden and swimming pool.
CC: MC, Visa, DC **$$**

Mulhouse
Hôtel Wir
1 Porte de Bâle, 68100 Mulhouse,
Haut-Rhin
tel: 03 89 56 13 22
fax: 03 89 46 44 91
Comfortable, centrally located, with moderately priced rooms and a recommended restaurant.
CC: Amex, DC, Visa **$**

Nancy
Grand Hôtel de la Reine
2 Place Stanislas, 54000 Nancy
Meurthe-et-Moselle
tel: 03 83 35 03 01
fax: 03 83 32 86 04
Marie-Antoinette once stayed at this majestic 18th-century hotel on Place Stanislas.
CC: Amex, DC, Visa **$$$**

Reims

Le Boyer Les Crayères
64 Boulevard Henri Vasnier,
51100 Reims, Marne
tel: 03 26 82 80 80
fax: 03 26 82 65 52
Relais et Châteaux hotel. Luxurious
chateau in its own park close to
centre, with celebrated restaurant.
CC: Amex, DC, Visa **$$$**

Hôtel De la Paix
9 Rue Buirette, 51100 Reims,
Marne
tel: 03 26 40 04 08
fax: 03 26 47 75 04
Reasonably priced central hotel with
pool and garden.
CC: Amex, DC, Visa **$$**

Ste-Menehould

Le Cheval Rouge
1 Rue Chanzy, 51800
Ste-Menehould, Marne
tel: 03 26 60 81 04
fax: 03 26 60 93 11
Charming, rustic hotel with
brasserie and restaurant. **$**

Strasbourg

Hannong
15 Rue du 22-novembre,
67000 Strasbourg, Bas-Rhin
tel: 03 88 32 16 22
fax: 03 88 22 63 87
Charming town house hotel,
convenient for the old town, with a
good wine bar.
CC: Amex, DC, Visa **$$**

Monopole-Métropole
16 Rue Kuhn,
67000 Strasbourg, Bas-Rhin
tel: 03 88 14 39 14
fax: 88 32 82 55
Elegant wood-beamed hotel, some
rooms with antique furniture, close
to Petite France historic area.
CC: Amex, DC, Visa **$$**

Troyes

Hôtel De la Poste
35 Rue Emile Zola,
10000 Troyes, Aube
tel: 03 25 73 05 05
fax: 03 25 73 80 76
Centrally located in historic town;
comfortable, with two restaurants.
CC: Amex, Visa **$$**

Verdun

Le Coq Hardi
8 Avenue de la Victoire,
55100 Verdun, Meuse
tel: 03 29 86 36 36
fax: 03 29 86 09 21
Friendly hotel with individually styled
rooms and fine restaurant.
CC: Amex, DC, Visa **$$**

LANGUEDOC & ROUSSILLON

Aiguës-Mortes: Gard

St-Louis
10 Rue Amiral Courbet,
30220 Aiguës-Mortes
tel: 04 66 53 72 68
fax: 04 66 53 75 92
Charming balconied hotel in walled
town, with a patio garden next to
the ramparts.
Closed January to mid-March. **$**

Carcassonne

Le Montmorency
2 Rue Camille St-Saëns,
11000 Carcassonne, Aude
Tel: 04 68 25 19 92
Fax: 04 68 25 43 15
At the foot of the medieval
ramparts, a reasonably priced hotel
with terrace, swimming-pool and log
fire in winter.
CC: Amex, DC, Visa **$$**

Ceret: Pyrénées-Or

La Terrasse au Soleil
Route de Fontfrède,
66400 Ceret
tel: 04 68 87 01 94
fax: 04 68 87 39 24
18th-century farmhouse with superb
restaurant and views of the
mountains from its elegant terrace.
Heated pool. Closed Nov–Feb.
CC: Amex, MC, Visa **$$$**

Collioure: Pyrénées-Or

Casa Pairal
Impasse des Palmiers,
66190 Collioure
tel: 04 68 82 05 81
fax: 04 68 82 52 10
Delightful villa in shady gardens of
palms, magnolias and fountains in
a quiet cul de sac close to village
and sea. Open from 22 March–12

Nov. Private parking. Outdoor pool.
CC: Amex, CB **$$**

Cordes: Tarn

Le Grand Ecuyer
Haut de la Cité,
81170 Cordes
tel: 05 63 53 79 50
fax: 05 63 53 79 51
Hotel in historic building, once
residence of the Counts of
Toulouse, with antique furniture and
stone walls. Acclaimed chef Yves
Thuriès cooks in restaurant.
CC: Amex, MC, Visa **$$**

Llo: Pyrénées-Or

Auberge Atalya
66800 Llo
tel: 04 68 04 70 04
fax: 04 68 04 01 29
Intriguing little hotel in a rebuilt
stone farmhouse, with antique
furniture, and peaceful terraces in
uplands between France and Spain
(2 km east of Saillagouse).
Swimming pool. Closed Nov.
CC: MC, Visa **$$**

Montpellier: Hérault

Demeure des Brousses
Route de Vaugières,
34000 Montpellier
tel: 04 67 65 77 66
fax: 04 67 22 22 17
18th-century provençal farmhouse in
peaceful shaded grounds. No
restaurant, but meals can be
arranged with advance notice. CC:
Amex, DC **$$**

Narbonne

Grand Hôtel du Languedoc
22 Boulevard Gambetta,
Aude 11100
tel: 04 68 65 14 74
Traditional grand hotel in centre of
town, with restaurant.
CC: Amex, DC, Visa **$$**

Sète Hérault

Grand Hôtel
17 Quai de Lattre-de-Tassigny,
34200 Séte
tel: 04 67 74 71 77
fax: 04 67 74 29 27
Belle Epoque hotel with fine glass
atrium, overlooking the Grand Canal.
CC: Amex, DC, CB **$$**

Toulouse
Grand Hôtel de l'Opéra
Place du Capitole,
31000 Toulouse, Haute-Garonne
tel: 05 21 82 04 66
fax: 05 23 41 04
Elegant hotel with fine restaurant at
the heart of the old city.
CC: Amex, DC, Visa **$$**

LIMOUSIN, PERIGORD & BORDEAUX

Bordeaux: Gironde
Le Bayonne Etche-Ona
15 Cours de l'Intendance,
33000 Bordeaux
tel: 05 56 48 00 88
fax: 05 56 48 41 60
A grand, central hotel in the Triangle
d'Or district with an 18th century
facade and a modern interior. No
restaurant.
CC: All **$$**

Grand Hôtel Français
12 Rue du Temple,
33000 Bordeaux, Gironde
tel: 05 56 48 10 35
fax: 05 56 81 76 18
All modern comforts in this
gracefully elegant 18th-century
mansion in the centre of town;
close to the cathedral, museums,
wine centre and theatre. There is no
restaurant.
CC: Amex, DC, Visa **$$**

Brantôme: Dordogne
Le Chatenet
24310 Brantôme, Dordogne
(D78 exit SW Brantôme)
tel: 05 53 05 81 08
fax: 05 53 05 85 52
A 17th-century country manor
standing in its own grounds.
Spacious, elegantly furnished
bedrooms and family ambiance.
CC: MC, Visa **$$**

Brive: Corrèze
La Truffe Noire
22 Boulevard Anatole-France,
19100 Brive-le-Gaillard, Corrèze
tel: 05 55 92 45 00
fax: 05 55 92 45 13
This recently restored town hotel
combines a rustic style with modern

comforts. There are several dining
rooms and the stone-arched cellar
restaurant offers regional dishes.
CC: Amex, DC, EU, MC, Visa **$$**

Cahors: Lot
Le Terminus
5 Avenue Charles-de-Freycinet,
46000 Cahors, Lot
tel: 05 65 35 24 50
fax: 05 65 22 06 40
A small, grand-hôtel from the turn of
the century offering warm
hospitality and graciously decorated
rooms. Gastronomic restaurant, Le
Balandre.
CC: Amex, DC, EU, MC, Visa **$$**

Capbreton: Landes
Aquitaine
66 Avenue Maréchal de Lattre de
Tassigny, 40130 Capbreton,
Landes
tel: 05 58 72 38 11
fax: 05 58 49 30 82
A modern hotel next to the beach;
with its own swimming pool and the
pool-side dining. **$**

**Champagnac-de-Belair:
Dordogne**
Le Moulin de Roc
24530 Champagnac-de-Belair,
Dordogne
tel: 05 53 02 86 00
fax: 05 53 54 21 31
A 17th-century former watermill with
great character. Bedrooms are
pretty and cosy and there are lovely
waterside gardens. The cuisine is
recommended.
CC: Amex, DC, Visa **$$**

Coly: Dordogne
Manoire d'Hautegente Terrasson
24120 Coly, Dordogne
tel: 05 53 51 68 03
fax: 05 53 50 38 52
A lovely old 13th-century manor
house in wooded grounds. Originally
a forge, later a mill, the house has
been in the same family for 300
years. Spacious, comfortable
bedrooms, furnished with antiques
and a vaulted dining room with
excellent food.
CC: MC, Visa **$$**

Condom: Gers
Hôtel des Trois Lys
32100 Condom, Gers
tel: 05 62 28 33 33
fax: 05 62 28 41 85
Formerly a private mansion, this
charming hotel with its 18th-century
façade and light, airy rooms offers
stylish comfort. There is a bar, a
swimming pool and a restaurant Le
Dauphin.
CC: all **$$**

Domme: Dordogne
La Daille
Florimont-Gaumiers,
24250 Domme, Dordogne
tel: 05 53 28 40 71
Small, English-run, farmhouse
hotel, with gardens, in beautiful,
countryside. Comfortable rooms in
a modern separate building; dining
room in the farmhouse serves light
cuisine based on local produce.
Minimum three nights.
No credit cards **$$**

Les Eyzies: Dordogne
Le Centenaire
Rocher de la Penne, 24620 Les-
Eyzies-de-Tayac, Dordogne
tel: 05 33 06 68 68
fax: 05 53 06 92 41
Situated at the foot of Les Eyzies,
the hotel combines sophisticated
amenities and a country style. Four-
star restaurant, (the International),
heated outdoor pool, sauna,
exercise room, and gardens.
CC: Amex, DC, EU, MC, Visa **$$**

Gourdon: Lot
Bissonier la Bonne Auberge
51 boulevard des Martyrs,
46300 Gourdon, Lot
tel: 05 65 41 02 48
fax: 05 65 41 44 67
An attractive hotel-restaurant near
the medieval centre of town. There
are good views from the terrace and
a pretty courtyard. Modern
bedrooms.
CC: Amex, Visa **$$**

Margaux: Gironde
Relais de Margaux
Chemin de l'Ile Vincent
33460 Margaux, Gironde
tel: 05 57 88 38 30

fax: 05 57 88 31 73
In a large park in the heart of the Medoc, this former wine cellar belonging to the chateau has been transformed into a luxury hotel with comfortably individual rooms. **$$$**

Pauillac: Gironde
Château Cordeillan-Bages
Route des Châteaux
33250 Pauillac, Gironde
tel: 05 56 59 24 24
fax: 05 59 59 01 89
A 17th-century Bordeaux style château, recently elegantly restored, and now housing the Bordeaux school of wine.
CC: Amex, DC, Visa **$$$**

La Pélissaria: Lot
46330 St-Cirq-Lapopie, Lot
tel: 05 65 31 25 14
fax: 05 65 30 25 52
A 13th-century house built on the hillside with lovely views out over the valley. There is a little terraced garden.
CC: MC, Visa **$$**

Rocamadour: Lot
Ste-Marie
Place des Senhals,
46500 Rocamadour, Lot
tel: 05 65 33 63 07
fax: 05 65 33 69 08
Built on a ledge on the rocks with a splendid view out over the countryside and medieval town, particularly from the terrace-café. Modern bedrooms, rustic decor in the public rooms.
CC: EU, MC, Visa **$**

La Rochelle: Charente-Maritime
Hôtel de France d'Angleterre et Champlain
20 Rue Rambaud, 17000 La Rochelle, Charente-Maritime
tel: 05 46 41 23 99
fax: 05 46 41 15 19
A former town house with a garden, trees and shrubbery, this charming hotel evokes the romance of days gone by. The bedrooms are modern in style.
CC: Amex, DC, EU, MC, Visa **$$**

St-Cirq-Lapopie: Lot
Auberge du Sombral
46330 St-Cirq-Lapopie, Lot
tel: 05 65 31 26 08
fax: 05 65 30 26 37
A peaceful old country inn with restaurant *Les Bonnes Choses*
CC: EU, MC, Visa **$**

St-Etienne-de-Baigorry
Arcé
64430 St-Etienne-de-Baigorry, Pyrénées Atlantique
tel: 05 59 37 40 14
fax: 05 59 37 40 27
By a river in a Basque village, with a beautiful, overhanging, dining terrace. A very popular hotel with airy public rooms and charming bedrooms.
CC: MC, Visa **$$**

Hotel Prices

$ = Budget under FF350
$$ = Moderate FF400–750
$$$ = Expensive FF800+
Prices are per double room.

LOIRE VALLEY

Amboise
Le Choiseul
36 Quai Charles Guinot,
37400 Amboise, Indre-et-Loire
tel: 02 47 30 45 45
fax: 02 47 30 46 10
Beautiful, refurbished 18th-century mansion facing the river, with a garden and pool. A member of the Relais et Chateau group. Good restaurant.
CC: MC, Visa **$$**

Angers: Maine-et-Loire
Anjou
1 Blvd. Maréchal Foch
49100 Angers
tel: 02 41 88 24 82
fax: 02 41 87 22 21
Old hotel recently restored and modernised with large, well equipped rooms. Restaurant Salamandre.
CC: Amex, DC, MC, Visa **$$**

Hôtel du Mail
8 Rue Ursules,
49100 Angers, Maine-et-Loire
tel: 02 41 25 05 25
fax: 02 41 86 91 20.
Built in the 17th century as part of a convent; an old-fashioned hotel in a central yet quiet location.
CC: Amex, DC, Visa **$**

Azay-le-Rideau
Le Grand Monarque
3 Place de la République, 37190 Azay-le-Rideau, Indre-et-Loire
tel: 02 47 45 40 08
fax: 02 47 45 46 25
Close to the chateau, the hotel has been charmingly renovated to combine the rustic atmosphere of an old manor house with modern comfort. A pretty courtyard and a good restaurant.
CC: Amex, DC, MC, Visa **$$**

Blois-Ouchamps
Relais des Landes
(A10 exit Blois South, direction Montrichard)
41120 Blois-Ouchamps, Loir-et-Cher
tel: 02 54 44 40 40
fax: 02 54 44 03 89
A comfortably appointed, 17th-century mansion in a large, peaceful park with trees.
CC: Amex, DC, Visa **$$**

Blois
Anne de Bretagne
31 avenue Jean-Laigret,
41000 Blois, Loir-et-Cher
tel: 02 54 78 05 38
fax: 02 54 74 37 79
A popular and cheerful little logis quietly located close to the chateau. No restaurant.
CC: Amex, DC, Visa **$**

Chinon
La Boule D'Or
21 Rue Rabelais,
37500 Chinon, Indre-et-Loire
tel: 02 47 98 40 88
fax: 02 47 93 24 25
An old, family-run hotel-restaurant in the centre of town facing the Vienne. Large dining room and terrace. **$**

La Flèche
Le Relais Cicero
18 Boulevard d'Alger,
72200 La Flèche, Sarthe
tel: 02 43 94 14 14
fax: 02 43 45 98 96
A peaceful, 17th-century house with
garden. No restaurant.
CC: MC, Visa **$$**

Fontevraud-l'Abbaye
La Croix Blanche
Place des Plantagenets,
49590 Fontevraud l'Abbaye,
Maine-et-Loire
tel: 02 41 51 71 11
fax: 02 41 38 15 38
Delightful hotel with wooden beams
and stone fireplaces, close to the
abbey. Good food.
CC: MC, Visa **$$**

Loches
Le Domaine de Mestré
Mestré, 49590 Fontevraud
l'Abbaye, Maine-et-Loire
tel: 02 41 51 75 87
fax: 02 41 51 71 90
This is the abbey's 13th-century
farmhouse, offering a warm, family
welcome and the farm's own
produce for the table. **$**

George Sand
39 Rue Quintefol,
37600 Loches, Indre-et-Loire
tel: 02 47 59 39 74
fax: 0247 91 55 75
An old coaching inn under the
castle ramparts, full of medieval
character. (Demi-pension obligatory
during high season).
CC: MC, Visa **$$**

Montreuil-Bellay
**Splendid and Relais de Bellay
(annexe)**
139 Rue du Docteur Gaudrez,
49260 Montreuil-Bellay,
Maine-et-Loire
tel: 02 41 53 10 00
fax: 02 41 52 45 17
A large hotel standing in its own
grounds with a swimming pool and
view of the chateau. Comfortable
rooms, good food.
CC: Visa **$$**

Nantes
Astoria
11 Rue de Richebourg, 44000
Nantes, Loire-Atlantique
tel: 02 40 74 39 90
fax: 02 40 14 05 49
A comfortable, traditional hotel,
close to the château, museums and
the Botanical gardens.
CC: Visa **$**

Orléans
Jackhotel
18 Rue Cloître Saint-Aignan
45000 Orléans, Loiret
tel: 02 38 54 48 48
fax: 02 38 77 17 59
Small, central hotel in a former
cloister behind the church. **$**

Sancerre
Panoramic
Rempart des Augustins
18300 Sancerre, Cher
tel: 02 48 54 22 44
fax: 02 48 54 39 55
Modern hotel, with a swimming pool
and wide view over the river Loire
and surrounding vineyards.
CC: Amex, MC, Visa **$**

Saumur
Anne d'Anjou
32–33 Quai Mayaud, 49400
Saumur, Maine-et-Loire
tel: 02 41 67 30 30
fax: 02 41 67 51 00
One of the region's best, set in a
charming, 18th-century building with
an internal courtyard and gardens
beneath the château and beside the
river Loire.
CC: Amex, DC, MC, Visa **$**

Le Clos des Bénédictins
4 Rue des Lilas, Saint-Hilaire-Saint-
Florent, 49400 Saumur
Maine-et-Loire
tel: 02 41 67 28 48
fax: 02 41 67 13 71
A new hotel in a peaceful setting,

overlooking the town and the river.
CC: Visa **$$**

Tours
Jean Bardet
57 Rue Groison
37100 Tours, Indre-et-Loire
tel: 02 47 41 41 11
fax: 02 47 51 68 72
An elegant, rambling villa in a park,
with beautifully furnished rooms, a
swimming pool and chauffeur-driven
Rolls for hire. CC: Amex, DC, MC,
Visa **$$$**

Vendôme
Le Vendôme
15 Faubourg Chartrain, 41100
Vendôme, Loire-et-Cher
tel: 02 54 77 02 88
fax: 02 54 73 90 71
Built on the site of an old auberge
used by pilgrims on their way to
Santiago de Compostela, close to
the centre of the old town.
CC: MC, Visa **$**

LE NORD

Abbeville: Somme
De France
19 Place du Pilori,
80100 Abbeville
tel: 03 22 24 00 42
fax: 03 22 24 26 15
An attractive, grand hotel in the
centre of town. Comfortably well
equipped with all amenities.
CC: Amex, DC, Visa **$$**

Amiens: Somme
Le Postillon
19 Place au Feurre,
80000 Amiens
tel: 03 22 22 00 20
fax: 03 22 91 86 57
Close to the cathedral. Rooms have
half timbered ceilings and all
modern amenities. There is a cosy
lounge bar.
CC: Amex, Visa **$$**

Boulogne-sur-Mer: Pas-de-Calais
Métropole
51 Rue Thiers,
62200 Boulogne
tel: 03 21 31 54 30

fax: 03 21 30 45 72
Standing between the ramparts of the upper town and the sea. Rooms are spacious and attractive. Elegant breakfast room and pretty garden.
CC: Amex, Visa **$$**

Calais: Pas-de-Calais
Meurice
5 Rue E. Roche,
62100 Calais
tel: 21 34 57 03
fax: 21 34 14 71
One of the first luxury hotels. Large, comfortable sitting room, conservatory-breakfast room and well-known restaurant.
CC: Amex, DC, Visa **$$**

Compiègne: Oise
De Flandre
16 Quai de la République,
60200 Compiègne
tel: 03 44 83 24 40
fax: 03 44 90 02 75
Simple but good. Pleasant hotel, situated close to the centre of town. facing the river.
CC: DC, Visa **$**

Dunkerque: Nord
Europ Hôtel
13 Rue du Leughenaer,
59140 Dunkerque
tel: 03 28 66 29 07
fax: 03 28 63 67 87
A large, modern hotel at the entrance to the harbour, near to the beaches and next door to the casino.
CC: Amex, DC, Visa **$$**

Lille: Nord
Carlton
3 Rue de Paris,
59000 Lille
tel: 03 20 13 03 33 13
fax: 03 20 51 48 17
A grand hotel with furnishings in the styles of Louis XV and XVI and marble bathrooms. Conveniently situated for the city centre and Opera house.
CC: Amex, DC, Visa **$$$**

Grand Hôtel Bellevue
5 Rue Jean-Roisin,
59800 Lille
tel: 03 20 57 45 64

fax: 03 20 40 07 93
A gracious,18th-century Bourbon hotel that can boast Mozart amongst its earliest guests. Close to the Opera and Palais de Musique.
CC: Amex, DC, Visa **$$**

Montreuil-sur-Mer: Pas de Calais
Auberge de Grenouillère
La Madelaine-sous-Montreuil.
62170
tel: 03 21 06 07 22
fax: 03 21 8 36 36
A Picardy-style farmhouse with great character and a Michelin starred restaurant. Individual and well-equipped rooms.
CC: Amex, DC, Visa **$$**

Recques-sur-Hem: Pas de Calais
Château de Cocove
62890 Recques-sur-Hem
tel: 03 21 82 68 29
fax: 03 21 82 72 59
Restored 18th century château in a wooded park a few kilometres from the port. Extremely comfortable with a good restaurant and wine cellar.
CC: Amex, DC, Visa **$$**

PARIS

Luxury
de Crillon
10 Place de la Concorde, 75008
tel: 01 44 71 15 01
fax: 01 44 71 15 03
Built for Louis XV in the 18th century, on the beautiful Place de la Concorde, the Crillon is one of Paris' truly grand hotels, accommodating everyone from visiting royalty to fashion models. A splendid mansion with marble reception hall, winter-garden tea room, presidential suites, piano bar, fitness centre and two restaurants, Les Ambassadeurs and L'Obélisque, all on a most luxurious scale.
CC: Amex, DC, MC, Visa

George V
31 Avenue George V, 75008
tel: 01 47 23 54 00

fax: 01 47 20 40 00
Fabulous antiques, paintings and tapestries adorn this vast famous hotel, celebrated for its lavish style.
CC: Amex, DC, Visa

Marignan-Elysées
12 Rue Marignan
75008
tel: 01 40 76 34 56
fax: 01 40 76 34 34
A luxury hotel between the Champs Elysées and the fashionable avenue Montaigne, with an Art-Deco façade and modern interior focussed round La Verrière, the glass roofed reception and bar. A gilded and sculpted ceiling in the foyer depicts the hotel's history . The restaurant, La Table du Marché is a favourite with personalities from the worlds of fashion, film and media.
CC: Amex, DC, Visa

Paris Hilton
18 Avenue de Suffren
75740, cedex 15
tel: 01 44 38 56 21
fax: 01 44 38 56 23
A large, modern hotel very close to the Eiffel tower, overlooking the Palais de Chaillot and the Trocadero Gardens. Shopping gallery, large conference centre, restaurants, bars.
CC: Amex, DC, Visa

Plaza-Athénée
25 Avenue Montaigne, 75008
tel: 01 53 67 66 65
fax: 01 53 67 64 66
A magnificent 19th-century hotel built and furnished in the Empire style. Close to the Théatre des

Paris Hotel Prices

In common with most capital cities, Paris has a wider range of accomodation – and prices – than you would expect to find in the rest of France. Paris hotels have been arranged by category, as follows:
Luxury FF2,000+
Expensive FF1,000–2,000
Moderate FF500–1,000
Budget under FF500

Champs-Elysées and a favourite with performers and composers. Fitness club, beauty parlour and two restaurants, La Régence and Le Relais Plaza.
CC: Amex, DC, MC, Visa

Ritz
15 Place Vendôme, 75001
tel: 01 43 16 30 30
fax: 01 43 16 31 78
Guaranteed elegance with original marble and chandeliers, the Ritz is still the place to stay for many of the world's wealthiest people. Unashamed luxury on one of the most famous squares in the capital.
CC: Amex, DC, Visa

Expensive

de l'Abbaye
10 Rue Cassette, 75006
tel: 01 45 44 38 11
fax: 01 45 48 07 86
A tastefully converted former abbey with a chic air. The public rooms are comfortably large and filled with fresh flowers and there is a charming conservatory- style breakfast room/bar in the old chapel with french windows out onto the courtyard garden.
CC: Amex, MC, Visa

Lutetia
45 Boulevard Raspail, 75007
tel: 49 54 46 46
fax: 49 54 46 00
Opulent art nouveau hotel on the Left Bank, exquisitely decorated in thirties style. Bar is a fashionable literary venue.
CC: Amex, DC, EC, MC, Visa

Montalambert
3 Rue de la Montalambert, 75007
tel: 45 48 68 11
fax: 42 22 58 19
Beautifully restored hotel with fashionable bar and immaculate designer furnishings. You can choose between antique or sleek modern décor in the bedrooms. There are splendid views from the eighth floor.
CC: Amex, DC, MC, Visa

Pavillon de la Reine
28 Place des Vosges, 75003
tel: 01 40 29 19 19
fax: 01 40 29 19 20
The best hotel in the Marais, ideally located on the Place des Vosges, but with a quiet courtyard. Beautifully furnished with antiques
CC: Amex, DC, CB

Regina
2 Place des Pyramides, 75001
tel: 01 42 60 31 10
fax: 01 40 15 95 16
Antique furnishings and art-nouveau details make this delightful hotel by the Rue de Rivoli a favourite for film sets.
CC: Amex, CB, D

Relais Christine
3 Rue Christine, 75006
tel: 01 40 51 60 80
fax: 01 40 51 60 81
Calm and tranquillity in the middle of St Germain-des-Prés, in this exquisite hotel in the cloisters and chapel of a 16th-century abbey. Courtyard, tiled reception hall, stone vaulted breakfast room with massive fireplace and beautifully decorated bedrooms.
CC: Amex, CB, D

St Beuve
9 Rue Saint Beuve, 75006
tel: 01 45 48 20 07
fax: 01 45 48 67 52
Discreet, cosy hotel with fireplace and country antiques in the salon, a favourite with the art scene, tastefully decorated and hung with contemporary paintings. Excellent policy of upgrading guests to a more expensive room than booked whenever possible.
CC: MC, Amex, Visa

de Vieux Paris
Relais Hôtel du Vieux Paris
9, Rue Gît le Coeur, 75006
tel: 01 44 32 15 90
fax: 01 43 26 00 15
19th-century hotel which was a favourite in the 1950s and 60s with American Beat Generation writers William Burroughs and Allen Ginsberg. Today, it is a more luxurious establishment, all

exposed beams, marble bathrooms and limousines and is attracting a new generation of aspiring artists.
CC: EU, Visa, MC, Amex

Moderate

de l'Angleterre
44 Rue Jacob, 75006
tel: 01 42 60 34 72
fax: 01 42 60 16 93
Formerly the British Embassy (Benjamin Franklin refused to enter to sign the Treaty of Paris because he considered it to be British soil), the hotel maintains a faintly English air. Well proportioned, elegant rooms, often with splendid bathrooms. There is a beautiful staircase with trompe l'oeil murals and a lovely courtyard garden.
CC: Amex, DC, MC, Visa

de Banville
166 Boulevard Berthier, 75017
tel: 01 42 67 70 16
fax: 01 44 40 42 77
A 1930's Art-Deco style town house with an elegantly furnished piano bar. Bedrooms are tastefully and comfortably decorated and the service is of an old fashioned excellence.
CC: Amex, MC, Visa

Ducs de Bourgogne
19 Rue du Pont-Neuf, 75001
tel: 01 42 33 95 64
fax: 01 40 39 01 25
Ideally situated for the Châtelet and the Louvre. Furnished with antiques, the public rooms are warm and welcoming. The bedrooms are modern and well- appointed.
CC: Amex, DC, Visa

Duc de St-Simon
14 Rue de Saint-Simon, 75007
tel: 01 42 20 07 52
fax: 01 45 48 68 25
A charming, 18th- and 19th-century hotel just off the boulevard St-Germain. There is a little secret garden and a courtyard. The salon is beautifully furnished and the bedrooms elegant yet cosy. There is no restaurant but two famous cafés – the Deux Magots and the Flore – are only a few minutes' walk away.
CC: not accepted

de Fleurie
32 Rue Grégoire-de-Tours, 75006
tel: 01 53 73 70 00
fax: 01 53 73 70 20
A very popular, family-run hotel which successfully combines elegance and cosiness. There is a sitting room with stone walls and exposed beams, a bar and breakfast room and bedrooms are prettily decorated.
CC: Amex, DC, MC, Visa

Jeu de Paume
54 Rue Saint-Louis-en-Ile, 75004
tel: 01 43 26 14 18
fax: 01 40 46 02 76
A 17th-century building that began life as a palm-game court (the forerunner of tennis) and is now a very original hotel with stone walls and exposed beams and a glass-walled lift. There is a courtyard garden and a sauna.
CC: Amex, DC, MC, Visa

Saint-Germain
50 Rue du Four, 75006
tel: 01 45 48 91 64
fax: 01 45 48 46 22
In the heart of St-Germain, close to the Sorbonne and the Luxembourg Gardens, the hotel has a warm and friendly atmosphere and comfortable bedrooms decorated in Laura-Ashley style.
CC: Amex, DC, Visa

Saint-Louis
75 Rue Saint-Louis-en-Ile, 75004
tel: 01 46 34 04 80
fax: 01 46 34 02 13
Smart, old-fashioned hotel on the Ile St Louis, with warm, rustic decor and furnished with antiques. Close to the Marais and Notre Dame.
CC: MC, Visa

Saint-Louis-Marais
1 Rue Charles-V, 75004
tel: 01 48 87 87 04
fax: 01 48 87 33 26
The sister hotel to St-Louis-en-Ile with exposed beams, tiled floors and attractively decorated rooms.
CC: MC, Visa

Saint-Thomas-d'Aquin
3 Rue Pré-aux-Clercs, 75007
tel: 01 42 61 01 22

fax: 01 42 61 41 43
In the heart of the left bank close to the Louvre and Musée d'Orsay. An attractively fronted town house with plain, modern interiors.
CC: Amex, DC, Visa

Budget

Chopin
10 Boulevard Montmartre
(46 passage Jouffroy), 75009
tel: 01 47 70 58 10
fax: 01 42 47 00 70
Well back from the main road at the end of a 19th-century glass-and-steel roofed arcade, this is a quiet and friendly hotel. Simply but thoughtfully furnished.
CC: Amex, DC, MC, Visa

Ermitage

Paris Hotel Prices

Luxury FF2,000+
Expensive FF1,000–2,000
Moderate FF500–1,000
Budget under FF500

24 Rue Lamarck, 75018
tel: 01 42 64 79 22
fax: 01 42 64 10 33
Tucked away behind the Sacré-Coeur, a friendly little hotel filled with surprises. An old fashioned parlour with antiques, prints and photographs; walls, glass panels, skirtings and doors painted with scenes of Montmartre by artist Du Buc. Light, spacious bedrooms with tiny bathrooms.
CC not accepted

Grand Hôtel l'Evêque
29 Rue Cler, 75007
tel: 01 47 05 49 15
fax: 01 45 50 49 36
On a lively, market street on the left bank, the hotel has been entirely renovated to a modest, modern standard.
CC: Amex, MC, Visa

Grand Hôtel des Balcons
3 Rue Casimir-Delvigne, 75006
tel: 01 46 34 78 50
fax: 01 46 34 06 27
A wrought-iron balcony fronted hotel with an Art-Nouveau theme. An

exceptionally substantial breakfast is served (bacon, eggs, sausages) for those about to embark on a hard day's sight seeing.
CC: MC, Visa

de Nice
42 bis Rue de Rivoli, 75004
tel: 01 42 78 55 29
fax: 01 42 78 36 07
The delightful result of collectors turned hoteliers with antique mirrors and doors, and period engravings, prints and fabrics. Basic amenities but a wealth of charm and character.
CC: MC, Visa

de Nesle
7 Rue de Nesle, 75006
tel: 01 43 54 62 41
A laid-back, student and backpackers hotel with no advance booking, basic facilities and delightful, spotless bedrooms with murals, furnished to various eclectic themes. There is also a garden with a pond and a palm tree.
CC not accepted

Saint-André-des-Arts
66 Rue Saint-André-des-Arts, 75006
tel: 01 43 26 96 16
fax: 01 43 29 73 34
A late 16th-century hotel that was originally built to house the king's musketeers and now sports an old shop-front facade. In the entrance, you will find an old choir stall (complete with misericords) and a listed staircase. The warren of plain, thin-walled bedrooms are all different, but not without their charm.
CC: MC, Visa

AROUND PARIS (ILE DE FRANCE)

Auberge du Gros Marronier
3 place de l'Eglise, 78720 Senlisse
tel: 01 30 52 51 69
fax: 01 30 52 55 91
Rustic little inn in the village of Senlisse, near Rambouillet and Versailles. Conservatory, terrace,

dining room with big open fire and large, pretty bedrooms.
CC: Amex, Visa **$**

Climat de France
32 Avenue de la Victoire,
77100 Meaux
tel: 01 64 33 15 46
fax: 01 60 23 11 64
Functional modern hotel with restaurant in old town of Meaux, with a regular 10-minute bus service to Disneyland Paris.
CC: Amex, Visa **$**

Hostellerie du Moulin
2 Rue du Moulin, 77940 Flagy
tel: 01 60 96 67 89
fax: 01 60 96 69 51
Imaginatively converted flour mill with garden, cosy sitting room and quirky wood-beamed bedrooms. Very reasonable prices and quite adventurous cooking. Convenient for Fontainebleu or Sens.
CC: Amex, DC, MC, Visa **$$**

Napoléon
9 Rue Grande,
77300 Fontainebleau
tel: 01 60 39 50 50
fax: 01 64 22 20 87
Fine old hotel with elegant salon, open fire, charming garden and restaurant. The hotel is convenient for the Fontainebleau Palace.
CC: Amex, DC, Visa **$$**

Pavillon Henri IV
21 Rue Thiers,
78100 St Germain-en-Laye
tel: 01 39 10 15 15
fax: 01 39 73 93 73
The birthplace of Louis XIV and now a small hotel in the grand style with views over Paris from the light and airy dining room, the terrace and front bedrooms. Convenient for the Château de Saint-Germain-en-Laye.
CC: Amex, DC, MC, Visa **$$$**

Le Prieuré
Chevet de l'Eglise,
60440 Eremenonville
tel: 03 44 54 00 44
fax: 03 44 54 02 21
Next to the church in the village of Ermenonville and convenient for Senlis and Chantilly. An intimate

impeccably furnished hotel, full of antiques. The best bedrooms overlook a pretty English rose garden.
CC: MC, Visa **$$**

PROVENCE & CÔTE D'AZUR

Arles
D'Arlatan
26 Rue du Sauvage,
13200 Aries, Bouches-du-Rhône,
tel: 04 90 93 56 66
fax: 04 90 49 68 45
Ancient provençal mansion, once residence of the Counts of Arlatan with, many period details, carved ceilings and antiques.
CC: Amex, DC, Visa **$$**

Aix-en-Provence
Hôtel des Augustins
3 Rue de la Masse,
13100 Aix-en-Provence, Bouches-du-Rhone,
tel: 04 42 27 28 59
fax: 04 42 26 74 87
Spacious converted 15th-century priory with vaulted ceilings and elegantly decorated rooms, open all year.
CC: Amex, CB, DC, Visa **$$$**

Hotel Prices

$ = Budget under FF350
$$ = Moderate FF400–750
$$$ = Expensive FF800+
Prices are per double room.

Avignon: Vaucluse
Cité des Papes
1 Rue J.-Villar,
84000 Avignon
tel: 04 90 86 22 45
fax: 04 90 27 39 21
Convenient location near the papal palace with excellent views of the ancient city.
CC: Amex, DC, Visa **$$**

Beaulieu-sur-Mer
La Réserve de Beaulieu
5 Boulevard Leclerc,
06310 Beaulieu-sur-Mer,
Alpes-Maritimes
tel: 04 93 01 00 01

fax: 04 93 01 28 99
Luxurious Renaissance-style pink villa dominating the sea front private beach and sea water swimming-pool.
CC: Amex, DC, Visa **$$$**

Cagnes-sur-Mer
Le Cagnard
Rue du Pontis-Long,
06800 Cagnes-sur-Mer,
Alpes-Maritimes
tel: 04 04 93 20 73 21
fax: 04 93 22 06 39
Exquisite small hotel in the old village near Grimaldi castle, with romantic beamed bedrooms and excellent restaurant. A member of the Relais and Châteaux group.
CC: Amex, DC, Visa **$$$**

Cannes
Carlton Intercontinental
58 Boulevard Croisette,
06322 Cannes, Alpes-Maritimes
tel: 04 93 06 40 06
fax: 04 93 06 40 25
Glamorous Croisette hotel: the most celebrated place to stay during the Cannes film festival and the Brasserie is the place to eat.
CC: Amex, DC, MC, Visa **$$$**

Eze
Château Eza
06360 Eze, Alpes-Maritimes
tel: 04 93 41 12 24
fax: 04 93 41 16 64
Fabulous castle hotel perched on rocks, with antique furnishing..
CC: Amex, DC, Visa **$$$**

Grimaud
La Boulangerie
Route de Collobrières,
83310 Grimaud, Var
tel: 04 94 43 23 16.
fax 04 94 43 38 27
Charming hotel in the Maures hills outside St Tropez, with Mediterranean garden and swimming-pool.
CC: Visa **$$$**

Juan-les-Pins
Belles Rives
Boulevard Baudoin,
06160 Juan-les-pins,

Alpes-Maritimes
tel: 04 93 61 02 79
fax: 04 93 67 43 51
1930s hotel, in exquisite period style, once the home of Scott and Zelda Fitzgerald. Balconies and private beach
CC: Amex, DC, MC, Visa $$$

Le Lavandou
Les Roches
Aiguebelle,
83980 Le Lavandou, Var
tel: 04 94 71 05 07
Perched on the cliffs at Aiguebelle outside Le Lavandou, tasteful modern hotel with fabulous sea views and its own private beach.
CC: Amex, DC, MC, Visa $$$

Marseille
Novotel Vieux Port
36 Boulevard Ch.-Livon,
13007 Marseille
Bouches-du-Rhône
tel: 04 91 59 22 22
fax: 04 91 31 15 48
Modern, comfortable hotel, convenient for sightseeing around the old port district.
CC: Amex, DC, Visa $$

Menton
Chambord
6 Avenue Boyer,
06500 Menton, Alpes-Maritimes
tel: 04 93 35 94 19
fax: 04 93 41 30 55
Very reasonable and well situated, just off the Promenade du Soleil.
CC: Amex, DC, Visa $$

Monaco
Hermitage
Square Beaumarchais
98000 Monte Carlo, Monaco
tel: 04 92 16 40 00
fax: 04 93 50 47 12
Total luxury in gorgeous Belle Epoque building with baroque dining room and wonderful terrace.
CC: Amex, DC, MC, Visa $$$

de Paris
Place du Casino,
98000 Monte Carlo, Monaco
tel: 92 16 30 00
fax: 04 93 25 59 17
Monaco's most famous hotel

offering the ultimate in luxury including Alain Ducasse's famous restaurant.
CC: Amex, DC, MC, Visa $$$

Mougins
Le Mas Candille
Boulevard Rebuffel,
06250 Mougins,
Alpes-Maritimes
tel: 04 93 90 00 85
Old farmhouse outside Mougins, charmingly renovated with pool and terrace with mountain views
Open all year round.
CC: Amex, DC, MC, Visa $$$

Nice
Négresco
37 Promenade des Anglais, 06000 Nice, Alpes-Maritimes
tel: 04 93 88 39 51
fax: 04 93 88 35 68
Nice's most glorious hotel, its great pink dome dominating the Promenade des Anglais, offering every luxury, and impeccable service.
CC: Amex, DC, MC, Visa $$$

La Pérouse
11 Quai Rauba-Capeu,
06000 Nice
tel: 04 93 62 34 63
fax: 04 93 62 59 41
Great view of Baie des Anges with terrace, swimming pool and garden restaurant. Open all year round. Air conditioning.
CC: Amex, DC $$$

Hotel Windsor
11 Rue Dalpozzo,
06000 Nice
tel: 04 93 88 59 35
fax: 04 93 88 94 57
Very reasonably priced, funky hotel, with every room decorated by a different artist. Charming small garden and pool.
CC: Amex, DC, MC, Visa $$

Nîmes
L'Orangerie
755 Rue de la Tour Eveque,
30900 Nîmes, Gard
tel: 04 66 84 50 57
Friendly charming hotel just outside

centre with pretty garden, small pool and good restaurant. Open all year.
CC: Amex, DC, CB $$

Ile de Port Cros
Le Manoir
83145 Ile de Port Cros, Var
tel: 04 94 05 90 52
fax: 04 94 05 90 89
Colonial-style house in large, tropical garden on this quiet island off Hyères. Closed from October–May.
CC: MC, Visa, DC $$$

St-Jean-Cap-Ferrat: Alpes-Maritimes
Brise Marine
58 Avenue Jean Mermoz,
06230 St. Jean-Cap-Ferrat
tel: 04 93 76 04 36
fax: 04 93 76 11 49
Sweet hotel in superb location; some rooms with sea views and an attractive terraced garden.
CC: Visa $$

St-Rémy-de-Provence
Mas des Carassins
1 Chemin Gaulois,
13210 St-Rémy-de-Provence
tel: 04 90 92 15 48
Sweet converted farmhouse in secluded gardens with intimate old-fashioned atmosphere and friendly hosts.
CC: MC, Visa, DC $$

St. Tropez
Le Yaca
1 Boulevard d'Aumale,
83990 St. Tropez
tel: 04 94 97 11 79
fax: 04 94 97 58 50
A lovely old provençal residence in the town with a swimming-pool and garden.
CC: Amex, DC, Visa $$$

Vence
La Roseraie
Avenue Henri-Giraud,
06140 Vence,
Alpes-Maritimes
tel: 04 93 58 02 20
fax: 04 93 58 99 31
Small friendly hotel in 1930s villa with a pretty garden and swimming-pool.
CC: Amex, Visa, DC $$

PYRENEES

Argelès-Gazost
Le Relais
25 Rue du Maréchal-Foch,
65400 Argelès-Gazost
Hautes-Pyrénées
tel: 05 62 97 01 27
Mountain hotel with wonderful
views, restaurant and garden.
CC: Visa **$**

Auch: Gers
Hôtel de France
Place de la Libération,
32000 Auch
tel: 05 62 61 71 84
fax: 05 62 61 71 81
A splendid hotel on the main square
of Auch run by chef André Daguin,
well-known for his promotion of
Gascon cooking.
CC: Amex, DC, Visa **$$**

Ax-les-Thermes: Ariège
Hôtel des Pyrénées
09110 Ax-les-Thermes
tel: 05 61 64 21 01
fax: 05 61 64 38 91
A family-run Logis de France hotel
convenient for skiing or walking in the
surrounding area. Open all year. **$**

Biarritz
Hotel du Palais
1 Avenue de l'Impératrice,
Pyrénées-Atlantiques 64200
tel: 05 59 41 64 00
fax: 05 59 41 33 67 99
Splendid hotel overlooking the
Grand Plage, originally built for the
Empress Eugenie. Excellent
facilities: thalassotherapy and sea-
water swimming pool
CC: Amex, DC, Visa **$$$**
Rooms: FF1500–2850

Foix
Lons
6 Place Georges Duthil, Foix
tel: 05 61 65 52 44
fax: 05 61 0 68 18
Pleasant hotel in the middle of town
with terrace restaurant overlooking
the river. Hotel is closed from 20
December – 15 January.
CC: Amex, DC, CB **$**

Pau
Continental
2 Rue du Maréchal-Foch
64000 Pau,
Pyrénées-Atlantiques
tel: 05 59 27 69 31
fax: 05 59 27 99 84
Prestigious elegant hotel which is
well-situated near the centre of
town.
CC: Amex, DC, Visa **$$**

Sauveterre de Comminges
Hostellerie des 7 Molles
31510 Sauveterre-de-Comminges
Haute-Garonne
tel: 05 61 88 30 87
fax: 05 61 88 36 42
Spacious hotel surrounded by
meadows and trees. The home farm
supplies sausages, foie gras and
trout and other home-made
products. Swimming pool.
CC: Amex, DC, CB **$$**

> ### Hotel Prices
>
> **$ = Budget** under FF350
> **$$ = Moderate** FF400–750
> **$$$ = Expensive** FF800+
> Prices are per double room.

St-Jean-de-Luz: Pyrénées-Atlantiques
Chantaco
Golf de Chantaco,
64500 St-Jean-de-Luz
tel: 05 59 26 14 76
fax: 05 59 26 35 97
Luxurious amenities in a beautiful
Spanish-style building with huge
fireplaces and French windows onto
the garden and pool. Good
restaurant.
CC: Amex, DC, Visa **$$$**

St-Jean-Pied-de-Port: Pyrénées-Atlantiques
Les Pyrénées
19 Place Charles-de-Gaulle,
64220 St-Jean-Pied-de-Port
tel: 05 59 37 01 01
fax: 05 59 37 18 97
Friendly hotel with authentic Basque
cooking, plus a garden and
swimming-pool.
CC: Amex **$$**

RHONE VALLEY & THE ALPS

Albertville: Savoie
Le Roma
Route National 90,
73200 Albertville
tel: 04 79 37 15 56
fax: 04 79 37 01 31
A modern and very comfortable
hotel-village complex. with a bar,
restaurant, swimming pool, exercise
room and sauna as well as pretty
and airy bedrooms.
CC: Amex, DC, Visa **$$**

Aix-les-Bains: Savoie
Le Manoir
37 Rue George 1er, BP 512,
73105 Aix-les-Bains
tel: 04 79 61 44 00
fax: 04 79 35 67 67
Warm and welcoming, large country
manor with rooms overlooking lovely
garden, park and woodlands. Close
to the hot springs. Member of the
Relais de Silence group.
CC: DC, Visa **$$**

Briançon: Hautes-Alpes
Auberge le Mont-Porel
5 Rue R.-Froger,
05100 Briançon
tel: 04 92 20 22 88
A small, traditional chalet-hotel
close to the ski lift. Warm
atmosphere, comfortable rooms.
CC: Amex, DC, Visa **$$**

Chamonix: Haute-Savoie
Auberge du Bois Prin
69 Chemin de l'Hermine
Les Moussoux,
74400 Chamonix
tel: 04 50 53 33 51
fax: 04 50 53 48 75
Friendly, exclusive, chalet-auberge
with a pretty garden and wide views
of Mont Blanc. Beautiful rooms and
very good resturant.
CC: Amex, DC, MC, Visa **$$$**

Divonne-les-Bains: Ain
Château de Divonne
01220 Divonne-les-Bains
tel: 04 50 20 00 32
fax: 04 50 20 03 73
Charming 19th-century mansion in
a large park with views of Mont

Blanc and Lake Geneva.
Exceptionally good cuisine.
CC: Amex, DC, MC, Visa $$$

Grenoble: Isère
D'Angleterre
5 Place Victor-Hugo,
38000 Grenoble
tel: 04 76 87 37 21
fax: 04 76 50 94 10
A central, modern hotel beside the
gardens of Place Victor Hugo, and
facing the mountains. Large rooms
with all amenities.
CC: Amex, DC, MC, Visa $$

Lyon: Rhône
Carlton
Place de la République
4 Rue Jussieu, 69002 Lyon
tel: 04 78 42 56 51
fax: 04 78 42 10 71
A very grand, central hotel with
richly and individually furnished
guest rooms.
CC: Amex, DC, Visa $$

Grand Hôtel des Beaux Arts
73–75 Rue du Président
69002 Lyon,
Edouard Herriot
tel: 04 78 38 09 50
fax: 04 78 42 19 19
A typically Lyonnaise building,
between the Rhône and the Saône.
Art-Deco style interior, individually
designed bedrooms.
CC: Amex, DC, MC,Visa $$

Mégève: Haute-Savoie
Au Vieux Moulin
188 Rue Ambroise-Martin,
74120 Mégève
tel: 04 50 21 22 29
fax: 04 50 93 07 91
Recently renovated, traditional
Alpine hotel-restaurant. Peaceful,
yet convenient for all local
amenities. Solidly and comfortably
furnished rooms.The hotel also
features a swimming-pool.
CC: Amex, MC, Visa $$

Montélimar: Drôme
Relais de l'Empereur
1 Place Marx Dormoy,
26200 Montélimar
tel: 04 75 01 29 00
fax: 04 75 01 32 21

Charming, comfortably appointed,
central hotel with a continuing
history of famous guests.
Traditional and regional cuisine;
breakfast in the garden or on the
terrace.
CC: Amex, DC, MC, Visa $$

Nantua: Ain
De l'Embarcadère
Avenue du Lac,
01130 Nantua
tel: 04 74 75 22 88
fax: 04 74 75 22 25
Very comfortably appointed, modern
hotel with three star restaurant and
beautiful views of the lake and
forest.
CC: MC, Visa $$

Val-d'Isère
Christiana
BP 48, 73152 Val d'Isère Cedex
tel: 04 79 06 08 25
fax: 04 79 41 11 10
Luxurious, modern, ski-chalet hotel
with fitness centre and massage
and beauty facilities. All rooms have
balconies.
CC: Visa $$$

Villard-de-Lans: Isère
Le Pré-Fleuri
Route des Cochettes,
38250 Villard-de-Lans
tel: 04 76 95 10 96
fax: 04 76 95 56 23
A quiet hotel close to the centre of
the village. Simple but fully
equipped rooms with lovely views of
the pretty garden.
CC: MC, Visa $

Where to Eat

How to Choose

France is full of wonderful
restaurants, from the grand classics
to the tiny auberge serving perhaps
only one menu of home-grown food.
The French pay very serious
attention to their food and it is only
recently that fast foods have started
to creep into French supermarkets,
and on to the high streets. It may be
argued, however, that the French
have always enjoyed convenience
foods provided by their splendid
traiteurs and *charcutiers*. Visit a
delicatessen (*charcuterie*) and pick
a selection of their prepared dishes
for a delicious picnic.

Each region has its own
specialities: the creamy sauces of
Normandy, the traditional *confits* of
duck and goose in the southwest,
choucroute in the east, *coq au vin*
in Burgundy and wonderful seafood
all around the coast.

It is still difficult to get a bad
meal, except occasionally in Paris
or the Côte d'Azur. It is always worth
seeking out the local regional food;
it is likely to be freshest and most
skilfully cooked and is the best way
to truly get the flavour of a region,
complemented by the local wine.
French regional cooking is in fashion
these days and many of the most
popular restaurants in Paris specialise in cuisine of the provinces.

Restaurant Listings

The following is a selection of some
of the best restaurants in the
regions, worth looking out for or
even making a special detour. The
restaurants are listed alphabetically
by region and then alphabetically by
town. Most specialise in the food of
their region, cooking local ingredients

with traditional skill and sometimes a more modern twist. The Paris selection includes classics you should not miss and the latest stars.

Menu prices are a rough guide to the cost, per head, of a three-course meal with a half bottle of wine. They are categorised as follows:

$ = Budget under FF150
$$ = Moderate FF150–300
$$$ = Expensive FF300+
CC means credit cards accepted (specified as Amex, American Express; DC, Diners Club; MC, MasterCard; EU, Eurocard, and Visa).

AUVERGNE & MASSIF CENTRAL

Aurillac
La Reine Margot
19 Rue G de Veyre,
15000 Aurillac
tel: 04 71 48 26 46
fax: 04 71 48 92 39
Popular Aurillac restaurant excellent for tasting the regional cuisine especially the locally reared pork and beef dishes cooked to ancient recipes.
CC: MC, Visa **$$**

Clermont-Ferrand
Gérard Anglard
17 Rue Lamartine,
63000 Clermont-Ferrand
tel: 04 73 93 52 25
fax: 04 73 93 29 25
Comfortable bourgeois restaurant with a terrace where you can sample Auvergnat delicacies with a subtle modern touch; local freshwater salmon with ginger butter, for example.
CC: Amex, MC, Visa **$$**

Conques
Hotel Ste-Foy
Rue Principale
12320 Conques
One of Aveyron's best hotels, a charming stone and timber building beautifully restored with intimate but spacious dining room and flowery courtyard. Inventive cooking and menu changed daily.
CC: Amex, DC, MC, Visa **$$**

Najac
Longcol
Aveyron, 12270 Najac
tel: 05 65 29 63 36
Beautifully restored 17th century farm restaurant offers simple local dishes.
CC: Amex, MC, Visa **$$**
Menus from FF145–245

Plaisance
Les Magnolias
Plaisance
12550 Aveyron
tel: 05 65 99 77 34
fax: 05 65 99 70 57
Enchanting 17th century village house owned by chef Francis Roussel with a garden full of ancient magnolia trees, where you can eat local food.
CC: Amex, DC, MC, Visa **$$**

Restaurant Prices

$ = Budget under FF150
$$ = Moderate FF150–300
$$$ = Expensive FF300+

BURGUNDY & RHONE-ALPS

Chambéry
L'Essentiel
183 Place Gare,
7300 Chambéry
tel: 04 79 96 97 27
fax: 04 79 96 17 18
Acclaimed as one of the best in Savoie where local specialities are superbly cooked; try the excellent Savoie freshwater salmon or the duck caramelized with spices.
CC: Amex, MC, Visa **$$**

Courchevel
Chabichou
73120 Courchevel
tel: 04 79 08 00 55
fax: 04 79 08 33 58
One of the most popular restaurants in Courchevel with fabulous mountain views from huge picture windows. Imaginative dishes include langouste carbonara with wild mushrooms, or chocolate tart.
CC: Amex, D, MC, Visa **$$$**

Dijon
Pré aux Clercs
13 Place Libération,
21000 Dijon
tel: 03 80 38 05 05
fax: 03 80 38 16 16
Rich traditional Burgundian cuisine cooked with panache by one of Dijon's star chefs, Jean-Pierre Billoux, and served with a delectable choice of prestigious wines.
CC: Amex, D, MC, Visa **$$$**

Juliénas
Le Coq au Vin
Place Marché,
69840 Juliénas
tel: 04 74 04 41 98
fax: 04 74 04 41 44
Sit on the terrace of this traditional Beaujolais bistro which serves the best of traditional, regional cuisine, not least its very own Coq au Vin recipe.
CC: Amex, Diner, MC, Visa **$$**

Lyons
Pierre Orsi
3 Place Kleber
69000 Lyon
tel: 04 78 89 57 68
fax: 04 72 44 93 34
One of Lyon's top chefs runs this luxurious bourgeois restaurant with a charming courtyard garden for dining on summer days. The roast pigeon and foie gras ravioli are especially recommended.
CC: Amex, MC, Visa **$$$**

Les Muses de l'Opéra
Place Comedie
69000 Lyon
tel: 04 72 00 45 58
fax: 04 78 29 34 01
Fashionable restaurant on the seventh floor of architect Jean Nouvel's new addition to the Opera house with wonderful views. Try stylish dishes like lentil terrine with chicken livers or lamb with apricots.
CC: Amex, MC, Visa **$**

Saint Agrève
Domaine de Rilhac
07320 St-Agrève, Ardèche
tel: 04 75 30 20 20

Magnificent mountain views and a rustic setting in an old Ardèche farmhouse for traditional country dishes cooked with style.
CC: MC, Visa **$$**

Saulieu
Côte d'Or
2 Rue Argentine,
21210 Saulieu
tel: 03 80 64 07 66
fax: 03 80 64 08 92
Chef Bernard Loiseau's much acclaimed restaurant with its pretty flower garden, serving an elegant and innovative cuisine, accompanied by equally prestigious wines. Special dishes might include frogs legs in garlic purée or pike in shallot fondue.
CC: Amex, DC, MC, Visa **$$**

Vézelay
L'Espérance
St-Père, 89450 Vézelay
tel: 03 86 33 39 10
fax: 03 86 33 26 15
Booking is essential at chef Marc Meneau's celebrated hotel/restaurant, with its glass conservatory-dining room that feels like part of the garden. Exceptionally good, inventive cuisine based on traditional Burgundy ingredients.
CC: Amex, DC, MC, Visa **$$$**

La Bouzerotte
21200 Bouze-lès-Beaune
tel/fax: 03 80 26 01 37
Dine outside on the sunny terrace or indoors beside the cosy fire according to the season. Traditional, regional cuisine.
CC: MC, Visa **$$**

LANGUEDOC & ROUSSILLON

Bouzigues
Côte Bleue
34140 Mèze
tel: 04 67 78 30 87
Large family restaurant overlooking the Bassin de Thau which is the best place to sample a vast variety of shellfish, mussels, langoustines, and the local Bouzigues oysters.
CC: Amex, MC, Visa **$$**

Carcassonne
Le Languedoc
32 Allée d'Iéna
tel: 04 68 25 22 17
fax: 04 68 47 13 22
After visiting the medieval Cité head for this local restaurant in the Bas Ville for an authentic *cassoulet*, the regional languedoc dish of beans, pork, duck and sausages.
CC: Amex, DC, MC, Visa **$$**

Céret
La Cerisaie
Route Fontfrède
tel: 04 68 87 01 94
fax: 04 68 87 39 24
Classy Paris cooking in a renovated farmhouse with fabulous views in the foothills of the Pyrenees above Céret. Try the soufflé of foie gras with artichokes, baked *rouget*, stuffed courgette flowers and excellent Roussillon wines.
CC: Amex, DC, MC, Visa **$$**

Collioure
Les Templiers
12 Quai de l'Amirauté,
66190 Collioure
tel: 04 68 98 31 10
fax: 04 68 98 01 24
Restaurant and hotel famous for the many artists who stayed here, Matisse and Braque among them.
CC: Amex, MC, Visa **$**

Cordes
Grand Ecuyer
Rue St-Michel,
81170 Cordes-sur-Ciel
tel: 05 63 53 79 50
fax: 05 63 53 79 51
Wonderful views over the valley from the terrace of this Gothic building. Try authentic *cassoulet* or delicious fish dishes.
CC: Amex, DC, MC, Visa **$$**

Perpignan
Casa Sansa
2 Rue Fabrique Nadal and 3 Rue Fabrique Couverte
66000 Perpignan
tel: 04 68 34 21 84
fax: 04 68 35 02 78
Authentic Catalan restaurant in the narrow streets of the old town, very popular with locals and always

lively. Try the rabbit with figs or beef daube with orange.
CC: Amex, DC, MC, Visa
Menus from FF150–200

Toulouse
Brasserie des Beaux-Arts
1 Quai de la Daurade,
31000 Toulouse
tel: 05 61 21 12 12
Lively popular brasserie on the corner of the quai by the river. The shellfish is displayed outside and the oysters are especially recommended.
CC: Amex, DC, MC, Visa **$$**

LIMOUSIN, PERIGORD & BORDEAUX

Bordeaux
Le Chapon Fin
5 Rue du Montesquieu,
33000 Bordeaux
tel: 05 56 79 10 10
Head for this classic Bordeaux restaurant with original turn of the century decor, to sample dishes like pigeon soup, lobster gazpacho, eel and red wine stew with wines from Côtes de Blaye and Graves.
CC: Amex, DC, MC, Visa **$$$**

Brantôme
Le Moulin de L'Abbaye
1 Route de Bourdeilles,
24310 Brantôme
tel: 05 53 05 80 22
fax: 05 53 05 75 27
Beautiful old mill with peaceful terrace overlooking the river Dronne, where you can sample traditional Périgord dishes with a nouvelle touch; try the pigeon with cèpes and crème brûlée with local Perigord strawberries. Excellent Bergerac wines and courteous service.
CC: Amex, DC, MC, Visa **$$**

Domme
L'Esplanade
24250 Domme, Dordogne
tel: 05 53 28 31 41
Wonderful views of the Dordogne from this hotel perched above Domme. Try trout, salmon or rack of lamb or their truffle specialities.
CC: Amex, D, MC, Visa **$$**
Menus from FF180–380

Limoges
Les Petits Ventres
20 Rue Boucherie,
87000 Limoges
tel: 05 55 33 34 02
A medieval building with a charming
terrace, the place to try the local
specialities, in particular the pot au
feu.
CC: MC, Visa **$$**

Monbazillac
Château de Monbazillac
24240, Monbazillac
tel: 05 53 58 38 93
fax: 05 53 57 82 50
Make a tour of the château before
sitting down on the terrace to enjoy
the restaurant's classical cuisine,
with dishes such as croustillant de
foie gras aux poires, bavaroise au
Monbazillac.
CC: Amex, MC, Visa **$$$**

Poudenas
Le Moulin de la Belle Gasconne
Poudenas,
47170 Lot-et-Garonne
tel: 05 53 65 71 58
Mme Garcia is author of a
cookbook on south-western French
food and cooks it to perfection in
her tranquil stone-built riverside
mill. Dine on the terrace and try the
Grand Repas Gascon.
CC: Amex, DC, MC, Visa **$$$**

St-Emilion
Hostellerie de Plaisance
Place du Clocher,
33330 St-Emilion
tel: 05 27 24 72 32
Splendid views of the exquisite
medieval town of St Emilion and
surrounding vineyards as you dine
on local cuisine and, of course,
local wine at the heart of wine
country.
CC: Amex, DC, MC, Visa **$$**

LOIRE VALLEY

Auch
Hôtel de France
2 Place de la Liberation,
32000 Auch
tel: 05 62 61 71 71
fax: 05 62 61 71 81

One of the best places to sample
the best of south-west cooking from
a kitchen presided over by the
celebrated chef, André Daguin,
most responsible for creating
interest in the rich rustic cuisine of
Gascony with its essential
ingredients of duck, goose, garlic
and red wine.
CC: Amex, DC, MC, Visa **$$**

Blois
La Péniche
Promenade du Mail,
41000 Blois
tel: 02 54 74 37 23
Fish dishes are the speciality when
you dine on this charmingly
restored river barge moored to the
quayside.
CC: Amex, DC, MC, Visa **$**

Chinon
Au Plaisir Gourmand
2 Rue Parmentier,
37500 Chinon
tel: 02 47 98 46 46
fax: 02 47 98 35 44
In the old town below the château is
this charming and highly regarded
restaurant with a sunny flowered
terrace. Try the ravioli escargots or
sandre (pike) with beurre blanc.
CC: Amex, MC, Visa **$$**

Eugénie-les-Bains
Les Prés d'Eugénie

Restaurant lore

It is now law in France to have
separate eating areas for
smokers and non-smokers.
Unfortunately, it must be one
of the most commonly flouted
laws in existence. Many French
still puff constantly throughout
a meal.

Menus must be displayed by
law outside any establishment.
Most places will offer a prix
fixe menu – a set meal at a
particular price, sometimes
including wine. Otherwise you
order separate items from La
Carte. Eating a menu is nearly
always the best value, unless
you really only want one dish.

40320 Eugénie-les-Bains
tel: 05 58 05 06 07
fax: 05 58 51 10 10
Michel Guérard, inventor of cuisine
minceur, runs two restaurants here
along with an immensely luxurious
spa hotel and rustic auberge.
Restaurant Michel Guérard offers
food with the emphasis on healthy
eating with great style, and La
Ferme aux Grives offers very
reasonably priced country style
lunches and dinners.
CC: Amex, DC, MC, Visa **$$**

Lamotte-Beuvron
Hotel Tatin
5 Avenue de Vierzon,
41600 Lamotte-Beuvron
tel: 54 88 00 03
This was where the famous Tarte
Tatin, the now ubiquitous caramelized
apple tart, was first invented so it is
always on the menu along with local
game and fish dishes.
CC: Amex, DC, MC, Visa **$$**

Nantes
La Cigale
4 Place Graslin, 44000 Nantes
tel: 02 40 69 76 41
This historic Nantes cafe is
decorated in exuberant Belle
Epoque style; good for drinks or
snacks but also serves excellent
fish and seafood.
CC: MC, Visa **$**

Orléans
La Chancellerie
27 Place du Matroi,
45000 Orléans
tel: 02 38 53 57 54
Popular brasserie with outside
tables in centre of Orléans, always
full at lunchtime for good local and
traditional dishes with Loire wines.
CC: Amex, MC, Visa **$**

Saumur
Auberge St Pierre
6 Place St Pierre,
49400 Saumur
tel: 02 41 51 26 25
Not far from the château in the old
town is this charming little
restaurant; try the delicious pike or
coq au vin.
CC: MC, Visa **$**

Tours
Jean Bardet
57 Rue Groison, 37100 Tours
tel: 02 47 41 41 11
Jean Bardet is the Loire's great chef and here he presides over an exquisite mansion, cooking superb dishes which draw on the vegetables and herbs grown in the gardens.
CC: Amex, D, MC, Visa **$$**

Les Hautes Roches
86 Quai Loire, Rochecorbon, 37210 Tours, Indre-et-Loire
tel: 02 47 52 88 88
The Loire's fanciest troglodyte hotel has a fine restaurant on a terrace overlooking the Loire river. Try the rabbit and foie gras terrine with fresh herb gelées, and Grand Marnier soufflé.
CC: Amex, MC, Visa **$$**

Les Caves de Marson
49400 Rou-Marson
tel: 02 41 50 50 05
For the total troglodyte experience head for this restaurant near Saumur with its rooms carved out of limestone caves. Try the *fouaces*, wheat pancakes cooked in an old wood-fired oven and stuffed with a variety of fillings.
CC: Visa **$$**

Vouvray
Château de Noizay
37210 Vouvray
tel: 02 47 52 11 01
fax: 02 47 52 04 64
16th century château in its own park, with a superb restaurant; try the smoked pigeon with local mushrooms or goat's cheese salad, complemented by Vouvray wine.
CC: Amex, MC, Visa **$$**

LE NORD

Brittany & Normandy
Auberge St. Saveur
6 Rue St. Saveur,
35000 Rennes
tel: 02 99 79 32 56
A half-timbered building in the old town that survived the great fire of 1750, with an interior that retains

its distinctive character. Traditional cuisine includes Breton lobster, fish and shellfish.
CC: Amex, Visa **$$**

Calais
La Diligence
Hôtel Meurice,
5 Rue Edmond Roche,
62100 Calais
tel: 03 21 34 14 71
Built in 1818 this was among the first of the luxury hotels in Europe. Refined cuisine includes such delicacies as fricassée of sole and crayfish or snails with mushrooms.
CC: Amex, DC, MC, Visa **$$**

Restaurant Prices

$ = Budget under FF150
$$ = Moderate FF150–300
$$$ = Expensive FF300+

Colmar
Maison des Têtes
19 Rue des Têtes,
68000 Colmar
tel: 03 89 24 43 43
fax: 03 89 24 58 34
Wonderfully authentic 17th century brasserie with a magnificent façade now classified as an historic monument; the place to go for Alsatian classics like choucroute.
CC: Amex, DC, MC, Visa **$$**

Dieppe
Auberge Clos Normand
Martin-Eglise, 76200
tel: 02 35 04 40 34
Farmhouse restaurant outside Dieppe, in summer food can be eaten in the orchard by the trout stream. All very good value (some rooms available too).
CC: Amex, MC, Visa **$$**

Kaysersberg
Le Bistrot
Residence Chambard, 13 Rue Général de Gaulle,
68240 Kaysersberg
tel: 03 89 47 10 17
fax: 03 89 47 35 03
A few steps away from this elegant, traditional inn is its popular restaurant, Le Bistrot. Try its fish

dishes or the excellent pot au feu.
CC: Amex, MC, Visa **$$**

Lille
L'Huîtrière
3 Rue des Chats-Bossus, 59800 Lille
tel: 03 20 55 43 41
fax: 03 20 55 23 10
Splendid choice of seafood as well as other traditional dishes in this stylish restaurant with a beautiful tiled Art Deco interior in the old section of Lille.
CC: Amex, DC, MC, Visa
Menus from FF260–600

Marlenheim
Le Cerf
30 Rue du Général-de-Gaulle,
67520 Marlenheim
tel: 03 88 87 73 73
fax: 03 88 87 68 08
Charming village inn makes a good place to try typical Alsatian dishes such as tête de veau and choucroute cooked with style.
CC: Amex, DC, MC, Visa **$$**

Mittelbergheim
Hotel Gilg
1 Route du Vin,
67140 Mittelberghelm
tel: 03 88 08 91 37
fax: 03 88 08 45 17
Charming traditional half timbered *winstub* on the Alsace wine route where you can complement wine tasting with delicious fish dishes.
CC: Amex, DC, MC, Visa **$$**

Reims
Les Crayères
64 Boulevard Henry Vasnier, 51100 Reims
tel: 03 26 82 80 80
fax: 03 26 82 65 52
Reims is full of top class chefs to complement its champagne, none more so than Gérard Boyer in his magnificent château. Try pigs trotters stuffed with foie gras, or the truffled lamb en croute; the chocolate soufflé is legendary.
CC: Amex, DC, MC, Visa **$$**

Riec-sur-Belon
Chez Jacky
Port de Belon,
29340 Riec-sur-Belon
tel: 02 98 06 90 32
fax: 02 98 6 49 72
Great place to eat exquisite Belon oysters and other seafood combined with local muscadet wine. **$$**

Roscoff, Finistère
Le Temps de Vivre
Place Eglise,
29680 Roscoff
tel: 02 98 61 27 28
Splendid sea views from light spacious dining room where you can sample excellent fish dishes, especially the John Dory and the steamed sole.
CC: Amex, MC, Visa **$$**

Crêperie des Remparts
31 Rue Théophile Louarn,
Ville close, 29900 Concarneau
tel: 02 98 50 65 66
In the middle of the ancient walled town is this restaurant where you can eat your fill of excellent crêpes and galettes. CC: MC, Visa **$$**

St-Malo
Hotel Tirel-Guerin
La Gouesnière,
35400 St-Malo
tel: 02 99 89 10 46
Friendly family run restaurant with specialities of tête de veau and lobster and delicious ice cream. Charming service.
CC: Amex, D, MC, Visa **$$**

Strasbourg
Buerehiesel
4 parc Orangerie,
67000 Strasbourg
tel: 03 88 45 56 65
fax: 03 88 61 32 00
This traditional Alsatian, half-timbered farmhouse has been reconstructed in the Orangerie park in Strasbourg and is home to one of the city's best restaurants. The restaurant is presided over by top chef Antoine Westermann. Try pike quenelles or roast John Dory. And for dessert brioche with pear and beer flavoured ice cream.
CC: Amex, DC, MC, Visa **$$**

L'Ami Schultz
1 Rue Ponts Couverts,
67000 Strasbourg
tel: 03 88 32 76 98
fax: 03 88 32 54 30
A warm, rustic restaurant with a terrace overlooking the river and close to the historic Petite France district. Wholesome, traditional, Alsatian cuisine cooked with beer. Open all year round.
CC: Amex, DC, MC, Visa **$$**

Charleville Mézières
Abbaye de Sept Fontaines, 08090 Fagnon
tel: 03 24 37 38 24
fax: 03 24 37 58 75
A château surrounded by park and golf course in the Ardennes countryside near the Belgian border, which offers traditional regional cuisine.
CC: Amex, DC, MC, Visa **$$**

Restaurant Prices

$ = Budget under FF150
$$ = Moderate FF150–300
$$$ = Expensive FF300+

Trouville-sur-Mer
Les Vapeurs
160 Boulevard F. Moreaux,
14360 Trouville-sur-Mer
tel: 02 31 88 15 24
Fashionable place for seafood, close to the fish market, with good fresh dishes available at all times.
CC: Amex, MC, Visa **$$**

Rouen
La Couronne
31 Place du Vieux Marché,
76000 Rouen
tel: 35 71 40 90
Oldest auberge in France, on the square where Joan of Arc was burned. An elegantly decorated interior provides a backdrop to excellent regional cooking. Speciality is the canard au sang (duck cooked in its own blood).
CC: Amex, DC, MC, Visa **$$**

La Mère Poulard
Mont St Michel, 50116
tel: 02 33 60 14 01

Visitors come from far and wide to sample the famous omelettes at Mère Poulard. Other specialities include grilled lobster and rack of lamb.
CC: Amex, DC, Visa **$$**.

PARIS

L'Arpège
84 Rue de Varenne, 75007
tel: 01 45 51 47 33
Fashionable restaurant near the Musée Rodin with svelte modern décor, highly creative cooking and a good wine list. Book well in advance.)
CC: Amex, DC, MC, Visa **$$$**

Au Pied de Cochon
6 Rue Coquillière, 75001
Famous old Les Halles market brasserie open around the clock for lashings of onion soup, pigs trotters and seafood.
CC: Amex, DC, Visa **$**

Brasserie Bofinger
5–7 Rue de la Bastille, 75004
tel: 01 42 72 87 82
Huge brasserie with exquisite Belle-Epoque décor, serving specialities like foie gras, oysters, and choucroute.
CC: Amex, DC, MC, Visa **$$**

Brasserie Flo
7 cour des Petites Ecuries, 75010
tel: 01 47 70 13 59
Flo is a traditional favourite, a jolly 1886 inn serving classic seafood dishes, choucroute, beer and Alsatian wine.
CC: Amex, DC, MC, Visa **$**

Brasserie Lipp
151 Blvd St Germain, 75006
tel: 01 45 48 53 91
Once a favourite of Sartre and de Beauvoir, Brasserie Lipp continues to be popular with the cognoscenti. The speciality here is steaming plates of choucroute.
CC: Amex, MC, Visa, DC **$$**

Le Bretagne
Bateaux Parisiens, Port de la
Bourdonnais, 75007
tel: 01 44 11 33 55
For the ultimate Paris experience
dine aboard the yacht Le Bretagne
for a luxurious meal while cruising
down the Seine.
CC: Amex, Visa **$$$**

Café de la Paix
12 Blvd des Capucines, 75009
tel: 01 40 07 30 20
This stunningly beautiful cafe with
decor by Charles Garnier is classified
as a historic monument; great
people-watching from the terrace.
CC: Amex, MC, Visa, DC **$$**

Chez Jenny
9 Blvd du Temple,
Paris 75003
tel: 01 42 74 75 75
This classic brasserie with 1930s
décor is the place to try Alsatian
specialities like choucroute and
suckling pig.
CC: Amex, D, MC, Visa **$$**

La Closerie des Lilas
171 Boulevard du Montparnasse,
75006
tel: 01 43 26 70 50
A period piece – a cocktail bar once
the haunt of the writers Joyce and
Hemingway and still popular with
artists and intellectuals.
CC: Amex, DC, MC, Visa

Costes
239 Rue St Honoré, 75001
tel: 01 42 44 50 25
A relaxed restaurant favoured by the
fashion crowd in a luxury hotel with
comfortable décor and traditional
dishes including light snacks.
CC: Amex, MC, DC, Visa **$$**

La Coupole
102 Boulevard du Montparnasse,
75014
tel: 01 43 20 14 20
fax: 01 43 35 46 14
Huge and ever-popular art deco
brasserie, recently restored to its
former glory. Serves good
choucroute, steak au poivre, lamb
curry and huge platters of seafood.
CC: AE, DC **$$**

Le Dôme
108 Boulevard du Montparnasse,
75014
tel: 01 43 35 25 81
Along the road from the other
famous café, La Coupole, this is
one of the most popular seafood
restaurants in Paris. Try the
bouillabaisse (fish stew).
CC: Amex, D, MC, Visa **$$**

Harry's New York Bar
5 Rue Daunou, 75002
tel: 01 42 61 71 14
Authentic New York bar brought over
piece by piece, once the favourite
hang-out of Hemingway, Fitzgerald
and company. Still the best place
for Bloody Marys. Lunch and
snacks available and a piano bar in
the basement.
CC: Amex

Jules Verne
Eiffel Tower, Second Floor, Paris,
75007
tel: 01 45 55 61 44
Innovative chef Alain Reix is
becoming well known as is his
restaurant on the second level of
the Eiffel Tower, where you can
combine excellent food and great
sightseeing.
CC: Amex, DC, MC, Visa **$$**

Le Munich
7 Rue Saint Benoît, 75006
tel: 01 42 61 12 70
Wonderful Left Bank brasserie with
traditional red velvet banquettes. A
great place for platters of seafood.
CC: Amex, DC, Visa **$**

Pegotys
79 Ave Bosquet, 75007
tel: 01 45 55 84 50
Charming English tearoom for those
feeling a bit homesick. Good for
breakfast and snacks as well as
afternoon tea.
CC: MC, Visa **$$**

Le Procope
13 Rue de l'Ancienne Comédie,
75006
tel: 01 40 46 79 00
This restaurant has been opening
its doors to the "glitterati" of Paris
(including Voltaire and Balzac) since

1686. and has now been
completely renovated.
CC: Amex, DC, MC, Visa **$**

La Tour d'Argent
15–17 quai de la Tournelle, 75001
tel: 01 43 54 23 31
The ultimate luxury Paris
restaurant, established since the
16th century; the ground floor has
a museum of gastronomy.
CC: Amex, Visa, MC, DC **$$$**

Violin d'Ingres
135 Rue St-Dominique, 75007
tel: 01 45 55 15 05
New restaurant fast becoming very
fashionable. Traditional cooking
with an updated twist; try pig's
trotter tart, egg mousseline, or
chocolate tart.
CC: Amex, Visa **$$**

PROVENCE & COTE D'AZUR

Antibes
Bacon
Boulevard Bacon,
06600 Cap d'Antibes
tel: 04 93 61 50 02
fax: 04 93 61 65 19
Celebrated restaurant famous for
its fish dishes, in particular its
spectacular bouillabaisse.
CC: Amex, D, MC, Visa **$$**

Avignon
La Vieille Fontaine
Hotel d'Europe
12 Place Crillon,
84000 Avignon
tel: 04 90 14 76 76
fax: 04 90 85 43 66
This grand 16th century townhouse
has a charming courtyard and
terrace, a perfect setting for original
cuisine such as roast sea bream
with tomato tart.
CC: Amex, DC, MC, Visa **$$**

Les Baux
Oustau de Baumanière
13520 Les Baux de Provence
tel: 04 90 54 33 07
fax: 04 90 54 40 46
Well known gourmet restaurant in a
16th century building in the strange

ruined town of Les Baux. A new chef has further enhanced its reputation but the favourite dishes are still truffle ravioli and *gigot d'agneau* en croute.
CC: Amex, DC, MC, Visa **$$**

Beaurecueil
Relais Ste-Victoire
13100 Beaurecueil
tel: 04 42 66 94 98
Gaze at Cézanne's much painted mountain from the terrace of this Provençal farmhouse outside Aix. Here you can enjoy Provençal cooking at its best including the treasured truffles of the Vaucluse.
CC: Amex, MC, Visa **$$**

Cannes
Belle Otero
Hotel Carlton,
58 Boulevard de la Croisette,
06400 Cannes
tel: 04 92 99 51 10
fax: 04 92 99 51 19
Opulent restaurant on the seventh floor of the Carlton Hotel with magnificent sea views. This much glamour is expensive so stick to the

Restaurant Prices

$ = Budget under FF150
$$ = Moderate FF150–300
$$$ = Expensive FF300+

fixed price menus. Don't miss the artichoke risotto when it's in season.
CC: Amex, D, MC, Visa **$$$**

Monaco
Café de Paris
Place Casino,
98000 Monte Carlo
tel: 92 16 20 20
fax: 92 16 38 58
A wonderfully renovated brasserie in the Belle Epoque style is one of the sights of Monte Carlo, a great way to sample the glamour without breaking the bank.
CC: Amex, D, MC, Visa
Menus from FF210

Mougins
Le Moulin de Mougins
Avenue Notre Dame de Vie,
06250 Mougins
tel: 04 93 75 78 24

fax: 04 93 90 18 55
Roger Vergé is the chef most responsible for promoting the fashion for Provençal cuisine, what he calls "Cuisine du Soleil" (cuisine of the sun). Here in his original restaurant, in an ancient olive mill, you can sample classics enhanced with imaginative panache, the courgette flowers stuffed with truffles, for example or *beignets* of flower blossoms
CC: Amex, DC, MC, Visa **$$$**

Nice
La Merenda
4 Rue Terrace, 06300 Nice
This little bistro tucked away in the old town of Nice has a big reputation; cognoscenti drop into make a reservation, since there is no phone. It is celebrated for its classic Niçoise cuisine now cooked by renowned chef Dominique le Stanc who can be seen at his stove producing much loved specialities like stockfish, stuffed courgette flowers and beef daube. Tables are chummily close so be ready to make conversation.
No credit cards **$$**

Reading the Label

Wines are graded according to their quality and this must be shown on the label. The grades are as follows:
● *Vin de table*: usually inexpensive everyday table wine. The quality can vary.
● *Vin de pays*: local wine.
● VDQS (*vin délimité de qualité supérieure*): wine from a specific area, of higher quality than *vin de table*.
● AOC (*appellation d'origine controlée*): Good quality wine from a specific area or château where strict controls are imposed on the amount of wine produced each year.
● *Mis en bouteille au château*: bottled at the vineyard. This is also indicated by the words, *récoltant* or *producteur* around the cap.
● *Négociant*: a wine that has been bought by a dealer and usually bottled away from the estate.

However, this is not necessarily to the detriment of the wine; there are many excellent *négociants* in business today.
The French are fiercely proud of their wines and keen to educate visitors about their production. In all the regions of wine production you will find roadside signs offering visits to cellars open to the public for tours, tastings and sale of wine. The following organizations disseminate information about wines and viticulture, organize courses and produce lists of cellars open to the public.

Fédération Interprofessionelle des Vins de Bourgogne, 12 Boulevard Bretonnière, 21200 Beaune, tel: 80 25 04 80. Also at 520 Avenue de Lattre de Tassigny, 71000 Mâcon,
tel: 03 85 38 20 15.

Comité Interprofessionel du Vin de Champagne, 5 Rue Henry-Martin, 51200 Epernay, tel: 03 26 51 19 30.
Professional Trade Council for Bordeaux Wines (CIVB), 1 Cours du 30 Juillet, 33075 Bordeaux, tel: 05 56 00 22 66.
Some tourist organisations in France offer wine tours and holiday courses, mostly lasting a weekend. For information, contact the professional bodies or the Loisirs Accueil services in the *départements* plants abound in the clear waters which bathe the coast. Outstanding sub-aqua areas with good facilities and experienced locals are the waters around Oban, the Summer Isles aqua Club, 16 Royal Crescent, Glasgow G3 7SL (Tel: 0141-aqua Club, 16 Royal Crescent, Glasgow G3 7SL (Tel: 0141-332 Glasgow 7SL (Tel: 0141-

St-Paul-de-Vence
Colombe d'Or
Place des Ormeaux-Place de Gaulle,
06570 St Paul de Vence
tel: 04 93 32 80 02
fax: 04 93 32 77 78
The Colombe d'Or has long been
known as an exquisite small hotel
and gorgeous restaurant, full of
stunning artworks donated by
Picasso, Braque, Miro and many
more when they came to what was
then a village cafe in the 1920s.
The terrace is the place to eat, and
the serving of fifteen different hors
d'oeuvres makes for delightful
surprises.
CC: Amex, DC, MC, Visa **$$**

PYRENEES

Barcus
Hôtel Chilo
64130 Barcus
tel: 05 59 28 90 79
fax: 05 59 28 93 10
Friendly hotel in small village near
the Spanish border serving
exceptional food which draws
visitors from far and wide;
imaginative Basque specialities
cooked by the Chilo family from the
fresh game, fruit and vegetables
they collect every day from the
market.
CC: Amex, DC, MC, Visa **$**

Biarritz
Le Galion
17 Boulevard Gen de Gaulle,
64200 Biarritz
tel: 05 59 24 20 32
fax: 05 59 24 67 54
In a wonderful position with terrace
overlooking beach and casino
gardens, for well prepared sea food
with a Basque flavour; especially
good are the stuffed squid in a
sauce of their own ink.
CC: MC, Visa **$$**

Espelette
Euzkadi
64250 Espelette
tel: 05 59 93 91 88
A restaurant in the full Basque
spirit. The house has a half
timbered façade hung with clusters

of Espelette peppers in the autumn
and the cuisine captures the best
of Basque tradition.
CC: MC, Visa **$$**

Wine

Vines have been cultivated in
France since the ancient Romans
first planted them. To exclude wine
from the dinner table is almost like
forgetting the salt and pepper. It is
not regarded as a luxury; everyday
wine (*vin de table*) is produced for
everyday consumption. On the other
hand France produces some of the
finest vintages in the world, and the
pomp, ceremony and snobbery that
accompany their production show
just how important it is to the
culture and economy of France.

The main regions of wine
production are Bordeaux (clarets
and sweet sauternes), Burgundy
(some say this area produces the
finest wines in the world),
Champagne (only wine from here
can truly call itself champagne), the
Loire valley where we find Muscadet
and other dry white wines, and
Alsace which produces white wine
of a similar style to its German
neighbours. A lot of red wine is also
produced in Languedoc and
Provence, and although their wines
are rapidly gaining a good
reputation, they have not yet
acquired the cachet of Burgundy
and Bordeaux.

Culture

Live Entertainment

There is a huge variety of live
entertainment in France, much of it
appears in Paris and other major
cities. In the summer, many major
cities (and even small towns)
present a programme of events,
including music and drama festivals
(often including street theatre and
other live outdoor performances).

An annual programme listing all
major festivals and *fêtes* throughout
the country is published each year.
The programme is available from
the French Government Tourist
Offices around the world.

Son-et-lumière displays are now a
popular way of presenting historical
events; these started at the
châteaux in the Loire Valley and have
spread to historic monuments all
around the country. Performances
are normally at around 9 or 10pm,
with, often, several shows a night in
July and August.

For information and reservations
contact the local tourist offices; a
national guide of historical shows is
published annually and is available
from the Fédération Nationale des
Fêtes et Spectacles Historiques,
Hôtel de Ville, 60000 Beauvais,
tel: 03 44 79 40 00.

THEATRE & OPERA
The Comédie Française and the
Opéra Garnier perfom at major
venues and are most famous for
their classical productions, but
there is a good choice of theatre,
concerts, opera and ballet for all
tastes to be enjoyed in the capital.
Some of the major venues are
listed below.
Comédie Française, 2 Rue
Richelieu, 75001 Paris,

tel: 01 44 58 15 15.
Opéra National, Palais Garnier,
Place de l'Opera, 75009 Paris, tel:
01 40 01 17 89, fax: 01 40 01 16
16.
Opéra Bastille, 2bis Place de la
Bastille, 75012 Paris,
tel: 01 40 01 17 89,
fax: 01 40 01 16 16.
Théâtre du Châtelet, 1 Place du
Châtelet, 75001 Paris,
tel: 01 40 28 28 28,
fax: 01 42 36 89 75.
Théâtre Madeleine, 19 Rue de
Surène, 75008 Paris,
tel: 01 42 65 07 09.
Théâtre Palais Royal, 38 Rue
Montpensier, 75001 Paris, tel: 01
42 97 59 81.

Diary of Events

Listed here are brief details of the
main annual events. For more
specific information, contact the
local tourist offices.
January: Paris Fashion Shows;
Limoux Carnival.
February: Menton Lemon Festival;
Nice Carnival.
March: Monte Carlo festival of
contemporary film music.
April: Lourdes Sacred Music
Festival.
May: Cannes Film Festival; Grasse
international rose show; Mâcon
wine fair; Nice Art Jonction
International Music Festival;
Bordeaux Musical May; Auvers-sur-
Oise music festival; gipsy
pilgrimage, Stes-Marie-de-la-Mer.
June: Strasbourg Music Festival;
Touraine Music Festival and Tours
international choral music
competition; Les Imaginaires at
Mont-Saint-Michel; Chartres
International Organ Festival; Noirlac
Music Festival.
July: Aix-en-Provence Festival; Anjou
Festival; Antibes Jazz; Festival;
Avignon Festival; Bastille Day –
celebrated throughout France on
the 14th; Nice Jazz Festival
Quimper – Fêtes de Cornouailles.
August: Antibes International
fireworks festival; Lorient Celtic
Festival; Marciac Jazz Festival;
Menton International Chamber
Music Festival; Dijon grape harvest

and folk fair; flower festival,
Bagnères de Luchon.
October: Dijon International
Gastronomy Fair; Paris Motor Show;
Paris Jazz Festival; and Montmartre
Harvest Festival.
November: Beaujolais Nouveau
celebrations; Beaune Wine Auction;
Dijon Gastronomic Fair.
December: Paris Boat Show;
Strasbourg Christmas market.

Cinema in Paris

Cinema programmes in Paris
change every Wednesday. Films
marked V.O. (*version originale*) are
screened in the original language
(not dubbed into French).

The following cinemas often
show films in their original
language:
**Les Forums Cinemas Orient
Express**, Rue de l'Orient-Express,
75001 Paris,
tel: 08 36 68 60 06.
Gaumont Champs-Elysées, 66
Avenue des Champs-Elysées,
75008 Paris,
tel: 01 42 56 37 01.
Le Grand Rex, 1 Boulevard
Poissonière, 75002 Paris,
tel: 01 42 36 83 93. Le Grand
Rex is a single theatre with the
largest cinema screen in Paris.

Nightlife

Where to go

Paris, of course, offers the best in
nightlife, with a huge choice of
venues and entertainment; in the
provinces you need to be in the
major towns. Many towns now
organize festivals which run through
the summer for the local people
and tourists. If you are staying on a
farm or in a country area, you may
be invited to join in local festivities.
Almost every town and village has
its own fête during the summer;
these range from simple boules
competitions with a dance, hosted
by an enthusiastic (sometimes
excruciating) band, playing
traditional music (or, if you're
unlucky, ancient pop songs), to a
full-blown carnival with street
theatre, fireworks and sophisticated
entertainment.

Information about nightclubs,
cinemas and other entertainment in
the provinces is available from the
tourist offices, or at your hotel.

Nightlife in Paris

As one of the most concentrated
cities in Europe the action starts in
Paris as soon as the sun goes
down. Bars and clubs are all over
the city, but particularly in the
central areas around the Louvre,
the Grand Boulevards, Marais,
Bastille, Montmartre, Pigalle and
the Latin Quarter. Some of the most
famous and popular nightspots in
Paris include:

Cabaret
The Crazy Horse Saloon, 12 Avenue
George V, 75008 Paris, tel: 01 47
23 32 32, fax: 01 47 23 48 26.
Famous music hall, with two or
three shows nightly.

Paradis Latin, 28 Rue du Cardinal Lemoine, 75005 Paris, tel: 01 43 25 28 28, fax: 01 43 26 62 56. Originally built in 1889 by Eiffel, and reopened as a theatre in 1977. **La Nouvelle Eve**, 25 Rue de La Fontaine, 75009 Paris, tel: 01 48 74 69 25, fax: 01 40 82 92 35. Offers genuine Pigalle music hall, but without the vulgarity. It has a good dinner menu; show starts at 10.30pm.

Night Clubs
Régine's, 49-51 Rue de Ponthieu, 75008 Paris, tel: 01 43 59 21 13. The most famous night club in Paris, frequented by the rich and famous, and hard to get into (membership usually necessary). The disco is open 11.30pm–dawn; also a restaurant.
Les Bains Douches, 7 Rue du Bourg-l'Abbé, 75003 Paris, tel: 01 48 87 01 80. Trendy venue, converted from an old public baths. Disco from midnight until dawn, plus a restaurant.
Folies Pigalle, 11 Place Pigalle, 75009 Paris, tel: 01 48 78 25 56. Fashionable disco in a district alive at night.
Le Balajo, 9 Rue de Lappe, 75011 Paris, tel: 01 47 00 07 87. Old-fashioned hall attracting a chic crowd, near the Bastille.

Jazz Clubs
Caveau de la Huchette, 5 Rue de la Huchette, 75005 Paris, tel: 01 43 26 65 05. Opens at 9.30pm.
New Morning, 7–9 Rue des Petites Ecuries, 75010 Paris, tel: 01 45 23 51 41. Sets generally start around 9pm.
Le Sunset, 60 Rue des Lombards, 75001 Paris, tel: 01 40 26 46 60. Dine in the ground-floor restaurant, then descend to the basement for the jazz at 10.30pm.

Shopping

Where to Shop
Over the past couple of decades, most major towns in France have made the sensible decision to keep town centres for small boutiques and individual shops. Many of these areas are pedestrianised and very attractive (although beware – some cars ignore the *voie piétonnée* signs). The large supermarkets, hypermarkets, furniture stores and do-it-yourself outlets collect on the outskirts of town, mostly designated as a *Centre Commercial*.

These centres, although aesthetically unappealing, are fine for bulk shopping for self-catering or for finding a selection of reasonably priced wine to take home. But for gifts and general window-shopping the town centres are far more interesting. It is here that you will find the individual souvenirs with a particularly local flavour, alongside the beautifully dressed windows of delicatessens and patisseries.

Clothing Sizes
Most shops are happy to let you try clothes on (*essayer*) before buying. Children's sizes, in particular, tend to be small compared with British and US age ranges. Hypermarkets are good for inexpensive children's clothes.

Shop for Lunch

If you want to buy a picnic lunch, remember to buy everything you need before midday. Good delicatessens (charcuterie) have delicious ready-prepared dishes, which make picnicking a delight.

Standard Fare

AOC, Appellation d'Origine Contrôlée, is a legal regulation for cheeses and poultry as well as wines, and it ensures the products conform to a particular standard

Opening Hours
Food shops, especially bakers, tend to open early; boutiques and department stores open from 9am, but sometimes not until 10am. In most town centres, just about everything closes from noon until 2.30 or 3pm but in Paris and other major tourist areas, stores and some other shops stay open. Most shops close in the evening at 7pm. Out of town, the hypermarkets are usually open all day until 8 or even 9pm.

Most shops are closed Monday mornings and many all day Monday.

Market Shopping
The heart of every French town is its market; they mostly start early in the morning and close at midday, although some bigger ones are open in the afternoon too. The French themselves usually visit early to get the best of the produce. Markets are a riot of colour and bustle; the best have all kinds of stalls from flowers to domestic animals (do not be deceived – these are for the pot). Local cheeses, honey, wine, pâté and other specialities are often offered for tasting to encourage browsers to buy.

There are more and more antique or second-hand (*brocante*) markets springing up around the provinces, as well as flea markets (*marchés aux puces*), which are also fun to look around – you may find a genuine bargain antique amongst all the old junk. The most famous of these, indeed the biggest flea market in the world, is Les Puces de St-Ouen at Porte de Clignancourt in Paris, open Saturday to Monday 6am–7.30pm.

Look out for special fairs held all

Market Etiquette

In a market all goods have to be marked with the price by law. Prices are usually by the kilo or by the *pièce*, that is, each item priced individually. Usually the stall holder (*marchand*) will select the goods for you. Sometimes there is a serve-yourself system – observe everyone else! If you are choosing cheese, for example, you may be offered a taste to try first; *un goûter*. Here are a few useful words:

bag	*le sac*
basket	*le panier*
flavour	*le parfum*
organic	*la biologique*
tasting	*la dégustation*

over the country at various times throughout the year, such as harvest times. Some of the most important are listed in "Diary of Events". For others, check with the local tourist office for details.

Shopping by Area

The different regions of France are famous for particular products, for example Breton lace, Limoges porcelain, Provençal fabrics, perfume from Grasse, to name but a few. Paris, naturally, has a fascinating range of shops from the fashion houses in the 8th arrondissement, particularly around the Faubourg St-Honoré, to the more affordable, but still chic department stores such as the famous Galeries Lafayette and Le Printemps (which boasts the largest perfume department in the world), both on the Boulevard Haussman, 75009 Paris.

The newest shopping arcade in Paris is Les Trois Quartiers at the Madeleine in the 8th arrondissement. Also worth a visit is the Forum des Halles, 75001 Paris, for a diverse selection of stores.

Buying Direct

Around the country, you may be tempted by all the signs you see along the road for *dégustations* (tastings). Many wine producers and farmers will invite you to try their wines and other produce with an eye to selling you a case, or maybe a few jars of pâté. This is a good way to try before you buy and can sometimes include a visit to a wine cellar.

Sometimes farm produce is more expensive to buy this way than in the supermarkets – do not forget that it is home-produced and not factory-processed, and it will be a lot fresher.

Export Procedures

On most purchases, the price includes TVA (VAT or value added tax). The base rate is currently 20.6 percent, but can be as high as 33 percent on luxury items. Foreign visitors can claim back TVA; this is worth doing if you spend in one place more than FF4,200 (FF2,000 for non-EU residents). Ask the store for a *bordereau* (export sales invoice). This must be completed and shown, together with the goods, to customs officers on leaving the country. It is wise to pack the items separately for ease of access. You then mail the form back to the retailer who will refund the TVA in a month or two. Certain items purchased (e.g. antiques) may need special customs clearance.

If you have a complaint about any purchase, return it in the first place to the shop as soon as possible. You will need your till slip as proof of purchase. In the case of a serious dispute, contact the local Direction Départementale de la Concurrence et de la Consommation et de la Répression des Fraudes (see phone directory for number).

Sport

In general, sports facilities are first-rate throughout France. Most towns have swimming pools and even small villages often have a tennis court, but you may have to become a temporary member to use it – enquire at the local tourist office or *mairie* (town hall) which will also be able to provide details of other local sporting activities.

It seems to be a quirk of the French tourist industry that they do not always take full advantage of their facilities. Even though there may be good weather in early summer and autumn, open-air swimming pools and other venues often limit their seasons to the period of the school holidays.

Many companies offer sporting and activity holidays in France; these are often organized too by the tourist offices in individual *départements*; write to the Services Loisirs Accueil at the destination of your choice (*see Useful Addresses*).

Water Sports

All over France water sports can be enjoyed at a Base de Loisirs. These centres, found not just on the coast, but inland on lakes and quiet river stretches, offer various leisure activities – not just water sports. They usually have a café or bar, maybe even a restaurant, as well as picnic areas.

Many such centres offer tuition in the various sports available – canoeing, wind-surfing etc; fees are usually charged at an hourly or half-hourly rate. Where boating and windsurfing is permitted, equipment is often available for hire, or bring your own.

The following addresses are the

central offices of the various water sports organizations in France; they will supply addresses of regional members and clubs.

Canoeing

Fédération Française de Canoë-Kayak de France, 47 Quai Louis Ferber, 94360 Bry-sur-Marne, tel: 01 48 81 54 26.

Sailing

Fédération Française de Voile, 55 Avenue Kléber, 75784 Paris Cedex 16, tel: 01 44 05 81 00, fax: 01 47 04 90 12.

Rowing

Fédération Française des Sociétés d'Aviron, 17 bd de la Marne, 94736 Nogent sur Marne, tel: 01 45 14 26 40.

Swimming

Fédération Française de Natation, 148 Avenue Gambetta, 75020 Paris, tel: 01 40 31 17 70.

Rafting

Société AN Rafting, 45 Rue de Paris, 92110 Clichy, tel: 01 47 37 08 77.

Water Skiing

Fédération Française de Ski Nautique, 16 Rue Clément-Marot, 75008 Paris, tel: 01 47 20 05 00, fax: 01 47 20 43 74.

Underwater Sports

Fédération Française d'Etudes et de Sports Sous-Marins, 24 Quai de Rive-Neuve, 13284 Marseille, tel: 04 91 33 99 31, fax: 04 91 54 77 43.

Fishing

With its wealth of waterways and lakes, fishing is a popular activity in France. It is possible to book fishing holidays (a weekend or longer) with accommodation; try the Loisirs Accueil services (see Useful Addresses). A permit (permis) is usually required for coarse fishing; enquire at local tourist offices. Sea

fishing trips are widely available on the coast – look out for sign boards advertising trips on the quayside. For regional fishing information contact Maison de la France, Paris, tel: 01 42 96 10 23.

Cycling

To take your own velo to France is easy – they are carried free on most ferries and trains – or you can rent cycles for a reasonable cost; main railway stations usually have them for hire and you can often arrange to pick up at one station and leave at another. Alternatively, try bicycle retailers/repairers or ask at the local tourist office.

Some youth hostels rent cycles and also arrange tours with accommodation in hostels or under canvas. For more information, contact the YHA (see Where to Stay).

Cycling Holidays

Cycling holidays are offered by various organizations; with campsite or hotel accommodation and the advantage that your luggage is often transported for you to your next destination. Some operators are listed below:

Fédération Française de Cyclotourisme, 8 Rue Jean-Marie-Jégo, 75013 Paris, tel: 01 44 16 88 88, fax: 01 44 16 88 99. More than 60 guided tours offered each year, all over France, 60–100 km (40–60 miles) per day. Bring your own bike. **Fédération Française de Cyclisme**, Bâtiment Jean-Monnet, 5 Rue de Rome, 93561 Rosny-sous-Bois Cedex, tel: 01 49 35 69 00, fax: 01 48 94 09 97.

Cresta Holidays, Tabley Court, 32 Victoria Street, Altrincham, Cheshire WA14 1EZ, tel: (0161) 927 7000.

Cyclists Touring Club, Cotterell House, 69 Meadrow, Godalming, Surrey GU7 3HS, tel: (01483) 417217.

Headwater Holidays, 146 London Road, Northwich CW9 5HH, tel: (01606) 48699. Hotel accommodation, and your luggage transported.

Susi Madron's Cycling for Softies, 2–4 Birch Polygon, Rusholme, Manchester M14 5HX, tel: (0161) 248 8282. Well-established with a good reputation, offers holidays with good accommodation in many parts of France.

It is advisable to take out insurance before you go. The normal rules of the road apply to cyclists (see Getting Around). Advice and information can be obtained from The Touring Department of the Cyclists Touring Club (address above). Their service to members includes competitive cycle and travel insurance, free detailed touring itineraries and general information sheets about France. The club's French counterpart, Fédération Française de Cyclotourisme (see above) offers a similar service. Rob Hunter's book Cycle Touring in France is also useful as a handbook, and the IGN Cyclists' Map No. 906 France Velo carries a mass of information.

Cycling Clubs

Such is the French passion for cycling that local clubs organize many trips lasting a day or more and visitors are often more than welcome to join in. Weekend or longer tours are organized by the national Bicyclub (address above). Lists of clubs and events are also organised by local members of the Fédération Française de Cyclotourisme (address above); write to them for regional or departmental offices. They also produce leaflets giving suggested cycle tours for independent travellers, ranging from easy terrain to very hard going for the more experienced cyclist, with details of accommodation, cycle repairers and other facilities en route.

Mountain Biking

This sport has really taken off in recent years, particularly among the French, many of whom are already dedicated cyclists. Many of the organizations listed under Cycling offer mountain bike holidays.

Mountain bikes (in French VTT – Vélo Tout Terrain) and protective gear can be hired locally, try the local tourist office, or cycle shops/repairers.

Horseback Riding

Riding holidays in France come under the umbrella of the Syndicat National du Tourisme Equestre, apte France, 60 Grande Rue, 60510 La Neuville-en-Hez, tel: 08 00 02 59 10. This organization embraces 220 specialist riding centres; contact them for regional or local branches who can also provide information about marked bridleways, maps, riding centres and insurance.

Treks lasting a day or more and also longer holidays on horseback can be organized locally. Information can be obtained from the organizations mentioned above, from tourist offices and from the Loisirs Accueil services of the individual *départements* (*see Useful Addresses*).

Golf

In recent years, golf has caught on in a big way in France and the Regional Tourist Boards have joined forces with the French Golf Federation in an effort to promote it better and set standards. The resulting organisation, France Golf International, embraces over 100 golf courses around the country which must provide a certain standard of facilities to all. They require courses to have weekend reservation systems, and have multilingual staff on hand.

Information can be obtained from the individual Comité Régional du Tourisme (see *Useful Addresses*) or the Féderation Française de Golf, 69 Avenue Victor Hugo, 75783 Paris Cedex 16, tel: 01 44 17 63 00; fax: 01 44 17 63 63.

Winter and Mountain Sports

Snow Sports
From the famous resorts, such as La Clusaz and Chamonix, founded early this century, to the state of

the art facilities provided for the 1992 Olympics at Albertville, France offers plenty of scope for skiers of all abilities and all ages. The newest resorts at Valmorel and Valfréjus make an effort to keep the activity as environmentally friendly as possible.

Ski France is the major winter sports body in France, grouping over 100 resorts and providing accommodation reservations. It also offers a 24-hour telephone ski bulletin from mid-December to mid-April, tel: 01 47 42 23 32, fax: 01 42 61 23 16. For information, contact them at 61 Boulevard Haussman, 75008 Paris.

Other useful addresses are the Fédération Française de Ski, 50 Rue des Marquisats 74000 Annecy, tel: 04 50 51 40 34; and Ecoles de Ski Français, 6 Allée des Mitaillères, 38246 Meylan, tel: 04 76 90 67 36 for information about lessons.

The most famous and popular ski resorts are to be found in the Alps, but the sport is also available in the Pyrenees and the Massif Central. The peak period for winter sports is February, although in some resorts it is still possible to ski in May. There are now several variations on traditional skiing, which are practised at many resorts. Cross-country skiing has been popular for some years now and marked trails are checked every day. Monoskiing was started in Chamonix and has quickly spread to other resorts, while snowsurfing is relatively new, particularly attractive to inexperienced skiers.

Other increasingly popular activities are snowshoe walking, which needs no particular skills, climbing frozen waterfalls (which does), and dog-sleigh driving, now recognised as a competitive sport. Information on these is available from tourist offices.

Organisations exist for the promotion of mountain climbing, caving and potholing – all practised in France – and dissemination of information:

Mountain Climbing
The following agents' are useful for organising mountain climbs in France:

France: Fédération Française de la Montagne et de l'Escalade, 8 Quai de la Marne, 75019 Paris, tel: 01 40 18 75 50.

UK: Sherpa Expeditions, 131a Heston Road, Hounslow, Middlesex TW5 0RD, tel: (0181) 577 2717, are specialists in mountain walking holidays. They also have agents abroad.

US: Himalayan Travel, 112 Prospect Street, 2nd Floor, Stamford CT 06901, tel: 800 225 2380.

Australia: Passport Travel, Suite 11a St Kilda Rd, Melbourne, Victoria 3004, tel: (03) 986 73888.

New Zealand: Venture Treks, PO Box 37610, 164 Parnell Road, Auckland, tel: (09) 799 855.

Potholing

For information on potholing in France write to: Fédération Française de Spéléologie, 130 Rue St-Maur, 75011 Paris, tel: 01 43 57 56 54.

Spectator Sports

Details of events can be obtained from the nearest tourist office, or from national organizers of events. Some of the better known competitive events are the Tour de France, a 22-day, 2,500-mile (4,000-km) bicycle race in July; the 24-hour car race at Le Mans in June; the Monaco Grand Prix in May and the Monte Carlo Motor Rally in January. May in Paris sees the International Tennis Championships and the Prix de Diane-Hermès, the French Derby, is held at Chantilly in June.

Language

French is the native language of more than 90 million people and the acquired language of 180 million. It is a Romance language descended from the Vulgar Latin spoken by the Roman conquerors of Gaul. It still carries the reputation of being the most cultured language in the world and, for what it's worth, the most beautiful. People often tell stories about the impatience of the French towards foreigners not blessed with fluency in their language. In general, however, if you attempt to communicate with them in French, they will be helpful.

Since much of the English vocabulary is related to French, thanks to the Norman Conquest of 1066, travellers will often recognise many helpful cognates: words such as *hôtel*, *café* and *bagages* hardly need to be translated. You should be aware, however, of some misleading "false friends" (*see above right*).

Words & Phrases

How much is it? *C'est combien?*
What is your name?
Comment vous appelez-vous?
My name is... *Je m'appelle...*
Do you speak English?
Parlez-vous anglais?
I am English/American
Je suis anglais/américain

Time

At what time? *A quelle heure?*
When? *Quand?*
What time is it? *Quelle heure est-il?*
● Note that the French generally use the 24-hour clock.

I don't understand
Je ne comprends pas
Please speak more slowly
Parlez plus lentement, s'il vous plaît
Can you help me?
Pouvez-vous m'aider?
I'm looking for... *Je cherche*
Where is...? *Où est...?*
I'm sorry *Excusez-moi/Pardon*
I don't know *Je ne sais pas*
No problem *Pas de problème*
Have a good day! *Bonne journée!*
That's it *C'est ça*
Here it is *Voici*
There it is *Voilà*
Let's go *On y va. Allons-y*
See you tomorrow *A demain*
See you soon *A bientôt*
Show me the word in the book
Montrez-moi le mot dans le livre
yes *oui*
no *non*
please *s'il vous plaît*
thank you *merci*
(very much) *(beaucoup)*
you're welcome *de rien*
excuse me *excusez-moi*
hello *bonjour*
OK *d'accord*
goodbye *au revoir*
good evening *bonsoir*
here *ici*
there *là*
today *aujourd'hui*
yesterday *hier*
tomorrow *demain*
now *maintenant*
later *plus tard*
this morning *ce matin*
this afternoon *cet après-midi*
this evening *ce soir*

On Arrival

I want to get off at...
Je voudrais descendre à...
Is there a bus to the Louvre?
Est-ce qui'il ya un bus pour le Louvre?
What street is this? *A quelle rue sommes-nous?*
Which line do I take for...? *Quelle ligne dois-je prendre pour...?*
How far is...?
A quelle distance se trouve...?
Validate your ticket
Compostez votre billet
airport *l'aéroport*
train station *la gare*

False Friends

False friends are words that look like English words but mean something different.
le car motorcoach, also railway carriage
le conducteur bus driver
la monnaie change (coins)
l'argent money/silver
ça marche can sometimes mean walk, but is usually used to mean working (the TV, the car etc.) or going well
actuel "present time" (*la situation actuelle* the present situation)
rester to stay
location hiring/renting
personne person or nobody, according to context
le médecin doctor

bus station *la gare routière*
Métro stop *la station de Métro*
bus *l'autobus, le car*
bus stop *l'arrêt*
platform *le quai*
ticket *le billet*
return ticket *aller-retour*
hitchhiking *l'autostop*
toilets *les toilettes*
This is the hotel address
C'est l'adresse de l'hôtel
I'd like a (single/double) room...
Je voudrais une chambre (pour une/deux personnes) ...
....with shower *avec douche*
....with a bath *avec salle de bain*
....with a view *avec vue*
Does that include breakfast?
Le prix comprend-il le petit déjeuner?
May I see the room?
Je peux voir la chambre?
washbasin *le lavabo*
bed *le lit*
key *la cléf*
elevator *l'ascenseur*
air conditioned *climatisé*

On the Road

Where is the spare wheel?
Où est la roue de secours?
Where is the nearest garage?
Où est le garage le plus proche?
Our car has broken down
Notre voiture est en panne

The Alphabet

Learning the pronunciation of the French alphabet is a good idea. In particular, learn how to spell out your name.
a=ah, **b**=bay, **c**=say, **d**=day **e**=er, **f**=ef, **g**=zhay, **h**=ash. **i**=ee, **j**=zhee, **k**=ka, **l**=el, **m**=em, **n** =en, **o**=oh, **p**=pay, **q**=kew, **r**=ehr, **s**=ess, **t**=tay, **u**=ew, **v**=vay, **w**=dooblah vay, **x**-=eex, **y** ee grek, **z**=zed

I want to have my car repaired
Je veux faire réparer ma voiture
It's not your right of way
Vous n'avez pas la priorité
I think I must have put diesel in the car by mistake
Je crois que j'ai mis du gasoil dans la voiture par erreur

the road to...	la route pour...
left	gauche
right	droite
straight on	tout droit
far	loin
near	près d'ici
opposite	en face
beside	à côté de
car park	parking
over there	là-bas
at the end	au bout
on foot	à pied
by car	en voiture
town map	le plan

Emergencies

Help! *Au secours!*
Stop! *Arrêtez!*
Call a doctor
Appelez un médecin
Call an ambulance *Appelez une ambulance*
Call the police *Appelez la police*
Call the fire brigade
Appelez les pompiers
Where is the nearest telephone?
Où est le téléphone le plus proche?
Where is the nearest hospital?
Où est l'hôpital le plus proche?
I am sick *Je suis malade*
I have lost my passport/purse
J'ai perdu mon passeport/ porte-monnaie

road map	la carte
street	la rue
square	la place
give way	céder le passage
dead end	impasse
no parking	stationnement interdit
motorway	l'autoroute
toll	le péage
speed limit	la limitation de vitesse
petrol	l'essence
unleaded	sans plomb
diesel	le gasoil
water/oil	l'eau/l'huile
puncture	un pneu de crevé
bulb	l'ampoule
wipers	les essuies-glace

Shopping

Where is the nearest bank (post office)?
Où est la banque/Poste/PTT la plus proche?
I'd like to buy *Je voudrais acheter*
How much is it? *C'est combien?*
Do you take credit cards?
Est-ce que vous acceptez les cartes de crédit?
I'm just looking *Je regarde seulement*
Have you got? *Avez-vous...?*
I'll take it *Je le prends*
I'll take this one/that one
Je prends celui-ci/celui-là
What size is it? *C'est de quelle taille?*
Anything else? *Avec ça?*

size (clothes)	la taille
size (shoes)	la pointure
cheap	bon marché
expensive	cher
enough	assez
too much	trop
a piece	un morceau de
each	la piece (eg ananas, 15F la pièce)
bill	la note
chemist	la pharmacie
bakery	la boulangerie
bookshop	la librairie
library	la bibliothèque
department store	le grand magasin
delicatessen	la charcuterie/ le traiteur
fishmonger's	la poissonerie

Slang

métro, boulot, dodo
nine-to-five syndrome
McDo McDonald's
branché trendy (literally "connected")
C'est du cinéma It's very unlikely
une copine/ un copain
friend/ chum
un ami friend but **mon ami**, boyfriend; also **mon copain**
un truc thing, "whatsit"
pas mal, not bad, good-looking
fantastic! fantastic! terrible!

grocery	l'alimentation/ l'épicerie
tobacconist	tabac (can also sell stamps and newspapers)
markets	le marché
supermarket	le supermarché
junk shop	la brocante

Sightseeing

town	la ville
old town	la vieille ville
abbey	l'abbaye
cathedral	la cathédrale
church	l'église
keep	le donjon
mansion	l'hôtel
hospital	l'hôpital
town hall	l'hôtel de ville/ la mairie
nave	la nef
stained glass	le vitrail
staircase	l'escalier
tower	la tour (La Tour Eiffel)
walk	le tour
country house/ castle	le château
Gothic	gothique
Roman	romain
Romanesque	roman
museum	la musée
art gallery	la galerie
exhibition	l'exposition
tourist information office	l'office de tourisme/le syndicat d'initiative
free	gratuit

Basic Rules

Even if you speak no French at all, it is worth trying to master a few simple phrases. The fact that you have made an effort is likely to get you a better response. More and more French people like practising their English on visitors, especially waiters in the cafés and restaurants and the younger generation. Pronunciation is the key; they really will not understand if you get it very wrong. Remember to **emphasise each syllable**, but not to pronounce the last consonant of a word as a rule (this includes the plural "s") and always to drop your "h"s. Whether to use "**vous**" or "**tu**" is a vexed question; increasingly the familiar form of "tu" is used by many people. However it is better to be too formal, and use "vous" if in doubt. It is very important to be polite; always address people as **Madame** or **Monsieur**, and address them by their surnames until you are confident first names are acceptable. When entering a shop always say, "Bonjour Monsieur/ Madame," and "Merci, au revoir," when leaving.

open	*ouvert*
closed	*fermé*
every day	*tous les jours*
all year	*toute l'année*
all day	*toute la journée*
swimming pool	*la piscine*
to book	*réserver*

Dining Out

Table d'hôte (the "host's table") is one set menu served at a set price. **Prix fixe** is a fixed price menu. **A la carte** means dishes from the menu are charged separately.

breakfast	*le petit déjeuner*
lunch	*le déjeuner*
dinner	*le dîner*
meal	*le repas*
first course	*l'entrée/les hors d'oeuvre*
main course	*le plat principal*
made to order	*sur commande*
drink included	*boisson compris*
wine list	*la carte des vins*
the bill	*l'addition*
fork	*la fourchette*
knife	*le couteau*
spoon	*la cuillère*
plate	*l'assiette*
glass	*le verre*
napkin	*la serviette*
ashtray	*le cendrier*

Breakfast and Snacks

baguette	**long thin loaf**
pain	**bread**
petits pains	**rolls**
beurre	**butter**

poivre	**pepper**
sel	**salt**
sucre	**sugar**
confiture	**jam**
oeufs	**eggs**
...à la coque	**boiled eggs**
...au bacon	**bacon and eggs**
...au jambon	**ham and eggs**
...sur le plat	**fried eggs**
...brouillés	**scrambled eggs**
tartine	**bread with butter**
yaourt	**yoghurt**
crêpe	**pancake**
croque-monsieur	**ham and cheese toasted sandwich**
croque-madame	**...with a fried egg on top**
galette	**type of pancake**
pan bagna	**bread roll stuffed with salad Niçoise**
quiche	**tart of eggs and cream with various fillings**
quiche lorraine	**quiche with bacon**

Numbers

0 *zéro*	11 *onze*	30 *trente*	**1000** *mille*
1 *un, une*	12 *douze*	40 *quarante*	**1,000,000** *un million*
2 *deux*	13 *treize*	50 *cinquante*	
3 *trois*	14 *quatorze*	60 *soixante*	
4 *quatre*	15 *quinze*	70 *soixante-dix*	● *The number 1 is often*
5 *cinq*	16 *seize*	80 *quatre-vingts*	*written like an*
6 *six*	17 *dix-sept*	90 *quatre-vingt-dix*	*upside down V,*
7 *sept*	18 *dix-huit*	100 *cent*	*and the*
8 *huit*	19 *dix-neuf*		*number 7 is*
9 *neuf*	20 *vingt*		*crossed.*
10 *dix*	21 *vingt-et-un*		

First course

An *amuse-bouche*, *amuse-gueule* or appetizer is something to "amuse the mouth", served before the first course

anchoiade	**sauce of olive oil, anchovies and garlic, served with raw vegetables**
assiette anglaise	**cold meats**
potage	**soup**
rillettes	**rich fatty paste of shredded duck, rabbit or pork**
tapenade	**spread of olives and anchovies**
pissaladière	**Provençal pizza with onions, olives and anchovies**

Meat and Fish

La Viande	Meat
bleu	**rare**
à point	**medium**
bien cuit	**well done**
grillé	**grilled**
agneau	**lamb**
andouille/ andouillette	**tripe sausage**
bifteck	**steak**
boudin	**sausage**
boudin noir	**black pudding**
boudin blanc	**white pudding (chicken or veal)**
blanquette	**stew of veal, lamb or chicken with a creamy egg sauce**
boeuf à la mode	**beef in red wine with carrots, mushroom and onions**
à la bordelaise	**beef with red wine and shallots**

à la Bourguignonne	cooked in red wine, onions and mushrooms
brochette	kebab
caille	quail
canard	duck
carbonnade	casserole of beef, beer and onions
carré d'agneau	rack of lamb
cassoulet	stew of beans, sausages, pork and duck, from southwest France
cervelle	brains (food)
chateaubriand	thick steak
choucroute	Alsace dish of sauerkraut, bacon and sausages
confit	duck or goose preserved in its own fat

Days and Months

Days of the week, seasons and months are not capitalised in French.

● **Days of the week**
Monday *lundi*
Tuesday *mardi*
Wednesday *mercredi*
Thursday *jeudi*
Friday *vendredi*
Saturday *samedi*
Sunday *dimanche*

● **Seasons**
spring *le printemps*
summer *l'été*
autumn *l'automne*
winter *l'hiver*

● **Months**
January *janvier*
February *février*
March *mars*
April *avril*
May *mai*
June *juin*
July *juillet*
August *août*
September *septembre*
October *octobre*
November *novembre*
December *décembre*

● **Saying the date**
20th October 1999, *le vingt octobre, dix-neuf cent quatre-vingt-dix-neuf*

Non, Non, Garçon

Garçon is the word for waiter but is never used directly; say *Monsieur* or *Madame* to attract his attention.

contre-filet	cut of sirloin steak
coq au vin	chicken in red wine
côte d'agneau	lamb chop
daube	beef stew with red wine, onions and tomatoes
dinde	turkey
entrecôte	beef rib steak
escargot	snail
faisan	pheasant
farci	stuffed
faux-filet	sirloin
feuilleté	puff pastry
foie	liver
foie de veau	calf's liver
foie gras	goose or duck liver pâté
gardiane	rich beef stew with olives and garlic, from the Camargue
cuisses de grenouille	frog's legs
grillade	grilled meat
hachis	minced meat
jambon	ham
lapin	rabbit
lardon	small pieces of bacon, often added to salads
magret de canard	breast of duck
médaillon	round meat
moelle	beef bone marrow
mouton navarin	stew of lamb with onions, carrots and turnips
oie	goose
perdrix	partridge
petit-gris	small snail
pieds de cochon	pig's trotters
pintade	guinea fowl
Pipérade	Basque dish of eggs, ham, peppers, onion
porc	pork
pot-au-feu	casserole of beef and vegetables
poulet	chicken
poussin	young chicken

rognons	kidneys
rôti	roast
sanglier	wild boar
saucisse	fresh sausage
saucisson	salami
veau	veal

Poissons	*Fish*
Armoricaine	made with white wine, tomatoes, butter and cognac
anchois	anchovies
anguille	eel
bar (or *loup*)	sea bass
barbue	brill
belon	Brittany oyster
bigorneau	sea snail
Bercy	sauce of fish stock, butter, white wine and shallots
bouillabaisse	fish soup, served with grated cheese, garlic croutons and *rouille*, a spicy sauce
brandade	salt cod purée
cabillaud	cod
calmars	squid
colin	hake
coquillage	shellfish
coquilles Saint-Jacques	scallops
crevette	shrimp
daurade	sea bream
flétan	halibut
fruits de mer	seafood
hareng	herring
homard	lobster
huître	oyster
langoustine	large prawn
limande	lemon sole
lotte	monkfish
morue	salt cod
moule	mussel
moules marinières	mussels in white wine and onions
oursin	sea urchin
raie	skate
saumon	salmon
thon	tuna
truite	trout

Légumes	*Vegetables*
ail	garlic
artichaut	artichoke
asperge	asparagus
aubergine	eggplant

French	English	French	English
avocat	avocado	citron vert	lime
bolets	boletus mushrooms	figue	fig
céleri	grated celery	fraise	strawberry
rémoulade	with mayonnaise	framboise	raspberry
champignon	mushroom	groseille	redcurrant
cèpes	boletus mushroom	mangue	mango
chanterelle	wild mushroom	mirabelle	yellow plum
cornichon	gherkin	pamplemousse	grapefruit
courgette	zucchini	pêche	peach
chips	potato crisps	poire	pear
chou	cabbage	pomme	apple
chou-fleur	cauliflower	raisin	grape
concombre	cucumber	prune	plum
cru	raw	pruneau	prune
crudités	raw vegetables	Reine claude	greengage
épinard	spinach		
frites	chips, French fries		
gratin dauphinois	sliced potatoes baked with cream		

Sauces / Sauces

Sauces	Sauces
aioli	garlic mayonnaise
béarnaise	sauce of egg, butter, wine and herbs
forestière	with mushrooms and bacon
hollandaise	egg, butter and lemon sauce
lyonnaise	with onions
meunière	fried fish with butter, lemon and parsley sauce
meurette	red wine sauce
Mornay	sauce of cream, egg and cheese
Parmentier	served with potatoes
paysan	rustic style, ingredients depend on the region
pistou	Provençal sauce of basil, garlic and olive oil; vegetable soup with the sauce.
provençale	sauce of tomatoes, garlic and olive oil.
papillotte	cooked in paper

(continued from main vegetable list)

haricot	dried bean
haricots verts	green beans
lentilles	lentils
maïs	corn
mange-tout	snow pea
mesclun	mixed leaf salad
navet	turnip
noix	nut, walnut
noisette	hazelnut
oignon	onion
panais	parsnip
persil	parsley
pignon	pine nut
poireau	leek
pois	pea
poivron	bell pepper
pomme de terre	potato
radis	radis
roquette	arugula, rocket
ratatouille	Provençal vegetable stew of aubergines, courgettes, tomatoes, peppers and olive oil
riz	rice
salade Niçoise	egg, tuna, olives, onions and tomato salad
salade verte	green salad
truffe	truffle

Fruits / Fruit

Fruits	Fruit
ananas	pineapple
cavaillon	fragrant sweet melon from Cavaillon in Provence
cerise	cherry
citron	lemon

Puddings / Dessert

Puddings	Dessert
Belle Hélène	fruit with ice cream and chocolate sauce
clafoutis	baked pudding of batter and cherries
coulis	purée of fruit or vegetables
gâteau	cake
île flottante	whisked egg whites in custard sauce
crème anglaise	custard
pêche melba	peaches with ice cream and raspberry sauce
tarte tatin	upside down tart of caramelised apples
crème caramel	caramelised egg custard
crème Chantilly	whipped cream
fromage	cheese
chèvre	goat's cheese

In the Café

If you sit at the bar (le zinc), drinks will be cheaper than at a table. Settle the bill when you leave; the waiter may leave a slip of paper on the table to keep track of the bill. The French enjoy bittersweet aperitifs, often diluted with ice and fizzy water.

drinks	les boissons
coffee	café
...with milk or cream	au lait or crème
...decaffeinated	déca/décaféiné
...black/espresso	express/noir
...American filtered coffee	filtre
tea	thé

Table Talk

I am a vegetarian Je suis végétarien
I am on a diet Je suis au régime
What do you recommend? Qu'est-ce que vous recommandez?
Do you have local specialities? Avez-vous des spécialités locales?
I'd like to order Je voudrais commander
That is not what I ordered Ce n'est pas ce que j'ai commandé
Is service included? Est-ce que le service est compris?
May I have more wine? Encore du vin, s'il vous plaît?
Enjoy your meal Bon appétit!

On the Telephone

How do I make an outside call? *Comment est-ce que je peux téléphoner à l'exterieur?*
I want to make an international (local) call *Je voudrais une communication pour l'étranger (une communication locale)*
What is the dialling code? *Quel est l'indicatif?*
I'd like an alarm call for 8 tomorrow morning. *Je voudrais être réveillé à huit heures demain martin*
Who's calling? *C'est qui à l'appareil?*
Hold on, please *Ne quittez pas s'il vous plaît*
The line is busy *La ligne est occupée*
I must have dialled the wrong number *J'ai dû faire un faux numéro*

...herb infusion	*tisane*
...camomile	*verveine*
hot chocolate	*chocolat chaud*
milk	*lait*
mineral water	*eau minérale*
fizzy	*gazeux*
non-fizzy	*non-gazeux*
fizzy lemonade	*limonade*
fresh lemon juice served with sugar	*citron pressé*
fresh squeezed orange juice	*orange pressé*
full (eg full cream milk)	*entier*
fresh or cold	*frais, fraîche*
beer	*bière*
...bottled	*en bouteille*
...on tap	*à la pression*
pre-dinner drink	*apéritif*
white wine with cassis, black-currant liqueur	*kir*
***kir* with champagne**	*kir royale*
with ice	*avec des glaçons*
neat	*sec*
red	*rouge*
white	*blanc*
rose	*rosé*

dry	*brut*
sweet	*doux*
sparkling wine	*crémant*
house wine	*vin de maison*
local wine	*vin de pays*
Where is this wine from?	*De quelle région vient ce vin?*
pitcher	*carafe/pichet*
...of water/wine	*d'eau/de vin*
half litre	*demi-carafe*
quarter litre	*quart*
mixed	*panaché*
after dinner drink	*digestif*
brandy from Armagnac region of France	*Armagnac*
Normandy apple brandy	*calvados*
cheers!	*santé!*
hangover	*gueule de bois*

Further Reading

Arts and Architecture

Art and Architecture in Medieval France, Whitney Stoddard. New York: Harper & Row, 1972.
Change, New Haven: Yale University Press, 1979. An illustrated architectural history of Paris.
France: A History in Art, by Bradley Smith. New York: Doubleday & Company, Inc. 1984. The history of France through the eyes of artists.
The Cathedral Builders, by Jean Gimpel. New York: Harper & Row, 1984. First published in French. The story of the hands and minds behind the cathedrals of France.

History and Social Commentary

A Concise History of France, by Douglas Johnson. New York: The Viking Press, 1971.
A Holiday History of France, by Ronald Hamilton. London: The Hogarth Press, 1985. An illustrated guide to history and architecture designed to be taken along on a trip.
A Traveller's History of France, by Robert Cole. London: The Windrush Press. Slim volume for background reading.
A Women's Life in the Court of the Sun King, by Duchesse d'Orléans. Introduction and translation by Elborg Forster. Baltimore: Johns Hopkins University Press, 1984. The letters of the Duchesse d'Orléans reveal the court-life of the 17th century.
France Today, by John Ardagh. London: Secker and Warburg. Up-to-date, hefty tome.
France Today, J.E. Flower (ed.). New York: Methuen & Co., Ltd, 1983. Essays on contemporary France.
The French, by François Nourissier. New York: Alfred A Knopf, 1968. A witty treatment of his compatriots, translated from the French.
The French, by Theodore Zeldin. New York: Random House, 1983.

A witty and insightful treatment of how the French live today.
The Identity of France, by Fernand Braudel. London: Fontana Press.
The Illustrated History of Paris and the Parisians, by Robert Laffont. New York: Doubleday & Co., 1958.

Belles Lettres

A Little Tour in France, by Henry James. New York: Farrar, Straus and Giroux, 1983. James originally published this account of his travels through France in 1885.
A Moveable Feast, by Ernest Hemingway. New York: Scribner, 1964. The life of the artist in Paris.
Mont-Saint-Michel and Chartres, by Henry Adams. New York: Doubleday and Co., Inc., 1959. Privately printed in 1905 and published in 1913, the book is an examination of architecture, literature and spirit.
Satori in Paris, by Jack Kerouac. New York: Grove Press, 1966. *Satori* is the Japanese word for sudden illumination. These are 10 days of travel à la Kerouac as he searches for Jean Louis Lebris de Kérouac in France.
Two Towns in Provence, by M.F.K. Fisher. New York: Vintage Books, 1983. A tribute to Aix-en-Provence and Marseille.
Village in the Vaucluse, by Laurence Wylie. 3rd ed. New York: Harper & Row, 1974.

French Literature

The Oxford Companion to French Literature, by Sir Paul Harvey and J.E. Heseltine. Oxford: Oxford University Press, 1959.

Classics by Date
La Chanson de Roland, c.1100.
François Rabelais, *Gargantua and Pantagruel*, 1532–64.
Jean Racine, *Phèdre*, 1677.
Voltaire, *Candide*, 1759.
Victor Hugo, *Nôtre-Dame de Paris*, 1831.
Gustave Flaubert, *Madame Bovary*, 1857.
Emile Zola, *Germinal*, 1885.
Marcel Proust, *Du côté de chez Swann*, 1913.

Food & Wine

The Food Lover's Guide to France, by Patricia Wells. London: Methuen. The best restaurants, food shops and markets in France, plus regional recipes.
French Regional Cooking, by Anne Willan. New York: William Morrow & Co., Inc., 1981. The founder of La Varenne's cooking school travels through the regions of France via her recipes. Both imperial and metric weights are given for each recipe.
Mastering the Art of French Cooking, by Simone Beck and Julia Child. New York: Alfred A. Knopf, 1983.
The New Larousse Gastronomique, by Prosper Montagné. New York: Crown Publishers, Inc, 1977. Translated from the French; a complete encyclopedia of the food, cooking techniques and dishes of the world, especially of France.
Wine Atlas of France, by Hugh Johnson and Hubrecht Duijker. London: Mitchell Beazley. Well-illustrated atlas, concentrating on wine and vineyards, but also supplementary information on history, architecture and culture.
The Wines and Winelands of France, Charles Pomerol (ed). London: Robertson McCarta. Guide to the wine regions of France, which focuses on the geology and science of the subject, plus itineraries and history.

Other Insight Guides

More than 20 other books from Apa Publications cover destinations in France. Companion **Insight Guides** include *Paris, Normandy, Brittany, Loire Valley, Alsace, Burgundy, Côte d'Azur,* and *Provence.* **Insight Pocket Guides**, containing personal recommendations and a fold-out map, cover *Paris, Brittany, Loire Valley, Alsace, Provence, Côte d'Azur* and *Corsica.* **Insight Compact Guides**, fact-packed easy-reference guides, cover *Paris, Normandy, Brittany, Burgundy* and *Provence.*

ART & PHOTO CREDITS

© 1998 Apa Publications GmbH & Co. Verlag KG (Singapore branch)

INSIGHT GUIDE
France

Cartographic Editor **Zoë Goodwin**
Production **Stuart Everitt**
Design Consultants
Klaus Geisler, Graham Mitchener
Picture Research **Hilary Genin**

Index

Numbers in italics refer to photographs

"I was first drawn to the Insight Guides by the excellent "Nepal" volume. I can think of no book which so effectively captures the essence of a country. Out of these pages leaped the Nepal I know – the captivating charm of a people and their culture. I've since discovered and enjoyed the entire Insight Guide series. Each volume deals with a country in the same sensitive depth, which is nowhere more evident than in the superb photography."

Sir Edmund Hillary

The World of Insight Guides

400 books in three complementary series cover every major destination in every continent.

Insight Guides

Alaska
Alsace
Amazon Wildlife
American Southwest
Amsterdam
Argentina
Atlanta
Athens
Australia
Austria
Bahamas
Bali
Baltic States
Bangkok
Barbados
Barcelona
Bay of Naples
Beijing
Belgium
Belize
Berlin
Bermuda
Boston
Brazil
Brittany
Brussels
Budapest
Buenos Aires
Burgundy
Burma (Myanmar)
Cairo
Calcutta
California
Canada
Caribbean
Catalonia
Channel Islands
Chicago
Chile
China
Cologne
Continental Europe
Corsica
Costa Rica
Crete
Crossing America
Cuba
Cyprus
Czech & Slovak Republics
Delhi, Jaipur, Agra
Denmark
Dresden
Dublin
Düsseldorf
East African Wildlife
East Asia
Eastern Europe
Ecuador
Edinburgh
Egypt
Finland
Florence
Florida
France
Frankfurt
French Riviera
Gambia & Senegal
Germany
Glasgow

Gran Canaria
Great Barrier Reef
Great Britain
Greece
Greek Islands
Hamburg
Hawaii
Hong Kong
Hungary
Iceland
India
India's Western Himalaya
Indian Wildlife
Indonesia
Ireland
Israel
Istanbul
Italy
Jamaica
Japan
Java
Jerusalem
Jordan
Kathmandu
Kenya
Korea
Lisbon
Loire Valley
London
Los Angeles
Madeira
Madrid
Malaysia
Mallorca & Ibiza
Malta
Marine Life in the South China Sea
Melbourne
Mexico
Mexico City
Miami
Montreal
Morocco
Moscow
Munich
Namibia
Native America
Nepal
Netherlands
New England
New Orleans
New York City
New York State
New Zealand
Nile
Normandy
Northern California
Northern Spain
Norway
Oman & the UAE
Oxford
Old South
Pacific Northwest
Pakistan
Paris
Peru
Philadelphia
Philippines
Poland
Portugal
Prague

Provence
Puerto Rico
Rajasthan
Rhine
Rio de Janeiro
Rockies
Rome
Russia
St Petersburg
San Francisco
Sardinia
Scotland
Seattle
Sicily
Singapore
South Africa
South America
South Asia
South India
South Tyrol
Southeast Asia
Southeast Asia Wildlife
Southern California
Southern Spain
Spain
Sri Lanka
Sweden
Switzerland
Sydney
Taiwan
Tenerife
Texas
Thailand
Tokyo
Trinidad & Tobago
Tunisia
Turkey
Turkish Coast
Tuscany
Umbria
US National Parks East
US National Parks West
Vancouver
Venezuela
Venice
Vienna
Vietnam
Wales
Washington DC
Waterways of Europe
Wild West
Yemen

Insight Pocket Guides

Aegean Islands★
Algarve★
Alsace
Amsterdam★
Athens★
Atlanta★
Bahamas★
Baja Peninsula★
Bali★
Bali Bird Walks
Bangkok★
Barbados★
Barcelona★
Bavaria★
Beijing★
Berlin★

Bermuda★
Bhutan★
Boston★
British Columbia★
Brittany★
Brussels★
Budapest & Surroundings★
Canton★
Chiang Mai★
Chicago★
Corsica★
Costa Blanca★
Costa Brava★
Costa del Sol/Marbella★
Costa Rica★
Crete★
Denmark★
Fiji★
Florence★
Florida★
Florida Keys★
French Riviera★
Gran Canaria★
Hawaii★
Hong Kong★
Hungary
Ibiza★
Ireland★
Ireland's Southwest★
Israel★
Istanbul★
Jakarta★
Jamaica★
Kathmandu Bikes & Hikes★
Kenya★
Kuala Lumpur★
Lisbon★
Loire Valley★
London★
Macau★
Madrid★
Malacca
Maldives
Mallorca★
Malta★
Mexico City★
Miami★
Milan★
Montreal★
Morocco★
Moscow
Nepal★
New Delhi
New Orleans★
New York City★
New Zealand★
Northern California★
Oslo/Bergen★
Paris★
Penang★
Phuket★
Prague★
Provence★
Puerto Rico★
Quebec★
Rhodes★
Rome★
Sabah★

St Petersburg★
San Francisco★
Sardinia
Scotland★
Seville★
Seychelles★
Sicily★
Sikkim
Singapore★
Southeast England
Southern California★
Southern Spain★
Sri Lanka★
Sydney★
Tenerife★
Thailand★
Tibet★
Toronto★
Tunisia★
Turkish Coast★
Tuscany★
Venice★
Vienna★
Vietnam★
Yogyakarta
Yucatan Peninsula★

★ = Insight Pocket Guides
with Pull out Maps

Insight Compact Guides

Algarve
Amsterdam
Bahamas
Bali
Bangkok
Barbados
Barcelona
Beijing
Belgium
Berlin
Brittany
Brussels
Budapest
Burgundy
Copenhagen
Costa Brava
Costa Rica
Crete
Cyprus
Czech Republic
Denmark
Dominican Republic
Dublin
Egypt
Finland
Florence
Gran Canaria
Greece
Holland
Hong Kong
Ireland
Israel
Italian Lakes
Italian Riviera
Jamaica
Jerusalem
Lisbon
Madeira
Mallorca
Malta

Milan
Moscow
Munich
Normandy
Norway
Paris
Poland
Portugal
Prague
Provence
Rhodes
Rome
St Petersburg
Salzburg
Singapore
Switzerland
Sydney
Tenerife
Thailand
Turkey
Turkish Coast
Tuscany
UK regional titles:
  Bath & Surroundings
  Cambridge & East Anglia
  Cornwall
  Cotswolds
  Devon & Exmoor
  Edinburgh
  Lake District
  London
  New Forest
  North York Moors
  Northumbria
  Oxford
  Peak District
  Scotland
  Scottish Highlands
  Shakespeare Country
  Snowdonia
  South Downs
  York
  Yorkshire Dales
USA regional titles:
  Boston
  Cape Cod
  Chicago
  Florida
  Florida Keys
  Hawaii: Maui
  Hawaii: Oahu
  Las Vegas
  Los Angeles
  Martha's Vineyard & Nantucket
  New York
  San Francisco
  Washington D.C.
Venice
Vienna
West of Ireland